physical education
FOR HIGH SCHOOL STUDENTS

A book of sports, athletics, and recreational activities for teen-age boys and girls

Second Edition—1970

American Association for Health, Physical Education, and Recreation

COPYRIGHT © 1955, 1960, 1970 BY
AMERICAN ASSOCIATION FOR HEALTH,
PHYSICAL EDUCATION, AND RECREATION

Printed in the United States of America. All rights reserved. This book, or parts thereof, may not be reproduced in any form without permission of the publisher. For information, address the Association, 1201 Sixteenth Street, N.W., Washington, D.C. 20036.

Library of Congress Catalog Card Number 79-136473

First Edition—1955
Revised Edition—1960
Second Edition—1970

Single copy, clothbound $5 (Stock No. 245-25116); paperbound $4 (Stock No. 245-25114). Discounts on quantity orders: 2-9 copies, 10 percent; 10 or more copies, 20 percent. All orders must be prepaid except those on official purchase order forms. Shipping and handling charges will be added to billed orders. Order from Publications–Sales Section, National Education Association, 1201 Sixteenth Street, N.W., Washington, D.C.

Foreword

This book about physical activity has been written especially for high school students. The first edition, published over a decade ago, met with instant success because it presented basic information about a subject that was highly important to high school boys and girls, in a way that was designed to make good reading for them. When it appeared, *Physical Education for High School Students* was a "first," a pioneering effort in giving background information, rules, strategy, officiating techniques, and safety requirements in what for too long was considered merely an "exercise" course. Today, when it is generally accepted that physical activity both involves and develops intellectual ability and that fitness and mental capacity cannot be separated in the individual, this textbook is still the outstanding effort to provide in one volume the necessary reading material to accompany a sound program of physical education.

The first edition and now this completely revised and up-to-date second edition resulted from the efforts of a national professional organization. Both editions were envisioned and carried to completion through the cooperative endeavors of almost 200 leaders in education. Authors and committee members made their contributions without compensation, as a professional service, thus making it possible to produce this book at a nominal cost to the student. It is the hope of all members of the American Association for Health, Physical Education, and Recreation that the book will help bring high school students closer to a knowledge of the joys of participation in physical activity—during their school days and as productive adult members of our society.

CARL A. TROESTER, JR.
Executive Secretary, AAHPER

Acknowledgments

Editor:
William H. Savage
Oakton High School
Vienna, Va.

Physical Education and You:
Donald Jones
Fairfax County (Va.) Public Schools

Angling and Casting:
Clifford L. Netherton
Northern Virginia Community College
Annandale, Va.

Archery:
Fred Schuette
Flint Community Junior College
Flint, Mich.

Badminton:
Virginia Hicks
Texas Women's University
Denton, Texas

James Poole
Tulane University
New Orleans, La.

John Shaw
Syracuse University
Syracuse, N.Y.

Baseball and Softball:
Gordon Gillespie
Lewis College
Lockport, Ill.

Becky Sisley
University of Oregon
Eugene, Oreg.

Basketball:
Edward Ashnault
Colgate University
Hamilton, N.Y.

Jannette Sayre
University of Nebraska
Lincoln, Nebr.

Bowling:
Clare Allom
Rockville High School
Rockville, Conn.

Lyndon Lee
Lifetime Sports Foundation
Washington, D.C.

Dance:
M. Frances Dougherty
University of Oregon
Eugene, Oreg.

Fencing:
Mrs. Kirsten Gardner
National Education Association
Washington, D.C.

Field Hockey:
Betty Shellenberger
Stevens School
Chestnut Hill, Pa.

Golf:
Mary Ann Ryder
Chico State College
Chico, Calif.

Gymnastics and Tumbling:
Mrs. Carolyn Bowers
Ohio State University
Columbus, Ohio

Alfred Sylvia
Auburn Public Schools
Auburn, Mass.

Riflery:
Stanley Mate
National Rifle Association
Washington, D.C.

Soccer:
  Flo Grebner
  Glenbard East High School
  Lombard, Ill.

  Glenn Warner
  U.S. Naval Academy
  Annapolis, Md.

Speedball:
  Hollis Fait
  University of Connecticut
  Storrs, Conn.

  George Van Bibber
  University of Connecticut
  Storrs, Conn.

Swimming:
  Charles Arnold
  University of New Hampshire
  Durham, N.H.

Tennis:
  Betty Brown
  Newcomb College, Tulane University
  New Orleans, La.

  Elaine Mason
  Fresno State College
  Fresno, Calif.

Touch Football:
  Robert T. Bronzan
  San Jose State College
  San Jose, Calif.

  Morris Patterson
  William Jewell College
  Liberty, Mo.

Track and Field:
  John F. Warner
  Cornell University
  Ithaca, N.Y.

  Phoebe Wienke
  School District No. 21
  Wheeling, Ill.

Volleyball:
  Nancy L. Chapman
  Indian Hill Junior High School
  Cincinnati, Ohio

  Mary Frances Kellam
  University of North Carolina
  Chapel Hill, N.C.

Wrestling:
  Irwin T. Hess
  University of New Hampshire
  Durham, N.H.

Art and Design:
  Tom Gladden
  Washington, D.C.

Special thanks go to Dorothy R. Mohr, Sacramento State College (Calif.), and Elmon L. Vernier, Board of Education, Baltimore (Md.) Public Schools, who served as editors of the original edition. Over the years, many other persons contributed to this publication. Their contribution is gratefully acknowledged.

The 1970 edition profited by the critical reading and comments of the students and teachers of the Fairfax County (Va.) Public Schools.

Contents

		Page
1	Physical Education and You	9
2	Angling and Casting	13
3	Archery	29
4	Badminton	45
5	Baseball and Softball	59
6	Basketball	81
7	Bowling	97
8	Dance	107
9	Fencing	121
10	Field Hockey	135
11	Golf	151
12	Gymnastics and Tumbling	165
13	Riflery	205
14	Soccer	219
15	Speedball	235
16	Swimming	249
17	Tennis	289
18	Touch Football	307
19	Track and Field	321
20	Volleyball	351

		Page
21	**Wrestling**	363
22	**Organization of Competition**	387
23	**Keeping Physically Fit**	393
24	**Career Information**	399

Physical Education and You

What is physical education all about? Does it mean learning sport skills, developing good health habits, providing situations for self-expression and exploration? In essence, it means all of this and more. Physical education offers valuable experiences for you as an individual and for society as a whole. It opens a whole new world of the future where recreation will increase 300 percent by the year 2000.

Physical education is basically an activity-oriented program. From the time you were born, physical activity has been a most important part of your development. At your present point in development, however, you have been exposed to many formal and informal types of physical activity in school. Let's review some of them.

During your elementary years, most of your physical education program was comprised of basic skills, movement exploration, and self-testing activities, along with some team-oriented sports. This was a good beginning, and hopefully continued through your junior high school years. The development of basic movement and sport skills is intricate and exacting, and it takes much practice to attain proficiency.

The skills which you pursue now in your physical education class should not be completely new to you. You already have learned the basic movements which have prepared you for today's physical education programs, designed to present skills and game situations to help meet your individual physical needs and interests. The sports skills which you learn now will be a great asset to you during future leisure time. Just how well you learn to use these skills is up to you.

Physical education classes help provide the regular amount of vigorous physical activity which is so vital for the maintenance of good health. They can help you establish a pattern of regular exercise for later in life.

Research has established that inactivity is a prime factor in the steadily increasing rate of heart, respiratory, and circulatory disease in this country, whether one is a teenager or adult. Regular strenuous physical activity of some sort is a must. Not that exercise will prevent or cure all ills; it *will* help your body to perform more efficiently, and this should be a goal for all of us.

What else will physical education mean to you? Does everything center around the physical learning which takes place? Hopefully not. As an outgrowth of your physical education program, you should be forming valuable personal assets in other aspects of life.

Your physical education course can help you acquire good health habits. Regular physical activity is one of these, but there is more to health than exercise. Diet is important not only for proper nutrition but for the control of your weight and your figure. Rest and sleep are also necessary for good health, along with a knowledge of how to take care of your body. Remember—a healthy, attractive, fully functioning body is your most prized asset and it is one of the aims of physical education to help you develop just this.

Games and sports have rules, and the rules are important. You can learn them in your physical education course, and you will also learn something about sportsmanship, both as a participant and as a spectator. You will be able to see more clearly the relationship of the rules of the game to the rules of life.

Taking part in sports as a member of a team will also teach you something about cooperation, about the responsibilities as well as the joys of being a member of a team. You can experience for yourself the values of working as a team; you will be able to act and react in various interpersonal situations and relationships involving active participation. You will find that you know yourself better at the conclusion of your physical education course; hopefully, you will also know your classmates better and will have experienced firsthand the cooperative efforts which form the basis of adult life in a democratic society.

People's interests and abilities vary in physical activities just as in other areas. A physical education course provides you with the opportunity to discover what sports you like best and where your outstanding abilities lie. But it is not necessary to be a champion in order to enjoy swimming or wrestling. Football, soccer, and basketball are exciting games, but unless you have the talent to become a professional athlete you probably will not have many chances to play them after you finish school. It is therefore advisable to learn some individual sports, while the instruction is available. Tennis, golf, and bowling are sports that will last you for a lifetime and may help you spend some of the vast amounts of leisure time which have been promised all of us in the future.

High school is the ideal time to acquire sport and game skills. Your body is sufficiently strong and developed and your knowledge of basic movements is sufficiently complete to handle the new physical demands which sport skills place on you. And the more you participate and practice in sports programs, the more you will develop your strength, skill, endurance, and general fitness. As an extra dividend for your efforts, you will find that you have a greater appreciation for and enjoyment of witnessing the performance of experts in our sports-conscious society.

A physical education course can help you to learn a more satisfying way of life. What you gain from your physical education experiences essentially will be up to you. Your teachers will introduce you to many skills and activities during your high school days, but only your active participation can make you a satisfactory performer. The following pages of this book can give you many facts about the history and rules of a variety of sports, but only your interest in absorbing this information can make a difference in your future life.

Angling and Casting

INTRODUCTION

Fishing techniques and equipment have been improved continually since man first fished for food and sport. Probably the first invention was a small object called a gorge. It was tied to the end of a line along with the bait and became lodged when swallowed by the fish.

The Hook

The next significant development was accomplished by bending a thin piece of metal and thereby shaping a hook. The distinguishing bend in the wire-like piece of metal initiated the term *angling*. The hook replaced the gorge and a barb was added to it. With both natural and artificial bait attached, the hook was being used by fisherman as early as 1200 B.C. This item of tackle has changed very little through the centuries except for size, some variation in shape, and the quality of metal used in its construction.

The Line

The early fishermen used lines made from hair and thin strips of animal skin. By the time the barbed hook came into use, there were fiber materials such as linen, cotton, silk, and wool to which the hook could be attached. The finest lines for fishing were developed from these fiber materials and were sometimes treated with oils and preservatives to improve their performance and to retard deterioration. At the present time, nylon and synthetics have almost completely replaced the use of other materials in the manufacturing of both monofilament and braided fishing lines. Nylon lines cast exceptionally well, are very durable, and are easily controlled in size, shape, color, and weight.

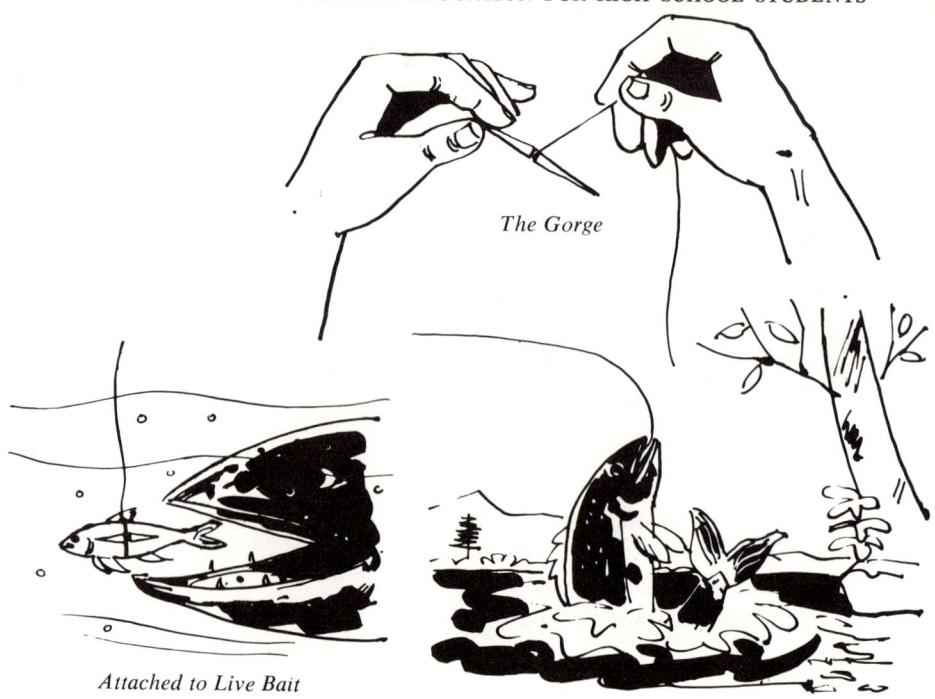

The Gorge

Attached to Live Bait

The Rod

Along with hooks and lines, the pole was used and developed to improve fishing. At first, branches from trees and then sticks selected and shaped to suit the angler were used as poles. Lines were tied to the end of the poles. This provided an obvious advantage to hand-line fishing. A new industry developed to manufacture solid wooden poles or rods of one, two, or three pieces. Following the development of the solid wooden rods came the creation and manufacture of skillfully designed and crafted split-bamboo rods. The split-bamboo rods were used and improved both in design and performance over a period of many years.

Early in the twentieth century, manufacturers introduced solid and tubular steel rods, which became very popular. These steel rods cast the line well, required little maintenance, and were more economical than the bamboo rods.

During the World War II era, newly developed plastics and fiberglass were molded into rods. These materials and processes have revolutionized the fishing rod industry. Almost all manufacturers feature this type of construction because of its advantages in terms of performance, weight, strength, durability, ease of maintenance, and cost.

ANGLING AND CASTING   15

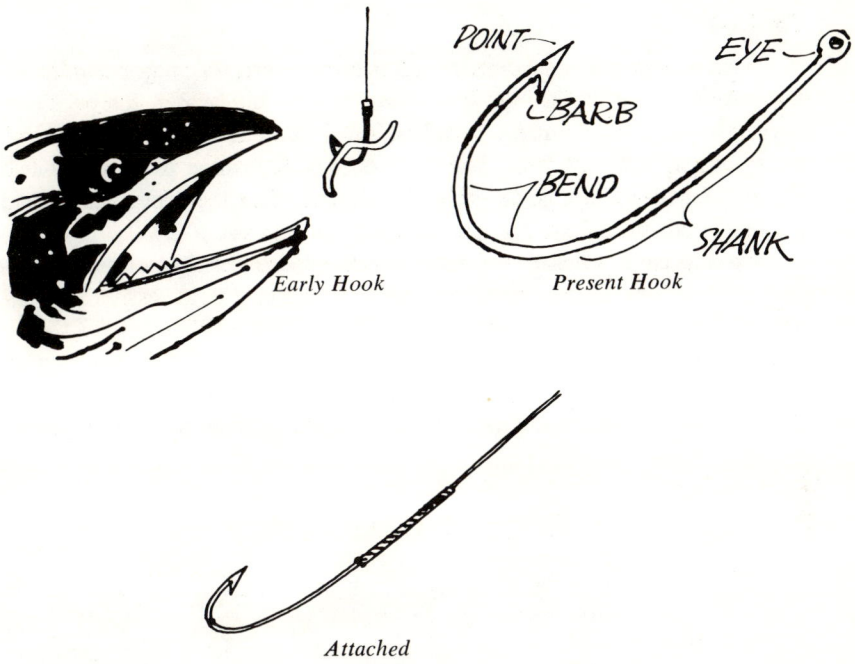

Early Hook   Present Hook

Attached

The Reel

For centuries, fishermen used hooks, natural or artificial bait and flies, lines, and rods without reels. Fishing without a reel as a part of the tackle is similar to cane pole fishing, which is an elementary but effective method of taking fish. The early fishermen pulled the excess line down through one or two guides on the rod and either held it in their hand or dropped it into a basket. The earliest reels were designed to store excess line.

The story of the invention of the casting reel by a Kentucky watchmaker is universally known. This reel did more than serve as a means of storing line. The reel, with its revolving spool, played out the line during the cast. The line was pulled from the spool by the weight of the bait or lure attached to the end. The action of the revolving spool reel enabled the fisherman to cast a greater distance with extreme accuracy and then to retrieve the line efficiently. It provided additional aid in playing and landing a fish. With the advantages afforded by the casting reel, the rods on which they were placed became shorter, making them more convenient to transport and more efficient in fishing either from a boat or near natural obstructions, such as trees and bushes.

The Cast

Fish specialists have determined that there are five major conditions that affect fish and fishing. These conditions are water temperature, oxygen supply, food supply, availability of protection for the fish, and the spawning cycle of fish. These conditions determine the kind of fish that may be found in a given body of water, whether the fisherman should use live or artificial bait, and the kind of tackle to use.

In any case, whether the fishing is to be done with natural or artificial bait or one type of tackle or another, casting is an essential technique. *The single most important contributing factor to successful fishing is successful casting. Successful casting is delivering the bait, either natural or artificial, to the area where fish may be taken with ease and accuracy and without endangering the safety of the fisherman or his fishing companions.*

FISHING EQUIPMENT

There are two types of fishing which are classified according to the techniques and equipment used. The two classifications are Fly Casting and Bait Casting. Fly Casting includes one basic kind of equipment and technique. Bait Casting includes three kinds: Spin Casting, Bait Casting, and Spinning. Spin Casting and Spinning have stationary spool reels that permit the line to "spin off" during the cast, and Bait Casting employs a revolving spool reel.

Equipment for Bait Casting

Spin Casting. The rod usually ranges in length from 5 to 6½ feet, has a light action, and is designed to cast ⅜ ounce lures. There are medium action rods designed for heavier lures and extra light action rods which are best for weights under ⅜ of an ounce. The push-button, stationary spool reel is attached on top of the handle. Monofilament lines, light lures, and live bait are used with Spin Casting equipment.

Bait Casting. Most Bait Casting rods range from 5 to 6 feet in length and have either medium or light action. They are designed to cast lures of ⅜, ½, and ⅝ ounce weights. The reel has a level wind device and should have a light, narrow spool and a large, light arbor.

Spinning. The rods range in length from 5½ to 7 feet and have light and medium action for fresh water fishing. They cast artificial lures weighing from ⅛ to ⅝ of an ounce and use monofilament lines testing

ANGLING AND CASTING

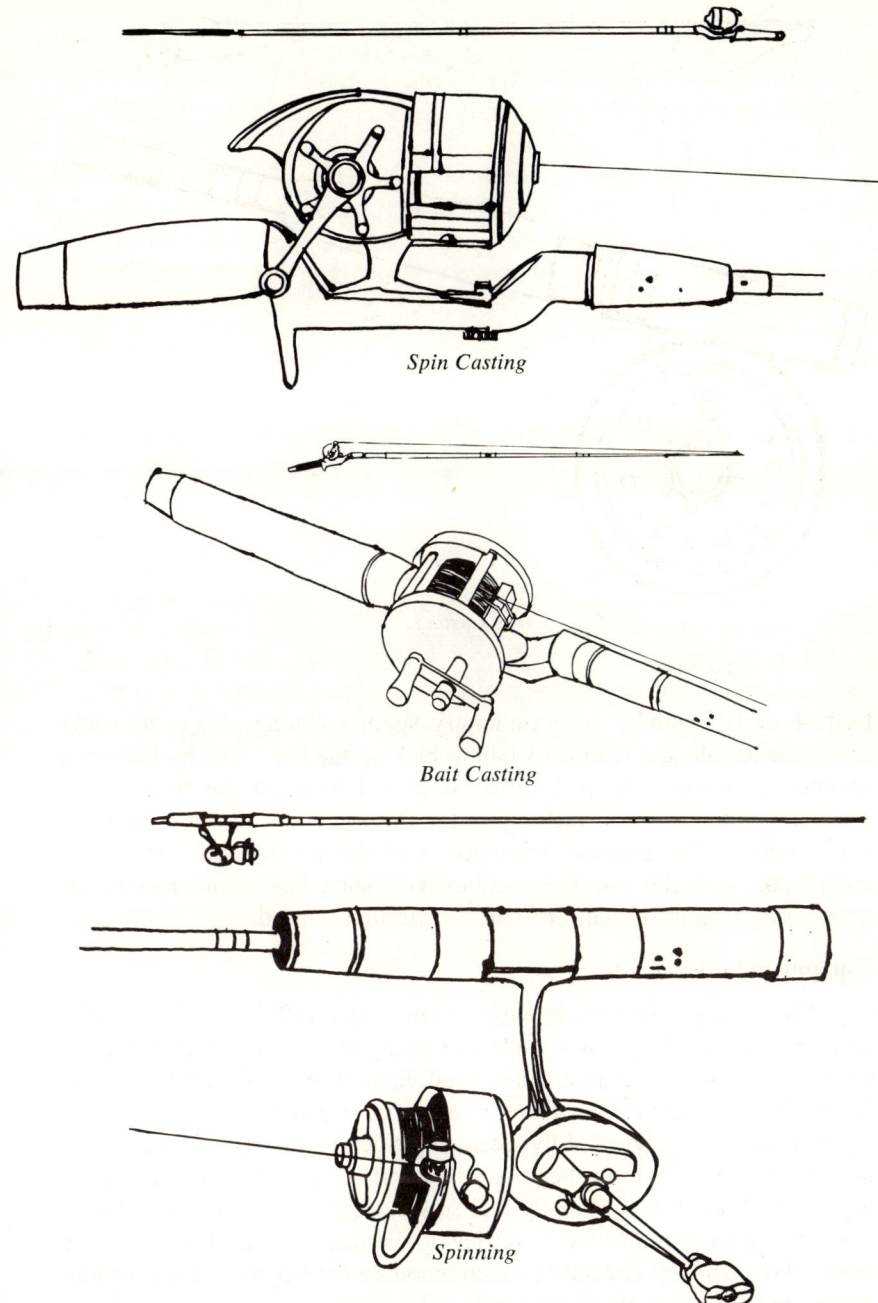

Spin Casting

Bait Casting

Spinning

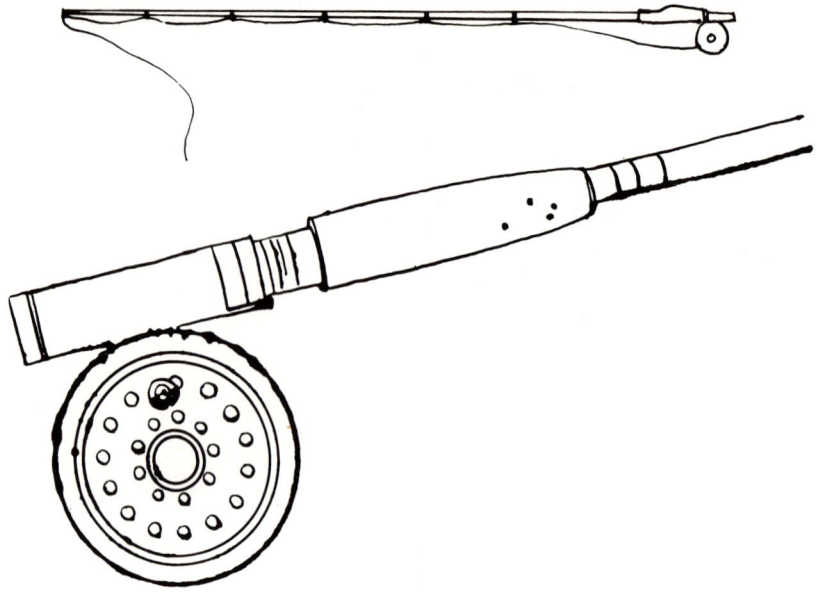

Fly Casting

from 4 to 10 pounds. The stationary spool spinning reel is attached under the handle and features a bail to pick up the line. The bail engages automatically when the reel handle is turned to begin the retrieve.

The equipment and techniques for fresh and salt water fishing are very similar. The greatest difference is in the weight and size of the equipment, with the salt water equipment being larger and heavier in most cases, and in the kind of bait or lure that is used.

Equipment for Fly Casting

Fly Casting rods vary in length from 6 feet to 9½ feet. Both light and heavier weight rods are made in varying lengths, but a light weight rod usually is shorter than a heavier rod; light weight rods average about 7½ or 8 feet, and heavy rods often are over 9 feet long.

There are two types of fly reels: single action and automatic. Single action reels are best for beginners and often are preferred by many experienced fishermen. The fly reel serves merely to store the line that is not being used and to aid in retrieving the line or fish. The reel must have a large enough capacity to accommodate the length and size of line to be used, plus an adequate amount of backing.

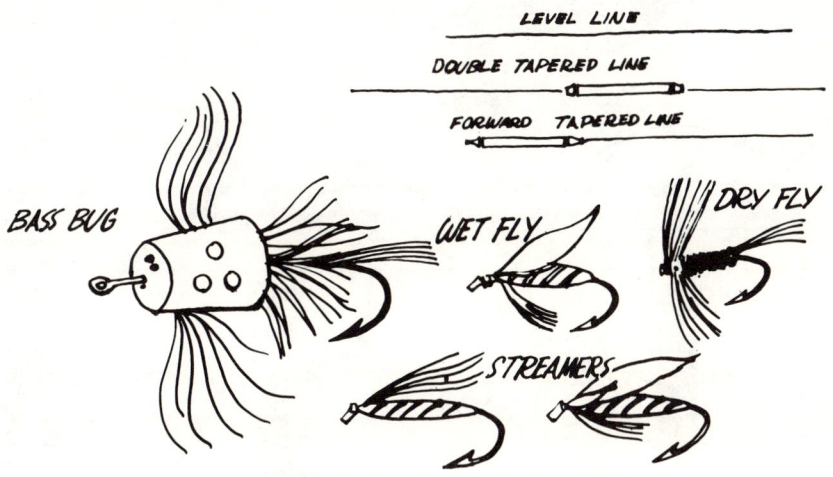

Fly lines have three basic designs: level, double tapered, and forward tapered. Level lines are the least expensive; double tapered lines are highly desirable for wet and dry fly fishing; and forward tapered lines are very efficient on extremely long casts. Further, fly lines are constructed to be either floating or sinking lines. All types will cast well if the line is matched to the rod on which it is to be used, as recommended by the manufacturer. The American Fishing Tackle Manufacturers Association (AFTMA) publishes a "table of standards," and line manufacturers publish various diagrams and charts showing comparative sizes, weights, and lengths of fly lines.

Leaders usually range in length from 6 to 9 feet. In most cases, tapered leaders work best. The leader may be made of different lengths and weights of monofilament nylon, or it may be purchased in a continuous, knotless taper. Leaders are manufactured in a variety of lengths, weights, tapers, and colors. Leader manufacturers publish charts indicating the conditions under which the various length, size, and color leaders should be used.

A wide variety of flies; streamers; spinners; plastic, rubber, or cork bugs; and lures may be attached to the leader.

Spin Casting

FISHING TECHNIQUES

Techniques of Spin Casting

Stand in a comfortable position with the right foot forward.* Grasp the rod handle so that the reel handle is on top. Place your thumb on the push button. The rod should be held a little above waist height and pointed directly above the target at the 10 o'clock position. The practice plug or fishing lure should hang down about 6 or 8 inches from the rod tip.

To begin the cast, press the push button all the way down with your thumb. Bring the rod directly up to the 12 o'clock position. Stop the backward cast when the rod is at the 12 o'clock position, even though the force of the lure or plug moving backward will cause the rod to continue back to about 12:30.

While the rod tip is still moving backward, begin the forward cast. Release the thumb from the push button at about the 11 o'clock position.

To retrieve the line, shift the rod and reel to the left hand, holding the reel and line. Have the line pass between the thumb and index finger of the left hand when being retrieved.

---

* All illustrations and descriptions of casting techniques are given for right-handed execution.

ANGLING AND CASTING   21

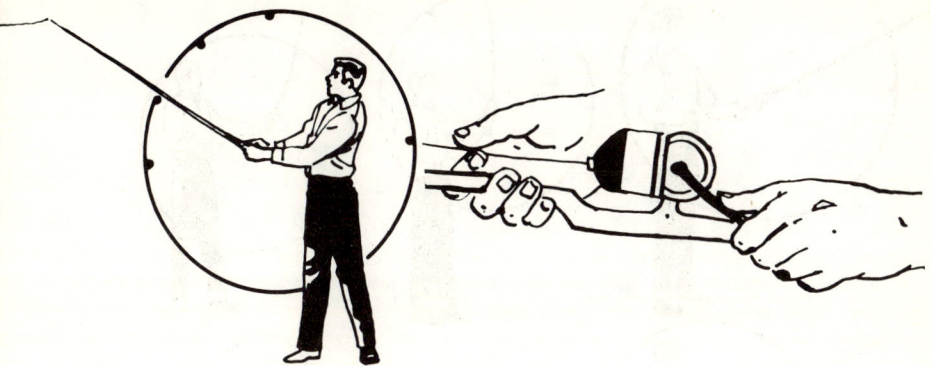

Spin Casting (cont.)

Techniques of Bait Casting

Stand in a comfortable position with the right foot forward. Grasp the rod handle so that the reel handle is on top. Place your thumb on the thumbing bar, putting pressure on the edge of the reel spool. The rod should be held a little above waist height and pointed directly above the target at the 10 o'clock position. The plug or lure should hang down about 6 to 8 inches from the rod tip.

To begin the cast, increase the pressure on the reel spool to keep it from turning. Bring the rod directly up to the 12 o'clock position. Stop the backward cast when the rod is at the 12 o'clock position, even though the force of the lure or plug moving backward will cause the rod tip to continue back to about 12:30.

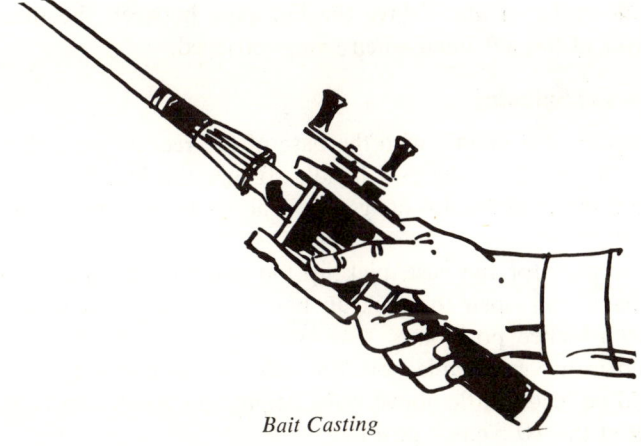

Bait Casting

Bait Casting (cont.)

While the rod tip is still moving backward, begin the forward cast. When the rod is at the 11 o'clock position on the forward cast, release the thumb pressure sufficiently to permit the spool to turn freely, but keep slight pressure on the spool at all times.

As the lure or plug approaches the target area, increase the thumb pressure on the reel spool, slowing it down. Stop the spool from turning completely just before the lure or bait touches the target.

To retrieve the line, shift the rod handle and reel to the left hand, holding the reel and line. Have the line pass between the thumb and index finger of the left hand when being retrieved.

Techniques of Spinning

Grasp the rod handle with the base of the reel between the second and third finger. Turn the reel handle so that the line is near the rod handle and the plug or lure hangs down about 6 or 8 inches below the rod tip.

To prepare for the cast, pick up the line with the index finger of the rod hand and open the pick-up bail by moving it across the reel spool into a locked position.

Stand in a comfortable position with the right foot forward. The rod should be held a little above waist height and pointed directly above the target at the 10 o'clock position.

ANGLING AND CASTING

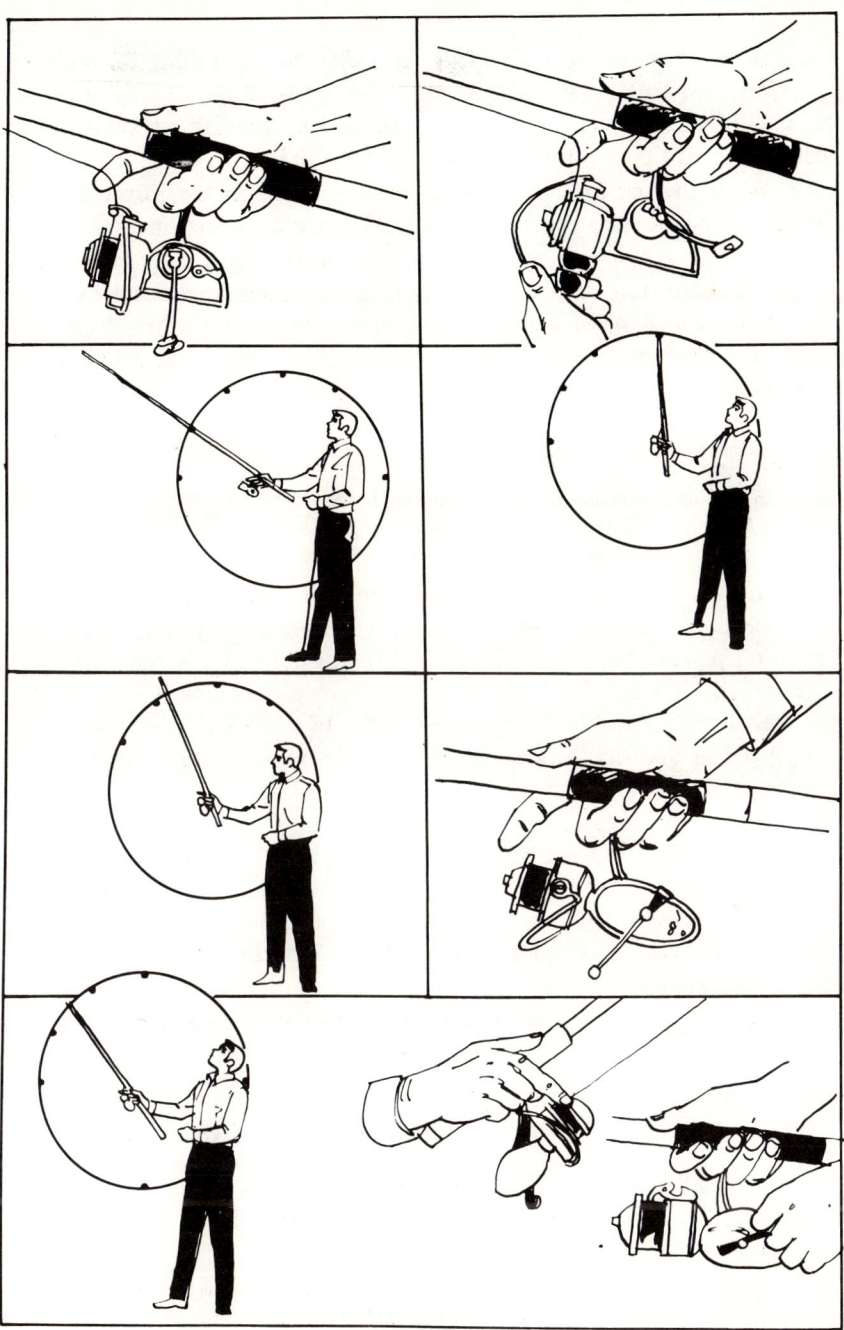

Spinning

Begin the cast by moving the rod directly up to the 12 o'clock position. Stop the backward cast when the rod is at the 12 o'clock position, even though the force of the plug or lure moving backward will cause the rod tip to continue back to about 12:30.

While the rod tip is still moving backward, begin the forward cast. When the rod is near the 11 o'clock position, release the line.

When the plug is in flight toward the target area, it may be slowed down or completely stopped by placing the index finger against the spool.

To retrieve the line, turn the reel handle in a counterclockwise direction. The pick-up bail engages automatically when the reel handle is turned.

Techniques of Fly Casting

Stand in a comfortable position with the right foot forward. Grasp the rod handle, placing your thumb directly on top and holding the line under your index finger. The rod handle should be held a little above waist height with the forearm about parallel to the ground.

Begin the cast with about 20 or 25 feet of line extended out from the rod tip, with the rod pointing at 9:30. For the pick up, begin moving the rod tip upward slowly with increasing speed until most of the line is lifted into the air. As the rod reaches the 10 o'clock position, increase the speed of the rod and flip the line directly up and back over the end of the rod tip.

For the back cast, bring the rod up to the 12 o'clock position and wait for the line to straighten out in the back. The weight of the line moving backward will cause the rod to bend back to about 1 o'clock.

As the line straightens out in the back, the forward cast brings the rod forward with increasing speed. This will cause a loop in the line to travel forward.

For the delivery, stop the forward motion of the rod at 10 o'clock and let the loop of the line travel forward until the line is straight.

PRACTICE AND COMPETITION IN CASTING

Like other sports, casting skills and techniques are improved with practice. Casting may be practiced on water, on a lawn, or on a gymnasium floor.

For all types of Bait Casting there are rubber and plastic practice plugs available in an assortment of weights, shapes, and sizes. For Fly

ANGLING AND CASTING

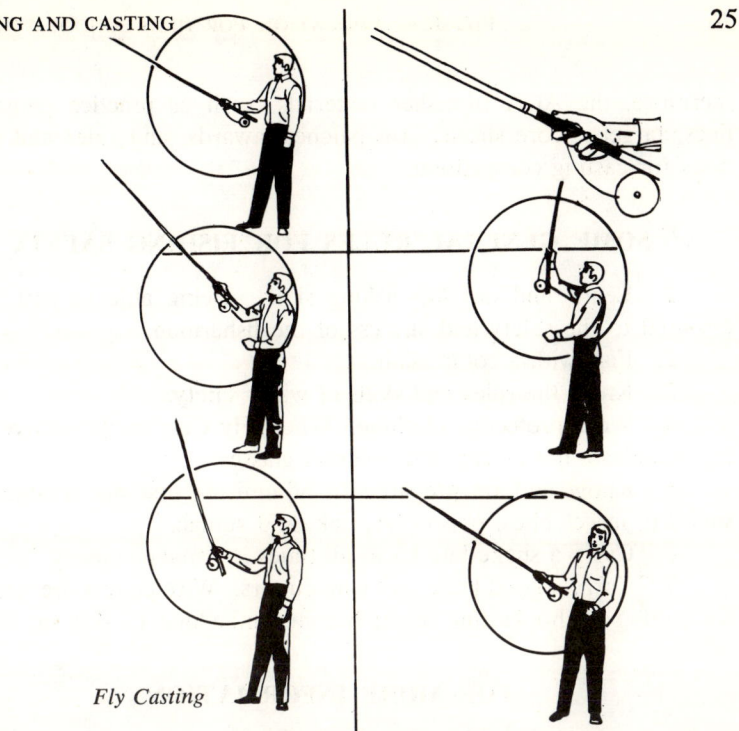

Fly Casting

Casting practice, a large visible fly with the barb cut from the hook is used.

For casting practice, it is highly desirable to use a target. Although many different objects may be used for this purpose, specific casting targets are made. These targets are either plywood discs or rings made of plastic or metal. The official size of the casting target used in all competition is 30 inches in diameter. The targets are designed for use on land or in the water.

The inclusion of some form of competition in casting practice is desirable for the interest it adds and for the opportunity it provides for skill improvement. Casting competition may be organized on a strictly informal basis, using only one or two targets. Casting competition may also be organized according to established rules and regulations as specified and sponsored by the American Casting Association (ACA).

The American Casting Association is the control organization for the sport of casting in America. The Association is a member of the AAU, the U.S. Olympic Association, and the International Casting Federation. The ACA sponsors and promotes casting tournaments on a local, regional, and national basis. Information may be obtained on sponsoring casting programs and tournaments through the ACA. Furthermore, the ACA furnishes materials, such as practice plugs, flies, lines, targets, score sheets, arm patches, awards, and rules and regulations for casting competition.

SOME GENERAL RULES FOR FISHING SAFETY

1. Learn and develop fishing skills. Being able to cast well is essential to the safety and success of the fisherman.
2. Fish with a companion.
3. Know the rules and skills of water safety.
4. Wear protective clothing. When Fly Casting, protective clothing includes a hat or cap and polaroid glasses.
5. Know and be prepared to administer first aid treatment for sunburn, insect bites, poison ivy, oak, and sumac.
6. Carry a snake bite kit at all times in "snake country."
7. Carry a good knife and wire cutters. Wire cutters are necessary for cutting off hooks that might become imbedded in skin or clothing.

FOR MORE INFORMATION

American Casting Association, P.O. Box 51, Nashville, Tenn. 37202

American Fishing Tackle Manufacturers Association and Fishermen's Information Bureau, 20 N. Wacker Drive, Chicago, Ill. 60606 (free listing of available motion picture films on fishing)

American Association for Health, Physical Education, and Recreation, 1201 16th Street, N.W., Washington, D.C. 20036 (*Casting and Angling*—Outdoor Education Series publication)

Athletic Institute, Merchandise Mart, Room 805, Chicago, Ill. 60654 (35mm slidefilm—"How To Improve Your Fishing"; pamphlet—"How To Catch Fish in Fresh Water," 25¢)

Catalogs and pamphlets showing equipment and fishing techniques may be obtained from fishing tackle manufacturers on request.

Archery

HISTORY

Archery belongs to a select group of activities that allow all ages—therefore entire families—to participate. Archery can be enjoyed in many forms: hunting; fishing; tournament shooting (both indoors and out); and games such as roving, tic-tac-toe, clout, and many others.

The introduction of the bow may have changed man's existence from a primitive to a civilized culture. In the beginning, the bow was used for hunting. But soon it came to be used in warfare. The first bows probably were made in the Stone Age.

Early bows were self-bows, a bow made from one piece of material, usually wood or bone. Later these materials were combined to make a composite bow.

Robin Hood and the English bowmen made the longbow famous. These were not the only well-known archers from England. Roger Ascham wrote the first known book on how to shoot a bow, *Toxophilus,* in 1545. Our American Indians are thought of as great archers, but their skill was in stalking the animal, shooting it at close range, and then tracking it down.

The first organized archery competition in the United States was held by the United Bowmen of Philadelphia in 1828. Since that time the National Archery Association was organized in 1879, the National Field Archery Association in 1939, the Professional Archers Association in 1961, and the American Archery Council in 1963.

With the development of our modern bow and interest in the out-of-doors, archery has become a very popular activity, evidenced by over 7 million active archers in the United States.

ROUNDS

Two rounds that have become popular among secondary school programs are the Modified Flint Round and the Modified Chicago Round. Both of these require a minimum of distance. The Modified Flint Round uses 12" and 18" field faces, scoring 5 and 3; and the Modified Chicago Round uses a five-color 36" face, scoring 5-4-3-2-1.

Modified Flint Round

Flights	Distance	Arrows	Face
1	17 yds.	4	18"
2	20 ft.	4	12"
3	20 yds.	4	18"
4	14 yds.	4	12"
5	15 yds.	4	18"
6	10 yds.	4	12"
7	20-17-15 14-10 yds. 20 ft.	6 (one for each distance)	18"

Modified Chicago Round

Flights	Distance	Arrows	Face
6	20 yds.	5	36"

The National Archery Association has developed a series of outdoor and indoor rounds that are excellent for developing club interest in your school. The following rounds are used for the intermediate (16-18) age group and score 9-7-5-3-1 on the five-color face.

American Round

Intermediate Boys and Girls—48" target

30 Arrows at 60 yards
30 Arrows at 50 yards
30 Arrows at 40 yards

National Round

Intermediate Girls—48" target

48 Arrows at 60 yards
24 Arrows at 50 yards

ARCHERY   31

Eye Dominance

Columbia Round

Intermediate Girls—48″ target
24 Arrows at 50 yards
24 Arrows at 40 yards
24 Arrows at 30 yards

Hereford Round

Intermediate Boys—48″ target
72 Arrows at 80 yards
48 Arrows at 60 yards
24 Arrows at 50 yards

    For those archers who like the out-of-doors and shooting in the woods, it is suggested that you look at the National Field Archery Association and their rounds. The Field Round consists of two 14 target courses, with target faces ranging in size from 6″ to 24″ and shooting distances varying from 15 feet to 80 yards.

SHOOTING TECHNIQUES

    There are two basic techniques of shooting: with and without a sight. Both require the use of 10 basic steps for consistency in shooting.
    Before attempting to shoot, eye dominance should be established. Overlap your two hands and thumbs so there is a small opening between

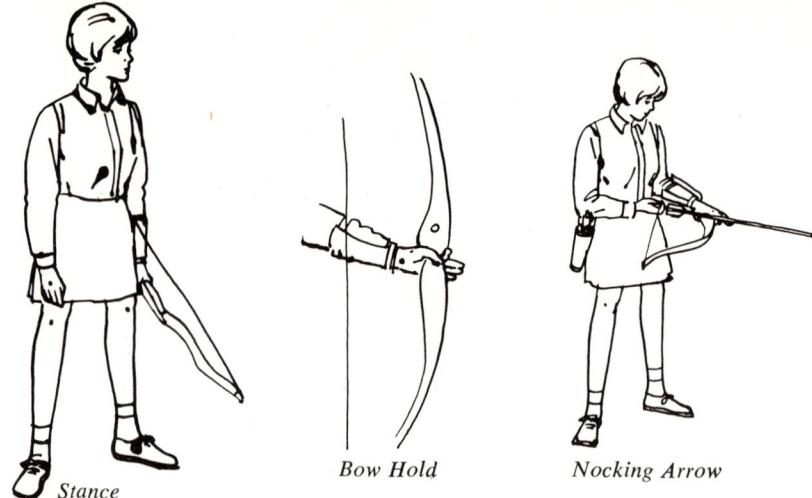

Stance   *Bow Hold*   *Nocking Arrow*

your hands. Extend your arms full length and with both eyes open, focus on a small object through the opening. Close your left eye; if the object remains focused in the opening, your right eye is dominant. Try this several times with each eye, but be sure to focus the object with both eyes open and then close one eye. Whichever eye keeps the object in the opening is your dominant eye. If your right eye is dominant, you are right-handed; and if your left eye is dominant, you are left-handed. The illustrations and descriptions which follow are for right-handed archers.

Stance

To establish your stance, stand with your left foot on the shooting line and your left shoulder toward the target. Your feet should be a shoulder-width apart. Move your rear foot forward until the heel of the rear foot is in line with the toe of your forward foot. Raise up on the balls of both feet and pivot one-eighth of a turn toward the target.

Hold the lower limb of the bow with your right hand. Raise the left hand with arm extended toward the target to shoulder level, then with the left hand in the handshake position, insert the bow handle. Wrap the index finger and thumb around the handle with the other fingers toward the target.

Nock Arrow

With the bow down at your side, rest the string on your hip and raise the bow until it is parallel with the ground. Lay the arrow on the bow with the cock feather up.

ARCHERY

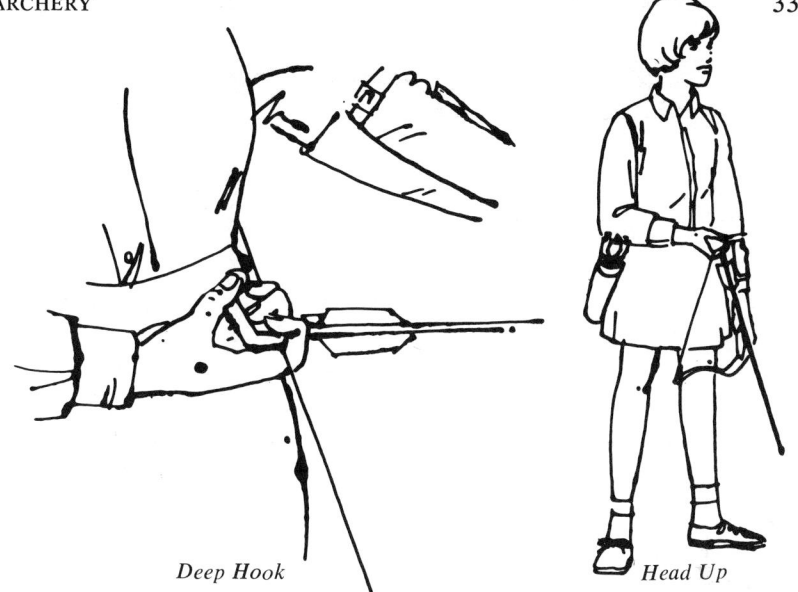

Deep Hook   *Head Up*

Set Hook

In setting your fingers on the bow string, position the fingers on your right hand in the boy scout salute (thumb on little finger with other fingers straight). Lay the bow string on the three extended fingers so the string is between the first and second joint of all three fingers. Now bend your fingers so they are pointing back up the arm.

Bow Hand and Arm

Again check the hold on the bow. The bow should be at your side and the bow arm naturally straight.

Head Up

After checking your bow hand and arm for correct position, you should bring your head up and focus your eyes on the target center.

Raise Unit

Bring the bow up to shoulder position with drawing elbow up and bow in the vertical position.

Draw—Anchor

Pull the string back to your anchor point, pulling with your back muscles. The pull should be on the string, and you should push on the bow.

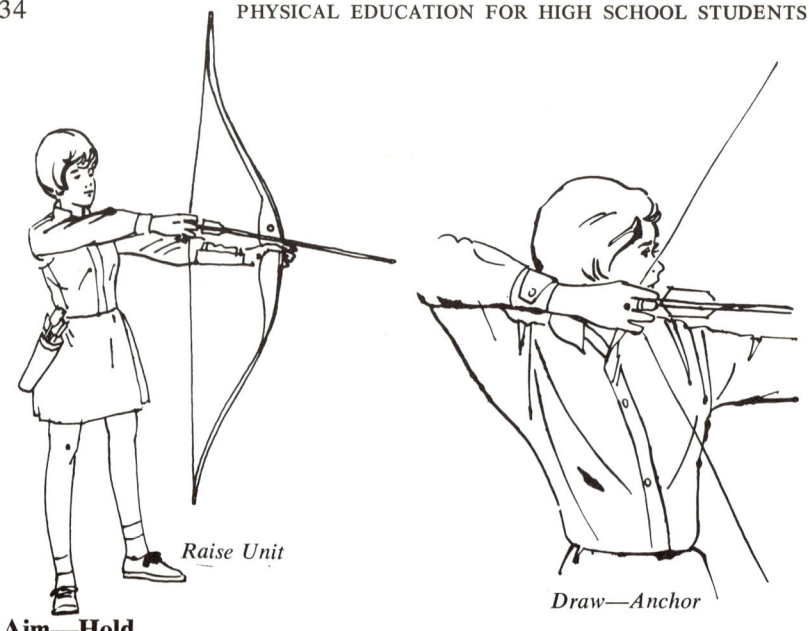

Raise Unit

Draw—Anchor

Aim—Hold

A momentary hold at the anchor point to steady the bow is essential. You should take a deep breath and hold while you tighten up your forward and rear shoulder. Aiming will be discussed later.

Aim—Release

Aiming is stressed in the last four steps because it is critical that you concentrate on looking at what you want to hit. To release, you simply relax the fingers on your drawing hand. The bow hold also should be relaxed as the arrow is released.

Aim—Follow-Through

Upon relaxing your drawing fingers, the drawing hand should move straight back. The bow should move slightly to the left and down, and the fingers of the bow hand should be relaxed, allowing the bow to swing freely in your hand.

AIMING

It would be advisable for you to start without a sight, using a high anchor point. The anchor point is a definite spot on the face which the index finger of the string hand must consistently touch in drawing. For aiming without a sight the anchor point would be the tip of the index finger (in the deep hook position) at the right corner of your mouth

Aim—Hold

and the "V" formed by your index finger and thumb hooking the back of the jaw. The hand should be solid against the face.

Now after you've tried the anchor point, you should work on aiming without a sight. As in throwing a ball to another person, you look at what you want to hit. Start at a distance of 20 feet from the target, closer if you like. Now raise your bow and without drawing look at the center of the target. Place the point of the arrow on the lower white circle (6 o'clock position), now shift your eyes back to the center of the target. Draw to your anchor point, hold, aim, and release. The important points to remember are the positioning of the bow before drawing (done by placing the arrow point at 6 o'clock) and looking at what you want to hit even during release and follow-through.

After you shoot several arrows and they hit in the same spot but not in the center, adjust where you place the point of the arrow. For example, if your arrows are going low, raise the point of the arrow up when establishing your "pre-gap" (i.e., 6 o'clock position on blue). Move it lower if your arrows are high. The farther back you get, the higher the pre-gap is raised; the closer you get, the lower the pre-gap is placed. Another point to work on is aligning the string in front of your dominant eye, down the shaft of the arrow, and through the center of the target. This will give you more consistent hits in relation to windage.

The use of a sight ensures that you will always put the bow at the right level. With a sight many use the low anchor point, especially when shooting long distances. The low anchor point is with the chin resting on the index finger and the string touching the center of the nose, lips, and chin. Use the same procedure established for bow elevation without a sight. Shoot several arrows at 20 feet, and note where the arrow is in relation to the target center. Raise your bow, establishing the pregap; now look along the edge of the bow window and the spot where the bow intersects the center of the target. That is the place to put the sight crossbar. Close your nondominant eye and forget the arrow; from now on you simply place the sight on the center of the target.

If the arrows don't hit the center but you do have them grouped, adjust the sight. The rule to remember for adjusting the sight is: Always move the sight in the direction you are off from the center of the target. Example: If your arrows are high, move the sight up; if the arrows are low, move the sight down; and if they are to the left, move the sight left.

After you have the sight adjusted for that distance, mark or record where it was. It will be correct for that bow at that distance every time you shoot. The sight should be adjusted for each distance you will be shooting from. You will raise it the closer you get and lower it the farther back you go.

STRINGING YOUR BOW

In stringing your bow, the end loop on the lower limb should be secured in the notch of the bow by a rubber band. With your feet shoulder-width apart, hold the bow with your right hand on the upper limb. Lay the lower limb across the ankle of your left foot and, taking the string with your left hand, step over the bow but under the string. The bow handle should be placed high behind your right thigh. Bring the string as far up on the bow as possible without putting pressure on the bow. Now, your right hand should be placed below the loop of the string. Raise your left heel off the ground and turn it out so the limb will not twist. Push with your right hand on the upper limb (keeping your right elbow high) so you push it down and in a straight line toward the lower limb.

Pressure at this point should be on the lower limb, handle, and upper limb, allowing slack in the string. With your left hand, slide the end loop up into the notch. Step out of the bow and, holding onto the string, check both the upper and lower notch to verify that the bow is strung properly. This is the step-through method of stringing your bow.

To unstring the bow, just reverse the above process.

ARCHERY

Stringing Bow

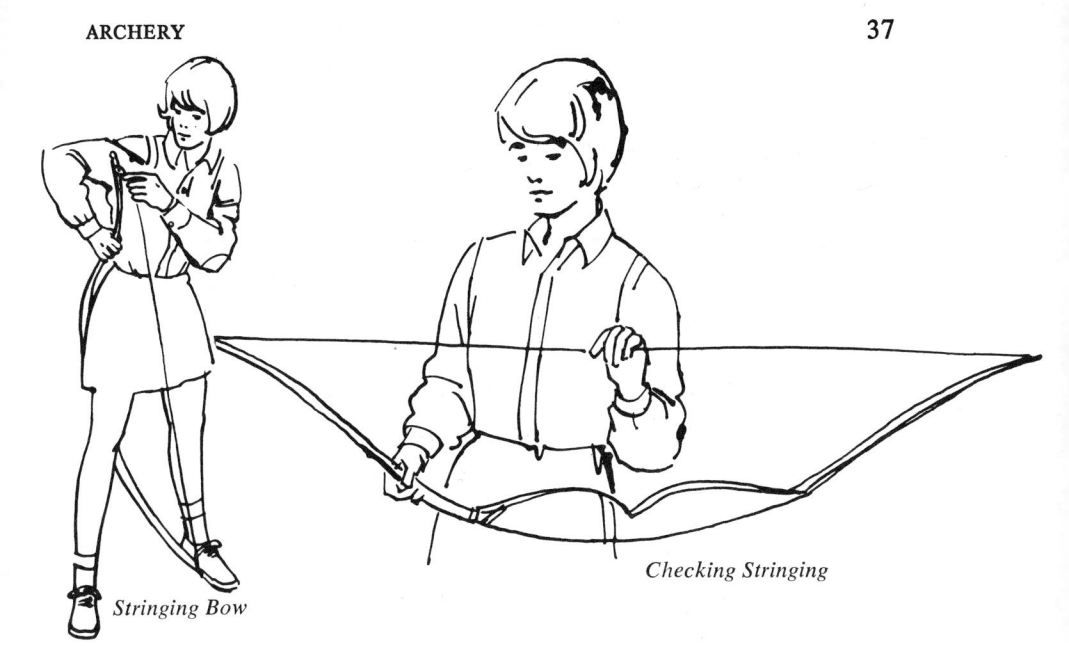

Checking Stringing

SELECTION AND CARE OF EQUIPMENT

The bow is the first item of importance to the archer. An average-priced bow with arrows matched in spine and weight would give you a good start.

Today's bows are made primarily from fiber glass or a combination of fiber glass and wood laminations. The prices range from around $10 to several hundred dollars.

Care for your equipment is essential to maintain its normal life expectancy. The bows, arrows, and leather goods should be stored in areas that are not excessively dry or moist. Temperatures should never exceed 85° or 90° for prolonged periods. A bow should be cleaned once a year with furniture wax, and strings should be waxed often. Your unstrung bow can be hung by the string on a wooden peg.

A light bow, 20 to 25 pound draw weight, is an excellent poundage for beginners. It is important, however, to have the recurve type, for it will have better cast.

Arrows are made from three basic materials: wood, fiber glass, and aluminum. Their cost increases in that order. For this reason, it is advisable to buy wooden arrows until your skill justifies using those made of the more expensive materials. The length of the arrow is most important. One way to determine arrow length is by placing the nock in the middle of your chest. Reach as far forward as you can with both

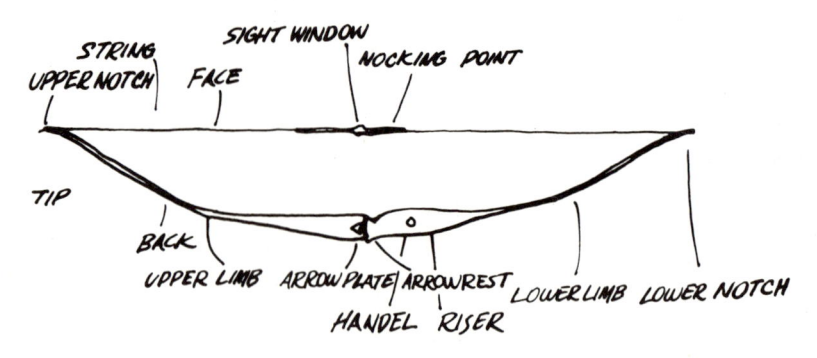

Parts of Bow

Parts of Arrow

arms, touching your fingers on the arrow shaft. The metal point must protrude beyond your finger tips; if it doesn't, get longer arrows.

Arrows, as well as bows, should be stored to maintain their shape. An inexpensive way to store your arrows is to take a cardboard box, turn it upside down, and punch holes in it. Insert the arrows in the holes and let them stand upright. They will remain straight in this position.

Any wooden arrow with a crack should be thrown away, for it may shatter upon release and could possibly injure you or others.

The quiver holds arrows and comes in many sizes and shapes. The most convenient type for general use is the hip quiver. It is placed on the right hip of the right-handed archer. Pocket quivers, ground quivers, back quivers, and bow quivers are also used by archers.

An arm guard is used for protection of your bow arm. It is important that it have a metal insert between the layers of leather. When putting on your arm guard, place it on the inside of the arm between the elbow and wrist with the narrow end toward the wrist.

The finger protector can be the tab or glove. For the beginner, the tab is recommended, especially when using the recommended deep hook.

A bow stringer is recommended when stringing and unstringing your bow, and they come in a variety of models.

A 36" mat is excellent for beginners to start with. It is fairly easy to move and is large enough to ensure hitting it. It is best for the beginner to place it on the ground so that arrows that go low need not be chased. The four-colored 36" face should be used initially, and then smaller ones as accuracy increases.

You should choose your shooting area with care. Many municipalities have laws against shooting a bow except on authorized ranges. If you have your own area, be sure no one will wander onto the range. This requires your taking the necessary precautions to ensure complete range safety. Thought should be given to the area beyond the targets. Shooting against a hill or with an open area behind the target is a good idea because you can see well beyond where the arrows will land if they go high.

SAFETY POINTS TO FOLLOW

1. Use care in handling and carrying equipment.
2. Never run with arrows held in your hand.
3. Never show your skill as an archer by using a human target or by permitting anyone to hold a target for you.
4. Always remember that a "loaded" bow is a deadly weapon.
5. Never shoot arrows that are too short.
6. Always use an arm guard and finger protector.
7. Never use imperfect or inferior equipment, such as cracked arrows or arrows without points or fletching.
8. Never use frayed bow strings.
9. Bows should be unstrung when stored.
10. Archery ranges should be supervised at all times.
11. Shooting should be at designated targets only.
12. Hanging arrows should be removed from the target face only after all archers have cleared the shooting line.
13. A bow falling in front of the shooting line should be retrieved only after all archers have unnocked their arrow.
14. When pulling arrows from the target, have all others stand to the side of the target so they will not be hit by the nock as arrows are withdrawn.

15. Only one person (i.e., Field Captain or Lady Paramount) should give the signal to shoot, retrieve arrows, or any other commands on the archery range.

16. When shooting field archery, always call "timber" before shooting.

17. When attempting to find lost arrows, have one person stand in front of the target so others will not shoot until the area is clear. If alone, place your strung bow across the face of the target.

18. An arrow falling in front of the shooting line and out of reach is considered "shot."

ARCHERY ETIQUETTE

1. Don't talk to or disturb shooters on either side when they are shooting.

2. Care should be taken with bow movement; avoid "jabbing" your neighbors in front or in back of you.

3. Avoid loud laughter or talk behind the shooting line; beginners sometimes mistake it for personal criticism.

4. Stay at the shooting line until your partner has shot his last arrow, then step back together. (It's much easier to shoot your final arrow when you're not the only one left on the line.)

5. Never shoot another person's personal bow. You may overdraw without realizing it, and you may damage the cast of the bow or break it.

6. Be honest when counting score. Always be a good sport.

ARCHERY TERMS

Anchor point. A certain spot on the shooter's face which the index finger of the string hand comes to on the draw to give consistency to shooting.

Arm guard. Protects the arm from the bow string; usually leather and worn on the inside of the forearm.

Arrow rest. An extraneous device on the bow to provide point contact; also a resting point.

Back. The side of the bow that is away from the shooter.

Blunt. A blunt-tipped arrow, often used for small game.

Bow arm. The arm that holds the bow and not the string.

Bow sight. A device that allows the shooter to sight directly on the target, which cannot be done with the arrow tip except at point-blank range.

Bow string. The string of a bow, usually made of dacron.
Broadhead. An arrow with sharpened metal tip for hunting live game.
Butt. Any backstop for holding arrows shot at a target.
Cast. The distance a bow can shoot an arrow.
Cock feather. The arrow feather at right angles to the nock; often of a different color than the other feathers.
Creeping. Letting the shooting hand edge forward before release.
Crest. Paint or decoration near the arrow feathers.
Draw. To pull the bow string back into the anchor position.
Drawing arm. The arm that draws the bow string back.
End. Number of arrows shot at one time (or position) before retiring.
End loop. That part of the string fitting over the bow nock.
Face. That part of the bow facing the shooter. Also, a target face.
Field archery. A competitive round shot at various distances and laid out like a golf course.
Field arrow. Arrow with field point, used outdoors for stump shooting, roving, and small game.
Finger tab. Tab worn on the drawing hand to protect the fingers and give a smoother release of the bow string.
Fletching. The feathers of the arrow.
Flight. Competitive round of shooting for distance; also, path of an arrow.
Free style. Shooting with the aid of a bow sight.
Glove. Worn to protect the fingers from the string.
Grip. The handle of the bow, held by the shooter when shooting.
Grouping. Arrows falling in a consistently small compact area on the target.
Head. The tip or point of an arrow.
Hen feathers. The two feathers not at right angles to the nock, usually the same color and used along with the cock feather to guide the arrow's flight.
Hold. To grip the bow; or to hesitate at full draw.
Index. A raised piece of plastic on the nock of an arrow that is in line with the cock feather.
Instinctive shooting. Aiming and shooting arrows instinctively, rather than with the aid of a bow sight.
Limbs. The two ends of a bow, from the handle riser out. The limbs bend and give the arrow the spring that propels it.
Laminate. A composite bow usually of wood and fiber glass.
Longbow. A bow with no recurve.

Nock. The groove in the end of an arrow in which the bow string fits.
Nocking point. The marked place on the bow string where the arrow nock is placed before drawing and releasing.
Notch. The grooves at both ends of the bow, which hold the bow string.
Overdraw. Drawing the arrow back too far, so that the tip passes the face of the bow. *Dangerous.*
Point. The tip on the end of the arrow.
Pre-gap. A method of aiming.
Quiver. Something to hold arrows; can be ground, back, or pocket.
Recurve. A bow curved on the ends.
Release. To let the bow string slip off the finger tips.
Self arrow. An arrow made entirely of one piece of wood.
Self bow. Bow made entirely of one piece of wood as opposed to bows of laminated construction.
Serving. The thread wrapped around the bow string to prevent fraying of the string.
Shelf. The place on the bow where the arrow rests.
Shooting tab. A device to protect the fingers of the string hand.
String. To prepare a bow for shooting. Also, the bow string.
String fingers. The three fingers used to draw back the bow string.
String height. The distance between the bow and the bow string at the handle. (Formerly, *fistmele*—a clenched fist with the thumb raised—was the approximate unit of measure for the correct distance.)
Solid bow. Common reference made to bow of fiber glass or plastics.
Target archery. A competitive round shot at fixed distances in an open field.
Target arrow. A lightweight arrow with target point.
Weight. The amount of effort (in pounds) required to pull the bow.
Windage. The amount of drift in the flight of an arrow caused by wind.

FOR MORE INFORMATION

American Association for Health, Physical Education, and Recreation. *Archery Skills Test Manual.* Washington, D.C.: the Association.

American Association for Health, Physical Education, and Recreation, Division for Girls and Women's Sports. *Archery-Riding Guide.* Current edition. Washington, D.C.: the Association. Published biannually.

Athletic Institute. *How To Improve Your Archery.* Chicago: the Institute.

Gillelan, G. Howard. *Modern ABC's of Bow and Arrow.* Harrisburg, Pa.: Stackpole Co., 1967.

Haugen, Arnold O., and Metcalf, Harlan G. *Field Archery and Bowhunting.* New York: Ronald Press, 1963.

Keaggy, David J., Sr. *Power Archery.* Revised edition. Riderwood, Md.: Archery World Magazine, 1968.

McKinney, Wayne C. *Archery.* Dubuque, Iowa: Wm. C. Brown Co., 1967.

Miller, Myrtle K. "General Archery Safety Rules" and "Practical Aids for Archery Instructors." 67 Old Stone Church Rd., Upper Saddle River, New Jersey.

Niemeyer, Roy K. *Beginning Archery.* Revised edition. Belmont, Calif.: Wadsworth Publishing Co., 1967.

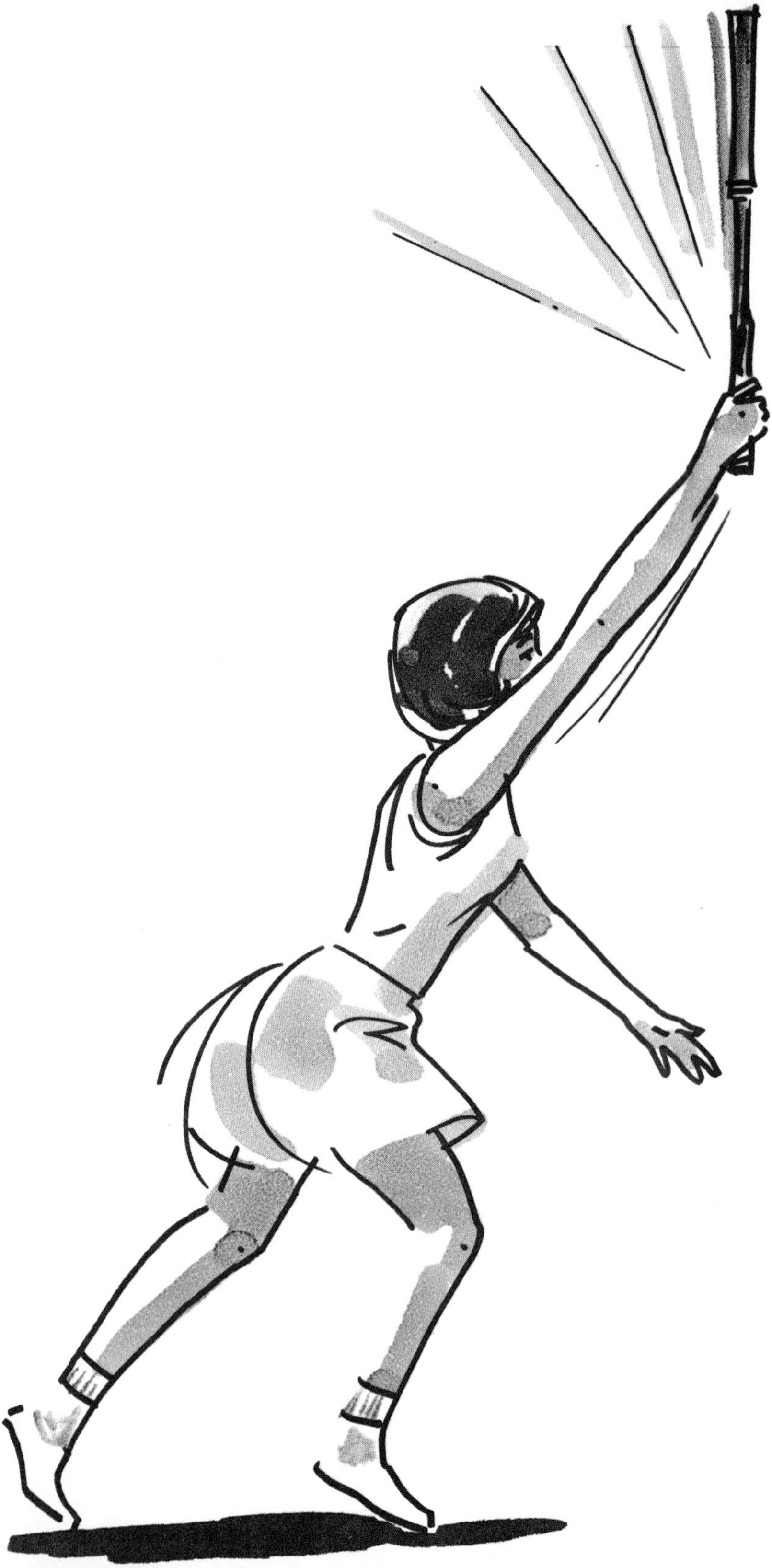

Badminton

Badminton comes to us from England. British army officers stationed in India learned to play a native game called Poona. They liked it so much that around 1860 they took equipment back to England and introduced the game to their friend, the Duke of Beaufort, who used Poona to entertain his guests at his country estate, Badminton House. The guests showed their appreciation by adding a few rules and renaming the game "Badminton."

In 1887, the Badminton Association was formed to standardize rules and to serve as a governing body for the game in England. Although the game was first played in New York City in 1878, very few Americans knew of its existence until 1918. Our soldiers stationed in England during World War I learned to play it and on their return home gave a boost to its popularity in this country.

Although badminton is now accepted as one of our most popular sports, the newspapers seldom carry reports of badminton matches. Many people do not know that the game is played on a local, sectional, national, and international basis. Just as tennis has its Davis Cup, badminton has the Thomas Cup for men and the Uber Cup for women. Both of these contests are held every three years.

There are many reasons why the game is so popular. Played by experts, it requires faster coordination and more physical stamina than does tennis. Beginning players, on the other hand, can enjoy it with very little technical skill. It is an ideal sport for boys and girls to play together, and it can be played indoors or outdoors. The tempo of the game depends on the players, thus making it a good game for players of all ages.

Badminton is similar to tennis, but the smaller courts and lighter racket require an entirely different use of the arm and wrist. The game

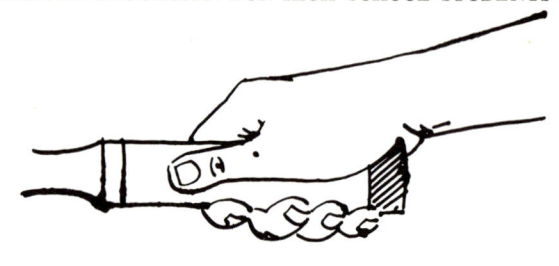

The Grip

is usually faster. Strength and endurance are very important in badminton, as is quick thinking, coordination, and skill in performing a variety of strokes.

The main purpose of the game is to score points by placing your shots so that your opponent cannot return the shuttle to your court. In order to play the game successfully, there are a few basic skills that you should learn.

BASIC SKILLS

The Grip

The first important thing is how you hold the racket. For forehand strokes and service, the grip is similar to the Eastern forehand grip in tennis. (All directions are for the right-handed player; reverse them if you are left-handed.) Put the racket handle in the palm of your right hand, with the flat face of the racket perpendicular to the ground or floor. Now wrap your middle, ring, and small fingers around the sides of the handle. Keep your fingers slightly spread. Set your forefinger like a "trigger" on a pistol and place the thumb around the handle on the left side. Now you will see that the index finger and thumb form a large "V" on top of the handle. Be sure you always have that "V" for forehand and service strokes.

For backhand strokes many players turn the racket slightly to the right and straighten the thumb a little along the flat edge of the handle. This might help you to get a little stronger whipping motion, for in all strokes a rotation of the forearm and wrist is essential.

The Serves

Now you are ready to serve the shuttle to your opponent. The short serve is used a great deal in doubles play and occasionally in singles for variety. For this serve, stand in a stride position with your left foot forward. Hold the shuttle by the tip of a feather in front and a little to the right of your body. Start with your weight on your right foot and shift it to the left just before the service. Use a short backswing with your wrist well cocked; drop the shuttle and sweep it across the net. Do not use your wrist. This action is like the swing of a gate. The shuttle should clear the net by a few inches.

For all serves the shuttle must not be above your waist when you hit it, and the head of your racket must be below any part of your hand. Also, you cannot move your feet while serving. To do a long serve, start with the weight on your right foot. Then transfer your weight to your left foot as you hit the shuttle. Swing the racket forward and hit the shuttle well in front of you, and follow through along the line of flight of the shuttle. The shuttle should travel high and deep into your opponent's court so that he is forced back to the base line to play it. This serve is used a great deal in singles and occasionally in doubles, although you cannot serve as deep in doubles due to the shortness of the service court. When you become a more advanced player, you will probably want to learn the drive serve also.

Some Exercises

Here are a few ways in which you can learn the feel of the racket and the shuttle. Hit the shuttle straight up into the air, and using plenty of arm rotation, count the number of consecutive hits you can make. Hit the shuttle upwards and catch it on your racket. Hit the shuttle against a smooth wall, starting near the wall and moving gradually, hitting continuously.

Forehand Overhead

Now suppose your opponent has hit the shuttle high to you, and it comes on your right side. You will want to make a forehand stroke to return it. If possible, hit the shuttle as far over your head as is comfortable. (You may have to move up or back a little.) Your body should face the right sideline, with your left foot closer to the net than your right. As you swing your racket up and behind your back with your hand close to your right ear, your weight goes to your right foot.

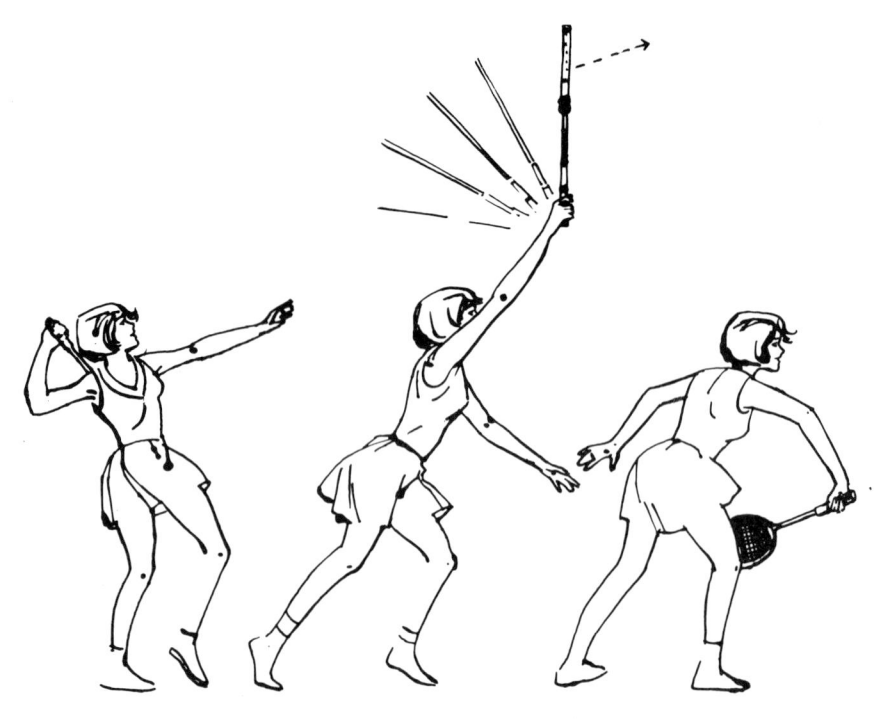

Overhead Clear

Cock your wrist. Now as you swing forward and upward extend your arm and transfer your weight to your left foot. Just as you hit the shuttle, rotate your forearm and wrist so the racket head is flat. Then follow through a little with your arm in the direction of the shuttle flight. This should be one continuous smooth motion. The forehand stroke should be used on all overhead strokes. The forearm rotation will vary depending on whether a clear, drop, or smash is required.

For the clear, you have the normal amount of rotation and at contact point the racket is pointing upwards. For the smash, which is only attempted when you are in the front half of the court, your rotation must be doubled in power and speed and your contact point is with your racket pointing downward.

The drop shot is a deceptive one. To your opponent it looks as if you are doing a clear, but you ease up on your rotation so that the shuttle just sails over the net and drops to the floor close to the net. Your opponent expects it to come to the back part of his court, and he may not be able to run up fast enough to hit it before it drops to the floor.

BADMINTON 49

Backhand

DRIVE

DROP

CLEAR

SMASH

Backhand Stroke

If the shuttle comes to you on your left side, you should return it with a backhand stroke. For this, face the left sideline, extend the right foot, and reverse all of the above directions for the forehand stroke. Rotate the forearm and wrist so the shuttle is contacted as high as possible. There is one backhand stroke in which the body faces more toward the net; this is called the round-the-head-stroke, but you will not need to learn that yet.

Drive Strokes

These are made both forehand and backhand on all shots to the side of the body that are contacted between shoulder and knee. Step with your right foot toward the shuttle and swing as in the overhead stroke. Extend your arm and rotate the forearm. The shuttle should travel in a line nearly parallel to the ground to your opponent's court.

Underhand Clears

The stroke for the forehand underhand clear is almost exactly like the deep singles serve. The forearm is rotated rapidly to sweep the shuttle high and deep into the back of the opponent's court. This is usually made when you want to hit over your opponent's head when he is near the net.

The backhand underhand clear is made almost like the forehand, with an unlocking of the wrist and a rotation of the forearm. On both these shots, contact the shuttle as close to the height of the net as is possible.

Footwork

In the waiting position the body should be bent slightly forward, with the weight more on the balls of the feet and the feet slightly more than a shoulder-width apart. As you move for a shot, use short steps to cover the court, perhaps ending with one long stride if necessary. Your last step should always be made with the racket foot. When moving toward the back of the court, never run backwards. Instead pivot and slide or run to the proper position. The pivot is something like the one you may have learned in basketball and is used a great deal in badminton to change your body direction quickly. Always try to return to your "home position" as soon as you have completed a shot so that you will be ready to move again for the next shot. Remember to keep your eyes on the bird, move quickly, get your balance, and keep far enough away from the shuttle to enable you to take your shot easily.

Net Shots

There are just a few more strokes you need to know about before you are ready to try a game. These are the net shots, and they are used when your opponent draws you close to the net with either a drop shot or a net shot of his own. One is a hairpin shot, in which the shuttle makes a hairpin curve. Either foot may be stretched forward, but with the right foot forward you will get a longer reach. Your racket should contact the shuttle as close to the height of the net as possible. You should strike the shuttle lightly with a lifting motion and with no rotation of the forearm.

If you are closer to a sideline than to the center of the court, you can try a cross-court net shot. This will be forehand when you are on the right and backhand when on the left. The shuttle must be contacted

BADMINTON   51

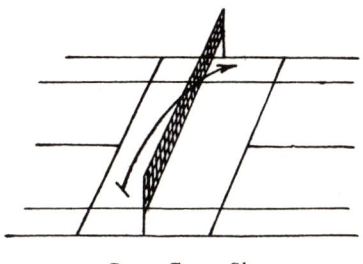

Cross-Court Shot

when it is close to the height of the net, and the entire action is done with a turn of the forearm, a little slower than the usual snap.

SINGLES PLAY

Now let's try a game. Get your friend Pat for an opponent. Suppose you serve first. You stand in your own right-hand service court. Pat stands in the diagonally opposite court. You must use an underhand serve, and remember that the shuttle, when hit, must be not above your waist and the head of the racket must be lower than any part of your hand. The shuttle must cross the net, clear the space between it and the short service line and reach Pat's receiving court.

If Pat fails to return the service or loses the rally, you win one point. You and Pat then move to the left-hand service courts, and you serve again. Until Pat wins a rally or you fail to make a good serve you continue serving from alternate courts. When Pat wins a rally and becomes the server for the first time, she has no score, as only the server can win points. She starts to serve from her right service court.

Suppose Pat won 2 points, then lost a rally, you are again the server, and the score is 3-2 in your favor. Take time out, while you learn a unique feature of badminton scoring in singles play. Whenever your score is zero or an *even* number of points, you serve from your *right-hand court*. But when your score is an *odd* number of points you serve from your *left-hand court*. As Pat has 2 points, she will serve from her right-hand court when next she becomes the server. This rule does not hold when you play doubles.

When playing singles, the court is narrow because the alleys are not used. So in most of your strategy you are trying to maneuver your opponent up and back in his court, although occasionally from side to side as well. Your opponent's backhand corner is usually an especially vulnerable spot; clears to that corner often set up smashes and net shots which become point winners.

For girls, the game is won by the first player to win 11 points, except when both players have 9 points or 10 points. If this happens see the list of terms below or a rule book for the explanation of "setting." For boys, the singles game normally ends when one player achieves a score of 15, although occasionally it is played to 21 points. A match is the best of 3 games.

DOUBLES PLAY

Now let us use the alleys of the court for both services and play. The line which is 2½ feet from the back boundary line is the back service line, but after service the entire court is used. Suppose you and Pat oppose Jean and Dick for a game of mixed doubles. You are the first server, so you serve from the right-hand court to the court diagonally opposite you. If you win the point, you move to the left-hand court and serve from there. You and Pat exchange courts for this, but Jean and Dick stay where they were. As long as you continue to win points, you continue to serve, alternating courts each time.

When you lose your serve, it goes to your opponents. If Jean is standing in the right court, she will serve next. When she loses her serve, Dick will serve next before it comes back to your side. He will serve from the court he happens to be in at that time. When he loses his serve, it comes back to your side. Whoever is in the right court will serve first, and when he loses his serve his partner will serve from the court where he happens to be at the time.

To summarize: On the first serve, the team starting gets only one term of service. This is usually called "hand down." Thereafter, each player on a team gets a term of service before the serve goes to the other team, or in badminton language, "two hands down." When the service changes sides, it is always started by the player who is in the right court, even though that player might have served last the last time the serve was on that side.

There are several different ways of playing in doubles. Sometimes the teammates prefer to be responsible for the entire right or left sides of the court, from the net to the back line. Sometimes, one player covers the front half of the court, all the way across, while his partner stays in the back part of the court. There are even some fancier ways to divide the court, like diagonally, or on a rotating basis. Perhaps for a start, you had better play side by side with your partner, and when you are ready for more advanced doubles play, your teacher can help you consider alternatives.

BADMINTON

A doubles game is won by the team getting 15 or 21 points, as agreed by the players before they start. The server should call the score before each serve, naming his team's score first and indicating how many hands are down. For example, you might call the score "6-3, one hand down," if your score is 6, your opponents' is 3, and Pat has already served during this inning. When both partners have completed their serves, it becomes two hands down. This completes an "inning," and the opponents get the serve.

HELPFUL HINTS

The following are helpful hints to improve your game:
1. Play singles whenever you can to develop an all-around game.
2. When possible reach upward to hit the shuttle.
3. For shots back of the short service line, have your side toward the net.
4. Use correct forearm rotation at all times.
5. Concentrate on placing the shuttle as far away from your opponent as possible. As you gain skill, begin to practice deception.
6. Risk clearing too far rather than not enough; otherwise you may set the shuttle up for your opponent to smash.
7. The smash is the chief attacking stroke; so learn it soon.
8. Clear deep to the corners of the court to avoid giving your opponent a smash.
9. In singles keep your opponent moving up and back in the court rather than from side to side.
10. Never be in a hurry to finish a rally; keep the shuttle in play until you have an opening for a winning shot.
11. Return to your home position after each shot.
12. In singles use a high deep serve to force the receiver back to his base line; fool him occasionally with a short serve.
13. Plan your attack with straight-ahead shots and only use cross-court shots when you have an opening for a sure point.

ETIQUETTE

Etiquette in badminton simply means the courtesy which players show each other in the game. Courtesy and good sportsmanship imply knowing how to win or lose gracefully and being able to accept all decisions in a good spirit. Some other specific points that apply to badminton follow:

1. The winner of the racket spin should have the choice of side or service.
2. The server keeps the score and calls it before each serve.
3. Never walk behind a court while a rally is under way.
4. Refrain from bothering another court for your shuttle until the rally is over.
5. Refrain from playing singles if others are waiting to play.
6. Be sure that your opponent is ready before you serve.
7. The losers of a match should congratulate the winners.
8. Help your partner, opponents, and any spectators enjoy the game by being courteous and cheerful.

SAFETY

You should always wear good tennis shoes to protect your ankles and good socks to protect your feet. Avoid any type of clothing which will hamper your arm or leg action. When playing doubles, get your signals straight with your partner so that you will not go after the shuttle at the same time and hurt each other. If you wear glasses, it is wise to wear a glasses protector. If you learn how to play a clever game, there is little danger of over-exhaustion from a badminton match.

OFFICIATING

In informal matches and games, no officials are needed, and the server calls the score each time before serving, naming the server's score first. Decisions are made by the players, and any disputed points are replayed. However, in tournaments it is desirable to have a tournament referee and umpires for each match. The umpires can be assisted by linesmen and net umpires. The umpires call each point clearly and record it on the official score card. For more details on how to become a good badminton official in your school, see the *Tennis-Badminton Guide,* published by the Division for Girls and Women's Sports of the American Association for Health, Physical Education, and Recreation.

SELECTION AND CARE OF EQUIPMENT

Wooden Frame Rackets

The price of rackets for badminton varies as much as the price for tennis rackets. A medium-priced racket will serve better in the long run than a cheap one. It pays to buy a good frame, as cheap frames break or warp when restrung. Get a weight and size you can handle easily. Nylon or gut strings are quite satisfactory. When not in use, the racket should be kept in a moisture-proof case and a press to prevent warping. Store it on a flat surface or hang it up in a place that is neither too hot nor too cold. Apply wax to the wood frame occasionally, and have broken strings repaired at once.

Metal Frame Rackets

These are relatively new in badminton and come from England. The advantage of these frames are (1) lightness—they weigh around 4 ounces; (2) they do not warp easily; and (3) they do not need a press. A disadvantage is that they are expensive. This disadvantage is offset by the fact that they should last for several years.

Feather Shuttles

Always try to play with a shuttlecock that is in good condition, because its flight will affect your game. Official matches usually are played with shuttles made of feathers. Store your shuttles in an upright position with the base down. Remove them from the box by the base. The feathers will be less brittle and last longer if they are kept in a moist place. Several hours before using, open the can and place a wad of wet paper in the bottom and top of the can. For outdoor play, be sure to get outdoor shuttles, which have a slightly heavier base than those for indoor play.

Nylon Shuttles

These are quite a bit cheaper than the feather shuttles and are more durable. The flight characteristics are slightly different than the feather ones, and, for this reason, they are not yet used in official tournaments. You need not be as careful in storage as you must for the feather shuttles.

Keep the net folded and stored flat when not in use. Repair any holes or tears with very strong thread. Never pull on the net once it is in place for use.

BADMINTON TERMS

Ace. One point, unit of scoring. Often used to denote an outright scoring point.
Bird. Shuttle or shuttlecock.

Clear. A high deep shot.

Down. Loss of service when the server or the serving side fails to score. In doubles each side has two downs, except in the first inning of a game when the serving side has one down.

Drive. To make a fast hard-hit shot parallel to the ground.

Fault. Denotes a violation of rules.

Game. Fifteen points in doubles, mixed doubles, and men's singles. Eleven points in women's singles.

Hairpin (net) flight. Short flight made from close to net. Ideally, bird should cross net close to net tape and fall close to other side of net.

High clear. A clear that goes high overhead and falls in the back court.

Inning. A side's turn at serving.

Let. Permitting the serve to be made over. Let may be given by the umpire for any unforeseen or accidental hindrance.

Match. The best of three games. Special arrangements may be made in informal play.

Pop-up. A slow high flight, the bird falling close to the net.

Rally. A play in which rapid returns are made by both sides.

Round-the-head-stroke. A circular "round-the-head" stroke used in returning overhead or shoulder-high flights on the left side of the body.

Setting. Increasing game points when the score is tied at 9-all, 10-all, 13-all, 14-all. In a 15-point game when the score is tied at 13, it may be set 5 points; when tied at 14, it may be set 3 points. In all 11-point games, when the game is tied at 9, it may be set 3 points; when tied at 10, it may be set 2 points. If the game is not "set," you play just to 15 or 11. The option of setting rests with the player or side first reaching the tied score.

Smash. A powerful stroke; the kill shot of the game.

Throw. An indistinct hit, usually caused by catching the feathers in the strings. This is considered a "fault."

Wood shot. Hitting the shuttle on the wood.

FOR MORE INFORMATION

American Association for Health, Physical Education, and Recreation, Division for Girls and Women's Sports. *Selected Tennis-Badminton Articles.* Washington, D.C.: the Association, 1970.

American Association for Health, Physical Education, and Recreation, Division for Girls and Women's Sports. *Tennis-Badminton Guide.* Current edition. Washington, D.C.: the Association.

American Association for Health, Physical Education, and Recreation, Lifetime Sports Education Project. *Ideas for Badminton Instruction.* Washington, D.C.: the Association, 1967.

Davidson, Ken. *How To Improve Your Badminton.* Chicago: Athletic Institute.

Devlin, Frank J., and Lardner, Rex. *Sports Illustrated Book of Badminton.* Philadelphia and New York: J. B. Lippincott Co., 1966.

Rutledge, Abbie, and Friedrich, John. *Beginning Badminton.* Belmont, Calif.: Wadsworth Publishing Co., 1965.

Varner, Margaret. *Badminton.* Dubuque, Iowa: Wm. C. Brown Co., 1967.

Badminton U.S.A. Edited by Mrs. Grace Devlin, Owings Mills, Md. A magazine published four times a year.

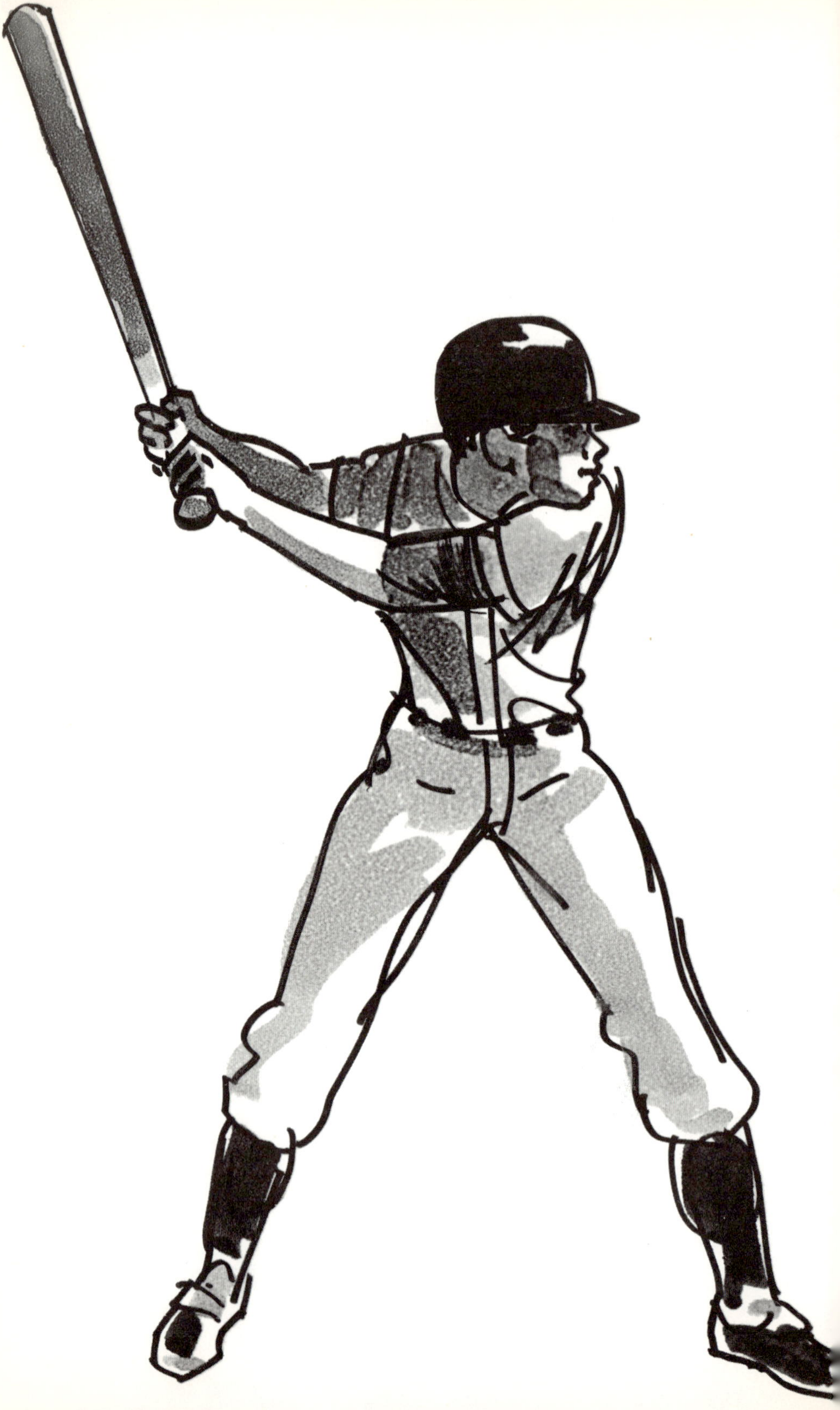

Baseball and Softball

I. BASEBALL

The true origin of baseball is a subject of much dispute. Abner Doubleday has been credited by some with founding baseball at Cooperstown, New York, in 1839. However, the baseball diamond as we now know it was drawn by Alexander Cartwright in 1845 in New York City. He was a member of the Knickerbocker Baseball Club whose members attempted to organize the then haphazard rules of many areas.

Baseball probably came from cricket, which was brought to America from England by early settlers. The children watched the adults play the game and improvised their own equipment and rules. When the upright stake used in cricket was abandoned for a rock or base (meaning station), the game received its name of baseball.

Early Beginnings

Early rules provided that the winner of a game was the first team to reach 21 "aces" (runs). Later this was discarded in favor of the nine-inning game. Many other rule changes have evolved over the years, but the distance between bases has remained at 90 feet.

At first the game was played solely for the recreation of the players, originally children, then adults also. Expense of travel and equipment grew to be quite an item, so a charge was made of spectators to defray expenses. As spectator interest mounted, occasional key players were paid for their services. Then in 1869 a team composed entirely of paid players made its debut in Cincinnati, Ohio.

During the Civil War Confederate prisoners of war saw Union soldiers playing baseball, and the game captured their fancy. When they returned home they introduced it in the South; thus knowledge of the game started spreading to different parts of the country.

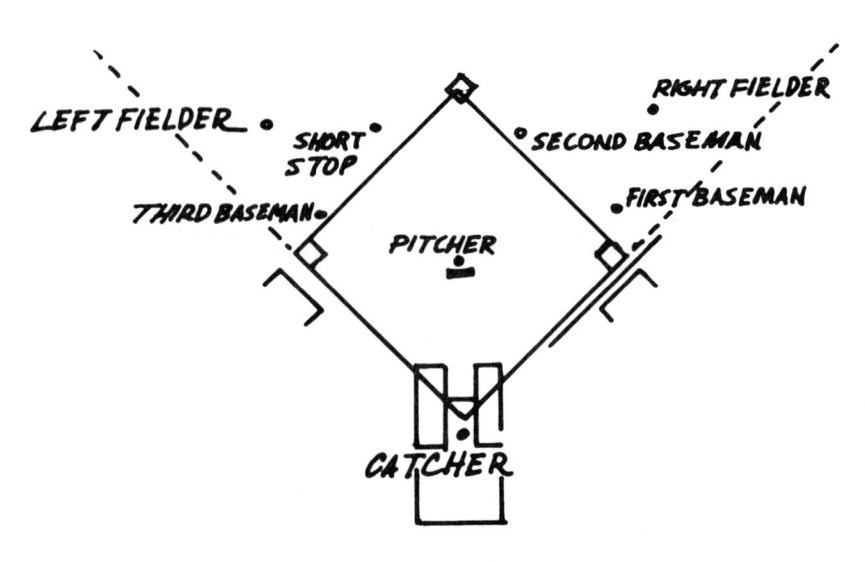

Diamond and Players

Popularity

The popularity of the game increased very rapidly. The National League was formed in 1875 and the American League in 1901. The World Series, held each year at the end of the season between the winning team of each league to determine the world champions, has contributed much toward the popularity of baseball.

Due to the advent of television, the farm teams of the major leagues have been decreased because the teams have not been able to survive financially. However, each major league still manages to maintain a few minor league teams to develop their younger players. Professional baseball is looking to the colleges throughout the United States to help produce and develop baseball talent, much the same as does professional football.

The Game

Baseball is a game between two teams of nine players each. The players and their designated numbers used in scoring are (1) pitcher; (2) catcher; (3) first, (4) second, and (5) third basemen; (6) shortstop; and (7) left, (8) center, and (9) right fielders. The field of play is a large area with a diamond near one end. The diamond, which is actually a square, is formed by four bases 90 feet apart. The pitcher's box or mound is 60 feet, 6 inches from the home base and on a straight line between home base and second base. It should also be 12 inches higher than home base.

The object of each team is to score more runs than the opponents. A game is divided into nine innings, and in each inning both teams are alternately on defense (in the field) and on offense (at bat) until each team has made three outs at bat. The home team starts the game by taking the field first. For class and intramural games the team to take the field first should be determined by the toss of a coin.

Baseball is composed of three distinct types of play or contest: (1) between the pitcher and the batter, (2) between the hitter and fielders, and (3) between the base runner and the fielders. A run is scored when an offensive player advances from batter to base runner and touches all four bases in order before his side is retired. An out is made when a batter is unsuccessful in reaching first base or when a base runner fails to advance to the next base.

Batting Rules

The batter may reach first base in many ways: by hitting the ball in fair territory and getting to first before the ball; by being hit with a pitched ball; by getting a walk when four "balls" have been thrown by the pitcher; by an error by a fielder; by the catcher's interfering with him; or by a fair-hit ball striking an umpire.

A runner may advance to another base if he reaches the base before being tagged with the ball. He may attempt to advance by free choice, or he may be forced to advance without penalty when a man at bat is walked on four balls or with possible penalty of being put out when a batter makes a hit and forces him to advance to another base. He may "steal" the next base, if that base is unoccupied, when the pitcher delivers the ball to the batter. This is considered a "stolen base" in baseball terminology, and base stealing is a very thrilling part of the game.

The batter is out under these conditions: when a fielder catches his batted fly ball; when a third strike is caught by the catcher, or on a third strike when first base is occupied and there are less than two outs; when he bunts foul on a third strike; when the batted ball is thrown to first before he arrives; when he hits a fly to the infield, if first and second base are occupied and there are less than two outs; when he interferes with players attempting to make the put-out; when he fails to bat in his proper order; or when he hits the ball while standing out of the batter's box.

Base-Running Rules

The base runner may advance if the pitcher balks or if a fielder obstructs his attempt to reach the next base. The base runner is out if he interferes with a fielder playing the ball; if he runs out of the basepath to keep from being tagged; if he fails to touch base after a fly ball is caught; if he is tagged while off base; if he is hit by a batted ball while off the base in fair territory; if he passes the runner ahead of him; or if he is off base when a fly is caught and the ball reaches the baseman before he can get back to the base.

Other Important Rules

All defensive players must be in the playing field before each pitch, except the catcher who must stay in his box behind home plate. However, fielders may run into foul territory to field a batted ball. A foul ball caught in the air by a fielder puts the batter out. If a foul fly is caught by the catcher (the ball must have reached the height of the batter's head to be considered a foul fly), the batter is ruled out. If it is caught below the batter's head level it is considered a foul tip and a strike on the batter. The pitcher is required to keep one foot on the "rubber" while pitching.

The strike zone is the area above the plate between the batter's arm pits and knees. A pitch through this zone is a "strike" on the batter. Any pitch passing outside the zone is a "ball," provided the batter does not swing at it. Three strikes make an "out," and four balls give the batter a "walk" to first base. Balls hit into foul territory are "foul balls" and are strikes unless there are already two strikes on the batter. After two strikes foul balls do not alter the count on the batter unless he bunts foul.

The batting order must be followed throughout the game unless there is a substitution. Failure to do so results in an out for the man who was to have batted. A substitute bats in place of the man whose place he took in the batting order.

A regulation game under High School Federation rules is seven innings; college and professional games are nine innings. In case of a tie at the end of the ninth inning, the game continues until one side is ahead at the end of an extra inning, or half inning in case the home team is ahead.

BASEBALL AND SOFTBALL

Pitching

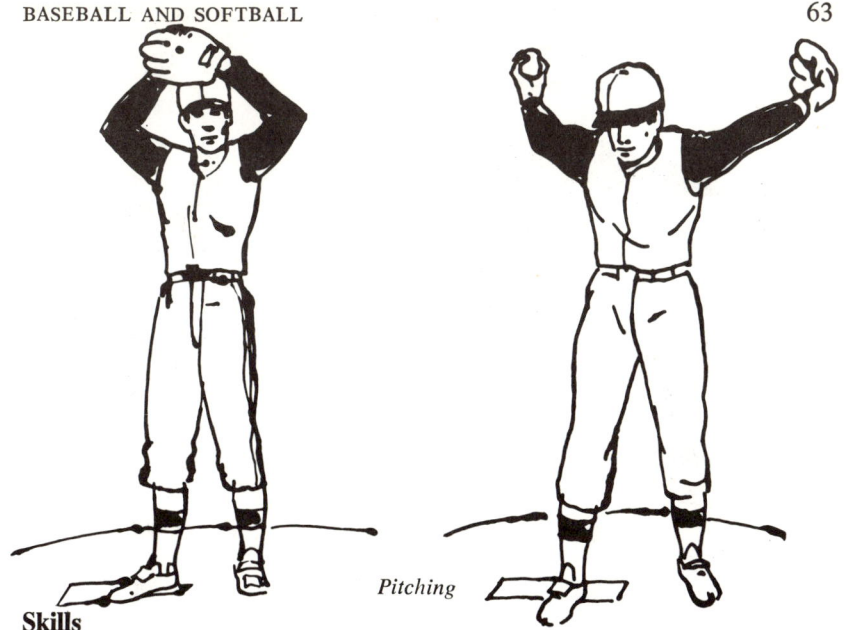

Skills

Baseball scouts and coaches check a player's potential ability primarily by three skills: speed in running, power of the throwing arm, and ability to hit. Though these qualities depend somewhat on "natural" ability, the great players are developed by hard work and by being truly dedicated to practicing the fundamentals for endless hours.

Pitching. If you are to be a successful baseball team you must develop a strong pitching staff. Pitching is considered 75 percent of defensive baseball. A good pitcher needs control and a fast ball. A curve and a change of pace delivery also are very desirable. To be a successful professional player you must be able to throw a curve ball for a strike, especially in crucial situations. Control is gained by throwing at a target from a legal pitcher's stance time and time again. Merely focusing on the strike zone is not enough. Working the corners by pitching within a few inches of a target is necessary. Throwing to a batter's weakness may not strike him out, but it should result in a weak grounder or a pop-up.

Physically, a pitcher relies upon his feet, legs, trunk, and arm to throw the ball. He uses his head to tell him how and where to throw. Proper footwork is important since over- or under-striding and turning the feet incorrectly may result in loss of speed and control. It has been said that a pitcher is only as good as his legs.

The right grip on the ball is important for the various pitches. Most deliveries are made with the two first fingers slightly separated

Pitching (cont.)

on one side of the ball and the thumb on the opposite side. Curves are made by turning the wrist inward or outward to impart a spin to the ball.

The change of pace is made in various ways. Generally, a pitcher depends upon a looser grip on the ball and less power. Palming the ball or grasping it with the knuckles or fingernails are other ways. A good pitcher will make these odd variations seem like regular pitches by not changing his pitching delivery when he is throwing his change of pace ball.

Catching

Catching. Proper placement of the hands in catching a ball can become a habit if these rules are followed. Balls above the chest should be caught with the elbows bent and the palms facing the ball with the thumbs toward each other, fingers up. A catch below the chest should be made with the arms extended downward and outward, the little fingers together, and the fingers pointing down.

Get in front of the ball on grounders and flies alike. Then if you miss the ball, you can block it with your body. Move quickly if the ball changes direction. Keep your eye on the ball and follow it into the glove. Reach out to meet the ball with relaxed arms and let them give a little with the momentum of the ball as you stop it and gain control.

When fielding grounders, keep the hips low and the weight controlled so that it may be quickly shifted so the body is in line with the path of the ball. The legs should be apart, with the left foot forward, knees and hips bent. The fingers of the glove should touch the ground, with the pocket open toward the oncoming ball. Stretch the arms out to meet the ball and then "give" to absorb the force of the ball. Continue to bring the arms back to prepare for the throw.

In fielding fly balls, get a quick start the instant the ball is hit. You must attempt to position yourself to catch the ball on the throwing side of the body. Good catches look easy because the fielder has judged the ball accurately. Errors in catching are usually the result of poor calculation.

Hitting

Throwing. All throws should be quick and accurate. The straightest throw is the overhand, but often a player must throw quickly from the position in which he fields the ball. This can be done by a side or underarm throw. If the distance is short, use a quick underhand toss. In any throw, step in the direction you intend to throw. Outfielders rarely use any but the overhand throw and should be taught to throw only from this position.

Hitting. Your object is to hit the ball safely. Keep your eye on it until the bat strikes it. Stand in a comfortable position from which you can reach the ball anywhere in the strike zone. Learn to swing only at good pitches. Don't try to outguess the pitcher. Instead, study the pitcher's delivery before your turn at bat. Hit the ball in front of the plate, not over it. As you swing, step toward the ball, pulling away from an inside pitch and leaning toward an outside one. Take a short controlled step toward the pitcher. Use a level swing and keep the elbows away from the body. Aim to meet the ball squarely and drive it through the center fielder rather than over his head. Stand steady in the box and move to meet the ball only after the pitcher starts his delivery. After two strikes, it is safer to choke up on the bat and just meet the ball. By choking the bat you are able to control your bat more and are more apt to put the ball in play. The most important factor in being a good hitter, after the basic fundamentals are understood and practiced, is your mental attitude. You must not fear being hit with the ball; you must attack the ball and feel that you can hit the ball against any pitcher. This positive approach can only be mastered by continual practice which builds confidence.

Bunting. Bunting is used to get on base or as a sacrifice to advance men already on base. The object of the sacrifice is to lay the ball down safely in fair territory so that runners may advance. Turn to face the pitcher as he starts the delivery; hold the bat loosely in front of you, level, with arms extended and hands separated, the upper hand close to the trademark; let the ball hit the bat and deflect either down first or third base line; then, and then only, take off for first base.

The bunter trying for a base hit shifts his feet as little as possible and starts for the base almost simultaneously with the bunt. Bunting, like any other phase of the game, is an art and must be practiced continuously. Bunting is like shooting pool; you must get the body low and get your eyes on a level with the bat and the ball.

Base Running. "Head-up" base running may determine the winner of a close game. Watch for signals from the base coach. Start your turn before you hit a base, and don't circle out too far from the base path. Touch the bag on the inside corner with whichever foot is convenient. Touch every base. When on base, watch the pitcher's feet; they will reveal where he will throw before his head turns. When advancing from one base to the next base, use a cross-over start. In the cross-over start your weight is on the leg closest to the next base; the travel leg is then crossed over the front leg to give you a faster start.

Sliding. A slide is used to stop the runner's speed and to avoid an infielder's tag. It is important to start the slide soon enough so that you don't hit the bag too hard. The four types of slides used by experienced players are the straight-leg slide, the bent-leg slide, the hook slide, and the head-first slide. Sliding should first be practiced wearing just socks on soft ground or a sawdust pit. If you make up your mind to slide do not change your mind. Many injuries are caused by halfway slides or slides which carry the body over the base.

Strategy

Certain situations in a ball game call for planning and cooperation on the part of the team. The way in which the offensive or defensive team plans and makes a play is called strategy.

The strategy often used by teams with a strong hitting power is to play for the big inning in which they hope to score enough runs to win the game. Other teams use what is frequently called "inside baseball" or "percentage ball." This means playing every inning for all that it is worth and making the most of each opportunity to score runs.

Teams depending upon the latter strategy rely upon the bunt, the hit-and-run, the squeeze, and steals to keep the defense on its toes.

The execution of the sacrifice bunt has already been mentioned and is normally used when runners are on first or second and there are no outs. The bunt is used to get men into scoring position and to lessen the possibility of a double play. The batter bunts only if the pitch is good, and the base runner goes only if the ball is bunted on the ground.

The Hit-and-Run Play. A double burden is placed on the short stop and second baseman when first base is occupied. In addition to being alert to fielding the ball, they must also try to prevent a steal. A runner on first starting with the pitch as if to steal second may pull the second baseman over and allow the batter to drive the ball through that hole for a hit. In addition, the man stealing second may be able to go to third by virtue of his early start. This is the hit-and-run play. A truer name would be the "run-and-hit" play, as the runner runs before the batter hits the ball. To protect the runner on this play the batter must swing at anything unless it is a wild pitch, one that the catcher is not able to catch and throw to the baseman to put the runner out.

The Squeeze Play. Late in the game when a run is needed badly and there is a man on third and less than two outs, a squeeze play may be in order. The runner goes with the pitch, and the batter must attempt to bunt the ball regardless of whether it is a good pitch or not. If he does not, the runner will probably be an easy out.

Stealing. Steals are executed when relatively fast runners are on base or when the catcher has trouble throwing to bases. The runner may steal to get into scoring position, to get into position to score on a fly or passed ball, or to take advantage of a napping defense. He may make his break on the pitch or delay his break until the catcher returns the ball to the pitcher. Occasionally two runners can advance on a direct or delayed double steal. There are many combinations of double steals, as you can well imagine. The first and third base steal situation is the most difficult for the defense to handle. The defense must practice its counter to this play for many hours. Of course, the team on offense will try to unnerve the defense by executing many offensive maneuvers in an effort to produce runs.

Signals. Regardless of the skill of individual members of a team, there must be team work for good strategy. In order for all to know what is going on signals are used. They should be easy to see and understand but clever enough to baffle the other team.

The coach and the team agree on a set of signals for such plays as steal, hit-and-run, squeeze, and bunt. Body signals given by the coach are the usual method. Examples of such signals are hands on hips, arms folded across the chest, left hand touching the right knee, and so forth. The more advanced the baseball players, the more disguised the signs must be to keep the opposition in the dark.

Position Play. The defense attempts to prevent the completion of offensive plays. It is important, then, that each man know just where to play during crucial situations. Normally, the first and third basemen play close in during a bunt situation, with the second baseman covering first and the shortstop covering second. If first base is the only base occupied, the catcher covers third when the third baseman has to make a play. If men are on first and second, the third baseman must protect his own base. The pitcher helps him cover part of his bunting territory.

In addition to the above plays each defensive man must know where and when to back up throws, to act as relay man, or to serve as a cut-off man. A good defensive player will think ahead of each play situation so that there is no hesitation during any play that may develop. To be sure that all situations are known by the players, defensive situations should be practiced almost daily so the players will know where to go and what to do.

Batting Order. Arranging the batting order so that each man can contribute in his own way is also a part of offensive strategy. Many coaches follow this batting order plan: (1) a man with ingenuity and a keen eye who can get on base one way or another; (2) a good hit-and-run man who can also bunt; (3) the best hitter; (4) a good long-ball hitter; (5) a long-ball but fair hitter; (6) the second lead-off man; (7) the second best hit-and-run man; (8) a poor hitter; (9) the poorest hitter—often the pitcher.

II. SOFTBALL

The game of softball was adapted from our national game of baseball by playground leaders and physical education instructors for indoor and playground use. A larger and softer ball is used, and the dimensions of the diamond are reduced.

During the Depression days of the early 1930's adults had more time on their hands; so they picked up playground ball as played by children and organized their own teams. Many different sets of rules and playing fields dimensions were used at this stage.

In 1934 the Amateur Softball Association was founded to standardize the rules and make them the same for boys and girls. The growth of softball since that time has been phenomenal. Young and old, men and women, boys and girls alike play it. There are many variations of softball, as has been mentioned. There is fast-pitch 12-inch ball, slow-pitch 12-inch ball played with 10 men (a fourth outfielder is used), and slow-pitch 16-inch ball prevalent in cities. Each of these games has enjoyed a great deal of popularity in the last decade. The slow-pitch games are more popular in most circles since the batter can put the ball in play on almost every pitch, thereby scoring more runs than is the case in fast-pitch 12-inch ball. In 16-inch slow-pitch games gloves are not used by the fielders. In addition there is a variation in the distance between bases, as well as other minor changes in the rules. Sixteen-inch softball is played with 10 men, and the fourth outfielder is called a short fielder.

Differences from Baseball

With a few exceptions softball is played the same as regulation baseball. The bases are 60 feet apart, and the pitching distance is 46 feet for men and 38 feet for women. The bat is smaller, but the ball is larger and softer than a baseball. Since bases are closer, runners cannot lead off base; they can leave only when the ball leaves the pitcher's hand. Also, since the pitcher is closer, he must pitch underhand, with the added rule that his wrist be no further away from his body than his elbow when the wrist passes below the hip. Seven innings constitute a regulation game. There are other minor differences, but they do not materially change the game.

Basic Skills

The following basic skills are essential in playing softball: batting, catching, fielding, running, and throwing. Batting and base running are considered offensive tactics in playing. Catching, fielding, and throwing are the defensive tactics. The skills discussed below are described for the right-handed player.

Batting. In batting, practice and drill are essential for developing timing, a level swing, and a "batting eye." It is seldom that two players will use identical batting techniques.

Whenever possible, use a bat which feels comfortable to swing. This involves the weight and length of the bat and the size of the grip in relation to the size of your hands.

While waiting for the pitcher to deliver the ball, hold the bat with a firm but relaxed grip. The left hand should be near the end of the bat, with the right hand above and close to the left hand. Hold the bat back and up by the right shoulder.

You should stand in a comfortable position facing home plate. Turn your head toward the pitcher so that you can look directly at the oncoming ball. Remember to watch the ball as it is released by the pitcher and step into your swing with your left foot.

Bring the bat round in a line with the pitched ball and hit the ball. Finish your swing with a follow-through over your left shoulder. Step toward first base with the right foot and run.

Base Running. The following suggestions will help improve your base running:

1. Watch the ball and advance additional bases whenever possible (that is, when four balls are called on the batter, on a throwback from catcher to pitcher, and on any poorly thrown ball).

2. Avoid wide turns when rounding a base.

3. Run on any hit ball when there are two outs.

4. Lead off after each pitch and advance if possible.

5. Run along the foul territory side of the line from third base to home to avoid being hit by a fairly batted ball.

6. Know the number of outs, inning, score, and count on the batter.

7. Avoid interferring with a player fielding a ball.

One of the most advanced elements of base running is the slide. Sliding is recommended only in advanced play and on suitable play surfaces such as grass and soft dirt. The skill of sliding is described in the section on baseball.

Throwing. The basic types of throws which you need to know are the overhand, underhand, and sidearm throw. The overhand snap and underhand whip throws are advanced techniques and are variations of basic throws.

Regardless of the type of throw you use, observe the following pointers:

1. Grip the ball with the first and second fingers on top of the ball and with the thumb under the ball.

2. On the wind-up, rotate the body by turning the left side toward the direction of the throw.

Overhand Throw

3. Rotate your body as you transfer the weight from the right to left foot.
4. Release the ball with the fingers pointing toward the target.
5. Follow through with the arm in the direction of the target.

The one thing that is different for each type of throw is the position of the palm of the hand as the ball is released. In the overhand throw the palm faces down; in the underhand throw the palm faces up; and in the sidearm throw the palm faces the body.

Since the ball can be thrown farther with the overhand throw, it should be used by catchers and outfielders; however, all players can use this more easily controlled and accurate throw when they have sufficient time to make a play. The sidearm throw is generally used by the infield players when they need to hurry a throw to a baseman. When passing the ball a short distance to a teammate, use an underhand throw. The underhand throw is also used by the pitcher.

Pitching. As a pitcher, learn how to grip the ball, release the ball, control the pitch, pitch the ball so that it cuts the corners, and be ready to field a batted ball.

In making a legal pitch you must assume a starting position with the ball held in both hands in front of your body and with both feet

BASEBALL AND SOFTBALL 73

Pitching

touching the pitcher's plate. In delivering the ball, keep your wrist closer to your body than the elbow when swinging the arm forward to release the ball. Use an underhand motion in releasing the ball. Take only one step toward the batter as the ball is released.

Catching and Fielding. In catching and fielding, you must gain possession and retain the ball in order to put out a batter or base runner. In performing this skill you should (1) watch the ball, (2) keep your body in front of the ball, and (3) relax and "give" with your hands as the ball is caught. Although there are some variations, the same general method for catching a ball is used for both baseball and softball players, and other suggestions will be found in the section on baseball.

If you wish to improve your catching and fielding ability remember the following points:
1. Watch the ball.
2. Use two hands whenever possible.
3. Move to get in line with a ball batted toward your position.
4. If possible, face toward home plate when catching a fly ball.
5. On a batted ball, call for the ball if more than one player is likely to try to field it.

6. As a baseman, be alert to move quickly to catch a poorly thrown ball—even to the extent of leaving your base.

7. As an infielder, field a bouncing ball either as it leaves the ground or near the height of the bounce.

8. As an outfielder, use your leg or body to block a rolling ball if you cannot reach it with your hands.

Position Play and Strategy

Position play for softball is much the same as that described for baseball. It is a good policy for teammates to talk with one another in working as an effective team unit. Being able to bat, run, catch, and throw is fun. Out-guessing your opponents adds to that enjoyment.

The strategy described for baseball is the same as that used by advanced softball players. The following hints on strategy will be helpful for less experienced players.

Elementary Strategy

1. As a member of the team in the field, always play for "one sure out."

2. As a base runner, touch all the bases.

3. As a base runner, when the ball is poorly thrown, run to the next base if time permits.

4. As a baseman or fielder, do no throw the ball to a base after the runner is there.

5. As a member of the team in field, catch the ball securely before trying to throw it.

6. As a fielder, call for the ball when more than one player is likely to try to catch a fly ball.

7. As an outfielder, after fielding the ball, throw the ball to an infield player as quickly as possible.

Intermediate Strategy

1. As a batter, when a base on balls occurs, if possible, continue on to second base.

2. As a baseman, when a base on balls occurs, be ready to prevent the runner from advancing another base.

3. As a batter, risk a called strike when you have a 3 and 0 count.

4. As a fielder, know the position of the base runners and the score. Know in advance what you should do before the ball is hit to you.

5. As a base runner, before there are two outs, leave the base after the ball is released by the pitcher, but stay near the base when a

BASEBALL AND SOFTBALL

fly ball is hit to the outfield. Return to your base if the fly ball is caught. If there is time after the catch, run to the next base. A runner on third base should stay on the base and run after the ball is caught.

6. As a base runner, when there are two outs, run when the batter hits the ball.

7. As a fielder, work, if possible, for a double play, but remember always to get one sure out.

8. As catcher, batter, or first baseman, know what to do on the third strike.

Advanced Strategy

1. As a batter, use the sacrifice-bunt play to advance a runner.

2. As a batter, use the base-hit bunt to get on base, and/or to score a run.

3. As a batter or base runner, use the hit-and-run play.

4. As an outfielder, generally throw a batted ball to the base ahead of the runner nearest home base.

5. As a member of the team in the field, move to "back up" a teammate on each throw or batted ball.

6. As a base runner on first base in the early part of the game, try to steal second base to determine the throwing ability and alertness of the catcher.

7. As a base runner, watch the base coach.

8. As a base coach, talk and/or signal to tell the runner to slide, stand up, stop at the base, or continue for additional bases.

Slow-Pitch Softball

The game of slow-pitch softball is almost identical to the regular (fast-pitch) game as far as bases, pitching distance, field conditions, and equipment are concerned. There are four basic rule differences. Ten players are used instead of nine, with the extra player being a roving, short fielder. The ball must be arched not higher than 10 feet nor less than 3 feet from the point where it leaves the pitcher's hand. This eliminates all fast pitching. Batters cannot lead off the base until the ball is hit, and no base stealing is allowed. Batters cannot bunt nor chop at the ball, but must swing away. Because of these differences there is greater participation on the part of all team members.

Sportsmanship

Courtesy and sportsmanship are as much a part of baseball and softball as are the rules. If in doubt, follow the Golden Rule: Do unto others as you would have them do unto you. We all like to win, but more important than winning is how we play the game. Be a good loser and a modest winner.

Never intentionally make a play that might injure an opponent or act in such a manner as to cause him to react in a way that will hurt him. Give encouragement to your teammates, and do not ridicule your opponents.

Know your place in the batting order and have your bat selected before it is time for you to bat. Don't delay the game by having to be paged when it is your turn to bat.

A good umpire is impartial. If a decision goes against you, remember he called it as he saw it. Any mistake that he might make is still official; you can protest, but his judgment is final. The rules state that no abusive language shall be used toward your opponent, the umpire, or the fans. Play hard and be a good sport.

Safety

The best equipment in the world cannot keep you from injury if you do not use good judgment and observe safety precautions. Be sure the playing area is free from hazards, such as broken glass, sharp stones, holes, barbed wire, poles, and slick places. Good equipment can protect you only if it is worn properly. Shoes too large may trip a runner. The catcher's body protector must cover the collar bones, and the mask should fit snugly so that it will not hang down and blind him.

If you have trouble holding on to a bat try taping the handle, using rosin, or using a bat with a large end. Never throw the bat when you have hit the ball. Drop it to the ground as you start to run.

Start the season and each game with a slow warm-up of the legs, back, and arms. Wear a sweater or a jacket if necessary to keep from getting chilled while waiting for your turn at bat. Unless it is very warm, the pitcher should wear a jacket when not pitching or batting.

To avoid accidents, keep the players' benches and equipment not in use away from the playing area. During warm-up practice keep all balls going in the same direction. Always watch the ball and bat to avoid being hit.

Treat all cuts and abrasions as soon as possible. Learn the basic skills properly. Above all, keep your eye on the ball.

Selection and Care of Equipment

The best practice in selecting equipment in both baseball and softball is to buy good merchandise. It is cheaper in the long run since it will last longer, give better service, and enable you to perform more skillfully. Any reputable sporting goods store can supply you.

The stamp *Official* on equipment refers only to size and weight and does not certify quality. Pick the type that will help you play best.

A bat should be selected in terms of balance for you. Don't worry about the length or weight if it feels right. Use it only to hit balls—never rocks. Bats with a close, narrow, straight grain are more alive and harder to break. Store bats in an upright position, and avoid exposure to excessive dryness or dampness.

In softball it is desirable for all players to wear a glove. The catcher and first baseman may use a mitt. Cowhide gloves, although more expensive, are more pliable than others. The horsehide glove will last longer, but it is a bit more stiff. Never over-oil a glove, but keep the pocket greased. Sitting on a glove may flatten the pocket and padding. Allow a wet or damp glove to dry naturally and then re-oil it.

Catchers must have the best of protection. They should get the best gear they can afford and make sure it covers them. The bar mask is lighter than the wire one and offers equal protection. The two types cost about the same.

Kangaroo leather shoes last longer, are lighter, yet are expensive. Selected calfskin or cowhide shoes are heavy, but they take scuffing better and are a little less expensive. Allow damp shoes to dry naturally and use a leather preservative to keep them soft.

The most serviceable uniform is probably a 50 percent wool and 50 percent cotton fabric. Occasional washing and mending will help it give long and useful service. As a precaution against injuries and infections, girls should wear knickers, slacks, or jeans and not shorts when playing softball. For sliding, sliding pads are advisable. These can be improvised with toweling or quilted padding.

FOR MORE INFORMATION

Allen, Archie P. *Baseball Coach's Handbook of Offensive Strategy and Techniques.* Englewood Cliffs, N.J.: Prentice-Hall, 1964.

American Association for Health, Physical Education, and Recreation. *Softball Skills Manual.* (Boys and Girls editions.) Washington, D.C.: the Association.

American Association for Health, Physical Education, and Recreation, Division for Girls and Women's Sports. *Selected Softball Articles.* Washington, D.C.: D.C.: the Association.

American Association for Health, Physical Education, and Recreation, Division for Girls and Women's Sports. *Selected Softball Articles.* Washington, D.C.: the Association, 1969.

Athletic Institute. *How To Improve Your Baseball.* Chicago: the Institute.

Coombs, J. W. *Baseball.* Third edition. Englewood Cliffs, N.J.: Prentice-Hall, 1967.

Irace, S. Charles. *Comparative Baseball Strategy.* Minneapolis: Burgess Publishing Co., 1967.

Kneer, Marian, and McCord, Charles L. *Softball.* Dubuque, Iowa: Wm. C. Brown Co., 1966.

Litwhiler, Danny. *Baseball Coach's Guide to Drills and Skills.* Englewood Cliffs, N.J.: Prentice-Hall, 1963.

Noren, Arthur T. *Softball with Official Rules.* New York: Ronald Press Co., 1966.

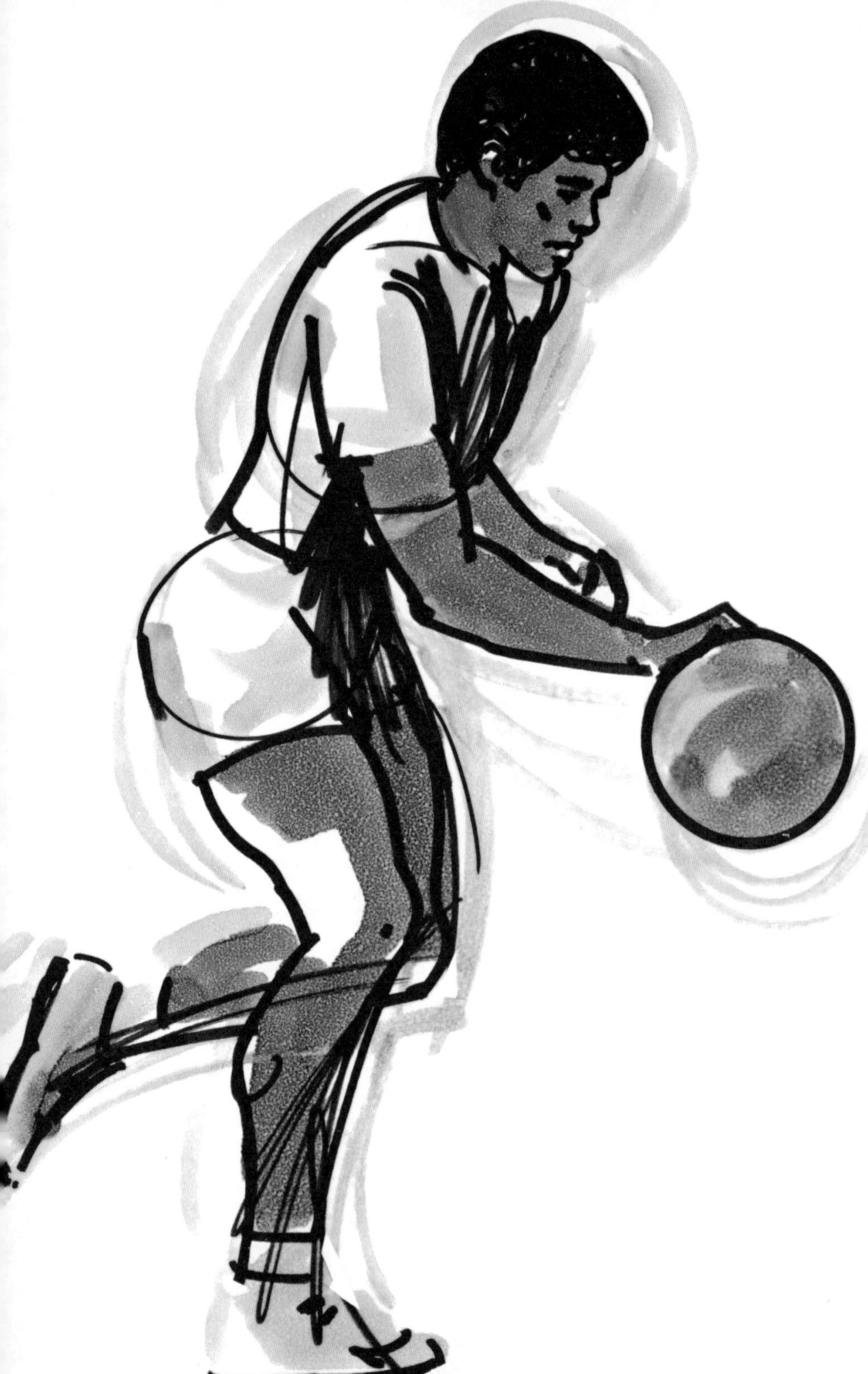

Basketball

Basketball is truly a great American game. It was invented by an American, developed to greatness in the United States, and became famous the world over—all in a few short years.

More high school boys and girls participate in basketball than in any other high school sport. Moreover, more high school boys and girls are spectators at basketball games than any other school sport. For this reason, it is important that you understand the rules for both boys and girls games. The games have much in common, but there are significant differences.

HOW IT BEGAN

In 1891, a Springfield, Massachusetts, YMCA leader, Dr. James Naismith, invented basketball to provide an indoor winter game for athletes. Peach baskets were used for goals, and so the game got its name.

At first, a soccer ball was used and players advanced the ball down the floor by rolling it. Later a special ball and the dribble were introduced.

In the beginning, any number of players from 9 to 50 could play; but within two years, the number was limited to 9, then to 7 and, in 1894, to 5, which became the standard number for boys games.

As the game became popular, many variations of rules developed. In 1933, the men's rules were standardized by a newly formed National Basketball Committee of the United States and Canada. Using these rules as a base, the Basketball Committee of the National Federation of State High School Athletic Associations adapts and publishes the rules for high school boys.

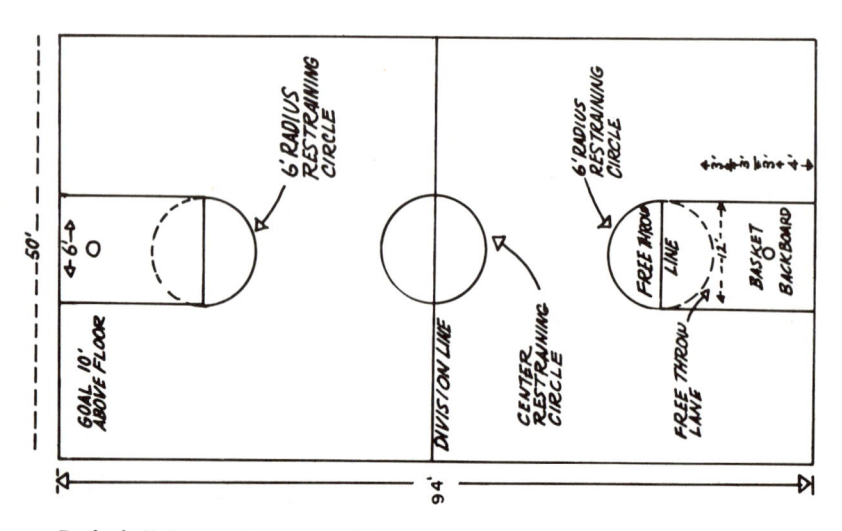

Basketball Court—Permanent Lines

The first girls game was played in March 1892. Dr. Naismith taught the group at the request of some women teachers in Springfield, Massachusetts. The men's rules were modified for the protection of the health and safety of girls, who do not possess the strength, speed, and ruggedness required for the boys game.

A women's rules committee was appointed in 1899. This committee was the parent of the long line of basketball committees of the Division for Girls and Women's Sports, which makes and publishes basketball rules for girls and women.

The original girls game called for five to nine players. Two types of courts were used in the past: the two-court game and the three-court game, with either six or nine players. The two-court game with six players became the official one in 1938.

THE GAME FOR BOYS

The playing area is called the court. The five players are designated center, right forward, left forward, right guard, and left guard. With the vast improvement of play due to the great number participating, many variations of the assigned positions mentioned have come about. That is, any player may be assigned different positions during play on offense.

Play begins with the referee's tossing up the ball in the center circle between the two centers, who jump to hit it to a teammate. The players advance the ball down the court by dribbling or passing until one is in a position to toss the ball through the opponent's basket. The defensive team tries to prevent scoring by the opposition and to secure possession of the ball. As soon as the defensive team gains possession of the ball, they advance it down the floor and attempt to score in their opponent's basket.

Points are made by two methods: Two points are scored if the ball goes through the goal when thrown from the field (field goal), and one point is scored for a successful free throw. The object of the game is to score more points than the opponents during the playing time. The game for high school boys is played in four quarters of 8 minutes each. If the score is tied at the end of the game, extra periods of 3 minutes each are played until one team is ahead at the end of an extra period.

In general, two types of defense are used: man-for-man and zone. In man-for-man defense each player is responsible for guarding a particular player on the opposing team. In zone defense each player is responsible for guarding any player entering his area of the floor. A team that plays zone defense should know all the fundamentals of man-for-man defense because a player on offense in a particular zone is guarded as if the defense were man-for-man.

Violations and Fouls

The rules establish legal procedures for the offense and the defense. An infraction of the rules is either a violation or foul. Some examples of violations are causing the ball to go out-of-bounds, failure of the offense to bring the ball across the center line within 10 seconds, dribbling a second time, and running with the ball. If you commit a violation, the ball is awarded to the opponents out-of-bounds on the sideline near where the violation occurred.

There are two types of fouls: technical fouls and personal fouls. Technical fouls include delaying the game, taking too many time-outs, leaving the court without permission, using unsportsmanlike tactics, and failing to report to the scorers table when entering the game as a substitute. Personal fouls are holding, pushing, charging, blocking, illegal use of hands, and impeding the progress of a player by an extended arm or leg. In general, if you commit a foul, a free throw is awarded to your opponents. If the team with the ball commits a foul, it is called an offensive foul and the defensive team is awarded the ball out-of-bounds where the infraction occurred. If you foul a player when he is in the act of shooting for a goal, he is awarded one free throw if the goal is made and two free throws if the goal is missed.

Two free throws may be awarded if the referee considers a foul a flagrant or intentional one. If a team commits four fouls in a half, an extra free throw is awarded if the first is successful as penalty for the common personal foul. In a personal foul, the player fouled is the one who must attempt the free throw, if physically able; any player may shoot a technical foul.

After a goal or free throw has been scored, the ball is put in play from behind the end line by a member of the team that did not make the score. At the beginning of each quarter and of extra playing periods and after a double foul, the ball is put in play by a jump ball in the center circle. When two opposing players have possession of the ball, it is a held ball. The ball is put in play by a jump ball at the nearest circle.

Officials

The game of basketball is officiated by a referee and an umpire. Two scorers and two timers assist them. A good official must know the rules thoroughly, know his or her duties as a referee or umpire in administering the game, be quick and agile, and be impartial in all decisions. An official should also merit and command the respect of the players. You might start learning to be a basketball official in your physical education class. Ask your teacher to help you. Both players and officials need to study the official rules each year because from time to time changes are made in the rules for basketball.

THE GAME FOR GIRLS

The playing court for the girls game is the same as that for boys. However, a girls team consists of six players: two offensive players, two defensive players, and two roving players. The offensive and defensive players are commonly called stationary players.

There is one basic difference between the boys and girls game. The center division line divides the court into two separate playing areas. Each half court is the front court of one team and the back court of the other team. The offensive players must remain in their own front court and the defensive players must remain in their own back court. The rovers may enter either the front or back court at any time and may even dribble across the center line. However, no team may have more than four players in either half of the court.

Any player who is fouled must take her own free throw unless she is injured or disqualified, in which case her substitute takes the free throw. This means that if a defensive player is fouled she must move to the front court to take her own free throw. One of the roving players temporarily replaces her in the back court. The fouled player may then remain in the front court or she may interchange positions with a teammate at any time.

This exchange of positions with another player is possible at any time during a game. Whenever a roving player wishes to become a stationary player, she may exchange positions with a teammate. Similarly, if a stationary player wants to become a rover, she trades places with a teammate. The ball does not even have to be dead, and it is not necessary to notify the officials of the change in positions.

Players may tie a ball that is in an opponent's possession by placing one or both hands firmly around the ball. A player may also take or tap the ball from an opponent.

Before the game begins, the captains meet with the officials, and the visiting team is given a choice of baskets. If there is no visiting team, a coin is tossed to determine choice.

At the beginning of each quarter and any overtime period, the ball is put in play by a jump in the center circle. Any player from both teams may jump. No player other than the jumpers may enter the restraining circle on any jump ball until the ball has been tapped. The jumpers may not catch the ball until it has hit the floor or been played by another player.

After a successful field goal or free throw, the ball is put in play by an opponent anywhere behind the end line. After a double foul, a jump is taken in the center circle. A field goal counts two points and a free throw one point.

The lineup for free throws differs from the boys game. Players from each team line up in alternate positions. At least one player from each team must line up along the free throw lane. The offensive team has the choice of either the left or right lane position nearest the basket. The defensive player takes her position at the other lane space nearest the basket. When the free throw is attempted, no player including the shooter may enter the free throw lane until the ball has touched the ring or backboard or has entered the basket. On a free throw the ball must hit the ring or enter the basket. If the free throw is missed, the ball remains in play.

Fouls

Blocking, charging, pushing, tagging, and unnecessary roughness are individual fouls. Other individual fouls are threatening the eyes of a player who has the ball, delaying the game, and unsportsmanlike conduct. The penalty for a foul is a free throw for the opponents. If a player is fouled in the act of shooting and misses the goal, she is awarded two free throws. During the last two minutes of the fourth quarter and throughout the duration of all overtime periods, a fouled player is awarded two free throws unless she scores a goal on the first, in which case only one free throw is awarded.

Individual fouls are charged against the player responsible for them, and when a player has committed five fouls, she is disqualified and must leave the game. A player may be disqualified for a single foul of unsportsmanlike conduct.

There are also team fouls, such as making an illegal substitution, leaving the court without the permission of an official, failing to provide scorers with the names and numbers of players, more than the legal number of time-outs, and coaching from the sidelines.

Violations are less serious infractions of the rules and are generally caused by incorrect methods of advancing the ball, such as traveling, holding the ball too long, illegal dribble, missing the basket entirely on a free throw, and stepping on a side line. The penalty for a violation is an out-of-bounds play awarded to the opposing team at the sideline near where the violation occurred.

BASIC SKILLS FOR BOYS AND GIRLS

Advanced skills, such as the jump shot, the hook shot, and mastering defense through hard work is essential in today's game of basketball. Basic skills are essential, as well. Ball control, speed, accuracy, and footwork depend on them. That is why your coach or teacher spends so much time in drill. Another method for improving a skill is to study a picture of it, and then practice the skill on the court. Almost all the skills you need are illustrated in this chapter. In each picture study (a) the starting position of all parts of the body and the ball, (b) the movement or action, and (c) the position or follow-through after the action is completed. It is important to note when the body weight is transferred from one foot to the other.

BASKETBALL

Jump Shot

In catching the ball a player should keep his eyes on the ball. The fingers should be relaxed with the hands forming a cup. The fingers should be spread and the ball should touch the fingertips first. Then the force of the pass should bring the ball to rest on the palm of the hand. The hands and arms should give slightly with the impact of the ball, and the arms should be placed immediately into position for a shot, drive, or pass.

Shooting

Shooting is the most emphasized skill in modern basketball. The latest and most useful type of shot is called the jump shot. It gets its name from the fact that a player jumps off the floor before shooting the ball.

The jump shot can be executed from either a running or standing position. It is a difficult shot for your opponent to anticipate and almost impossible to guard against. To make an accurate shot you need balance, coordination, and a clear view of the target.

In executing the jump shot from a running position, come to a quick stop and jump high into the air. Bring the ball over head with your shooting hand behind and under it. At the peak of the jump, when the body is no longer moving upward, release the ball.

Keep your eyes focused on the front of the basket and release the ball with a finger and wrist action rather than an arm movement. Try to put as much arch as possible on the ball and follow through with your wrist and arm.

Hook Shot

The hook shot is an advanced shot which you must learn to excel in the game. To make a hook shot, your back should be to the basket, with feet approximately a shoulder-width apart. Take a big step with your left foot. With your body protecting the ball from the defender, push hard off the left foot and jump into the air. Your right arm should be extended to full length and your left hand kept on the ball. Sweep your right arm upward to your right ear and release the ball and follow through with your wrist and hand.

When shooting the one-hand set shot, support the ball with your left hand (if right-handed), holding the back and bottom with your right hand. Push upward and outward, releasing the ball off the ends of your fingers with strong wrist action, and follow through with fingers and arms. It is important to keep your body well balanced and your eyes focused on the basket. Make it a habit to keep your right foot slightly advanced when using the one-hand set shot.

The one-hand set shot is used for the foul shot. It should be practiced every day because it is a free throw. You should make at least 60 percent of these shots.

One-Hand Set Shot

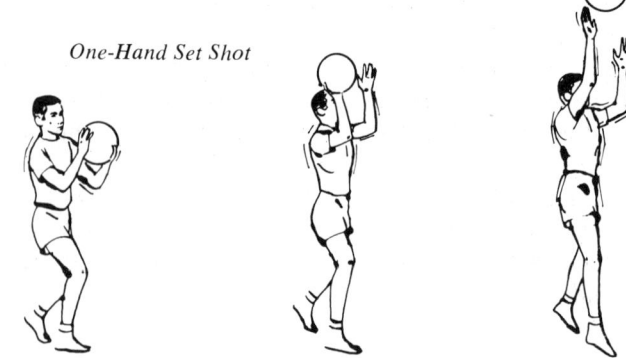

BASKETBALL

Lay-Up Shot

The lay-up is used when a player is running toward the basket. It is executed from a leap that carries the shooter beneath the backboard. You should step off on your left foot to make a right-handed lay-up shot. Release the ball at the height of your jump. When shooting from the side, lay the ball gently against the backboard so that it will drop through the basket. When shooting from the front of the basket also try to play the ball against the backboard.

Passing

Three basic passes, with variations, can be used to get the basketball from one player to another: the two-hand chest pass, the overhead pass, and the baseball pass. One- and two-hand underhand passes, as well as the hook pass, can be used.

The important thing to remember when throwing a basketball is to grip it with your fingers, not the palms of your hands. Learn to release the ball with a vigorous wrist-snap.

Individual players are allowed to move the ball from place to place on the court by dribbling (bouncing) it. Keep your head up and your body low, with the ball well out in front where it is easily controlled, fingers spread, hands relaxed. Push—do not bat the ball. Control it with your fingers. When closely guarded by a defensive player, bounce the ball low and protect it with your body. When dribbling the ball at full speed, the ball should be allowed to bounce higher and longer for greater speed.

Two-Handed Chest Pass

Overhead Pass

Baseball Pass

STRATEGY

The ability to use any part of your body—head, shoulders, or hips—to cause an opponent to think you are making a move other than what you plan is important to the good basketball player. Also of great importance is the ability to change direction fast. This requires a great deal of practice. Offensively, you must be constantly maneuvering with or without the ball.

At all times your body must be balanced and directly over your feet. On offense you must combine movement and quick changes of direction with abrupt stops. In making stops the weight must be back over the feet with hips down and head up. When coming to a stop, the feet should be positioned so that a pivot on one foot may be made.

On defense your feet must be spread, with the weight equally divided between both feet and concentrated on the balls of the feet and with heels on the floor. The hands should be raised and moving to keep an offensive man from passing easily to a teammate. As an offensive player gets closer to the basket, the hands and arms should be raised higher to keep the offensive man from getting a clear shot at the basket. Never allow an opponent to draw you off balance, and avoid crossing your legs when moving.

Tips to Individual Offense

1. Shoot when you have a good chance to score.
2. Always watch the ball, either directly or out of the corner of your eye.
3. Make quick stops and starts. Keep on the move.
4. Don't throw too hard when close to the receiver. Be sure a teammate is open before throwing him the ball. Learn to pass when in motion.
5. Remember that it takes a team to win a game and that you are only one of its members. Teamwork is all-important in basketball.

Tips to Individual Defense

1. Study your opponent. Find out if he is fast or slow, if he is shifty, and if he has favorite stunts and shots.
2. Always stay between your man and the basket. If he is a long way from it, give him more room; if he is close to it, stick to him like glue.
3. Never turn you head away from your man.
4. Watch for feints. Don't charge him. Keep your balance.

5. If he is dribbling, move with him, always keeping between him and the basket.

6. Get a rebounding position on your man if he or one of his teammates takes a shot. Keep inside him; box him out from the basket.

7. Talk to your teammates; warn them of offensive maneuvers.

8. When playing zone defense, get to your areas as quickly as possible and keep your eyes on the ball at all times. Keep your hands and arms up and moving.

9. Stay in a crouch, like a boxer, unless running full speed. Keep your balance and don't cross your legs when shuffling.

TEAM PLAY

Basketball is a series of stops and starts. A team gains possession of the ball, stops its defense, starts its offense; then it loses possession, stops offense, starts defense, and so forth. When playing effectively, teams make such transitions quickly and efficiently.

The key to team strategy is possession of the ball. Teams having possession maneuver the ball by passing and dribbling it, attempting to get a shot at the basket. The team not in possession operates to prevent successful shots and attempts to regain possession of the ball.

To become a good team player you should practice as an individual, with a second teammate, and so on against an equal number of opponents whenever you have time because this gives you the individual skills necessary for a good team player.

When on defense, your team has a choice of several styles of play. You can elect to play straight man-for-man, each player guarding a particular opponent, or you can use switching man-for-man, in which players change men when blocks and screens are set up. These are good, all-around defenses and are favored by countless coaches all over the world.

A zone defense also can be employed. Players guard particular areas of the floor rather than definite men, shifting when needed as protection to other players' territories.

To play truly effective basketball, your team should be well versed in what to do during special game situations, such as jump balls, free throws, and when the ball is thrown in from out-of-bounds.

Game play always is more complicated than practice drills. Your opponents are doing their best to outplay you. They will keep changing offenses and defenses, forcing you to do the same.

Your well-balanced attack will include variations to use when facing man-for-man, zone, and pressing (when they guard you all over the court) defenses. Your systems of defense should be designed to counter similar attacks by opponents.

A FEW GENERAL POINTERS

1. If the opponents are poor shooters, play them loosely so you can better cover a cutting game.

2. Always keep at least two players back when on offense, to pick up fast breakers in case you lose the ball.

3. After catching a rebound off the defensive board, look up instantly for free teammates downcourt.

4. Get the ball away from the defensive basket as quickly as possible.

5. Don't take a short, bounced dribble when you first get the ball. When you do so, you give up your right to dribble the ball.

6. Get a fast break against tall, slow teams.

7. Switch your defensive assignments around so your taller players are guarding big opponents.

8. Against a zone defense, break fast. Try to work the ball into scoring position before the zone can set up. If this doesn't work, move the ball rapidly, and overload the zone by putting two players in a single defensive player's territory.

9. Many teams stall to protect a lead late in the game. When stalling, keep spread so the defense cannot double-team; keep the center lane open for drive-ins; and keep the ball and players moving and keep threatening to score.

10. When on offense try to make the other team switch the men they are guarding, because a slow man may then be guarding a fast one.

COURTESY AND SPORTSMANSHIP

If your team has a reputation for friendliness and good sportsmanship, other teams will look forward to their games with you. The enjoyment of play and pleasant social relationships are important features of the game. However, one should play the game to win, as this does not compromise good sportsmanship and courtesy.

TIPS ON INDIVIDUAL EQUIPMENT

Your basketball clothing should permit freedom of body action, especially in the shoulders and legs. Well-fitted shorts are preferable for both boys and girls. Wear a clean pair of heavy socks at each practice and at each game. Wool socks are best; some athletes wear cotton socks inside their wool socks. Socks with holes should not be worn. Boys should always wear a good athletic supporter. Basketball suits should be laundered often.

Good sneakers will enable you to stop or change direction quickly. Your shoes should fit perfectly and should have arch supports and thick cushion insoles. Low-cut sneakers are suitable, but if your ankles are weak, it is better to wear a high shoe.

SAFETY

A health examination before you participate in sports is your best assurance that you are physically fit for strenuous activity. Basketball is strenuous. You probably will travel a mile or more during a game and much of it at top speed. You should secure a doctor's certificate before returning to play after recovering from an illness or injury. The certificate tells you and your coach whether you are ready to play again without risking re-injury or damage to your health.

Skills in basketball techniques are essential safety measures, too. Your play is handicapped if you lack good coordination. Awkwardness may cause injury to yourself and others. Drills help you develop a higher degree of skill. They also enable you to warm up gradually, so important in preventing injuries.

Jammed fingers can be avoided if you develop catching skill. Rings, watches, and other jewelry should not be worn because they may be damaged and are a hazard to other players. Your fingernails should be short.

If you wear glasses, wear guards; or, better yet, secure unbreakable lenses the next time you are fitted for glasses. They are inexpensive and provide adequate protection without lessening vision. Glasses with unbreakable rims or contact lenses are also desirable for athletes.

After play is over, shower immediately to remove perspiration and cool off your body gradually.

FOR MORE INFORMATION

American Association for Health, Physical Education, and Recreation. *Basketball Skills Test Manual.* (Boys and Girls editions.) Washington, D.C.: the Association.

American Association for Health, Physical Education, and Recreation, Division for Girls and Women's Sports. *Basketball Guide.* Current edition. Washington, D.C.: the Association.

American Association for Health, Physical Education, and Recreation, Division for Girls and Women's Sports. *Selected Basketball Articles.* Washington, D.C.: the Association, 1970.

Harkins, Mike. *Successful Team Techniques in Basketball.* Englewood Cliffs, N.J.: Prentice-Hall, 1966.

Lindeburg, Franklin A. *How To Play and Teach Basketball.* New York: Association Press, 1963.

National Federation of State High School Athletic Associations. *Official Basketball Rules.* Chicago: the Federation.

Neal, Patsy. *Basketball Techniques for Women.* New York: Ronald Press Co., 1966.

Schaafsma, Frances. *Women's Basketball.* Dubuque, Iowa: Wm. C. Brown Co., 1966.

Teague, Bertha. *Basketball for Girls.* New York: Ronald Press, 1962.

Wooden, John R. *Practical Modern Basketball.* New York: Ronald Press, 1966.

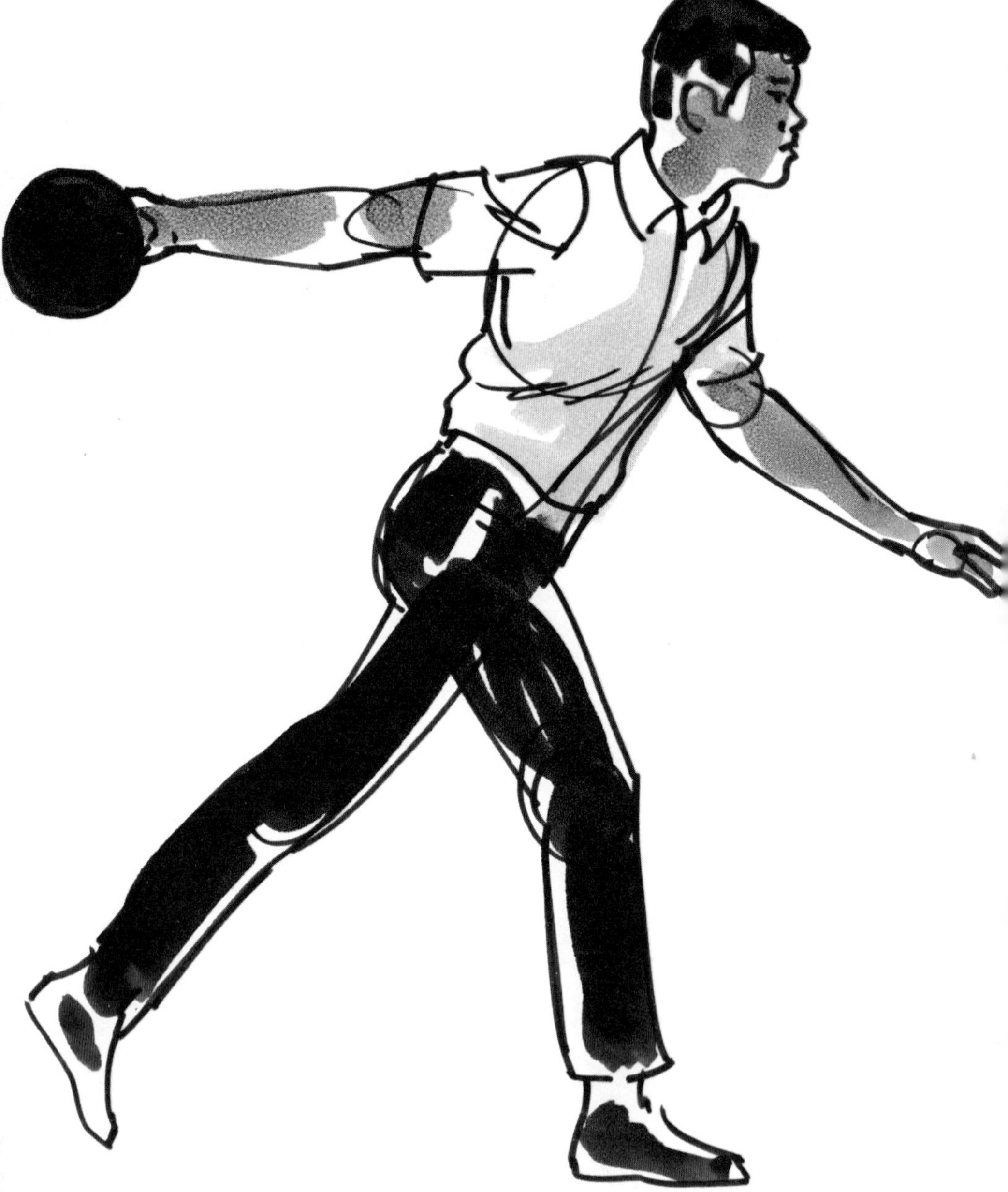

Bowling

The oldest known form of bowling dates back to 5200 B.C., according to Sir Flinders Petrie in his book, *The Making of Egypt*. The contents of a grave of an Egyptian child buried in 5200 B.C. revealed implements for playing a game similar to our present sport of ten pins.

The first record of bowling in America places the game in Manhattan in 1623. The settlers from Holland introduced the game in this country. Its popularity grew in New York City, and a bowling green was in use in the area around Battery Fort, now lower Broadway. Many similar bowling greens appeared, and by 1840 many indoor bowling establishments existed in New York City.

At this time there were only nine pins used in bowling, and they were arranged in the shape of a diamond. Indoor tournaments were held in the mid-nineteenth century, and the game began to suffer from exploitation by gamblers. Laws were passed in New York and Connecticut which prohibited the game of nine pins, but some enterprising soul added a tenth pin to avoid the law and so originated the game of ten pins. The pin setup was changed from a diamond-shaped arrangement to a triangular one.

In 1895, the American Bowling Congress was organized to set up universal laws for the game. This was the first American organization to set up rules and regulations governing bowling. More than any other group, this organization is responsible for the continued growth and expansion of bowling.

In 1961, the Woman's International Bowling Congress was organized in St. Louis, and this group has performed a similar service for ladies bowling.

In 1927, the National Duck Pin Bowling Congress was formed and arranged for the first national tournament the following year.

In 1936, the American Junior Bowling Congress was organized in Chicago, and this organization now supervises and furnishes a nation-wide program for more than 250,000 boys and girls in elementary, junior, and senior high schools in this country, Canada, the West Indies, and Germany.

Today bowling is America's most popular participant sport, with some 25 million men, women, and children of all ages and physical abilities bowling each year.

THE GAME

The American Bowling Congress rules state: "A Game of American ten pins shall consist of 10 frames. Each player shall bowl 2 balls in each of the first 9 frames except when he shall make a strike. A player who scores a strike or spare in the tenth frame shall deliver 3 balls." "A strike is recorded when the player completes a legal delivery and bowls down the full setup of ten pins on the first ball." "Any player who bowls down all ten pins with a legally delivered second ball in any frame has scored a spare."

BASIC SKILLS

Perhaps the most basic requirement necessary to become an expert bowler is the ability to coordinate the movements of your hands, arms, and shoulders with the movements of your hips, legs, and feet. This coordination aids greatly in delivering the ball in exactly the same motion each time. Practice helps any bowler achieve this coordination and consistency, which is necessary for high scoring.

After you have selected a ball which fits your fingers comfortably and is not too heavy or too light, you are ready to assume a bowling position or stance. Next, it is necessary to determine the number of steps to take before delivering the ball down the lane. The recommended four-step approach will probably suit you best. It is easy to measure the distance from the approach line to the foul line for the four-step delivery by pacing off the steps in the following manner. With your back to the pins, starting at the foul line walk four and one-half brisk paces away from the foul line. Stop, turn, and face the pins squarely. This, then, is your starting position.

The approach is started 12 to 15 feet from the foul line. Hold the ball at chest or waist level and shift it to the side as you face the pins

Four-Step Approach

squarely. Step forward on your right foot (if you are right-handed) with a natural walking step; push the ball forward and down in a smooth motion. On the second step, which should be longer and faster, your arm should continue to swing downward and to the rear in a pendulum-like motion. On your third step, which is longer and faster than the first two, the ball should be at the highest point of the backswing. Your delivery arm should be parallel to the floor, and your other arm out at the side for balance. The fourth and final step brings you up to the foul line in a graceful slide. Your left foot should be pointed at the foul line while the other foot drags behind the body to serve as a brake to check your slide. Keep the bowling wrist and forearm straight. Release the ball just above the floor well out over the foul line, making sure that you release the ball as your hand begins its upward movement. As you follow through with your hand and arm, your hand continues up to about shoulder level.

Types of Deliveries

There are two main types of deliveries used in bowling: the hook and the straight ball. After trying each type use the one that suits you best.

You should learn the hook ball first because it is the best working ball and gets the most pins when it is properly controlled. The hook ball travels in a straight line toward the 3 or 6 pin and then curves sharply into the 1-3 pocket.

Deliveries

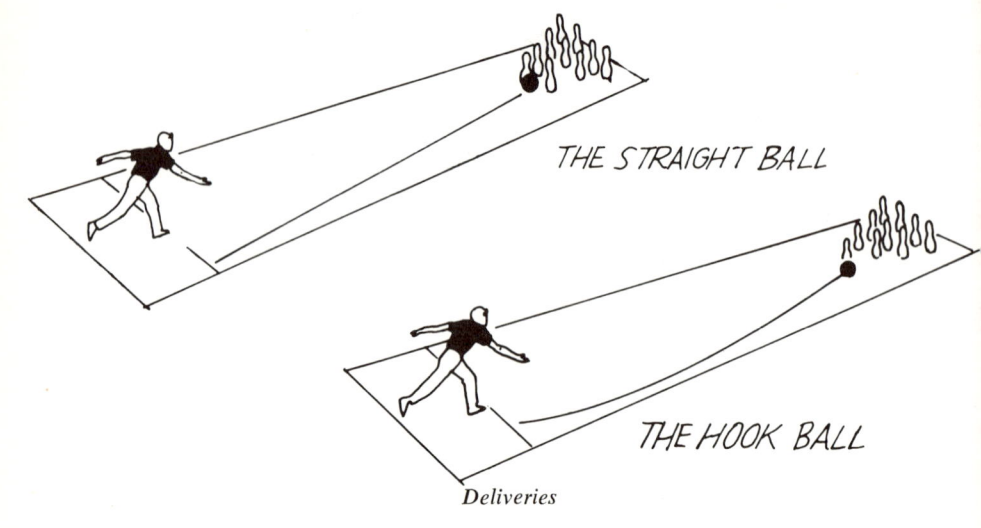

To deliver the hook, the ball is held with the thumb toward the body and the two fingers on the outside. Comparing this to a clock, the thumb position on the ball would be at 10 o'clock. Release the ball with your thumb in the same position to achieve just about the right amount of hook. The thumb is released before the fingers. For left-handers the thumb position would be at 2 o'clock.

The straight ball delivery goes straight to your mark, which is the 1-3 pocket. The ball is released on the final step of your approach almost 6 inches from the right side of the lane. Your thumb should be pointing directly at the pins. Again, when you release the ball your thumb leaves its hole before the other fingers so that you lay the ball on the lane rather than bounce it.

Aiming

There are two common methods of aiming: pin bowling and spot bowling. If you use the pin method, your eyes are concentrated on the 1-3 pocket throughout the approach, delivery, and follow-through. Spot bowling is the preferred method and is used by a greater number of bowlers, particularly when a hook ball is used. The ball is rolled along an imaginary line to the 1-3 pocket. The place where the imaginary line crosses the foul line is noted and another definite spot 10 or 15 feet down the lane is concentrated on until the ball has rolled across this spot. Do not look at the pins until the ball has crossed the spot which you have selected.

Strikes and Spares

You will find that it takes practice to make strikes (knocking all the pins down with the first ball) and spares (knocking all pins down with two balls). Success depends on how well you have learned the bowling fundamentals. Angle shooting is used for spares. Keep in mind, however, that you should use the same delivery on every bowl.

Tips to Help You

In practicing to improve your game, keep these things in mind:
1. A consistent delivery is necessary; you must be able to deliver a ball with approximately the same motion time after time.
2. Use your natural speed.
3. Get the ball out in front of you before you release it.
4. Concentrate on each delivery.
5. Don't forget to follow through correctly at the foul line.
6. Let your arm act as a pendulum.
7. Work on a normal backswing.
8. Relax and bowl easily; tense muscles cause jerkiness.
9. Work on good timing.
10. Use the correct angle when shooting for strikes or spares.
11. Keep your shoulders parallel to your target.
12. Keep your left foot pointed at your target as you approach the foul line.
13. Remember, control is more important than speed.
14. Walk in a straight line from approach to foul line in a four-step delivery.

SCORING

It is easy to score a bowling game. A perfect score is 300 points. A game consists of 10 frames. (A frame is similar to an inning in baseball.) Two balls are rolled in each frame, except when you score a strike. If you knock down all the pins with the first ball, it is a strike, marked (X). If all the pins are knocked down with two balls of the frame, you score a spare, marked (/).

For a strike, you get 10 pins plus the total pinfall on the next two balls. For a spare, you get 10 pins, plus the pinfall of the next ball. If you make a strike in the tenth frame, you get two additional balls to be rolled immediately; if you make a spare in the tenth frame, you get one more ball. You get merely the pinfall of any frame in which neither a strike nor a spare is scored.

1	2	3	4	5	6	7	8	9	10
[X]	[X]	[X]	[X]	[X]	[X]	[X]	[X]		X|X|X
29	49	69	99	129	158	177	186	195	225

Assume that this is your score card at the end of a game. At the end of the second frame, having made two strikes, you have a (X) in each upper-right box but no numerical score. In the third frame, you made a spare, bowling over 9 pins with your first ball and the remaining pin with your second ball. So you put down 29 for the first frame (10 plus your pinfall on the next two balls) and 49 for the second frame (29 plus the strike in the second frame plus the 9 for the first ball of the third frame). Now see if you can figure out the scoring in the seven remaining frames.

COURTESY AND SPORTSMANSHIP

Every sport has a code of ethics and rules. Bowling, too, has its etiquette. Among the more important items to remember are the following:

1. Always observe the foul line, even in practice when there is no one to check you.
2. Don't mar lane approaches or any other equipment in the bowling establishment. Proprietors have invested thousands of dollars in this equipment, and common sense should dictate proper care of it.
3. When it is not your turn to bowl, remain on the bench. Don't distract others who are trying to concentrate on their bowling.
4. Confine your activities to the lane on which you are bowling. In other words, don't wander off onto another approach in an effort to put "body English" on the ball.
5. Give the bowler on your right preference at all times. Let him deliver his ball first before you take your stance on the approach.
6. Don't waste time between shots.
7. Observe common courtesy toward other bowlers at all times. Avoid shouting or loud talking or laughing when anyone else is bowling.

SELECTION AND CARE OF EQUIPMENT

One reason why many people begin bowling is that they do not need to purchase their own equipment in order to participate. You can go in any bowling center in the country, rent a pair of bowling shoes, select a house ball provided without charge by the bowling establishment, and you are ready to bowl.

However, if you take up the game seriously and wish to improve your scoring, it is necessary to own your own bowling ball. In this way you can become accustomed to using the same ball each time you bowl. This will naturally help you perfect your game.

The most important feature of any bowling ball is the grip. Your local bowling proprietor or your local bowling store can measure you and fit you with a ball which has been drilled to meet your personal specifications. These bowling equipment experts can make sure you don't get a ball which has too wide or too narrow a span. They can also make sure the thumb and finger holes are not too large or too small.

Secondly, a bowling equipment expert can provide you with a ball which is the proper weight for you. Most normal adult men use a 16-pound ball, which is the maximum weight. Many top women bowlers use a 16-pound ball. However, for most women and for many smaller men and young bowlers, a somewhat lighter ball is recommended.

If you intend to do much bowling, it is also recommended that you own your own bowling shoes. Be certain your bowling shoes are comfortable so that your feet will not be pinched or cramped.

SAFETY PRECAUTIONS

Bowling does not present many safety problems. Perhaps that is one reason many youngsters, as well as adults, can enjoy the game. However, bowlers should be careful in handling the bowling ball because it is possible to drop it on one's foot, with very painful results.

In selecting your ball from the rack, be sure you pick it up with your hands on either side of the ball. Do not place your hand between your ball and the next ball as you may suffer a mashed finger.

Before bowling, always test the approach to see whether you can slide properly. Conditions on approaches vary greatly from one establishment to another. If you are in the habit of sliding on the approach, differences in the surfacing of the approach may throw you off balance.

FOR MORE INFORMATION

American Association for Health, Physical Education, and Recreation, Division for Girls and Women's Sports. *Bowling—Fencing—Golf Guide*. Current edition. Washington, D.C.: the Association.

American Association for Health, Physical Education, and Recreation, Division for Girls and Women's Sports. *Ideas for Bowling Instruction*. Washington, D.C.: the Association, 1970.

American Bowling Congress. *The Official A.B.C. Bowling Guide*. Milwaukee, Wis.: the Congress.

Archibald, John J. *Bowling for Boys and Girls*. Chicago: Follett Publishing Co., 1963.

Bellisimo, Lou. *The Bowlers' Manual*. Englewood Cliffs, N.J.: Prentice-Hall, 1965.

Kidwell, Kathro, and Smith, Paul, Jr. *Bowling Analyzed*. Dubuque, Iowa: Wm. C. Brown Co.

National Bowling Council. *How To Have the Most Bowling Fun*. Chicago, Ill.: the Council.

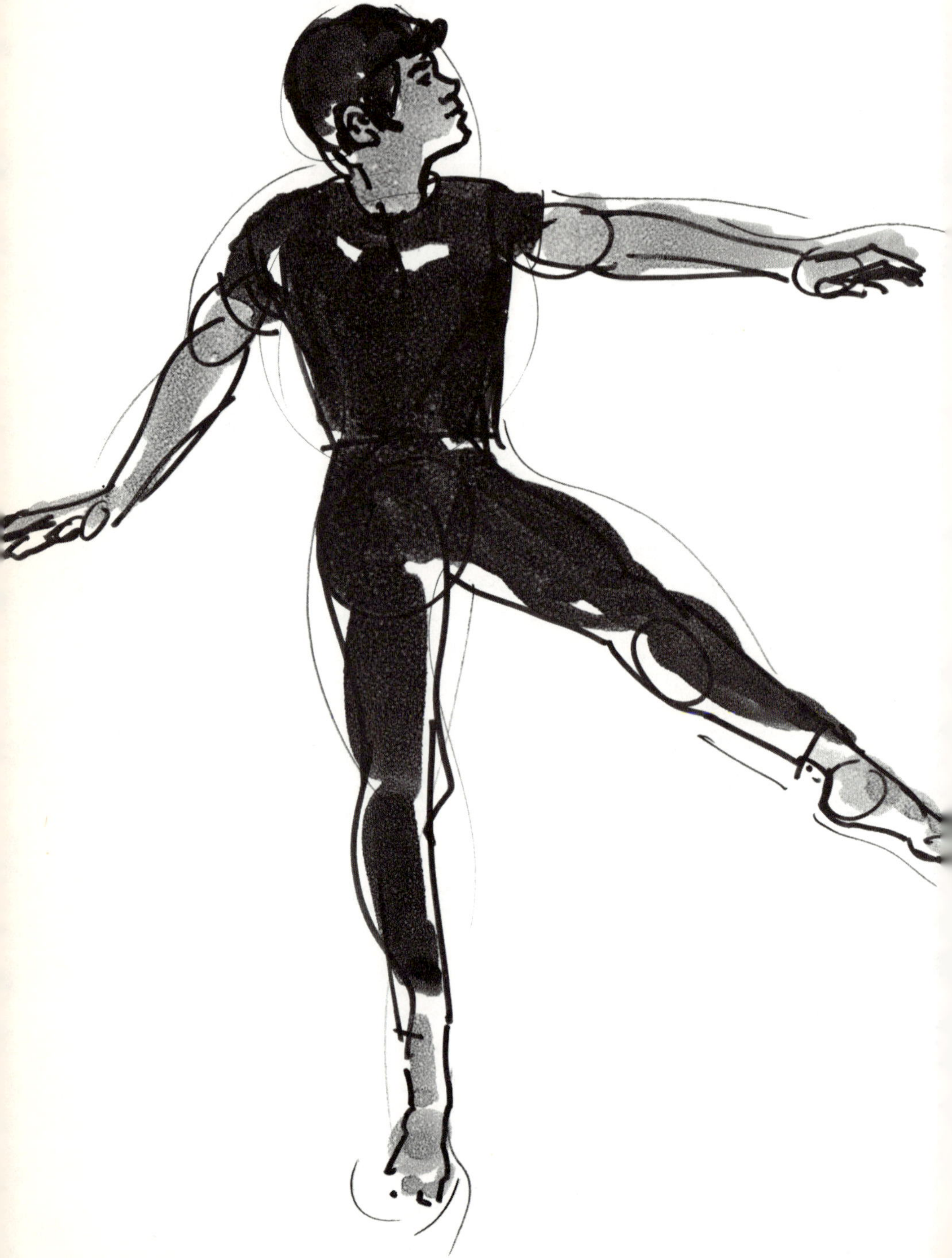

Dance

The ways in which the human body can move from any fixed base are relatively simple and limited in number. The trunk can bend and straighten in varying degrees in all directions, and it is possible to do some rotating or turning from side to side; it can resist the pull of gravity by remaining upright, or fall in the direction of that pull. The appendages—arms and legs—have the same movement possibilities, no different in kind and varying only in degree or range.

Ways of moving from one place to another through space are also simple and limited in number. Aside from rolling and crawling, it is possible to move from one place to another by walking, hopping, or jumping. These are called basic locomotor movements. Skipping, sliding, and leaping are combinations or variations of these simple ways of getting from place to place.

By combining these few basic forms of movement, the human body can perform highly specialized movements varying from the smallest, lightest action, such as catching a soap bubble, to athletic feats which win world championships. A dancer can whirl through space as though suspended in the air. Countless movement possibilities exist, and each individual selects from these possibilities those which serve his purpose—to work, to engage in sports and games, to dance.

Given the nature of the dance—folk, social, modern, jazz, or ballet—the same basic movements will be applied in different ways. The meaning or aim of dance determines what movements are selected and the kind of dance that results from these selections.

For many kinds of dance, such as ballet, folk, and square dance, tradition hands down the movements. Even with traditional forms, however, new combinations and selections are added from time to time. Other forms of dance, such as modern dance, jazz, and the kind of social dancing called "fad" dancing, involve constant changes.

Modern Dance

Dance is one of the most versatile and satisfying activities in which to participate, either occasionally for personal refreshment, or as a part of preparing for a future vocation. Not only can dance provide a wide variety of enjoyable ways to move, but it can supply opportunities for each person to learn more about the world he lives in, to gain more enjoyment from that world, and to communicate and share that joy with others.

SOME FORMS OF DANCE

Dance is a part of the cultural heritage of all races, for man has always danced. He has danced for many purposes and in many ways. The following forms are ways of dancing most commonly found in American culture.

Modern Dance

Early in the twentieth century, some dancers—most notably, Isadora Duncan—sought a dance expression not limited to the traditional ballet or folk dance forms. The stress was on dance as an expression of human emotions and the validity of any movements which are effective in communicating these emotions.

The theories of Isadora gained acceptance in some parts of Europe, but it was in America that modern dance developed most widely and rapidly. American dancers built on these theories to develop modern dance as an American art form. Modern dance provides opportunities for each person to discover ways in which the body can move to express ideas or feelings and gain pleasure from that expression, either as a dancer or as a viewer of the dance.

Skill in dance requires the following: a responsive instrument—the body; awareness of many kinds and qualities of materials—movements; practice and knowledge in the selection and organization of these materials—composition or choreography.

A dancer's body should be strong, flexible, coordinated, and capable of meeting great energy and endurance demands. Many of the activities of modern dance condition the body to meet these demands. Such activities are commonly referred to as "technique" and may include all the movements the body is capable of performing.

The range of bodily movements is extended by attention to the quality or texture of a movement and its suitability to the ideas to be expressed. Quality depends upon the way energy is released in executing a movement. Movement quality may vary from a sharp explosive release of energy (such as might be used in hammering a nail); to that which is slow, smooth, and controlled (like a drop of oil spreading over a surface); or light and airy (like a single dandelion seed carried by the wind). The most important factor in finding the quality of movement material needed is that it be not merely imitative but that it portray the feeling or idea that the dancer wishes to express. Some modern dance artists believe that movement need not stem from an idea or feeling; it can be merely aesthetically appealing.

Dance composition, or choreography, means the selection and organization of dance movements into a form. This is a process of problem solving; it is like fitting together the many pieces of a puzzle into a whole or like arranging musical sounds into a song. The problem may involve only a limited number of movements for a single dancer, or many and complex movements for a large group of dancers. There are no absolute rules for this kind of problem solving. Each dance artist must work in his own way. It is a process of exploration in organizing movement into shapes, mass, forms, patterns, or designs; of deciding upon the form which best expresses the ideas or purposes of the dance.

At some time in the process of selection, the dancer must experiment with the placement of movements in space. How much space is to be used? What directions through space will the movements take? Is design or pattern important? Should the design be angular, circular, or a combination of these? Developing a sensitivity to the space in which movement takes place is important in dance.

Another problem in choreography is to decide on how time will be used. What tempos or rates of speed are most effective for the ideas? What rhythms are set up as a result of accents? What degrees of intensity are most satisfying? Variety in the use of time elements contributes to the texture of movement in dance.

Developing the body for artistic expression, selecting movement materials appropriate to the ideas or feelings to be expressed, and organizing materials into compositional form are all part of dance. When these processes are completed the result is called a dance. A system of dance notation permits the recording of dance movements so that they can be communicated. It is possible to learn the complete ballet "Giselle" or the dances from "West Side Story," as composed by Jerome Robbins. A Hungarian czardas or a Swedish polka may be learned as originally composed. All may be danced for the enjoyment of the dancer or for the enjoyment of those watching the dancing. Dance in any or all of its forms provides an endless source of personal satisfaction.

Jazz

Jazz dance is hard to define. Certainly, as the term is used today, jazz is a kind of modern dance, but its movements and rhythmic roots have existed in traditional dance for countless centuries among many cultures. These movements have been adapted to suit the purposes of jazz dance. The ways in which energy is released, and how time and space are used, determine the style or form called jazz. No single jazz style exists, however. A strong syncopated beat and a high degree of improvisation is characteristic of jazz dance, as it is characteristic of jazz music.

The syncopated rhythm of jazz is a dominant part of the American musical environment. Jazz can be danced purely for self-enjoyment or to provide pleasure to a viewing audience. It can be performed alone, with a partner, or with a group of dancers. Much of the popularity of jazz dancing in the theater is credited to the many fine Black artists who have contributed to this part of the American music and dance heritage.

Ballet

Ballet is the oldest classical form of dance in Western culture. Although ballet dance experiences are limited in most high schools, many students have had technical training in ballet or seen it performed in the theater or elsewhere. However, the assumed relationship of ballet to certain forms of gymnastics has recently created interest in including ballet in high school activity programs.

Ballet stems from the European court dances of the sixteenth and seventeenth centuries. While court ballets were popular in several European countries, the French court was the center of its highest development and gave us ballet as we know it today. The development of ballet included specific rules for performing its movements. The French terms for ballet movement remain relatively unchanged and are used to represent the steps of ballet wherever it is taught or performed in the world today.

The movements for ballet include conventional poses or positions for the feet, the arms and hands, and the body. All positions are done standing in place, springing or leaping into the air, or traveling through space. The seven basic movements in ballet dancing are defined by the following French verbs: *plier,* to bend; *étendre,* to stretch; *relever,* to raise; *glisser,* to slide; *sauter,* to jump; *élencer,* to dart; *tourner,* to turn around. Similarly, each position and movement of the feet, legs, and arms is specifically named.

Some of the poses used in ballet tend to involve body positions which are somewhat unnatural. It is important that a teacher of this form of dance not only be well trained in ballet, but also understand the principles of human growth and development, and the proper use of the body to prevent injury or the establishment of improper movement or body alignment habits.

Ballets are usually composed by choreographers, rather than performing dancers. The leading female or star dancer is called a *ballerina,* and the leading male dancer a *danseur.* The chorus of dancers is called the *corps de ballet.*

To master the techniques of ballet requires many years of training, usually beginning at early ages. An appreciation of ballet as a form of dance art can be made more meaningful by learning experiences in some of the movement techniques provided in schools. The main purpose of ballet is exclusively performance, although the technical training has been used successfully to strengthen and correct some kinds of physical disabilities.

Folk Dance

Folk dancing is one of the most enjoyable and educational dance activities in which to participate. Full enjoyment of folk dancing depends upon an understanding of—and appreciation for—the many cultures of the world and upon skill in performing the steps appropriate to this form of dance. The steps used in folk dancing are combinations of fundamental ways of moving through space. Different combinations of walks, hops, and jumps result in different folk dance steps. For example: One way of walking may be a waltz step while another kind of walk will be a two-step. One combination of walking and hopping can be a polka step while a different way of combining these basics is a schottische step.

The walk, skip, hop, slide, polka, schottische, two-step, and waltz are some of the steps used in folk dancing. The ability to do these steps well and in rhythm with the music is the basis for enjoying folk dancing. The style in which these steps are performed depends upon the country from which the dance comes. A walking step is simply placing one foot in front of or behind the other in order to move in a specific direction. However, the strong forceful walk of a Cossack performing a hopak is far different in feeling and appearance than the small, tight walk of a Lebanese dancer performing the zaroura dance.

Many of the folk dances done today are handed down from one generation to another. The dances were created out of the life experiences of the people. These experiences have to do with work, play, religious beliefs, superstition, war, occupations, courtship and marriage, birth and death. There are gay dances and sad ones, dances of imitation

Folk Dancing

and of ritual, dances requiring little skill and others of great difficulty. The original meaning of many of the dances has been lost through the years, but the pride, the strength of character, and the feeling of unity exhibited by the dances of a particular culture are apparent when the dances are performed today.

Folk dancing provides desirable outcomes which are social, recreational, or physical in nature. On the social side are dancing with others and assuming individual responsibility for a part in the group. Recreational outcomes are realized in the joy and satisfaction in being a part of the dancing group. Physical outcomes are exhibited by improved states of physical well-being that result from folk dancing.

Folk dancing implies dancing with others. Some folk dances are done by couples; others are done by groups of people. The grouping may be in single, double, or concentric circles which move clockwise or counterclockwise. The dance grouping may call for single, double, or multiple lines, with dancers side by side or one behind the other and the lines moving forward, backward, or in a serpentine pattern. Each folk dance has a design of its own, although similarities exist among dances of a particular country and other countries which have shared common cultural influences. Many of the basic steps are similar, but the total design for each dance is unique, depending upon the way in which steps are combined, how dancers are grouped, and the style of the movement and the underlying purpose of the dance. The purpose may be the expression of joy, as in a dance of celebration, or a ritualistic prayer for rain for the crops. Most traditional folk dances once had a purpose, although as they are done today that purpose may no longer have meaning for the dancers.

Folk dancing is enjoyable for all ages. There are dances for children and for elders; there are dances for the novice and for the highly skilled dancer; there are dances for few or for many people. Folk dancing is for everyone and enjoyable for all. In addition to the many dances inherited from other cultures, an American folk dance form has emerged by adapting parts of that inheritance.

Square Dance

Square dancing is known as the folk dance of America. Some of the dances brought to the Colonies from Europe were the quadrille and contradanse. In the Colonies the European forms of these dances changed little by little to their new environment. Jigs and reels from the British Isles became the Virginia reel; stately French or Italian quadrilles became the lusty square dance. Clog dances from England and Ireland became the basis for the fast footwork contained in the famous "running sets" characteristic of the Appalachian mountain region.

The gold rush to the Western United States brought an intermingling of cultures and dances from those cultures. An evening program of dances might include quadrilles, contras, round dances, and called figure dances—the square dance. It was the added element of the "caller" which was uniquely American.

A caller does not dance but directs the interchanging movements of dancers into patterns called "figures," which make up the design of the dance. Several variations exist in the grouping of dancers; and characteristic groupings, styles, and movements are associated with various parts of the country. The most common formation is that of four couples arranged with the "head" couple standing with their backs to the caller at the beginning of the dance. The other couples are numbered two, three, and four in a counterclockwise direction around the square. Couples number one and three are known as "head" couples, and numbers two and four are the "side" couples.

Variations also exist in the steps used for square dancing. Walking, skipping, sliding, shuffling, and light running steps are used to move the dancers through intricate interweaving figures. The caller defines the movement and the figures to be danced and indicates which dancers are

DANCE 115

Square Dancing

to execute the call. The movements most commonly used in making up figures are *circle* (left or right), *swing your partner, allemande* (left or right), *grand right and left, right and left through,* and *ladies chain.* The style used in performing these movements varies, depending upon that which is popular in the particular part of the country, the particular group of dancers, the nature of the call, and the use of a figure by a particular caller.

The earliest American square dancing called for a different figure to be performed by each couple, while the other three couples waited their turn. Today a caller may have all eight dancers moving at the same time in the most intricate patterns. There are two general kinds of square dance calls in popular use today: the singing call and the patter call. The lyrics of a song are the call directions arranged in rhythm and set to a specific melody. The song is the call. The patter call consists of rhythmic, and often rapid, spoken directions for dance figures, mingled with humorous or nonsense phrases. The patter call is often used to create a fast dance with many changing figures. Dancers must pay close attention to the call to avoid entanglement in the interweaving of patterns and figures.

Square dancing is enjoyed by people of many ages. It can be relatively simple requiring little specialized dance skill. However, enjoyment is increased as more difficult figures are introduced as a challenge to the dancers. Square dancing is an ideal social activity because of the characteristic interchanging of partners and couples. Positive physical and recreational outcomes are the same as for other forms of folk dance. The usual costume for square dancing consists of a full skirt of medium or ankle length for women and Western-style shirts and trousers for men. While a special costume is not necessary for square dancing, it adds to enjoyment of this recreational dance activity.

SOCIAL DANCE

Folk and square dancing are most frequently done for recreation. This is almost exclusively true of the dance form called "social," "ballroom," or "popular" dance. The first two terms came about because certain dances were done on social occasions in a room designed for that purpose and called a "ballroom."

Social dancing, as we have come to know this couple dance form in America, was imported to the Colonies from Europe. During the sixteenth and seventeenth centuries, the social couple dances for royal courts in France, Italy, Spain, and England were modified and refined versions of more vigorous peasant dances. These were called court dances and included such dances as the courante, the pavana, the allemande, the gavotte, the gigue, and the galliard. The eighteenth and nineteenth centuries fostered the contredanse, quadrilles, and cotillions from which the American square dance evolved. Many European couple dances of the nineteenth century remained relatively unchanged in America. These included the polka, the schottische, the mazurka, and the waltz. These dances were popular in essentially the European form until the influence of syncopated music, first known as "ragtime" and later "jazz." This influence, too, was an import. It was imported from Africa and brought to America by slaves.

Recreational dance in any historical period has always been closely related to the popular music of that period. The popularity of jazz music in America led to many long-lasting dance innovations during the first three decades of the twentieth century. Today jazz provides the major dance music for social dancing over much of the world. Dances called the turkey trot, the bunny hug, the one-step, and the fox trot were popular in the early part of the twentieth century. The dances of the twenties reflected the Black influence in dance movement as well as Black music. Popular dances included the charleston, the shimmy, and the black bottom.

Social Dancing

Other music and dance imports to America came from Latin America. The tango was popular early in the twentieth century, and the rhumba was introduced in the thirties. From that time Latin dances have enjoyed popularity in America. The sixties saw the rise of such Latin dances as the cha-cha, the meringue, and the bossa nova. Moreover, in the sixties popular dancing took a different direction. Emphasis was placed on the individualistic style of discotheque dancing. Dances from this period include the twist, the watusi, the swim, the monkey, and many others.

A history of social dancing in America shows the tendency for innovation in the creation of dances. Dancing has provided a way for young people to find a means of reflecting their ideas instead of the ideas of an earlier age. It might be said that this characteristic is true of most Americans in their preference for new innovations in their culture.

Some of the ways of dancing created by youth are retained and become a part of our social dance heritage; others quickly lose their appeal and are dropped. Such dances are referred to as "fad" or "in" dances. New dances will continue to be created out of the same old material, since there is really nothing new in social dancing—only new ways of using the same basic social dance materials. New dances will emerge, and they will be as valid in their time as the waltz was in its time. Some of them like the waltz will become a part of our heritage.

The materials of social dancing are based mainly on walking, with the occasional use of a hop or jump. Skill in social dancing is based upon the quality, rhythm, and style applied to the use of these materials. Much social dancing requires learning various dance positions and the technique of leading or following and responding to a partner. Full enjoyment of social dancing comes from doing these things well.

To dance well requires more than merely learning the step patterns of a dance. A good dancer develops (a) an accurate response to the rhythm or beat of the accompaniment, (b) alertness in leading or following dance steps, (c) coordination and poise in the execution of steps, (d) consideration for a partner and other dancers, and (e) courtesy appropriate to the occasion. To achieve these skills requires attention and practice in performing a wide variety of steps, rhythms, positions, and styles. To dance well can provide pleasure for a lifetime. Learn early and continue long. The initial investment of time and effort can be a source of continuing satisfaction.

FOR MORE INFORMATION

Modern Dance

Cohan, Selma Jeanne. *The Modern Dance: Seven Statements of Belief.* Middletown, Conn.: Wesleyan Press, 1966.

Ellfeldt, Lois. *A Primer for Choreographers.* Palo Alto, Calif.: National Press Books, 1968.

Pease, Esther E. *Modern Dance.* Dubuque, Iowa: William C. Brown Co., 1966.

Ballet

Amberg, George. *Ballet in America: The Emergence of an American Art.* New York: Duell, Sloan, and Pearce, 1949.

Lawson, Joan. *Classical Ballet: Its Style and Technique.* New York: Macmillan Co., 1960-61.

Jazz

Mattox, Matt. "In Jazz Dance." *Focus on Dance V.* Washington, D.C.: American Association for Health, Physical Education, and Recreation, 1969.

Stearns, Marshall W. *The Story of Jazz.* New York: Oxford University Press, 1956.

Folk Dance

Gilbert, Cecile. *International Folk Dance at a Glance.* Minneapolis, Minn.: Burgess Publishing Co., 1969.

Lidster, Miriam D., and Tamburin, Dorothy H. *Folk Dance Progressions.* Belmont, Calif.: Wadsworth Publishing Co., 1965.

Square Dance

Jensen, Mary Bee, and Jensen, Clayne R. *Beginning Square Dance*. Belmont, Calif.: Wadsworth Publishing Co., 1968.

Phillips, Patricia A. *Contemporary Square Dance*. Dubuque, Iowa: William C. Brown Co., 1968.

Social Dance

Kraus, Richard G., and Sadlo, Lola. *Beginning Social Dance*. Belmont, Calif.: Wadsworth Publishing Co., 1964.

Youmans, John G. *Social Dance*. Physical Activities Series. Pacific Palisades, Calif.: Goodyear Publishing Co., 1969.

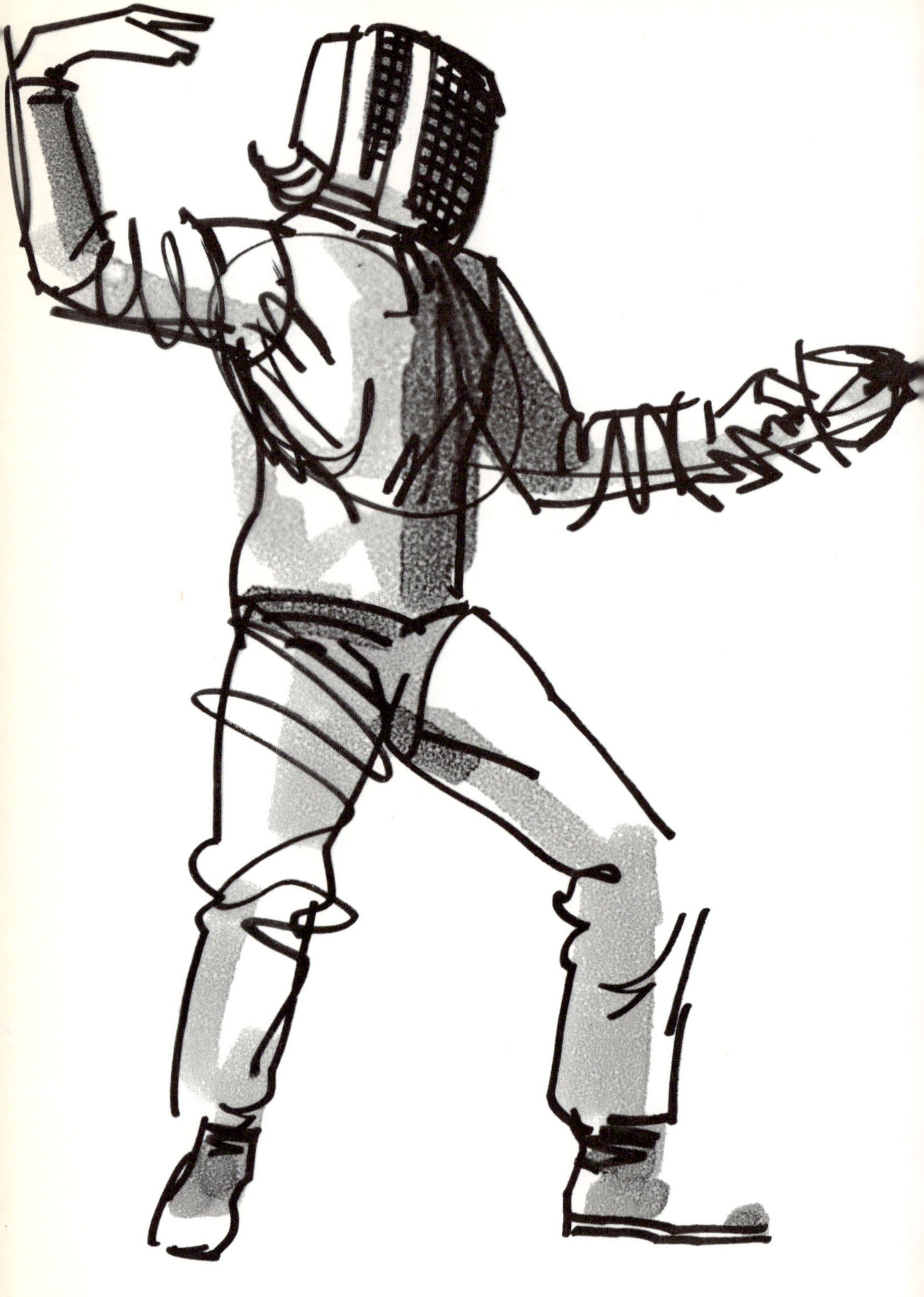

Fencing

Until the mid-eighteenth century fencing and swordplay were used primarily for life and death combat. Dueling was a brutal and often fatal practice. For some years duels to the death in defense of honor and fencing-as-sport existed side by side, but eventually duels were outlawed and swordsmanship became a pastime for sportsmen.

In most of the European countries fencing schools were established, primarily for young noblemen. Various nationalities developed their own methods of fencing; chief among these were the French and Italian schools. The schools vary in the weapon employed and in the methods of attack and defense. Grace and agility characterize the French approach, while the Italians emphasize powerful movements.

A GROWING SPORT

Fencing is growing more popular as a sport. Schools and colleges, as well as clubs and community centers, offer instruction in fencing. Both men and women, young and old, find fencing an excellent form of exercise and recreation. The sport is well organized. At the international level the Federation Internationale d'Escrime establishes rules and governs the annual world championship fencing matches. In the United States all contests are controlled by the Amateur Fencer's League of America, which was organized in 1894. Fencing is one of the events included in the Olympic Games.

DESCRIPTION

Fencing is a contest between two individuals with a weapon, each of whom tries to score a legal touch against his opponent. The encounter is confined within an area 40 feet long by 6 feet wide, called the strip. The middle of the strip is marked with a center line. On both sides of the center line, 6 feet 7 inches away, are the on-guard lines where the fencers assume their initial on-guard position. There is a warning line 9 feet 10 inches from each end of the strip. Points are scored for legally forcing an opponent off the end of the strip with both feet. If a fencer steps off the side of the strip, he is penalized by being required to retreat a certain distance from where he stepped off the strip, unless this puts him off the end of the strip.

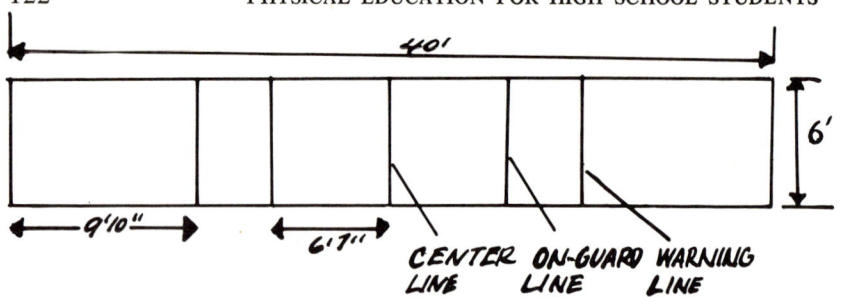

Certain very definite rules define what is a "legal touch." Official competitions are directed by a director and judged by a panel of four judges. Many official bouts utilize electrical scoring apparatus to scientifically determine when a touch has been made. This system requires electrically wired weapons and metal vests.

Mens bouts are usually 6 minutes long, with the first contestant to score five touches declared the winner. The womens bout is 5 minutes long, and the winner is she who first scores four touches. Aside from these differences, the rules for men and women fencers are the same.

THE WEAPON

Fencing is of three types, depending upon the weapon: foil, epee, and saber. The foil is the basic fencing weapon and the one which most fencers begin with. Many fencers limit themselves quite happily to the foil, as opposed to going on to the epee and the saber. This chapter will deal with foil fencing and merely mention in passing variations which the other two types of fencing entail.

The Foil

The foil has a slender, light blade which tapers from a thicker rigid section near the handle to a more slender and flexible region near the tip. The tip is in the form of a small button. The handle has a 3- to 4-inch

FENCING

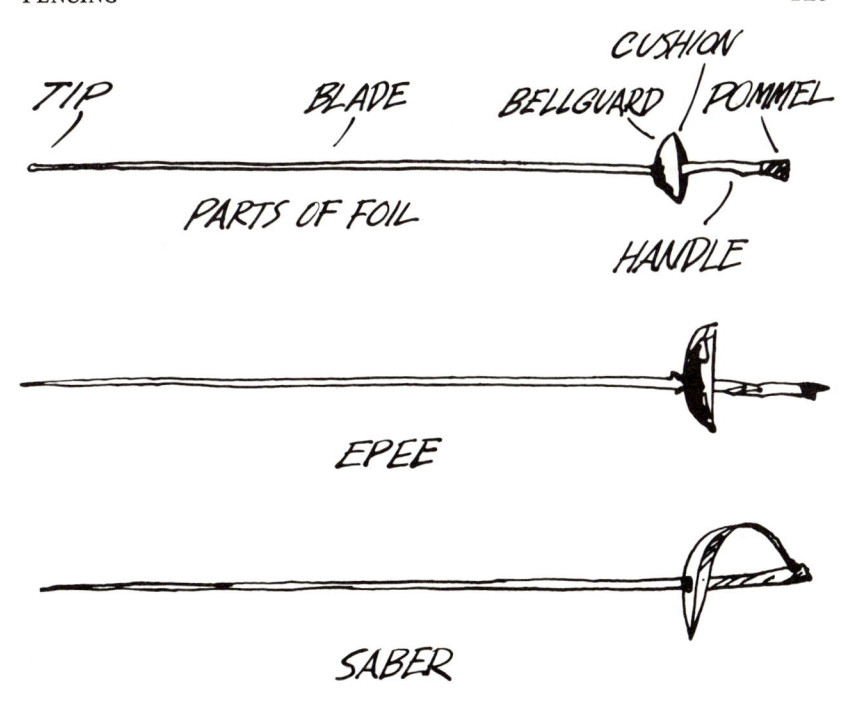

Parts of Foil: TIP, BLADE, BELLGUARD, CUSHION, POMMEL, HANDLE

EPEE

SABER

cup called the bell guard, which protects the hand. The inside of the guard is cushioned for further protection. The handle is composed of the grip and the pommel. The pommel is weighted to act as a counterbalance.

The Epee

The epee, or dueling sword, is similar to the foil and is a thrusting weapon. The blade is heavier and not as flexible. It has a larger guard and a small, flat, beveled steel tip.

The Saber

The saber, unlike the foil and the epee, is a cutting as well as a thrusting weapon. The hand guard on a saber curves around the hand to protect the knuckles from cuts.

EQUIPMENT

Besides his weapon a fencer needs a strong wire-mesh mask with a cloth bib which extends downward to protect the throat. Body protectors in the form of full or half jackets are necessary. These are made

Costumed Fencer

Lines of Engagement

of padded canvas. The full jacket covers the entire target area plus both the arms. The half jacket, which is less expensive, covers only one arm and the front, back, and one side of the body. A padded glove may be worn to protect the hand. Either tennis shoes or low-cut, leather-soled fencing shoes may be worn.

Care of Equipment

Steel blades should be oiled occasionally to prevent rusting. This precaution need not be taken with fiber glass blades. Fiber glass blades should never be used against steel blades. Masks and jackets should be hung to permit airing and drying. Jackets and bibs should be laundered often.

THE TARGET

In foil fencing the target on which legal touches may be scored includes the trunk from the top of the collar to the groin in front, and down to a horizontal line passing across the top of the hips in back. The target excludes the arms, legs, and mask and bib. (In epee fencing the target includes the entire body. In saber fencing the target includes all part of the body above the groin.) For the various attacks and defenses, the target is divided into four areas known as the lines of engagement.

FENCING 125

On-Guard

BASIC TECHNIQUES

In fencing there is considerable latitude for individual agility and dexterity. However, there are some conventional styles of attack and defense basic to the sport. Moreover, the progress of the match is strictly organized much as a dance is choreographed.

On-Guard

All attacking and defensive movements start from an on-guard position. If you are right-handed, stand with your right shoulder and the toes of your right foot toward your opponent. Your left foot should be at a right angle to your right foot and a shoulder-width away. Keep your knees bent and your weight evenly distributed over both feet. Keep your trunk erect, leaning neither forward nor backward.

Hold your weapon arm with the elbow raised about 6 inches from your ribs. The tip of your foil should point toward your opponent's face. Bend your rear arm at the elbow and raise it so that the upper arm is parallel to the floor and the forearm perpendicular to the floor. Let your hand and fingers drop toward your head in a relaxed position. There are slight variations in the basic stance for epee and saber fencing.

The on-guard position is one of great balance from which the fencer can either advance or retreat. The distance between opponents at the start of a bout is such that one fencer could almost, but not quite, touch

Lunge

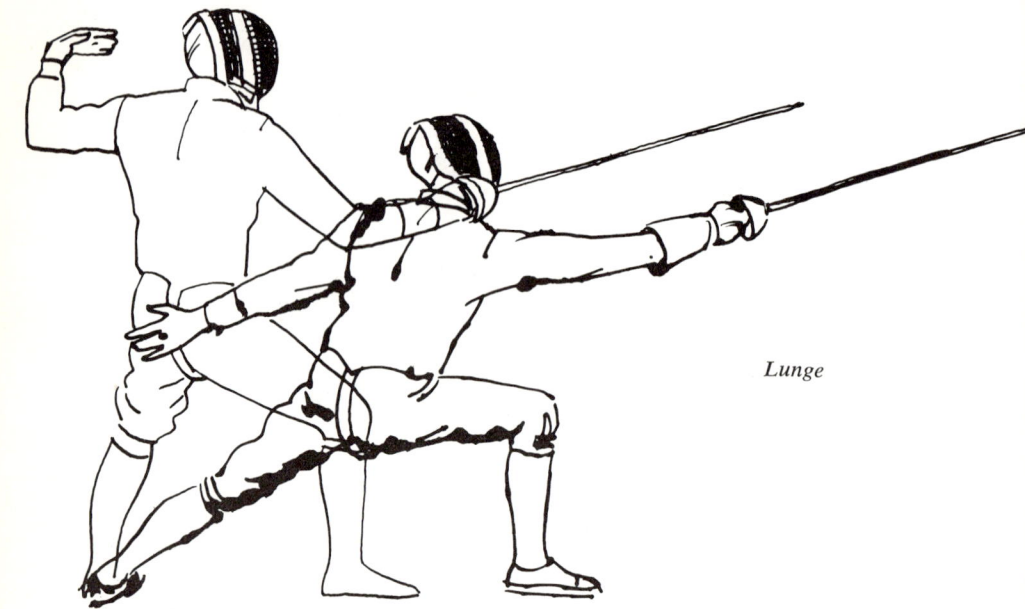

the other with a full forward lunge. In order to score a touch, therefore, the attacking fencer must close this distance. To defend himself, the defensive fencer often must reestablish the original distance. Hence, fencing is a series of advances and retreats. The on-guard position, which one assumes again and again throughout a bout, gives you the best stance from which to make both offensive and defensive moves. When you raise one foot from the on-guard position to make a move (either an advance or retreat) you are at your most vulnerable, because you cannot immediately change the direction of your movement. When moving, take short steps and keep your feet close to the floor.

Lunge

The lunge is a fundamental technique to reach your opponent with the tip of your foil when he is out of arm's reach. From the on-guard position, extend your weapon arm, with the tip of your foil slightly below your hand. This offensive movement gives you the right-of-way to pursue your line of attack. Propell your body forward by vigorously extending your rear leg while stepping forward on your right leg. At the same time swiftly lower your left arm and extend it to help maintain balance. Your rear foot remains on the floor with your leg extended. Your right knee will be bent and above the instep. To return to the on-guard position, the movements are reversed in one quick operation. The right leg is pulled back; the rear arm is raised.

Attacks

Attacks come under two headings: simple and composite. Simple attacks are executed in one movement. Composite attacks involve two or more movements, with a preliminary feint as the first move.

Straight Thrust. To make a straight thrust, extend your weapon arm without changing your line of engagement (the angle at which you hold the foil). Depending upon the distance between opponents, a lunge usually accompanies a thrust. Speed is essential in performing a straight thrust because it is easily defended against.

Disengage. Extend your weapon arm as in the straight thrust, but during the extension, pass your blade under your opponent's blade into the opposite line of engagement. This movement is usually followed by a lunge. Keep your foil close to your opponent's weapon during the disengage. Use only your wrist and fingers in executing this circular movement. The point in changing your line of engagement is to confuse your opponent and thereby cause him to defend the wrong side.

Cutover. This attack is similar to the disengage. Instead of passing your foil tip beneath your opponent's blade, you pass over it into the opposite side. Use only your wrist in executing this movement.

Double Disengage. This is literally two disengages. The first disengage is designed to make the defender parry hard in the threatened line, leaving his other side open for your second disengage in the original line. The first disengage is considered a feint, designed to confuse your opponent. It is best to initiate the attack as your opponent steps forward and momentarily has his foot off the floor. Before he can change his direction he finds himself too close to his opponent and thereby more likely to panic and be fooled by your feint.

Beat. On this attack you deflect your opponent's blade with the strong part of your foil (near the bell guard) pushing against the weaker section (near the tip) of your opponent's weapon. After deflecting his blade, thrust toward his exposed target. These steps should be accomplished in one continuous movement. During the beat your hand stays in place; only the point of your foil moves.

Defense

Attacks are directed against one of the four areas of the target (lines of engagement). Each parry, which is a defense against an attack, is named for the section it protects. Simple parries are primarily instinctive defensive actions to deflect the attacking blade. In parrying, you should use just enough deflecting motion to protect the threatened area. If you overprotect, moving the foil hand too far to one side, you are immediately vulnerable to a disengage or cutover.

There are two parries for each of the divisions of the target area. The two parries for any division are executed exactly alike except for the position of the hand, which is palm up in one parry and palm down in the other. The defender has an advantage in that he uses the strongest part of his foil to defend against the weakest part of the attacker's blade.

Parry Four. This parry defends the high inside line. Move your hand laterally from the normal position to the left at breast level, contacting your opponent's blade and deflecting it sideways. As you perform this parry, your hand will roll slightly.

Parry Six. The parry of six defends the high outside line. Turn your hand palm downward and move it to the right. Keep the tip of your foil at about eye level.

Parry Seven. In this and the following parry the blade moves downward rather than horizontally. Drop the point of your foil in a small half arc leftward, but keep your hand in the original position, although it will turn slightly.

Parry Eight. This parry is the reverse of the parry of seven in that as the blade is dropped it moves to the right to deflect the attacker's blade.

Circular or Counterparry. These parries defend the four and six areas. By moving your blade in a tight circle either clockwise or counterclockwise (depending upon the line of attack) with your wrist and fingers, you pick up your opponent's foil and force it through a small arc back to the line from which it started.

Riposte

After the defender has successfully parried an attack, he makes an immediate counterattack, called a riposte. This may be either simple or composite, direct or indirect. A simple thrust and lunge immediately following the parry is often best. The opponent attempts to parry the riposte, then execute a counter riposte, and so on. The sequence of a bout is attack (thrust)—defense (parry)—counterattack (riposte) over and over again. After a legal touch is scored or one opponent is forced off the end of the strip, the fencers return to the original on-guard position and start anew.

FENCING

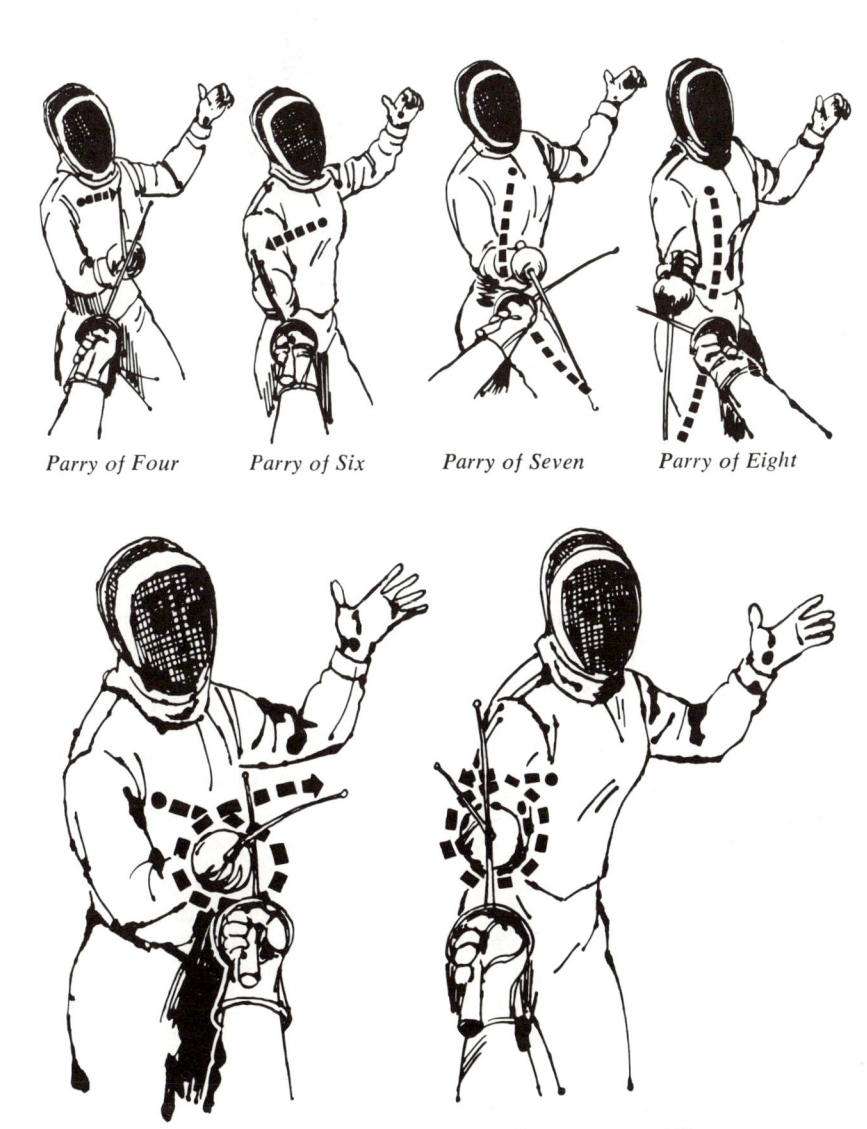

Parry of Four *Parry of Six* *Parry of Seven* *Parry of Eight*

Counterparry of Four *Counterparry of Six*

Stop Thrust

STRATEGY

The simpliest and most basic tactic to use on an opponent is to gain just enough distance to facilitate a hit. You can do this by pressing your opponent and forcing him to retreat. (Of course, your opponent at any time may seize the initiative with a counterattack.) Press on a step or two and then fall back (retreat), inviting your opponent to follow. Allow him to advance a step or two and then, at the precise moment he lifts his foot for another step, lunge forward suddenly toward him and attempt to score a touch.

Using a variety of attacks, parries, and feints helps to confuse your opponent and to cause him to move in and out of scoring distance. For a touch to be legal, the scorer must have the right-of-way. To gain this, you must always extend your weapon arm before a lunge. A defender must parry an attack before he can gain the right-of-way and respond with a riposte (counterattack).

SAFETY AND SPORTSMANSHIP

Injuries in fencing are the result of negligence, rather than the nature of the sport. Make sure your equipment is in good repair and *never* fence without protective clothing—the mask and jacket. Always carry your weapon with the tip toward the floor.

FENCING   131

If for any reason a fencer wants to halt a bout, he stamps his right foot twice. This signal should always be honored. In friendly matches where no judges are presiding, each fencer should call touches against himself, but never against his opponent. If judges are present, always accept their rulings without comment. Shake hands with your opponent at the end of the bout.

FENCING TERMS

Advance. To get within attacking distance by moving toward an opponent.

Attack. An offensive maneuver in which one fencer and his weapon move forward toward a target on his opponent.

Beat. To deflect an opponent's blade forcefully to the side to open a line of attack.

Bout. A contest between two fencers.

Feint. An attack or thrust which is not carried through; designed to mislead an opponent into defending one target and exposing the real target.

Lines of engagement. Division of the target into four quarters. Attacks are directed toward specific lines of engagement and defensive maneuvers are designed to protect each quarter as it is threatened.

Lunge. An attack executed by rapidy moving the front foot as far forward as possible while extending the rear leg and thrusting with the weapon.

On-guard. The basic position assumed at the beginning of a bout and from which offensive and defensive moves are made.

Parry. A defensive maneuver with the blade to deflect an opponent's thrust.

Retreat. To move away from an opponent.

Right-of-way. Gained by extending the weapon arm toward a valid target. The fencer with the right-of-way can proceed with his attack and legally score if he makes a touch.

Riposte. A counterattack immediately following a parry.

Strip. An area 6 feet by 40 feet on which a fencing bout is confined.

Target. The area on a fencer's body where legal touches can be scored. Divided into four lines of engagement.

Thrust. A basic offensive maneuver in which the weapon arm is rapidly extended toward a valid target; often accompanied by a lunge.

Touch. Achieved by touching a valid target area on an opponent with the tip of the weapon. If legally executed, the offensive fencer scores.

FOR MORE INFORMATION

American Association for Health, Physical Education, and Recreation, Division for Girls and Women's Sports. *Bowling—Fencing—Golf Guide.* Washington, D.C.: the Association.

Castello, Hugo, and Castello, James. *Fencing.* New York: Ronald Press Co., 1962.

Editors of Sports Illustrated. *Sports Illustrated Book of Fencing.* Philadelphia: J. B. Lippincott Co., 1962.

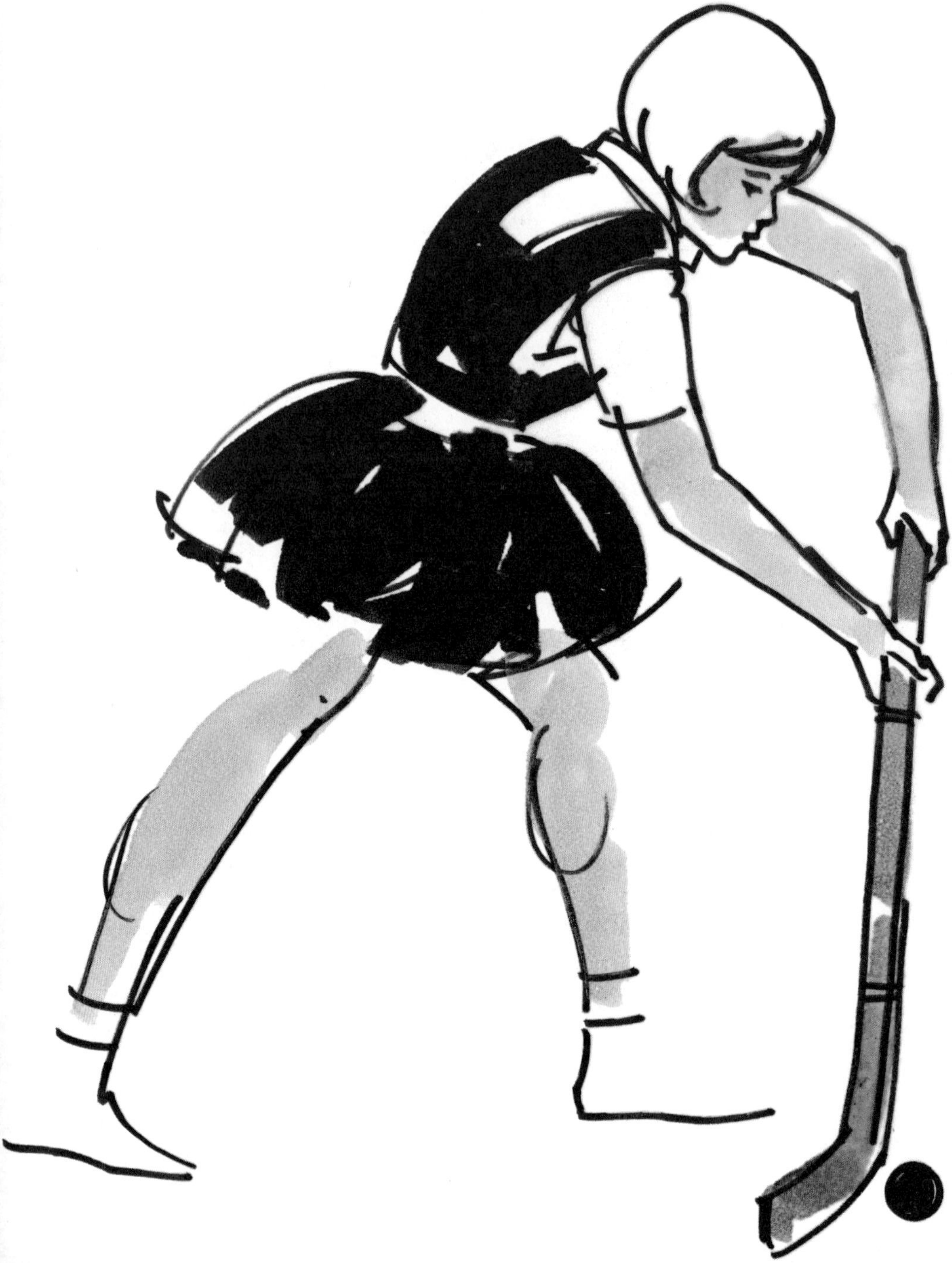

Field Hockey

Hockey is a very old game. The exact origin is not known, but there is reason to believe that a crude form of the game was played by the ancient Greeks, Romans, and Persians as early as 514 B.C. The modern game probably came from an early Scottish game, shinty—also played in London under the name of hackie. That the names well described the play is indicated by a rule which stated that "should a player come in on the wrong side as you were dribbling down, you were at liberty to hit him across the shins." The "weapons" were made of light oak, often weighted with lead to give them greater driving power.

Today's game of field hockey, however, is one of speed, skill, and wits, with no personal contact allowed. As early as 1885 women's teams were organized in the women's colleges of Oxford and Cambridge in England. About 1900 an Englishwoman, Miss Constance Applebee, introduced the game to several colleges in this country. From that time on, hockey has grown in popularity with girls and women here. The United States Field Hockey Association was formed in 1921, and at the present time there are many affiliated clubs throughout the country, which enable players to continue enjoying field hockey after they have graduated from school.

THE GAME

Field hockey is played between two teams of 11 players each. There are 5 forwards (center forward, left and right inners, and left and right wings) and 6 defense players (center halfback, left and right halfbacks, left and right backs, and a goalkeeper). The field is about the size of a football field, but the goals are much smaller.

The object of the game is for the attacking forwards, aided by their defense, to hit the ball past the opposing defending players and into the

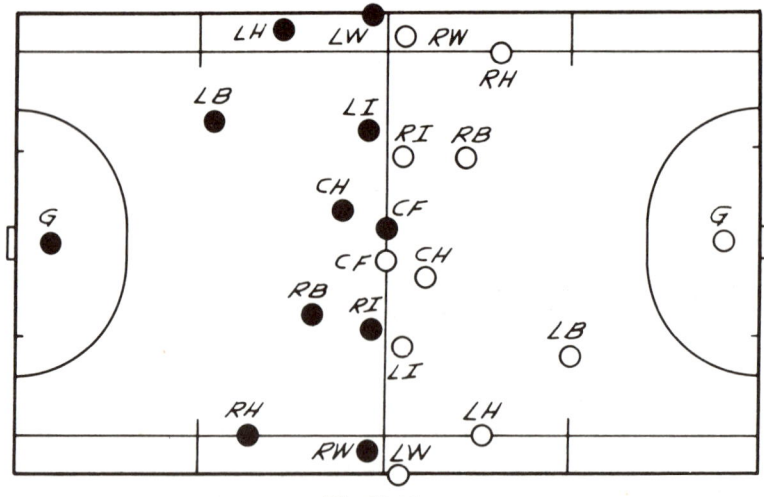

The Field

goal for one point. The aim of the opposing defense, of course, is to get the ball and clear it out to their forwards. The stick has a long handle and a curved blade flat on one side. The ball may be hit with the flat side only. It may not be advanced by any part of the player's body. The ball is a small leather-covered one.

To start the game, the teams line up as shown in the diagram. Although the forwards stand facing each other, they are not each other's closest opponents. It is the defense player standing most nearly opposite a forward who is responsible for seeing to it that she does not get the ball. This is called marking.

The two center forwards face each other, standing squarely with one foot on either side of the center line. The ball is between them. On the umpire's whistle, they start to bully. The bully is done by alternately touching the ground beside the ball and the opponent's stick three times. After the third touching of sticks, both players may try to get possession of the ball. Once learned, the bully is usually done rather rapidly— ground/sticks, ground/sticks, ground/sticks, hit!

After the ball is put in play by means of the bully, anyone may try to hit it. Actually the players remain in the general area of the field in which they started, progressing up and down the field but not across it. Players play the ball when it comes into their area, then pass it to a teammate in another area. The five forwards form the main attacking line and are followed and helped by their halfbacks and backs behind them. If they lose control of the ball, it is the duty of these players to

FIELD HOCKEY 137

The Bully

recover it. If all else fails, a team still has its well-padded goalie, who not only may hit but also may kick the ball.

A player may hit the ball to another player, or she may take it down the field herself by means of a series of taps, sending the ball a short distance ahead of her. This is called dribbling. She may try to dodge around an opponent.

To hold the stick correctly, place it in front of you with the toe of the blade pointing straight ahead. Grasp the top of the stick in your left hand. If you raise the stick in the air, the blade will now point back over your head. Lower the stick again and place your right hand just below your left. Now you have a correct grip for the drive. Place the ball in front and to the right of your right foot and hit it straight ahead, using an easy arm and shoulder swing. Let your right elbow bend a little on the back swing so that you don't have to bend your wrists very much, and follow through with the stick pointing in the direction the ball has gone. You may not raise your stick above shoulder level, for this is a foul called sticks.

SOME RULES

Other rules based on safety make it a foul to use personal contact or to hit dangerously as in slashing at or interfering with the opponent's stick, undercutting the ball so that it goes into the air, or hitting it directly at an opponent's legs.

Stopping the Ball

In keeping with the sportsmanlike spirit of the game is the rule of obstruction, which states that you may not go between an opponent and the ball. You must always give her a fair opportunity to get to it. If you always face your opponent when trying to get the ball from her, you will not commit this foul. Forwards may not go way down the field ahead of the ball to wait for it near the opponent's goal. A forward who does so probably will be ruled offside. As a forward, stay on a line with the rest of your forwards.

The penalty for making a foul is usually a free hit awarded to the other team on the spot where the foul occurred. This is an unguarded hit with all other players at least five yards away. A defense player nearly always takes the hit, and the forward line moves ahead to be ready to receive it.

BASIC SKILLS

Stopping the Ball

To stop a ball which has been hit to you, you should run to meet it with your stick pointing toward it. Turn the flat side of the blade toward the ball just as you get to it and reach with your left wrist leading. This will put the blade of the stick straight up and down, so the ball cannot hop over it. "Give" with your wrist as you meet the ball, and, if necessary, slide your right hand down the stick a little to get more control. However, you will be able to hit the ball more quickly if you do not change your drive hand position too much. Always use your stick to stop the ball, not your foot or hand. The hand stop is legal; but if you let the ball rebound the least bit, you have committed the foul called advancing.

Dribbling

When you have possession of the ball, the problem is what to do with it. If you wish to dribble, get the ball ahead of you and slightly to your right. Keeping your original grip on the stick, turn your wrists so that the blade of the stick facing away from you comes flat against the ball. You will probably find your ball control a little easier at first if you slide your right hand down the stick slightly as you did in stopping the ball. Now by wrist action propel the ball along just ahead and slightly to your right by a series of taps. The closer together you can keep your hands the better. Also, keep as erect a position as you can when you run. Learn to dribble so that you alternately watch the ball and keep track of the position of other players. Always dribble straight down the field. If you want the ball to go across the field, pass it to a teammate in that part of the field.

Passing

When you wish to drive or pass the ball to a teammate, be sure to bring your hands together at the top of the stick and let your right elbow bend a little. This is an arm and shoulder swing, not a wrist-action stroke. Passing to your left is easiest; do so when the ball is ahead of you. Passing to the right is harder as you have to turn the blade of your stick in order to hit with the flat side of it. Move ahead so that the ball is behind your right foot, turn your shoulders, and drive as you step forward with your right foot. Be sure the ball goes ahead of your teammate. Field hockey is a game of constant movement and your teammates will be running. Try to place the ball where your teammate can hit it on the run without having to slow down.

If an opponent is about to take the ball from you and you don't have time to get off a drive, you can use a push pass. Place the blade of the stick against the ball, slide your right hand down the handle, and push the ball as you step forward on your right foot.

Dodging

There are several dodges you can use to go around an opponent. In all of them the secret lies in doing them quickly and at the last moment so she cannot anticipate your move. Often it is good to mislead your opponent by making a feint in the opposite direction from which you intend to go and so get your opponent to shift her balance in that direction.

The non-stickside dodge is probably the easiest. As you and your opponent move toward each other, you can see that her stick blade is on her right and that a ball sent to that side will be easy for her to stop. Stopping it on her left will be much more difficult; so as she runs toward you, give the ball a quick, short push to her left or non-stick side, run past her on her right, and recover the ball behind her.

However, if she suspects you are going to use this dodge, you can fool her with a stickside dodge. Just as you meet your opponent, give the ball a sudden quick pull to your left, and as she runs past you, continue on your way. When your opponent is "on" to both these dodges, try the scoop. Just as she starts to take the ball from you, slide your hands apart, lay your stick back, blade facing up, and scoop or shovel the ball right over her stick.

Getting the Ball

Then there is the problem of how to get the ball away from the other team. This must be done with no personal contact and no interference with an opponent's stick. The trick then is to get the ball while it is off the opponent's stick. The easiest interception is, of course, on a pass from one player to another. Run to meet the ball with your stick low and pointing toward it. Reach for the ball and control it with your stick. It is not necessary to stop dead, but you must control it before you hit it or it may fly up into the air and hit someone. Run to meet the ball, control it, pass it.

Tackles

If your opponent is dribbling the ball and keeping it close, you can still get it by means of a tackle. Tackle means taking the control of the ball away from your opponent. Time your tackle so that you reach for the ball just as it leaves her stick and she has started on her back swing for the next hit of her dribble. If she is coming toward you, run to

FIELD HOCKEY 141

Scoop Tackle

Lunge Tackle

meet her with your stick down and reach for the ball just as you would to stop it. This is the straight-on tackle. Be sure to keep to the left just enough so that the other player will pass you on your right and not run head on into you.

If you miss this tackle and your opponent continues dribbling down the field, turn around and run after her, catching up with her on her stick side, but not too close (at least a stick's length away). Now you are ready to do a left-hand lunge. As you pass her and just as the ball leaves her stick, swing your stick to your left, letting go with your right hand and reaching with your left. Your aim is for the ground directly in front of the ball and the blade of your stick should rest there—don't let it swing on through and clip your opponent across the shins. Come to an immediate stop, turn around, put your right hand back on your stick, and the ball is yours—but get moving or the other player will be back to try a left-hand lunge on you.

Circular Tackle

Sometimes it is not possible to overtake a player on her stick side; it is necessary to tackle on the non-stick side. In this case, you will have to use the circular tackle, which is more difficult. As you overtake the player on her left or non-stick side, you will have to pass her and come around to get the ball almost facing her. If you just reach in, you will be obstructing with your stick or shoulder (putting your stick or shoulder between her and the ball). Come around almost facing her, reach for the ball, and keep going so that you make a semicircle round her.

TEAM PLAY

You must master the above skills of field hockey as an individual player and learn to do them all at top speed. Equally important is to learn to be a good team player.

Passing is a very important team skill. The best way to get the ball down the field to score a goal is by fast, accurate passing around your opponents. Learn to move so that you are ready to receive a pass where the opponents cannot get it or to draw your opponent out of the way so as to make a hole for the ball to be passed through to another teammate. And run! Speed counts in field hockey. Always keep both hands on your stick and carry it low, ready for action.

POSITIONS

Different positions call for different abilities. Try them all until you find the one for which you are best qualified.

Halfbacks

Halfbacks must have great speed and stamina, as they must be up the field on the attack with their forwards, often shooting for goal themselves, and then back on defense when the other team breaks through with the ball. The left and right halfbacks must be especially fast as they are responsible for the opposing wings—usually the fastest of the forwards.

Backs

The backs do not have much running to do, but their job requires lots of headwork to set up a defense that will outwit the other team. They are the players who do most interchanging (exchanging positions temporarily with another player). The backs always play diagonally with each other. For example, when the ball comes into the right back's territory, she goes on the attack, while the left back drops back and toward the goal to cover in case the right back is passed. In this way an aggressive back can often break up an attack on her side of the field before it really gets started.

In general, all defense players tend to play up, marking their opponents closely when the ball is on their side of the field and back in a covering position when the ball is on the opposite side of the field. The theory behind this is that the forward farthest from the ball is the least dangerous and can be loosely marked.

The Goalie

The goalie is that last brave soul standing between the opposition and a score. She either has no action or plenty of it all at once—no in-between for her! She must be smart, quick, and certainly not faint of heart. She should have the ability to direct the play of her defense.

The Wings

On the forward line the wings are usually the speediest players, as a very fast wing can often get the ball from her defense, dribble it down the field, and set it up in scoring position before the opposing defense can swing into action. By the time a wing reaches the 25-yard line on

Flick

the attack, she should have decided whether she will dribble in and shoot or pass. Generally, she should pass before she crosses the line. If she gets caught beyond it, she should dribble down to the corner and then pass back to another forward. She should dribble in to the striking circle only when she intends to take the shot herself.

The Center Forward

The center forward (and this is true of the center halfback position as well) must be an excellent team player, since she is in the best position to direct the play of her line. She often has the opportunity to switch the direction of the ball; so she should see that both sides of the field are played equally.

Inners

The inners are usually the team's highest scorers. They are in good scoring positions and should be very skillful at dodging, passing, and outsmarting the goalie.

Scores are not always made on hard-hit balls; often they are made on quick passes from one forward to another which pull the goalie out of position. Dodges, pushes, and flicks also contribute to scoring. The flick is a very effective scoring shot as it goes slightly off the ground and is difficult to stop. To flick, start as for a push pass, but instead of simply pushing the ball, give a quick, hard snap of the wrists so the toe of the stick blade ends pointing up. This puts a spin on the ball. Like

FIELD HOCKEY

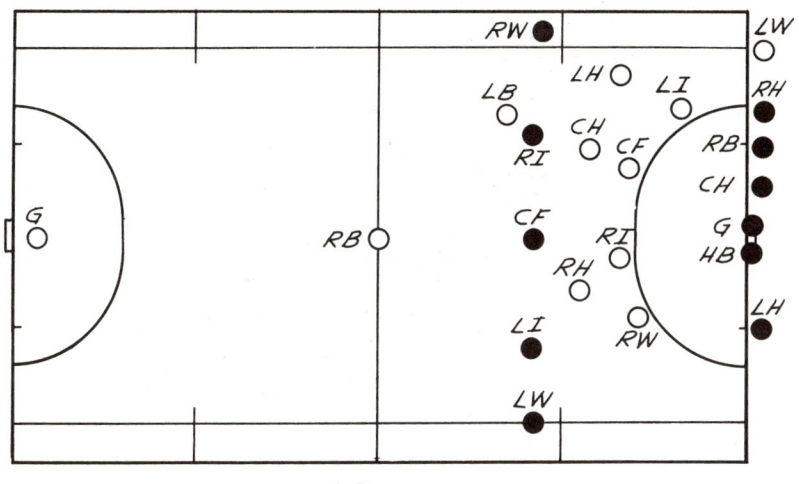

A Corner

the push pass, the flick should be done in a reaching position with the right foot forward. It is a fast stroke since there is no back swing. A left inner who finds herself in a difficult spot to drive for goal often can flick for the far corner away from the goalie, who is busy protecting the near corner.

STRATEGY

All forwards should shoot for goal as soon as the ball is in the striking circle (Goal does not count if hit from outside the circle.) and then follow up immediately. All forwards should not crowd the goal at once; some should drop back to the edge of the circle either to receive a back pass from a teammate or to intercept a ball hit by the defense.

If the forwards shoot and miss the goal and the ball goes out-of-bounds over the end line, play is resumed by a "defense hit" taken by placing the ball 15 yards from the end line opposite the spot where it went out. A member of the defensive team takes the hit with all other players at least 5 yards away. Occasionally the defending team hits the ball out over the end line. In this case, a corner is awarded the attacking team.

Corner

On a corner, players line up as shown in the diagram. The attacking wing on the side where the ball went out places the ball on the endline

Roll-In

at the alley line or on the sideline 5 yards from the corner. She hits the ball to any member of her team, all of whom must have their feet and sticks outside the striking circle until after the ball is hit. The player receiving the ball must stop it (not necessarily motionless) before shooting for goal. The ball may be deflected or passed but may not be shot for goal until it has been stopped. The six defense players of the defending team must stand with their feet and sticks behind their own goal line. Their forwards must be beyond the 25-yard line until the ball is hit.

Penalty Corner

A penalty corner is awarded when the defense intentionally hits the ball over the end line or foul inside the striking circle. For this type of corner the ball is hit out from a spot on the end line not less than 10 yards from the nearest goal post.

Roll-In

If the ball is hit out-of-bounds over a sideline, a player on the opposite team rolls it in. The ball must be rolled and must touch the ground inside the field within 1 yard of the point where it left the field. The player taking the roll-in must have both her feet and stick outside the sideline. She may not play the ball again until someone else has touched it. All other players must be out of the alley and within the field of play until the ball has left the hand of the player taking the roll-in. Whenever an occasion arises in which both teams should be given the ball, a bully is taken.

SAFETY

Injuries do not have to happen in field hockey. They happen more to beginners than to advanced players because of lack of skill, lack of familiarity with the rules, and failure to think before acting. If you learn to handle your stick skillfully—never hit into another player, never hit a moving ball without first controlling it—your game of field hockey should be fun and free from injuries. Always wear shinguards and see that your goalie wears regulation goal pads and foot protectors. If you need to wear your glasses while playing, protect them with a glasses guard. You can get a clear plastic one which gives unobstructed vision.

EQUIPMENT

Field hockey equipment is quite expensive and rather easily damaged if handled carelessly. If you are using school sticks, shinguards, and balls, treat them with respect—they have a rugged life. Good sticks, springy enough not to hurt your hands when you hit, cannot be too tough. Be careful how you use yours. Rubber grips are hard to replace—don't pull yours off or tear at it. Sticks come in various lengths and weights. Hold a stick in the drive position and swing it easily. If it just clears the ground, it is the right length. The usual lengths of sticks are from 33 to 36 inches. Sticks vary in weight, too. For most players a 17- or 18-ounce stick is best. Usually goalies and backs use heavier sticks. Sticks that are very heavy may get off a power drive, but they make it difficult for forwards and halfbacks to do the tricky fast stickwork necessary for passing, dodging, and handling the ball.

If you find it possible to own your own stick, do so by all means. Getting used to the feel of a stick helps a lot. Buy yours from a store that handles good hockey equipment. Most good sticks at the present time are made in England, India, or Pakistan. Short-toes sticks with mulberry heads are now the most popular and should be cared for with linseed oil. Long-toed sticks with heads of ash should be cared for with wax. If an edge of a stick splits, tape it with adhesive or electrician's tape before the split gets worse. Put on just enough tape to do the job; too much will throw your stick out of balance. The handle should have rubber inserts running down inside to act as shock absorbers. When you press the blade of the stick against the ground, you should feel some springiness in the handle.

Get a stick that feels comfortable; avoid one that is too heavy or too stiff. You will probably have to pay at least $7 for your stick, so take care of it. Wipe it dry after you play with it on wet grass. Store your stick lying flat so it will not warp. Keep it in a cool dry place. Heat dries out a stick and will cause it to break very easily.

While leather-covered balls are official for games, plastic balls are much cheaper, longer wearing, and just as good for practice. In fact, the newer plastic balls are being considered for "match" play.

When the ground or grass is slippery, it is important to wear shoes with rubber or plastic cleats or grooved soles. Shoes with metal cleats or spikes are not allowed.

OFFICIATING

Don't forget officiating. A field hockey game can't go on without good umpires. There should be two, one on either side of the field. Each umpire takes the half of the field to her right as she stands on the 50-yard line. She is responsible for roll-ins to her left on her side of the field and for any fouls she feels the other official cannot see. Umpires hold the whistle or refrain from calling a foul if it would be to the advantage of the offending team to do so. There are two official timekeepers and two official scorers. You can learn to officiate as you learn to play.

Remember, you will enjoy playing if you always act in a sportsmanlike manner. It is customary in field hockey for a player, when she knows she has committed a foul, to step back and let her opponent play the ball. When this happens, the umpire does not blow her whistle and the game continues. When it is necessary for the official to make a decision, respect that decision and be courteous to your opponents. Learn the rules and abide by them for clean and enjoyable play.

FOR MORE INFORMATION

American Association for Health, Physical Education, and Recreation, Division for Girls and Women's Sports. *Field Hockey-Lacrosse Guide.* Current edition. Washington, D.C.: the Association.

American Association for Health, Physical Education, and Recreation, Division for Girls and Women's Sports. *Official Field Hockey Scorebook for Girls and Women.* Washington, D.C.: the Association, 1970.

American Association for Health, Physical Education, and Recreation, Division for Girls and Women's Sports. *Selected Field Hockey-Lacrosse Articles.* Washington, D.C.: the Association.

Delano, Anne Lee. *Field Hockey.* Physical Education Series. Dubuque, Iowa: Wm. C. Brown Co., 1967.

Lees, Josephine, and Shellenberger, Betty. *Field Hockey.* Revised edition. New York: Ronald Press, 1967.

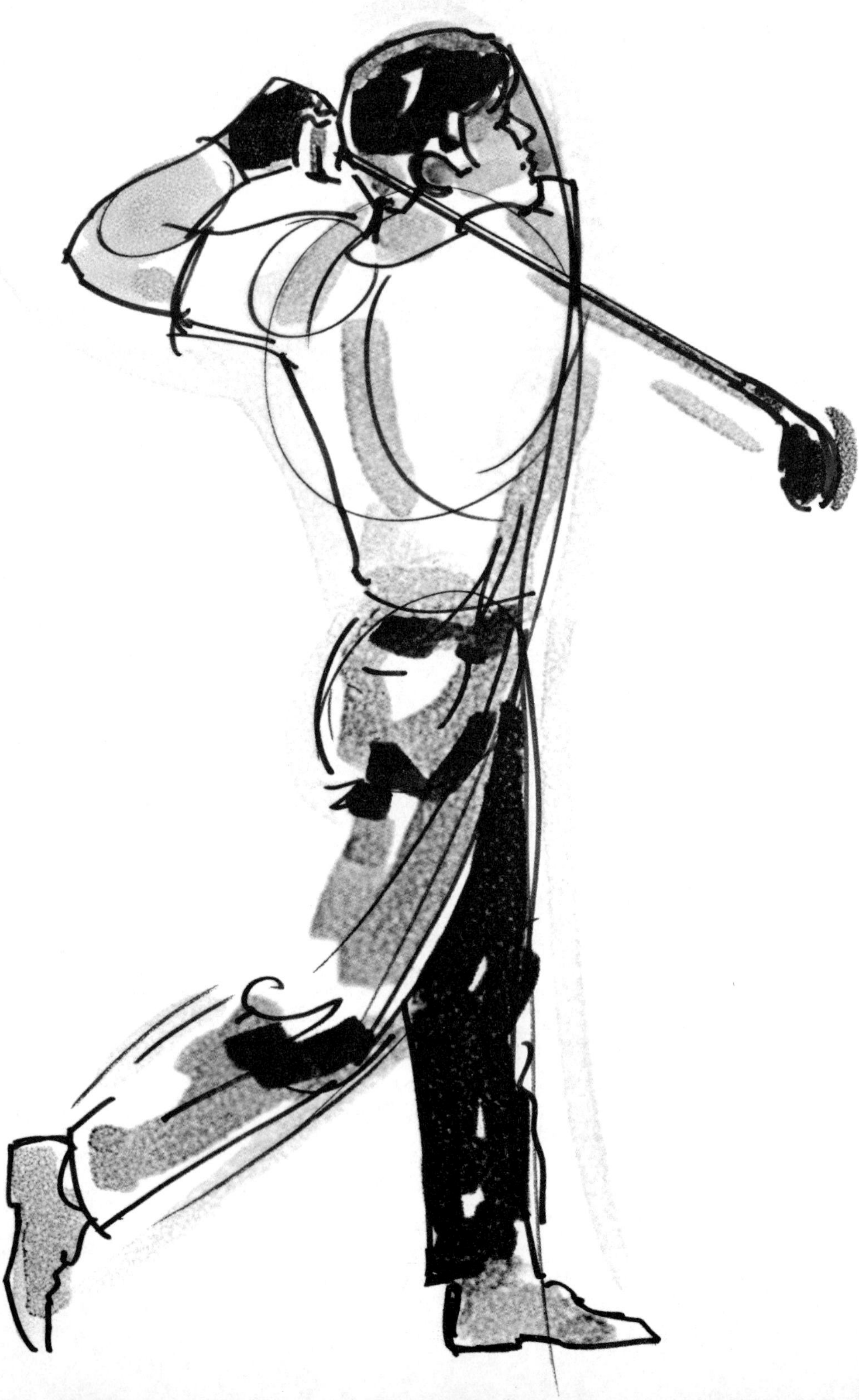

Golf

Golf probably originated in Scotland, although its exact beginnings are not known. Shepherds tending their flocks on pasturelands may have started the game by hitting pebbles with their crooks.

Golf was a popular game in Scotland in the fifteenth century. It was so popular that Parliament issued a decree banning the sport in 1457, because the men were neglecting their practice of archery to play golf. The ban was soon forgotten when the King of Scotland, James IV, was discovered playing golf. Mary, Queen of Scots, was the first woman golfer in the history of the game. Golf continued to be popular with royalty, noblemen, and commoners. The game was officially recognized in 1860, when the British Open Golf Tournament was first played.

A Scot promoted golf in the United States in the late nineteenth century. Since that time it has been played continuously here.

THE GOLF COURSE

A golf course is a large field divided into 18 areas called holes. Each hole consists of an area called the tee, from which play is begun; an area of mowed grass varying in length from under 100 yards to over 500 yards, called the fairway; and a small area of closely cut grass at the end of the fairway, called the putting green. Somewhere in the green a circular cup, about 4 inches in diameter and 6 inches deep, is sunk. On either side of the fairway there may be areas of long grass, trees, and bushes, called the rough. There are two types of hazards on the course: shallow to deep pits filled with sand, called sand traps; and water hazards, such as lakes and creeks.

One Hole

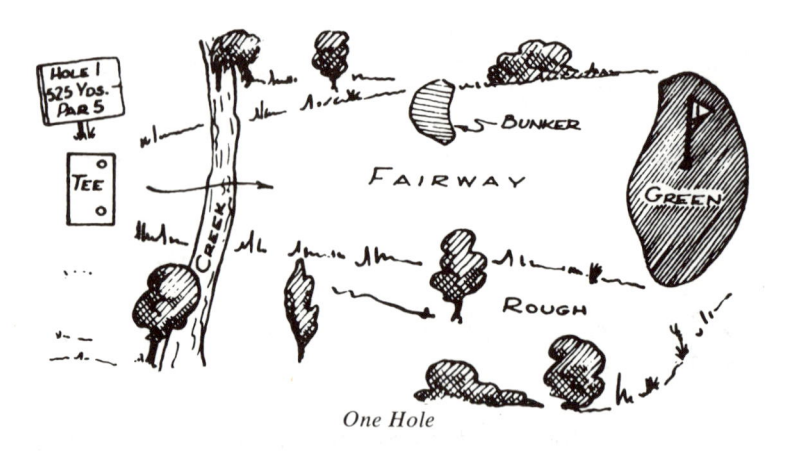

THE GAME

The game is played with a small, hard rubber ball, which is placed on the ground and hit with long-shafted clubs. The object of the game is to hit the ball from the teeing area to the green and into the cup with the fewest possible strokes.

At the teeing area for each hole, the ball may be placed upon a wooden peg, also called a tee. The player attempts to hit the ball from the tee down the fairway in the direction of the putting green. He continues to hit the ball from wherever it lies until it finally drops into the cup. The score for each hole is the number of strokes needed to get the ball from the tee into the cup. The score for the game is the total number of strokes for all 18 holes.

THE CLUBS

In playing golf it is necessary to hit the ball long and short distances. These distances will vary from over 200 yards to less than a foot. The ball must be hit from different surfaces, as from the fairway, rough, sand, and putting green. At times it is necessary to hit the ball high into the air to get over a tree or a hill; to hit the ball low to go under the branches of a tree; or to roll the ball along the grass. There are two types of clubs: woods and irons. These have special features to enable the player to hit the ball different distances under different conditions.

All of the clubs are numbered: the woods, one through five; the irons, two through nine. As the number of the club becomes higher, the club shaft is shorter and the slant to the face, the striking surface of the club, is greater.

The woods are so called because the head or striking end is made of a rounded block of wood. The woods all have longer shafts, or handles, than any of the irons. It is possible to hit the ball farther with the wood clubs than with the irons. The number one wood, the driver, is used at the start of a long hole to hit the ball off the tee. Since the face of this club has little slant, it is not used to hit a ball off the grass. If your ball is on the fairway and you still have a long distance to go to the cup, you should choose one of the other wood clubs. There is more slant, or loft, to the faces of the other woods, so you can more easily strike the ball off the grass into the air. Which particular club you choose depends upon the distance to the green and the position of the ball on the grass. The number two wood is called the brassic; the number three, the spoon.

The iron clubs have iron or steel heads. There is a name for each iron, but they are generally called only by number. The two iron will hit the ball farthest and lowest since this club has the longest shaft and the least loft. The higher-lofted irons will hit the ball shorter distances and higher into the air.

The medium and high-lofted irons, five through nine, are used to play various type shots. You may wish to hit the ball a shorter distance than is possible with a particular club. For this stroke, you grip down on the shaft and take a smaller swing at the ball.

When the ball is on the putting green, the club called the putter is used. The putter has the shortest shaft and the least loft. The ball is hit so that it rolls along the surface of the putting green toward the cup.

TECHNIQUE OF PLAYING

How To Hold the Club

The grip of the club is first in importance. Without a good grip the hands and wrists cannot work properly when you are swinging the club. The most popular grip is the overlapping grip. In this grip the left hand is at the top of the club and the right hand is directly below it, with the little finger of the right hand overlapping the index finger of the left. (If the player is left-handed and using left-handed clubs, he should do

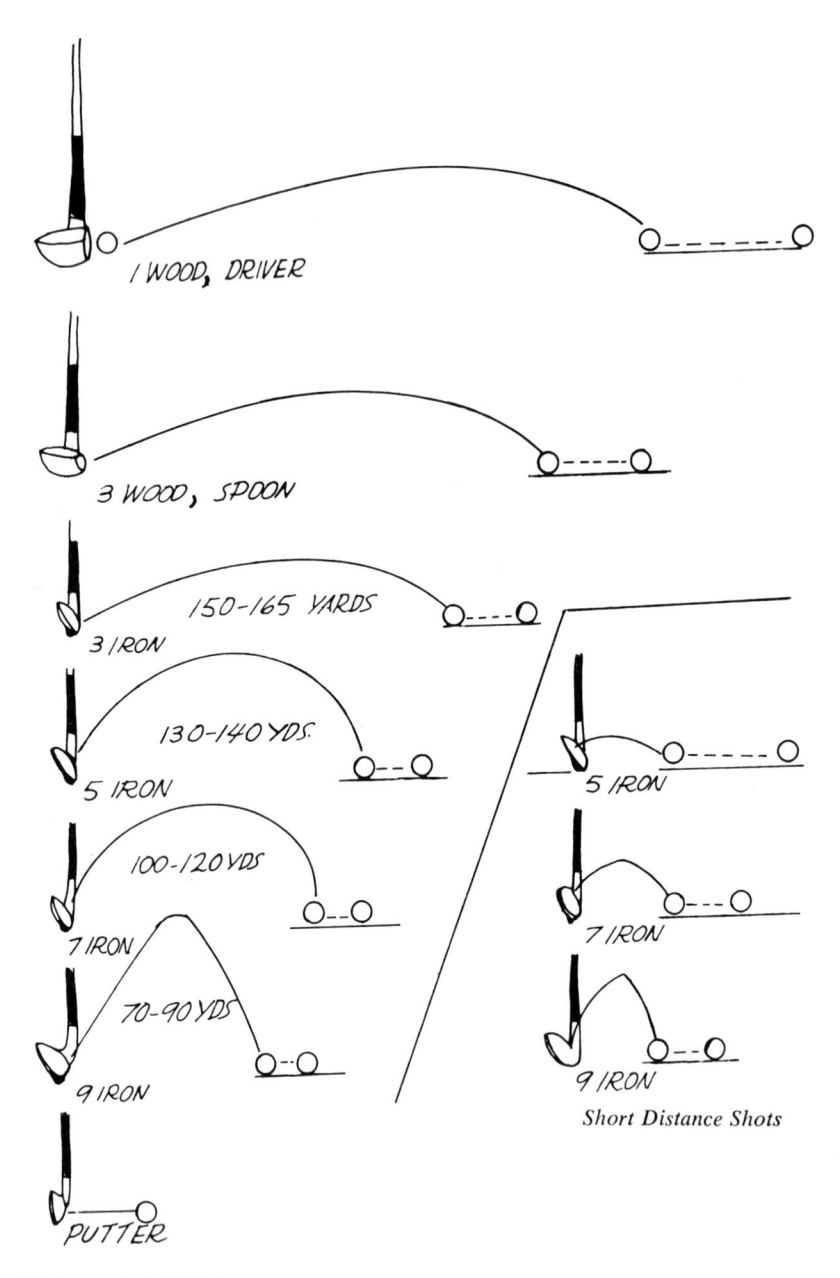

154   PHYSICAL EDUCATION FOR HIGH SCHOOL STUDENTS

Minimum Set of Clubs

Short Distance Shots

GOLF 155

Overlapping Grip

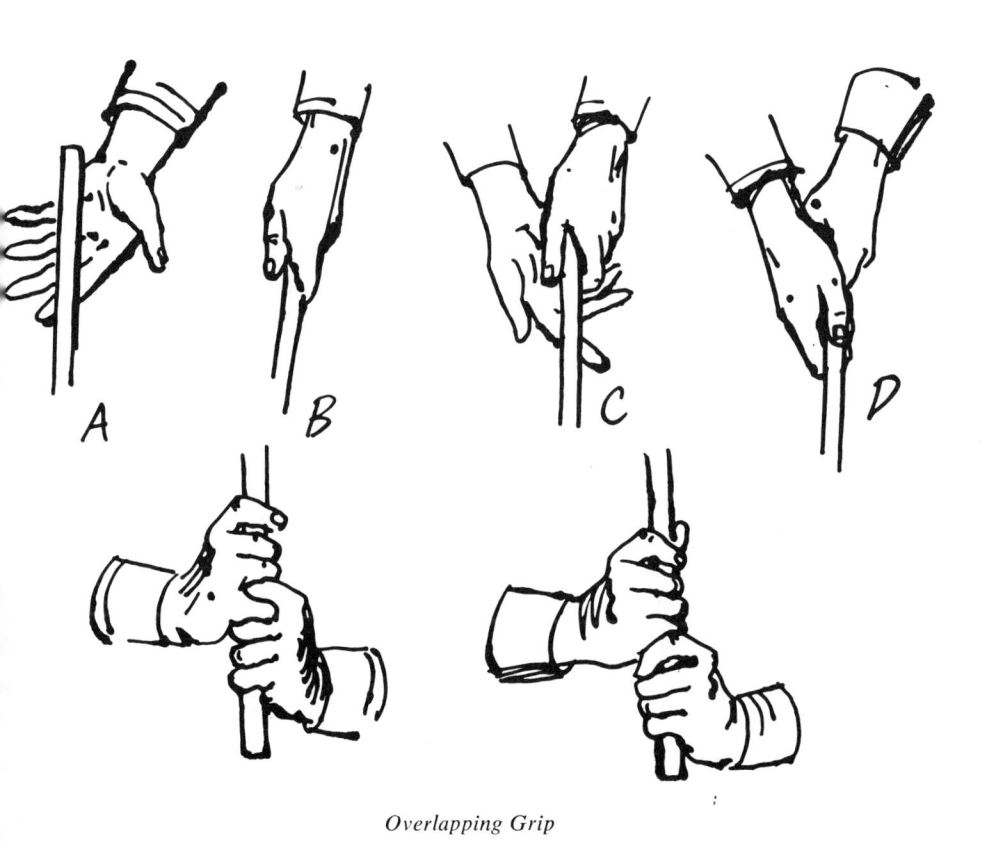

the reverse.) To grip the club, move your hands from the natural hanging position at the sides and take hold of the club on the leather grip. This is similar to shaking hands with the club. The palms face each other. The left thumb fits in the line of the right palm. The grip should be firm, but not tight. A tight grip will prevent you from swinging the club swiftly, which is necessary to hit the ball the intended distance.

Some golfers prefer the interlocking or the natural grip. The positions of the hands are the same for all the grips. In the interlocking grip the little finger of the right hand and index finger of the left hand interlock. In the natural grip the little finger of the right hand is placed on the club with the other three fingers.

```
                SQUARE
                STANCE
                
                CLOSED
                STANCE
                
                OPEN
                STANCE
```

Stance

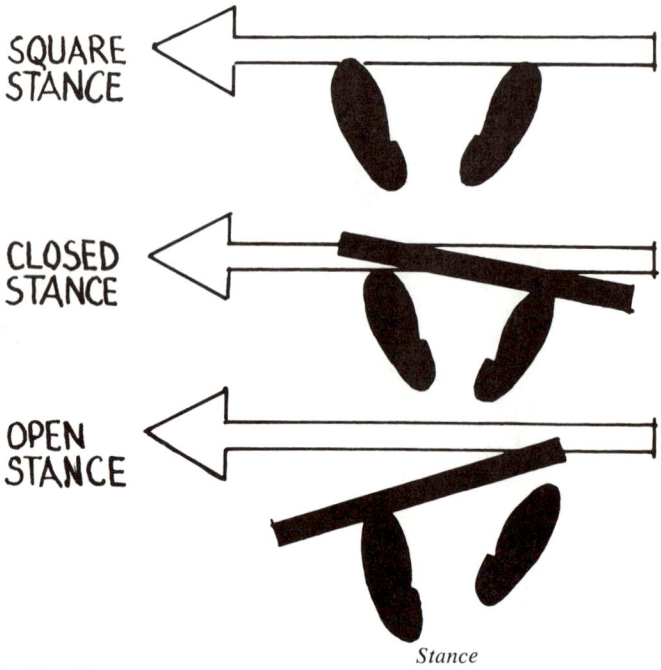

How To Stand

The stance (position) to take to hit a golf ball is relatively simple. If you wish to hit the ball a long distance, you place your feet about a shoulder-width apart, with the knees flexed as if you were about to sit down. For short distances, you should stand with your feet closer together, at a comfortable distance from the ball in a balanced position. The shaft of the club is at the center of the body and the club head rests evenly on the ground.

How To Hit the Ball a Long Distance

The movement to hit a golf ball is called a swing. To hit the ball far you must swing the head of the club swiftly, because the distance a ball will travel depends in part upon the speed of the club head. Consider how you would throw a ball a long distance. For a long distance you would swing your hand in a larger arc. So, to hit a golf ball a long distance, you must swing the club in as big a circle as you can and with control. In the swing away from the ball—the backswing—the club is swung to a position where the shaft is approximately over the right shoulder and horizontal to the ground. From this position the club head is swung toward the ball and distant target. It gains speed on the down-

Top of Backswing

swing, and this speed carries the club up over the left shoulder on the follow-through. This swing can be compared with the swing a baseball player takes to hit a ball. The actions are much the same, but since one ball is in the air and the other on the ground, the paths the bat and the golf club follow are different.

Let's look at this movement more closely. The club head is swung back from the ball close to the ground and rises gradually on the backswing. As the club swings through and contacts the ball, it remains close to the ground and again gradually rises on the follow-through. It is important that you do not try to swing the club up into the air. This will happen automatically.

During the backswing and on into the follow-through, the left arm remains fairly straight. There is an upward pull that keeps the left arm extended. The wrists bend, or "cock," naturally on the backswing and follow-through. This action of the wrists is like the natural action that occurs when you strike a nail with a hammer.

The weight of the body shifts with the action of the swing onto the foot away from the target (on the backswing) and then onto the foot closest to the target (as the club swings through the ball). With this shift the body turns, or "pivots." Because you watch the ball until you strike it, your head will remain fairly steady during the swing. It is like the hub of the wheel of the swing. After you strike the ball, your head will turn as your body turns to watch the ball in flight.

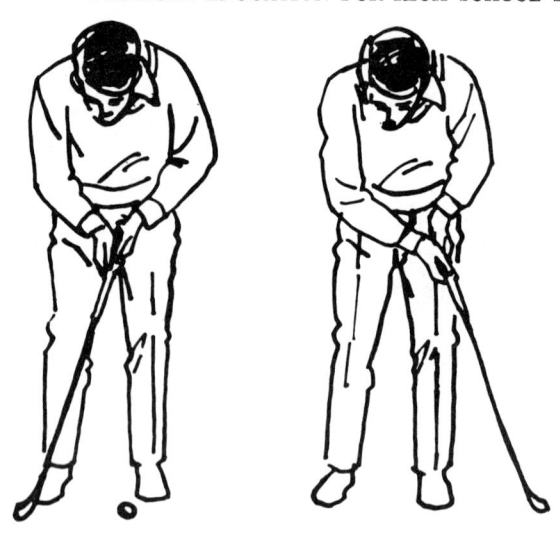

The skilled golfer has learned to hit the ball far and straight by developing a smooth, easy, and rhythmic swing. It is this graceful swing, not brute strength, that produces club head speed and accurate contact with the ball.

How To Hit the Ball a Short Distance

The golf shot to the putting green is called the approach shot. The shots requiring a smaller swing than the full swing are taken with the medium or high-lofted irons, numbers four through nine. On these strokes you wish to hit the ball near the cup; so to be more accurate, you take a short hold on the club.

This swing is an abbreviation of the full swing. It may be very short like the swing of a pendulum of a clock or it may be almost a full swing. You learn to sense by feel just how far you must swing a club for distances requiring less than a full stroke.

How To Putt a Ball

The putt is the stroke used on the putting green to roll the ball into the cup. The club head is swung a short distance away from the ball and then toward the cup. Because the swing is so small, there will be very little or no body action. The stroke is with the arms and wrists.

If you observe golfers, you will see that for this stroke there are many individual grips and stances. Putting is an individual stroke. Good skill in putting is important because about a third of the strokes for a round will be taken on the green.

Hole	Yds	Par	Hole	Yds	Par
1	535	5	10	385	4
2	208	3	11	176	3
3	392	4	12	393	4
4	551	5	13	583	5
5	445	4	14	187	3
6	403	4	15	404	4
7	354	4	16	396	4
8	225	3	17	396	4
9	363	4	18	469	5
Out	3476	36	In	3389	36

Score Card

SCORING

After playing each hole you write your score for the hole on the score card. The score card will show the length of each hole in yards and the par for each hole. Par for a hole is the number of strokes a good player needs to play a hole. Par for a hole varies from three to six, depending upon the length of the hole. If a hole is 153 yards long, a good player should be able to hit the ball from the tee to the green. Since par allows two strokes on the putting green, par for this hole is three; thus, on a 300-yard hole par would include two strokes to get onto the green and two putts, or four. Because men usually hit the ball farther than women, par on some holes is higher for women.

In playing golf you always have par to compete against. If you get one stroke less than par for a hole, you score a birdie. A score of two strokes under par is an eagle. A score of one over par is a bogey.

GOLF RULES

The fundamental rule of golf is that once you strike the ball from the tee, you do not touch it until you lift it out of the cup, except to strike it with the club. If it is impossible to strike the ball, there are rules to govern the situation.

The elementary rules are not difficult. As you continue playing golf, you will learn more rules as situations of play arise.

1. To start each hole, you tee your ball between the tee markers, or within an area two club lengths back of them.

2. You play from the tee according to honor. On the first tee you decide by lot who will play first. After the first tee, the person with the lowest score on the previous hole has the honor of playing first.

3. After teeing off, the ball farthest from the cup is played first.

4. You play the ball as it lies on the grass or in the sand, unless certain rules allow you to move the ball.

5. If your ball lies near such obstructions as ball washers, sprinklers, and hoses, you may move the ball without penalty.

6. You may not press down the ground near your ball or break or bend anything fixed or growing.

7. If loose impediments, such as fallen leaves or twigs, interfere, you may move them, except in a hazard.

8. In playing from hazard, you cannot touch the surface of the hazard before you take your swing to hit the ball.

9. The penalty for a lost ball or an unplayable ball is either (a) to shoot another ball from the spot where you played the previous one and add a penalty stroke, or (b) to drop a ball at any distance behind the point where the ball lies, adding a penalty stroke. In case the ball is in a bunker, the ball must be dropped in the bunker.

10. If your ball goes beyond the limits of the course—out-of-bounds—you must shoot another ball from the spot where you played the previous one.

11. The flag must be attended when you are on the green. If the ball hits the pole, the penalty is: match play, loss of hole; medal play, two strokes.

12. If your ball comes to rest on the wrong putting green, you must lift it from the green. Drop it off the green not nearer the cup you are playing for.

GOLF ETIQUETTE

Golf is usually played by four people called a foursome. There will be many foursomes on a course at one time. Playing is more enjoyable and safe if all golfers follow rules of etiquette. Your observance of these simple rules shows consideration for other players on the course.

1. Learn the rules of golf and abide by them.
2. When a golfer is making a shot, stand quietly to the side of him. Golf requires concentration; so do nothing that will disturb the player.
3. Wait until the players in front of you are out of range before playing your stroke.
4. When you have finished playing a hole, replace the flag in the cup and leave the green immediately. Mark your scores on the score card at the next tee.
5. If you dig any turf—a divot—replace it and press it down with your foot.
6. Be careful how you walk on the putting green so as not to mar the surface in any way. Never walk or stand near the cup.
7. After you have made a stroke in a sand trap, smooth out all marks made in the trap.
8. If a member of your group is looking for a ball, help him in his search. If you are delaying the players behind you, signal them to pass. Wait until they are out of range before continuing with your play.
9. Play without delay. If you are a beginner and players behind you play faster, invite them to play through.

SAFETY PRECAUTIONS

For the number of people playing golf, few accidents occur. Probably most that do happen are due to carelessness or lack of knowledge. Do you know that it is possible to swing the club at 100 miles per hour or more? The golf ball also travels at a high rate of speed. When you practice or play, follow these safety rules.

1. Before taking a practice swing, check your area to see that no one is in the range of your swing. When other people are swinging or taking practice swings while waiting to tee off, be careful where you walk.
2. When playing, never walk ahead of anyone making a golf shot.
3. If you hit a ball that possibly could strike someone, call "Fore" loudly.

4. Before playing golf, study the game. All players should have instruction before playing.

GOLF COMPETITION

Golf is a major individual sport. The sport pages of newspapers always carry stories on golf tournaments. There are two types of competition: stroke or medal play and match play. In a stroke or medal play tournament, the contestants play a certain number of rounds, usually four, and the winner is the person with the lowest total score. In a match play tournament, two players are matched against each other, and the competition is by holes. The person who wins the greatest number of holes is the winner. Winners keep playing until there is one winner of the tournament.

FOR MORE INFORMATION

American Association for Health, Physical Education, and Recreation, Division for Girls and Women's Sports. *Bowling-Fencing-Golf Guide.* Current edition. Washington, D.C.: the Association.

Boros, Julius. *Swing Easy, Hit Hard.* New York: Harper & Row, 1964.

National Golf Foundation. *Golf Lessons.* Chicago: the Foundation, 1968.

National Golf Foundation. *How To Improve Your Golf.* Chicago: the Foundation, 1963.

United States Golf Association. *The Conduct of Women's Golf.* New York: the Association, 1965.

United States Golf Association. *The Rules of Golf.* Current edition. New York: the Association.

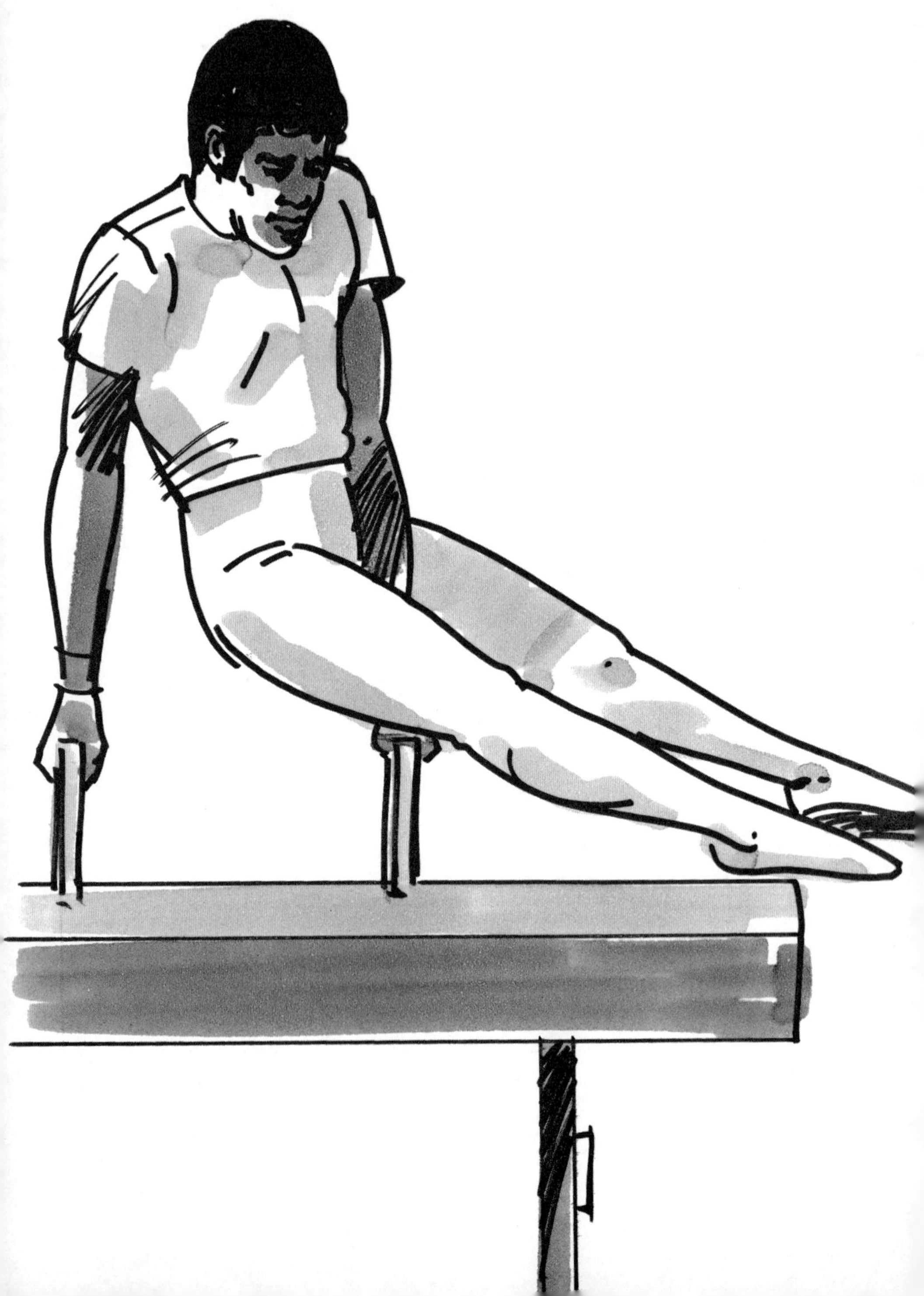

Gymnastics and Tumbling

BRIEF HISTORY

There is some difficulty in determining with preciseness when gymnastics and tumbling first came into prominence. However, there is some evidence which points out that as early as 2500 B.C. the Chinese and the Egyptians did some forms of gymnastics and tumbling. Later, the Greeks collected all of these ideas and formed them into a system of training which became an important part of general education. The word *gymnastics* is derived from Greek, and it was the Greeks who promoted gymnastics and many other forms of physical activity as no other nation in the world has done. To the Greek citizen, gymnastics and other forms of physical activity were as important as philosophy, politics, music, and art.

The Greek way in time came to an end. During the Roman period and the Middle Ages, gymnastics received little recognition. The only exception was the training of knights and the activities of acrobats who entertained the nobility. The writings of two prominent physicians, Hippocrates and Galen, went unnoticed by civilized nations, and physical activity was kept alive only because of military needs.

Competitive Gymnastics

Competitive gymnastics is a part of the sports and athletic programs of colleges, high schools, YMCA's, YWCA's, Turnvereins, Sokols, and other such organizations. Since the rebirth of the Olympic Games at Athens, Greece, in 1895, both men and women have competed in gymnastics. Founded in 1881, the International Federation of Gymnastics has done much to standardize events and also the scoring of events. In competitive gymnastics, performance is usually graded on the basis of the difficulty of the stunts performed and the form of the competitor and the smoothness with which his skills are combined into his total exercise. The performance begins when the gymnast touches the apparatus and ends when he dismounts. The events established by the International Federation of Gymnastics for Olympic competition include floor exercises (boys and girls), side horse vaulting (girls), long horse vaulting (boys), side horse support exercises (boys), still rings (boys), horizontal bar (boys), parallel bars (boys), uneven parallel bars (girls), and balance beam (girls). Other events which can be included in gymnastic competition include tumbling, trampoline, rope climbing, and flying rings.

Values

What will participation in gymnastics do for you? Here are a few of the ways it will help you:

1. Your upper body strength will be improved, and when trampoline and tumbling events are included, your all-round strength will increase.

2. Your coordination will improve. This means that you will be able to perform with more grace and less effort.

3. You will have added flexibility.

4. You will learn how to fall properly, and this will be helpful to you in all sports.

5. You will learn to be "cautiously" courageous. In other words, you will learn the dangers involved in certain stunts and will proceed to overcome these dangers through progressive mastery of skills.

6. You will take an interest in helping your classmates to learn stunts, and you will also be appreciative of the help they give you.

7. You will be provided with a sufficient number of skills so that you can arrange a routine of your own. In other words, you will be able to use your own talents in developing various stunt combinations.

SAFETY

A boy or girl may advance from simple to complex techniques in gymnastics and tumbling with little danger by following simple safety principles. Remember that all expert gymnasts followed these rules as they attained success:

GYMNASTICS AND TUMBLING

1. Warm up well with calisthenics or with elementary stunts in the activity in which you are to participate.
2. Inspect the equipment before using it. See that it does not move when you mount it.
3. Chalk your hands well before working on the apparatus.
4. Have only one person at a time working on the apparatus.
5. When learning advanced stunts, insist upon mature spotters.
6. Always have sufficient mats in fixed and proper positions.
7. Roll with a fall.
8. Learn your stunts in a progressive manner. Do not attempt stunts based upon lead-up stunts that you have not perfected.
9. Volunteer to spot your classmates.

Spotting

Spotting is positioning oneself so as to assist a performer in doing a stunt without fear of injury. This is done with or without the use of spotting belts. The following points should be kept in mind when spotting:

1. Spot by holding an appropriate part of the body for the activity in question. In spotting someone on the parallel bars, always spot below the bars.
2. When your classmate says "Spot me," know what he is going to do so that you can spot correctly.
3. When spotting on one knee in tumbling, the knee should be away from your classmate.
4. When spotting, stay as close as possible to both your classmate and the apparatus.
5. Realize that most people will have trouble with certain skills.
6. When spotting, concentrate on just what you are going to do and how you are going to do it. Look for such things as point of greatest momentum, changes in grip, shift of body position, and direction of possible falls.

BALANCE BEAM

The balance beam is an accepted event in all sanctioned gymnastic meets for girls. The beam is approximately 4 inches in width, 16 feet 4 inches in length, and between 2 feet 6 inches and 4 feet in height from the floor.

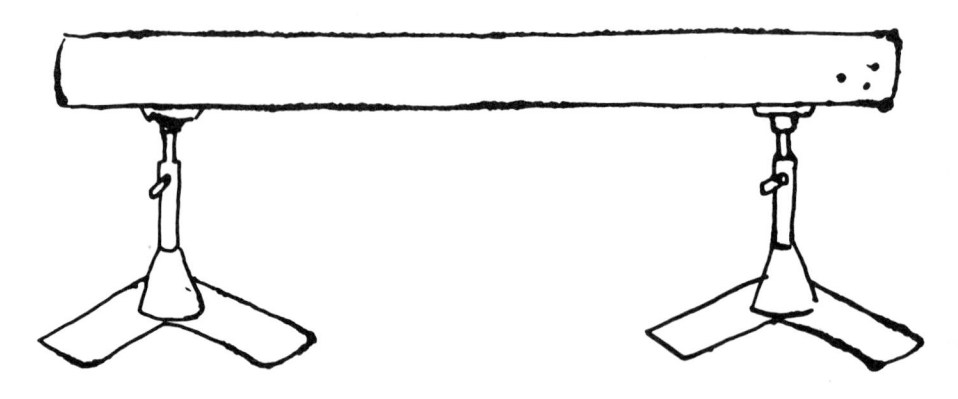

Balance Beam

In competition a routine must be of a specific duration—not more than 2 minutes nor much less than 1 minute and 30 seconds. A well-executed exercise should consist of a mount, graceful locomotion movements (walking, dance steps, turns, jumps), stunts and balances, and end with a dismount.

As a beginner you may find that your teacher will begin by having you balance along a line on the floor. This will help you orient your thinking to what it will be like performing on the beam itself. You will find that balance beam work will offer you many opportunities to develop a variety of graceful and feminine movements. As your confidence increases, you will develop greater skill in balancing on a very narrow and restricted area.

Jump to a Straight-Arm Front Support

Begin your mount by facing the middle of the beam at a distance of about 3 yards or so. A beat board or reuther board may be used to get added height on the mount. Taking off with both feet together, placing your hands about 2 feet apart on top of the beam, vault into your straight-arm support position. Look straight ahead, have your thighs resting on the beam, your legs together, and your toes pointed.

Straddle to a "V" Seat

From a front support position, swing your right leg over the beam and at the same time turn your body to the left so that you are facing the left end of the beam. Place both of your hands behind you under your lower back and lean backward and raise your legs with toes pointed into a "V" seat hold position.

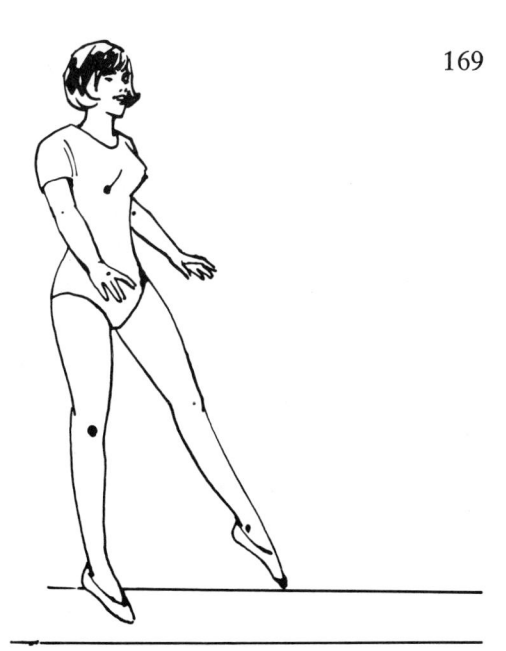

Stand from a Squat

From your "V" seat swing your legs down, straddle the beam until your feet reach the beam on the back swing. With both of your feet and knees on the beam and your hands in front of you, push yourself up to a standing position.

Walk, Run, Walk, Pivot Turn

From a standing position in the middle of the beam, take two short walking steps, three short running steps, and one walking step. You should now be at the left end of the beam. Raise up onto the balls of your feet and rotate your body toward your rear foot. As you make your one-half pivot turn, your arms should be gracefully held out and up and your head and chest should be erect.

Dip Steps into a Front Scale

Once you have made your pivot turn, take three moderate dip steps forward toward the middle of the beam. To make your dip steps look polished, keep the toes of your moving foot pointed. Your supporting leg will flex at the knee as your moving foot dips well below the top edge of the beam.

Front Scale

When you have made your third dip step, secure your weight on your forward foot, raise your left leg, and lower your chest so that your upper body and raised leg are parallel to the beam. Your head should be facing forward and your arms should be held away from your body in as graceful a manner as possible. Both of your legs should be straight, the toes of your raised leg should be pointed, and you should hold your scale for 3 seconds.

Pirouette and Step

From your front scale, swing your rear leg forward and as it passes your support foot, flex it at the knee. As the swinging leg passes across the front of your supporting foot, rotate your body 180 degrees and place your foot in front of your supporting foot. The foot which supported you in your scale balance is now brought forward as you get set for your jump change.

Two Jump Changes into a Deep Squat

Jump straight up with both of your feet momentarily leaving the beam. As you reach the peak of your jump, your rear foot comes forward and your forward foot goes to the rear. Repeat same procedure. Land in a deep squat position with your arms held gracefully out to the side and your head and chest directly over your rear foot.

Squat Turn—Duck Walk

From your deep squat position with your weight back on your rear foot, swing your arms in the direction of your half turn. Maintain your squat position and take two steps forward. As you perform the duck walk, look straight ahead and keep your arms out to the side for balance.

Stand—Swedish Fall—Front Dismount

From your duck walk, move to an upright stand position. Next, fall forward landing on your hands. Flex your arms as they make contact with the beam and at the same time extend one leg upward with your toes pointed as you lower your chest towards the bar. Once you have completed your Swedish fall, move your extended leg to the beam and assume a front leaning rest position. From this position, kick your left leg up and away from the beam, with your right leg quickly joining the left so that both legs are together. As both legs fall fully, extend with

GYMNASTICS AND TUMBLING 171

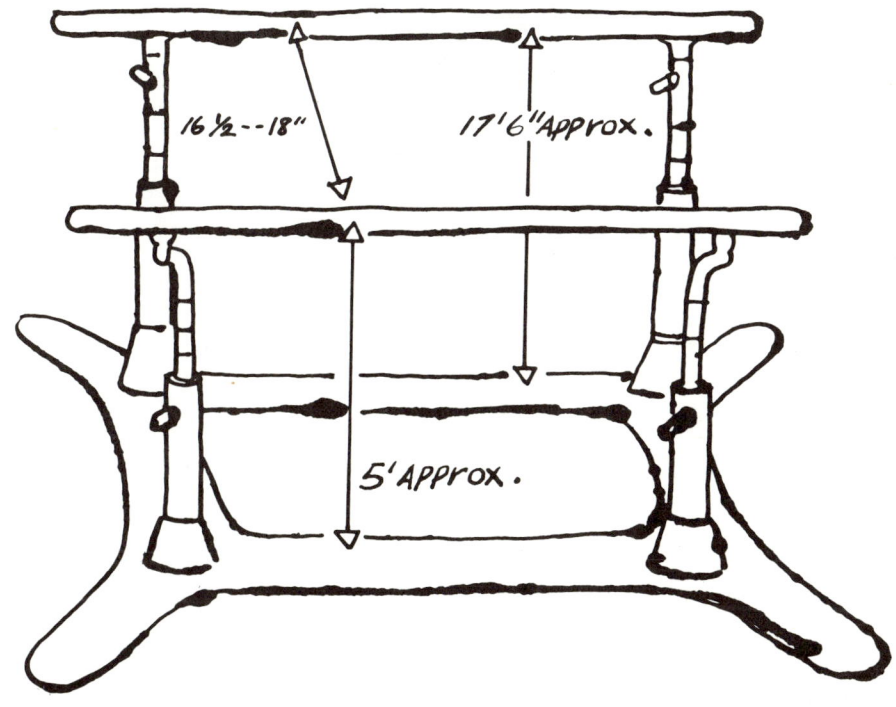

Uneven Parallel Bars

toes pointed, lift your left arm up and away from the beam in anticipation of your landing. Your right hand remains on the beam to assist you in controlling your landing.

UNEVEN PARALLEL BARS

The uneven parallel bars have only recently been accepted as a standard piece of equipment in girls gymnastic competition. In 1952, during the Fourteenth Olympic Games, the uneven parallel bars became a required event in women's international competition. Many feel that this event is the most spectacular of all the girls events.

A successful routine on the uneven parallel bars should consist primarily of swinging maneuvers and vaults, with the gymnast moving from bar to bar in a seemingly effortless performance. Emphasis should be placed on continuous graceful movement with no obvious display of strength. Support positions, either standing or sitting, should be of a

Straight-Arm Support

short duration and used sparingly. Usually no more than two balances opposite the bar or other stop positions are allowed in an exercise. A competitive uneven parallel bar routine begins with a mount from the floor or reuther board and ends with a dismount from either the high or low bar; the exercises should consist of at least 10 well-integrated skills.

The uneven bars are between 16 and 18 inches in width. The height of the high bar is about 7 feet 6 inches, and the height of the low bar is approximately 5 feet. This piece of equipment more than any other in girls gymnastics will develop strength and endurance in your arms, shoulders, and abdomen. It will also do much to develop your sense of balance and timing as you maneuver from one bar to the other. Your self-confidence in handling your body at different heights should increase greatly as you gain experience on the uneven parallel bars.

Jump to Straight-Arm Front Support

From a standing position facing both the low and high bar run forward, hitting the reuther board and using a regular grip. Vault to a straight-arm support position on the low bar facing the high bar. Your hands should be about a shoulder-width apart and your fingers should be over the bar, with your thumbs close to your hips underneath the bar. Your shoulders should be between the bars, your head looking forward, your legs straight, and your toes pointed.

GYMNASTICS AND TUMBLING   173

Crotch Seat

From your straight-arm front support position, swing your left leg over the bar, and at the same time release your left hand from the bar and lean laterally to the right. Regrasp the bar with your left hand as your leg goes over the bar and as you come into your crotch support, also changing your grasp with your right hand so that your thumb is on top and your fingers are on the bottom. Now remove your left hand from the low bar and grasp the high bar. When you have secured your grasp on the high bar move your right hand close to your thighs and make a quarter turn so that you are facing the right end of the bars.

Seat Balance

From your crotch straddle position, bring your right foot up onto the low bar, keeping it close to your body. Move your right hand behind your back and extend your left leg fully as in a "V" seat position.

Squat Stand to a Mixed Grip Swing on High Bar

With your right foot on the low bar, move your right hand in front of your right foot and swing your left leg back onto the bar beside your right foot. Reach up with your right hand and grasp the high bar with a reverse grip. Let your body swing from the low bar to the high bar. As your legs move under the high bar, release your left hand and make a one-half turn by turning your head to the left so that you are looking over the low bar. Regrasp the high bar with your left hand in a regular grip.

Raise Legs to a Standing Position on Low Bar

From a hang on the high bar, swing your legs forward so that both your feet land on top of the low bar. Extend your legs and change your hand position so that you are now standing on the low bar facing the high bar.

Scale on Low Bar

Turn your body so that you are facing the end of the bars with only one hand in contact with the high bar and the other hand out parallel to the low bar. Next, extend your inside leg back until it is parallel with both bars and in line with your extended arm. Hold the scale for at least 2 seconds.

Squat to a Front Support Position on Low Bar

From your scale position, bring your free hand down onto the low bar and flex your weight-supporting leg so that you are in a squat position. From this position take the hand from the high bar and place it about 2 feet forward of your left hand on the low bar. Keeping your arms fully extended allow your legs to drop below and between your arms on the low bar.

Cast Back—Backward Hip Circle on the Low Bar

From a front straight-arm support position on the low bar, swing your legs backwards so that your body comes about 3 feet away from the bar. As your legs come back toward the bar, flex your arms slightly, pike at the waist, throw your head back, and keep the bar in close to your abdomen. If you follow these directions, you will end up as you started in a front support position.

Single Leg Flank Vault Dismount

From your front support position with your back to the high bar, swing your left leg over the bar so that you are in a crotch seat. Place your right hand on the high bar and the fingers of your left hand on the underside of the low bar just behind your left leg. Swing your right leg up and over the low bar, pushing off the high bar with your right hand. Keep a hold on the lower bar with your left hand as your body makes a half turn to the left. As you land bring your legs together, anticipate your landing by extending your right arm up and keeping a firm hold on the bar with your left hand.

FLOOR EXERCISES

This is an Olympic event which is performed by both men and women in an area approximately 40 feet by 40 feet. However, there are some major differences between the routines developed by men and women. A girls routine should display graceful and effortless feminine movement which combines dance and tumbling skills into a unified rhythmic composition. Girls floor exercises should be done to music, which is not the case with boys. Boys routines are less dance-oriented and more tumbling-oriented, with one or two strength stunts incorporated into the routine. Flexibility is very much a part of the routine for both sexes and must be displayed if one is to have an acceptable performance.

GYMNASTICS AND TUMBLING   175

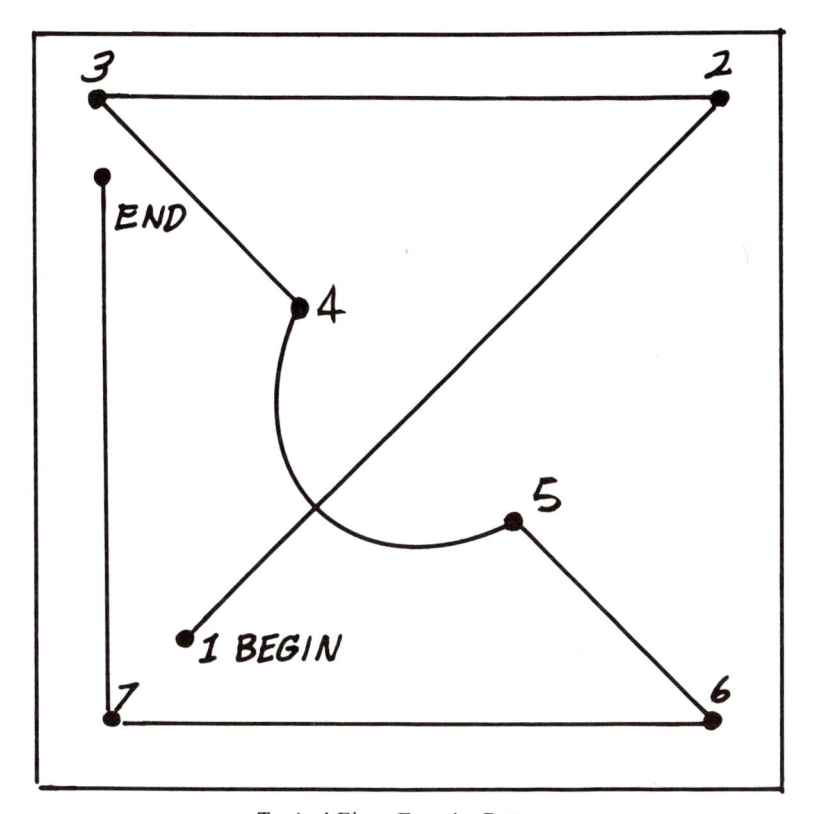

Typical Floor Exercise Pattern

Movement should not be in one direction; rather, it should be in a number of directions to provide an opportunity for the performer to demonstrate his varied abilities. The following series of stunts are suggested for a boys floor exercises routine; however, with the exception of the press head balance, all of these skills in combination with dance movements are suitable for girls.

Dive Forward Roll to a Stand

Stand at the corner of the mat facing the opposite corner. You can do this maneuver either from a stand or by running a few steps. Take off on both feet and keep your legs straight while in the air, flexing only at the hips. When you land, flex your arms and tuck both your legs into your chest and roll forward into a standing position.

Front Scale

From a standing position, lower your chest and raise your right leg so that your body forms a "T" position with your arms held straight out from your shoulders. Your right leg should be as straight as possible and your toes pointed. A balance position is usually held for 3 seconds to demonstrate that you are in full control.

Scale Turn into Two Backward Rolls

From your scale, swing your right leg forward. When it reaches a forward point even with your waist, simultaneously turn your right foot toward the floor and pivot to the left on the ball of your left foot. As you complete your half turn, place your right foot next to your left and lean backwards. Place your hands on top of your shoulders with your palms facing upwards, your thumbs just beneath your ears, and your elbows in close and in front of your chest. Your chin should be touching your chest and your knees should be brought into your chest as you make your roll. As your feet are passing over your head, you should be pushing with your hands so that your feet will land straightly flexed, ready to go directly into the next backward roll.

Jump Half—Pirouette—Straddle Stand

From your stand position spring straight up in the air and make a half turn so that you are facing in the opposite direction. As you land, spread your legs so that you land in a straddle position, with your body bent at the waist so that your chest is parallel to the floor. Your arms should be straight out from the shoulders and you should be looking forward.

Straddle Stand—Swedish Fall

Move into an upright straddle stand and let your right leg move toward your left foot as you let your upper body fall toward the floor. Your hands make contact with the floor partially flexed with one leg raised high. Hold this position for less than a second and then lower the raised leg and extend both arms so that you are in a push-up position.

Press to Headstand

From a push-up position, place the front of your head on the mat about a foot in front of your hands. Keeping your legs straight and toes pointed, slide your hips forward until they are just over your head. When

GYMNASTICS AND TUMBLING 177

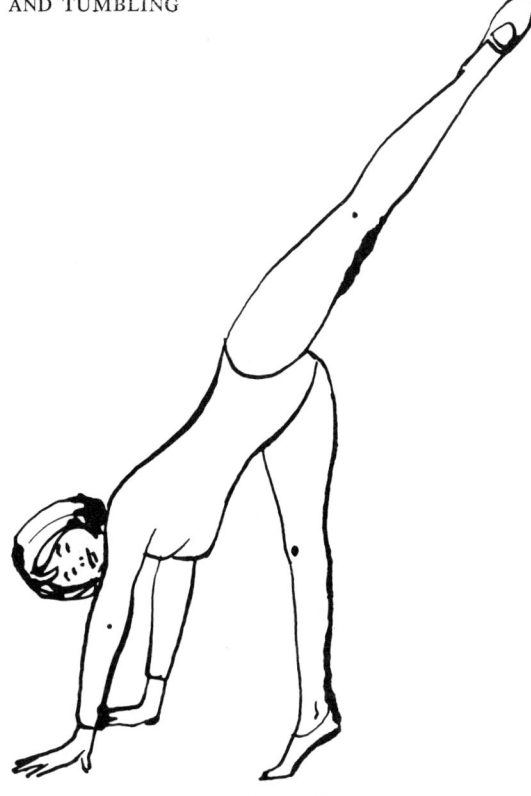

Swedish Fall

your hips are over your head, raise your legs so that your body is in one straight line from head to toe. Hold your head balance for approximately 3 seconds.

Forward Roll to Sit and Lower Head to Knees

From a headstand, arch your body so that your hips move beyond your head and you begin to feel off-balance. As your hips pass your head, apply pressure with your hands to lift your head off the mat and at the same time bring your chin to your chest. Your legs should be kept straight throughout the roll, and your arms should circle upward and then down fully extended on each side of your legs, with your head and chest also down and as close to your legs as possible.

Turn to Front Support and into Forward Roll Walkout

From a sitting position, place your left hand next to your hip and extend your left arm as you lift your hips from the mat and turn your

Forward Roll Walkout

body so that you are in a push-up position. Next, slide your feet forward and push off both feet into a forward roll keeping one leg extended and the other tucked so that you end in a standing stride position.

Walkout into Two Cartwheels

When you complete your walkout forward roll, go immediately into your cartwheels. If your right foot is forward, place your right hand on the mat about a foot or so in front of your right foot. Keeping your head up, push off your left foot and then off your right foot, all the while keeping your right arm as well as your left arm fully extended to support your weight. Your second cartwheel will be done just as the first, with the exception that you will be standing sideways.

Round-Off into a Front Lunge

From a sideways standing position, turn your body forward so that you are facing the center of the free exercise area. Take a few quick steps and move into a low hurdle movement with your left foot raised slightly. Lean forward and bend at your waist so you move toward the mat. Both of your hands approach the mat, with your left hand making contact first and your right hand following. The fingers of your right hand point toward your left hand, both arms are fully extended as you are momentarily in a sideways handstand position. As your legs pass the vertical, you make a quarter turn so that you are looking at the spot where you began the round-off. To conclude your routine, extend one

GYMNASTICS AND TUMBLING

Forward Roll Walkout (cont.)

leg back so that it is fully extended. Bring your arms forward so that they point upward, forming a "V" pattern with your shoulders.

PARALLEL BARS

The parallel bars require a certain amount of upper body strength, but one does not have to be exceptionally powerful to enjoy working on the bars. Most skills do require some form of balance, timing, and coordination. In competitive work, the gymnast's exercise usually consists of both above- and under-the-bar skills, combined with swinging and twisting maneuvers and at least one strength stunt, such as a press handstand. During competition the bars must be between 16½ inches and almost 19 inches and between 63 inches and 67 inches from the floor.

Jump Half Turn Mount

Facing the ends of both bars and with the bars less than 5 feet high, place your right hand on the end of the bar which is directly in front of your left shoulder. Make a vertical jump and as you reach the peak of your jump twist your body so that your back turns to the bars. As you are making your half turn, lean to your right. Your right arm should be perfectly straight when you reach the peak of your jump and your left hand should grasp the end of the other bar.

Scissor Turn to Cross-Riding Seat

Scissor Turn to Cross-Riding Seat

To make your scissor turn, get your body into motion with special emphasis on obtaining a high back swing. Your arms should remain straight, and your swing should be from the shoulders. As your legs rise above the bars on the back swing, your legs scissor so that your right leg goes over to the bar which is being held by your left hand and your left leg goes over to the bar which is held by your right hand. When you have assumed a cross-ride seat position, bring your hands from the end of the bars to a position in front of your knees. Throughout this maneuver your arms and legs should remain straight and your toes should be pointed.

GYMNASTICS AND TUMBLING 181

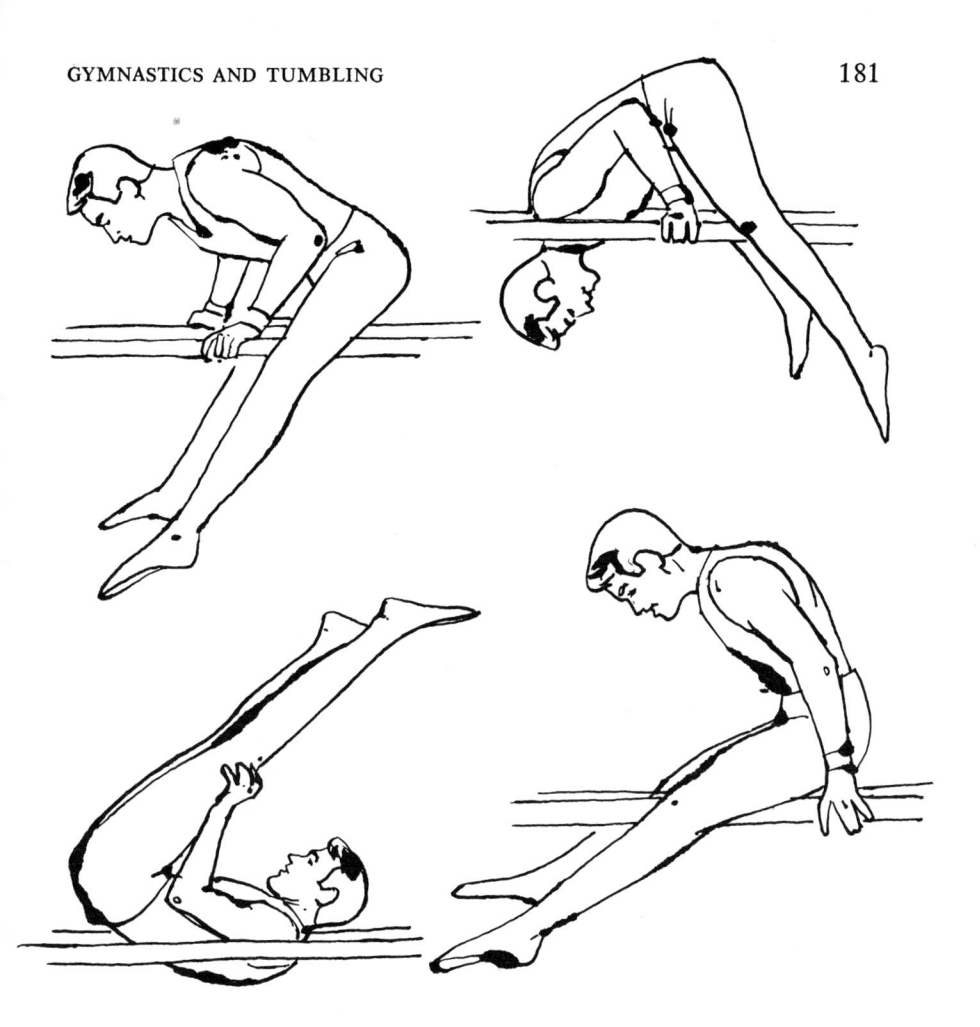

Straddle Forward Roll

Straddle Forward Roll

After completing your scissor turn, you are ready to begin your straddle forward roll. To perform this stunt well, you should keep your body in a piked straddle position, with your legs straight and toes pointed. You begin the roll by moving your head toward your chest and lifting your hip upward. Your elbows should be kept well away from your body so that the shoulder area of the arm makes contact with the bars. If this is not done, you will have difficulty with your shoulder balance and possibly may fall through the bars. A knowledgeable spotter should assist you as you practice this skill.

Straddle Press into a Shoulder Balance

Straddle Press into a Shoulder Balance

    Your head should be pushed back; that is, the chin should not be brought close to the chest as it was in the shoulder roll. Your hips should be elevated slowly and with control. As in the shoulder roll, your elbows must be kept well away from your body. When you complete the shoulder balance, your legs should be together and as straight as possible, with your toes pointed. To demonstrate that you are in full control of the balance, you should hold it for 2 or 3 seconds.

Back Uprise

    To go into a back uprise from a shoulder balance, you should begin by going into a forward roll with your legs together. As your legs come down, release your hands and quickly regrasp the bars in front of you. You are now temporarily in a bent-upper-arm support position, with your legs still in motion. As your legs pass the vertical position, you should drive your legs backward. The backward drive of your legs should allow you to press downward on your hands so that your arms can extend into a straight-arm support position. You will more than likely need to practice your back uprise as a single skill before you can go into it from a shoulder balance.

Cross-Riding Seat Travel to End of Bars

From your straight-arm support position, swing your legs forward. As they rise above the bars on the front swing, move them into a straddle so that you assume a cross-riding seat position. Next move your hands in front of your knees and at the same time push your legs up and back so that they come together on the back swing. As they rise above the bars on the forward swing, move them into a cross-riding seat position.

Straddle Dismount

To perform this dismount from a cross-riding seat, you must have your hands in front of your knees and about an inch or less from the end of the bars. Begin the dismount by swinging your legs backward vigorously so that they rise at least 3 feet above the bars. As your legs swing backwards, your arms should be fully extended, your shoulders should be forward of your hands, and your hips should move upward. When you reach the peak of your backswing, your legs go into a straddle position, your hands push your body up and away from the bars, your arms are brought up and away from your body, and your eyes focus straight ahead in anticipation of your landing. Upon landing, your legs should flex to cushion your fall, and you should then go into a position of attention to demonstrate full control of the dismount.

SIDE HORSE SUPPORT EXERCISES

Side horse support exercises are performed only by men in gymnastic competition. A regulation size horse is a leather-covered cylinder approximately 5 feet in length, 14 inches in diameter, and 4 feet in height. The height is measured from the mat to the top of the handle-like supports, which are called pommels.

Holding one pommel in each hand with your feet off the mat is the recommended beginner support position. From this position you should

Straddle Dismount

GYMNASTICS AND TUMBLING

begin to get a feel of how your body is to move in performing support exercises. A skilled performer's exercise should consist of a continuous series of swinging movements. His routine should carry him from one end of the horse to the other end, and in the process he should perform such skills as single and double leg circles, regular and reverse scissors, tromlets, moores, and some type of a loop dismount.

Suggestions for Improving Your Side Horse Performance

1. Your arms should be fully extended (straight) while performing.
2. Think of controlling your body from your shoulders down.
3. For the most part, your hips will stay between your arms. If this is not done, you will more than likely fall from the horse.
4. Your toes should be pointed and your legs straight when performing.
5. Most beginning movements are pendulum-like. This means the cutting and noncutting leg should swing together even though they are on different sides of the horse.
6. Practice your skills and with perseverance you will overcome most of your difficulties.

Half Leg Circle Mount

Stand facing the side horse with your body between one pommel and the end of the horse. Place your left hand on the pommel and your right hand on the end of the horse. Jump vertically off both feet and at the same time lean your shoulders laterally to the left while your legs move to the right. Go into a stride position so that your right leg goes over to the front side of the horse. Your right hand should be thrown off the end to allow your right leg to come over and then should return to its original position, with your fingers pointing toward the end of the horse.

Half Leg Travel

From your stride position on the end of the horse, move directly into half leg travel. To do this, shift your weight to your right arm and swing your left leg over the far pommel so that momentarily you are in a position in which both legs are straddling the right pommel. The shift of weight from your right arm and then over to right pommel is made with haste as your right leg comes over the top of the horse. Once you have both hands on the right pommel, swing your left leg back and at the same time move your left hand to the left pommel. This will bring you

Right Single Leg Circle

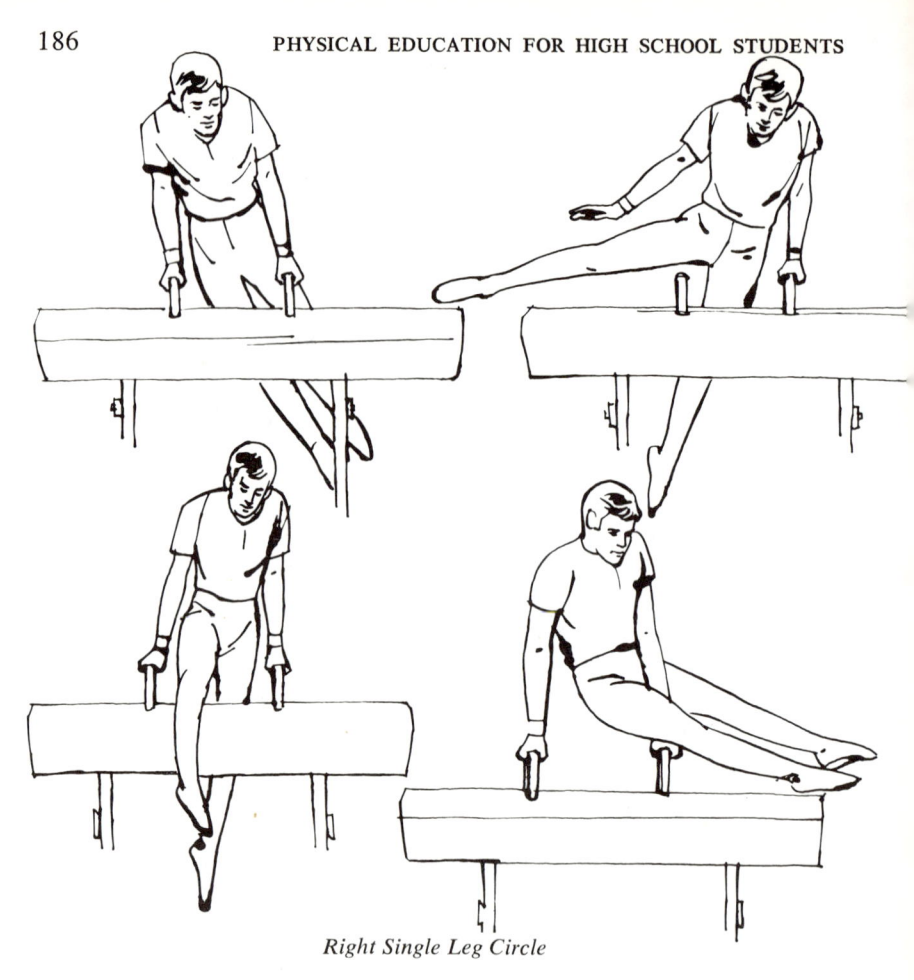

into a front support position with one hand on each pommel and both legs together.

Right Single Leg Circle

From your front support position, swing both legs to the right but concentrate on the right leg parting from the left and going over to the other side as you reach the peak of your swing. As you make your cut with your right hand, your shoulders lean toward the left pommel. Once the right leg is over the horse, regrasp the right pommel and shift your shoulders to your right so that your right leg will be able to cut back, bringing both legs and hands into the original front support position. It is important to remember that as your right leg is traveling on one side of the horse your left is also traveling on the other side.

Right Half Leg Circle

This skill is simply a repeat of the first half of the right single leg circle. The only exception is that the right leg does not cut over the left pommel.

Left Half Leg Circle

With both legs between the pommels but on different sides of the horse, shift your shoulders to your right side and swing both legs to the left. Remove your left hand so that your left leg can come over to meet your right leg. You are now in a rear support position.

Right Half Leg Circle Backwards

Swing both legs to the right, shifting your shoulders to the left, and swing your right leg back over the horse. As you do this, thrust your right hand off the pommel, with your right hip rotating backwards to allow your right leg to go over the horse with ease.

Left Half Leg Circle Backwards

As your legs swing to the left after your right leg has come over the other side and your right hand has regrasped the right pommel, your legs should continue moving to the left and you should shift your shoulders to the right. Your left leg should swing over to meet your right leg. You should end in a front support position.

Left Half Leg Circle into Single Rear Dismount

From your front support position, move into a left half leg circle forward. Your right leg should be at a right angle with your left leg as you begin your single rear dismount. Your weight should be over the right pommel and you should then push vigorously with your left hand which, along with a vigorous swing with your right leg, will enable you to make your half turn over the outside end of the side horse. As you perform this skill, your left hand should push vigorously off the left pommel, then move to the end of the horse and push your body upwards as your legs pass over the end. Your left hand will then come back onto the horse as you make your landing.

STILL RINGS

Skills performed on the still rings require more upper body strength than does any other piece of gymnastic equipment. You will find the

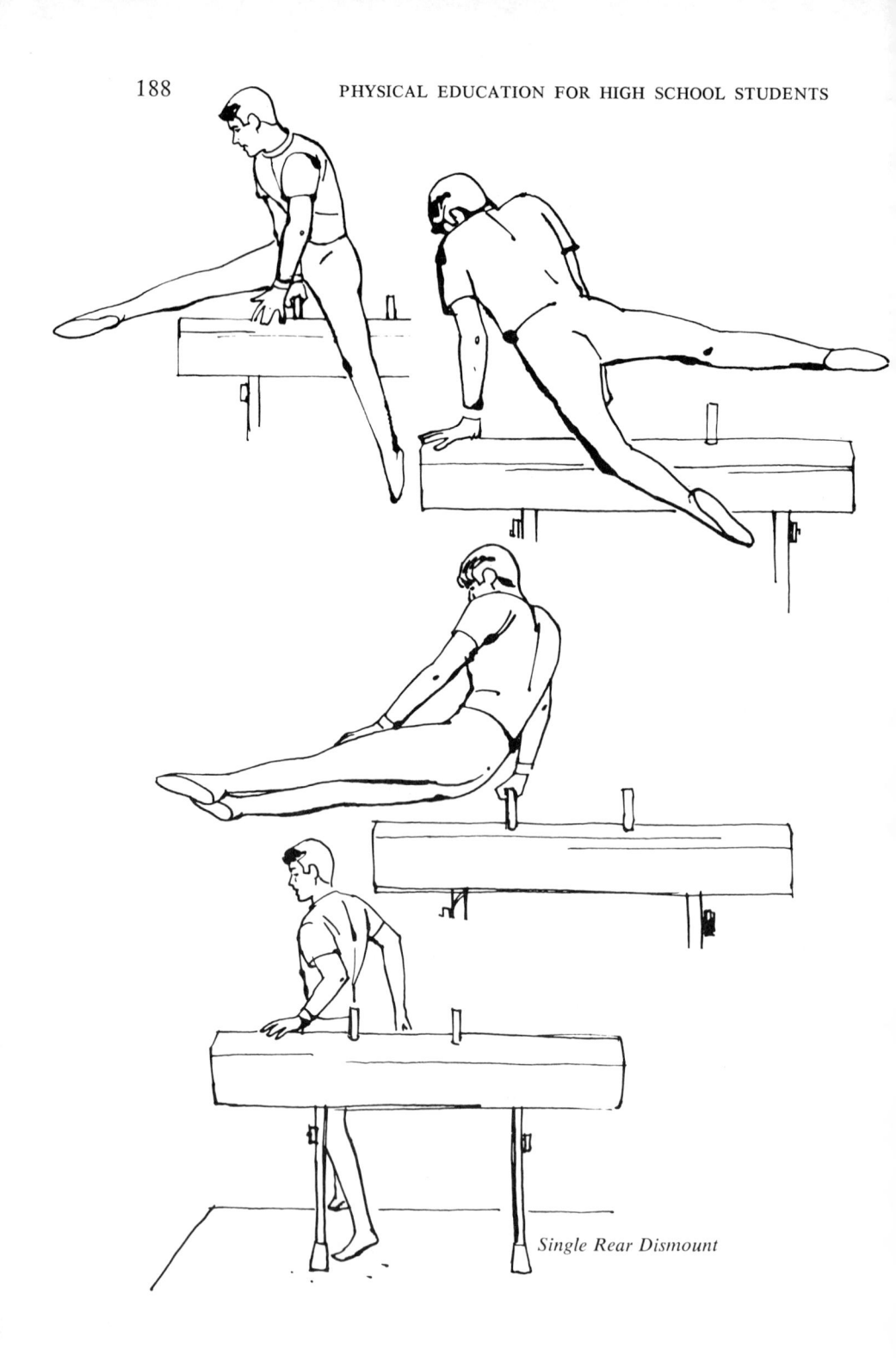

188   PHYSICAL EDUCATION FOR HIGH SCHOOL STUDENTS

Single Rear Dismount

GYMNASTICS AND TUMBLING   189

rings very challenging, and if you have a fairly strong upper body, you will find the following stunts well within your ability. In competitive gymnastics the rings are between 7 feet 10 inches and 8 feet 2½ inches from the floor and are between 19 inches and 20 inches apart. The ring itself is made of laminated wood and for best results is held by wire cables attached to ball bearing swivels, which, in turn, are attached to a ceiling beam. A competitive routine consists of stunts done below and above the rings—stunts such as swinging movements into balances or levers. Working both above and below the rings a skilled performer should demonstrate an ability to combine swinging combinations with balances and strength maneuvers in the development of his exercise. When performing on the rings there should be no movement except that of the gymnast.

Pull-Over (Skin the Cat)

This stunt is easily done if you keep your body in a tuck position throughout the pull-over and return. Once you have developed sufficient strength, you can do a pull-over in a pike position. From a still hand on the rings, bring your knees up to your chest and at the same time chin yourself. As your legs come up in between your arms which are bent, force your head back and allow your feet to pass between the rings and on down until your feet are pointed toward the mat. To return to your starting position, pull your body upward with your arms and lead with your hips while still maintaining your tuck position. Try to move slowly with control. You should have a spotter on either side of you.

Straight Body Inverted Hang

From a front hang position on the rings, move into the inverted hang in the same manner as you began the pull-over. Draw your legs up to your chest; pull up with your arms; and as your legs come between the rings extend both your arms and your legs so that you are in a straight inverted position. Your hands should be on the outside of your upper legs, head away from your chest, legs fully extended with your toes pointed. When you can do this with ease, try going into an inverted hang in a pike position. For an even greater challenge, try to do this stunt in a straight body position with no leg or hip flexion.

Pike Inverted Hang—Single Leg Cuts (Two)

From a straight body inverted hang, flex your body at your hips so that your legs are brought down and your head is brought toward your chest. You should be looking at your legs, and your back should be to the mat. Two spotters should be on each side of the mat close enough to you to catch you if the need arises. To make your first cut and catch, swing your legs forward in a straddle position. Swing your right leg, the cutting leg, toward your right forearm. As your leg hits your arm, release the ring and then quickly regrasp it as your right leg swings down to meet your left leg. Your arms should be flexed as you make your cut so that your chest will have added height. As you go into your single leg cut, your chin should come toward your chest, your arms should be flexed, and your eyes should be focused on the ring which is to be released and then regrasped. When you have completed your cut and catch, repeat the same maneuver with your left leg and hand.

Nest Hang—Bird's Nest

After completing your second single leg cut and catch, bring your legs up into a point between the rings. With your legs bent at the knees, place your left foot in the left ring and your right foot in the right ring. Your feet should enter the rings just behind your head, and the rings should cut across your insteps. Once you are in this position, bring your head away from your chest, push your legs to the rear, and arch your body so that your chest is facing the mat and you are looking straight ahead.

One Arm—One Leg Nest—Half Turn

From your bird's nest position, release your right foot and your left hand. Maintain your grip with your right hand and left foot. Hold this position for a second or so. Next, exert pressure on the ring with your left foot and turn your body so that your left hand swings around and regrasps the left ring. As you regrasp the ring, take your left foot out of the ring.

Backward Straddle Dismount

From a front hanging position, swing your legs upward. Keep them well apart, straddling the outside of your forearms. The upward swing should be vigorous so that when your legs make contact with your arms and you release the rings, your body will continue around. You should land on your feet, with legs flexed and arms outstretched for added balance and control. Spotters are essential in learning this maneuver.

HORIZONTAL BAR

For competitive purposes, a horizontal bar should be approximately 8 feet long, just over 8 feet above the mat, and should be made of 1⅛ inch diameter spring steel. A competitive routine should consist entirely of swinging skills, with possibly one vault included; there should be no stops in the exercise.

Performing on the horizontal bar can be very demanding on your hands. To protect yourself against blisters and palm tears, it is suggested that you chalk your hands well, keep the bar clean, and work for only short periods of time. It is recommended that the bar be lowered when learning new skills.

Mixed Grip Half Turn

Jump vertically, grasping the bar with the palm of one hand facing you and the back of the other hand facing you (regular grip). To make your half turn, release the hand whose back faces you. Swing the released hand and make a half turn so that the backs of both hands face you. Practice this from a still hanging position, using first one mixed grip and then reverse the hand positions.

Pull-Over

With both hands assuming a regular grip on the bar (backs of hands facing you), chin yourself and at the same time flex your body at the hips so that your legs move upwards toward the bar. Your chin should be well away from your chest as your legs begin to move up and over the bar. As your thighs make contact with the bar, lift your head up and move your body into a front support position above the bar.

Single Leg Cut into a Forward Single Knee Circle

Swing one leg up and over the bar, making a leg cut so that your leg rests on the bar between your hands. As you make your leg cut, lean slightly to the side opposite your cutting leg. Change your grip with both hands so that your thumbs are on top (reverse grip). To execute the forward knee circle, push your body upward off the bar, raise your hips and let the bar hook your leg behind your bent knee. Keep your arms straight and your head stretched forward. As you come up, your arms should flex a little and your extended leg should be driving you up into a position above the bar.

Backward Single Knee Circle

As you come into a controlled position above the bar, change your hands back into a regular grip and immediately go into your backward knee circle. Begin by allowing your body to fall backwards with your head and shoulders leading and at the same time swinging your fully extended leg vigorously forward. Your arms should be kept fairly straight as you make your backward single-knee circle. When you come into a controlled position above the bar you are ready for the next skill.

Single Leg Cut into a Backward Hip Circle

From a position of control above the bar, swing your hooked leg out from between your arms. As the leg cut is made, push your body up and away from the bar. Your body should travel less than a foot away from the bar and, then, as you come back into the bar, pike at the waist, keep the bar in close to your body, and have your legs circle the bar with your head and shoulders thrown backward to assist you in your backward movement.

Cast Back to Long Underswing

From your front support position above the bar, push your body up and away from the bar. As you are moving backward away from the bar, extend your arms so that your body is completely stretched out. Be sure not to push out and away too vigorously because this will provide you with too much forward momentum and present a possibility of your not being able to maintain your grip on the bar.

Pike Half Turn Dismount

On your second forward underswing, pike your body as you go under the bar itself. When you are out beyond the bar, release your hand grip and turn your body in toward the bar. You should land with both feet together facing the bar. A spotter should be at your side as you practice this skill.

ROPES

Rope climbing is a strenuous activity and is a very good way to develop upper body strength. You will find it helpful if you use chalk before climbing. Come down slowly to prevent hand burns. All gymnasts should climb the ropes several times daily for conditioning purposes.

GYMNASTICS AND TUMBLING 193

Climbing Rope with Legs

Climb Rope with Legs

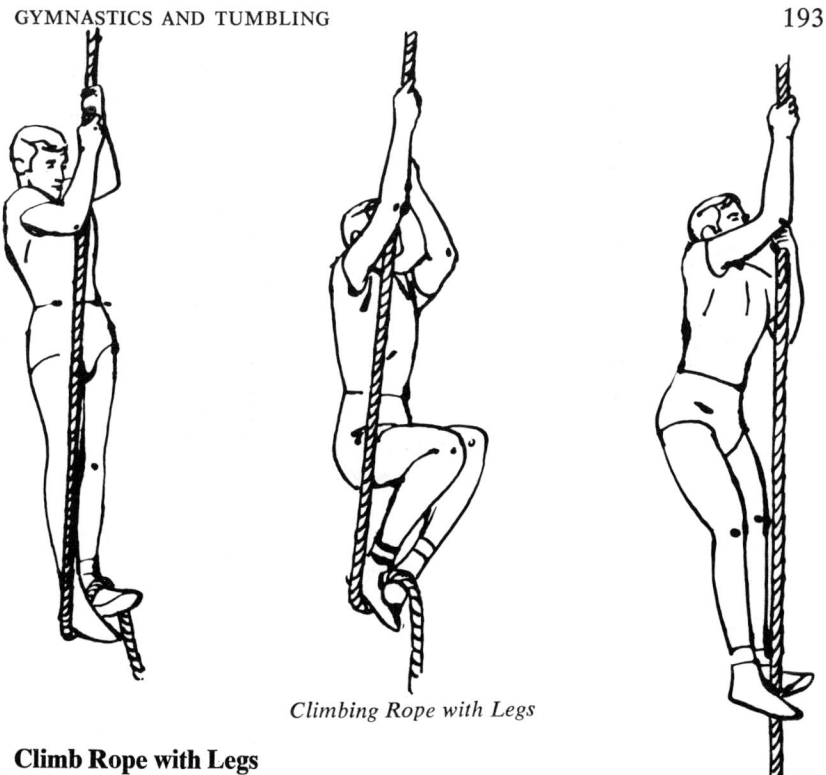

The rope passes down the side of your body under your right foot and over your left foot while your hands grasp the rope tightly. Flex your knees but keep the rope in the same relative position. Squeeze the rope tightly with your feet; straighten your legs; and reach higher with your hands. Continue up the rope.

Climb Rope Without Use of Legs

This should be attempted only after you have acquired sufficient strength and technique of climbing the rope with both hands and feet. Grasp the rope high above your head; pull up with your arms while keeping your legs in an "L" position with the rope between your legs. Increase the length of your reach as you progress.

Make Fast and Rest

Climb the rope at least 10 feet and allow it to pass between your legs and around the outside of your right leg and over the instep. Press the rope tightly against your right instep with the sole of your left foot. Squeeze the rope in your right armpit.

Climbing Without Use of Legs

Up Down—Up Down

Climb the rope either with or without using your legs. Return to within 12 inches of the floor and repeat.

VAULTING

Vaulting is one of the most interesting and exciting of all gymnastic activities. It includes running and diving as well as vaulting. Learn to approach the reuther board springboard or mini tramp with a few running steps and hit the center of the board or mini tramp with both feet. Practice this by springing up and forward onto a landing mat before attempting to vault. A reuther board should not be hit on the very end, but rather in the soft center where the board starts upward toward the curve.

More advanced technique for side horse vaulting may be accomplished by removing the pommels from the horse and covering the hole with tape. A better take-off from the board and push-off from the horse are then required.

Touch Toes

Spring in the air bringing your feet up with your legs apart. Touch your toes quickly and land on your feet.

Half Twist

Spring in the air and, when nearing maximum height, turn your head to the right. Bring your left hand upward and across your chest to give impetus to the turn. Complete the twist by facing in the direction of the springboard and land on both feet.

Straddle Over Human—Squat Position

A person stands erect, then places his hands firmly on his knees, with his back bent 45 degrees and one foot slightly in advance of the other. The performer springs, places his hand on the upper back of the other, and straddles over him.

Straddle Over Human—Standing Position

This should be practiced only after the straddle over squatting position has been mastered. A person stands erect, hands at sides, and with one foot in advance of the other. The performer springs, places his hands on the person's head, and straddles over him. When done correctly very little weight is placed on the person's head. When this stunt has been perfected, add more people for the performer to spring over. The performer always tries to place his hands on the head of the one farthest from the board. Although both boys and girls may vault, it is better to use only boys as the objects over whom others vault.

Squat Vault—Side Horse

Spring from the board as you grasp both pommels. Lift your knees high, keep them together, vault over the horse, and land on your feet on the other side. Without pommels, your hands should be placed flat on top of the horse after springing from the board. A quick push off the horse along with a lift of your head and shoulders will emphasize flight over the horse. (Have a contest to see who can come off the horse with the greatest height and furthest distance.)

Flank Vault—Side Horse

Spring from the board as you grasp both pommels. Bring both legs over the croup (right side) of horse. Legs should be straight and raised high. Keep weight supported on straight left arm.

Wolf Vault—Side Horse

This is a combination of squat and straddle vaults. Grasp both pommels as you spring from the board. Bring your left knee high between the pommels while your right leg is straight and to the outside.

Handspring—Side Horse

Grasp both pommels as you spring from the board. Lean forward slightly as you throw your legs high in the air. Arch your back and release your grasp on the pommels only after your feet are several feet past the horse.

Straddle—Side Horse

Grasp the pommels as you spring from the board. Place your legs wide apart. At your highest point, release your grasp and straighten up as you go over the horse. Land on your feet on the mat.

Straddle—Long Horse (Boys Only)

Detach the pommels and position the horse in such a way to allow you to work the long axis. You now have a long horse. You should not consider working this way until you have acquired a reasonable proficiency with the previously mentioned stunts. Run and spring from the board; then reach with both hands for the far end (neck). Push off hard with your hands; keep your legs spread; and land on the mat. At first, land lightly on the horse in the saddle; then increase your distance a few inches each time until you can clear the horse. As you progress, elevate the horse.

TUMBLING

Tumbling is probably one of the best all-around activities for physical development, and it is usually included as a part of gymnastics. Actually, tumbling is a form of gymnastics without the use of apparatus.

Forward Roll

From a squat, reach out and lean forward. Keep your weight on your arms. Tuck your head, placing the back of your head on the mat. Keep your legs close to the floor and straighten them to roll gently over the neck and shoulders. Tuck your legs rapidly and reach forward to come up on your feet.

Dive

Once you have mastered the forward roll, you can think about diving for distance and over classmates. Take off from both feet with a slight forward lean. When in mid-air, keep your eyes open and reach for the mat. Take the weight on your hands; tuck your head; land on the back of your neck. Stay tucked and continue rolling until you reach a standing position. As you progress, add more people to dive over.

Dive Between Legs

This stunt is performed by diving through the legs of another student doing a head balance with his feet spread wide apart.

Backward Roll

Stand with hands at sides. Squat and sit backwards with your head tucked to your chest and with your back rounded. Bring your hands next to your ears and your elbows near your sides as you push upwards over your shoulders. Stay in tuck position as your hips roll upward over your shoulders. As your legs reach over, push off the mat with your hands and head to bring your feet to the mat.

Backward Extension Roll

Follow the instructions for a forward roll. When your hips roll upwards over your shoulders, extend your legs over your head as you push off the mat. When your feet come to the mat, you will be standing in an upright rather than a tucked position.

Squat Balance

Squat with your knees resting on the outside of your elbows. Lean forward until your balance is held with hands and toes. Bend your arms slightly; keep your head up; and bring your toes off the mat. Keep your weight forward on your fingers.

Head Balance

From a squat balance lean forward gently until your head touches the mat. Make a triangle of your hands and head. Keep your hips high and arch your back as you extend your legs upwards.

Cartwheel

A cartwheel may be performed from a standing position by swinging your leading leg upwards and forcefully extending your other leg.

Your hands and feet should be in a straight line. To perform a running cartwheel, take a short run sideways. Place your left hand on the mat close to your left foot. Place your right hand on the mat a shoulder-width apart from your left hand to assist you into the inverted position. Bring your right leg down. Your left leg will follow, bringing you to a standing position facing in the direction from which you started.

Handspring

Take a short run forward. Hop on one foot to step forward with the other and place your hands with arms outstretched on the mat. Swing your free leg vigorously up toward the ceiling, push upwards with your supporting leg, and give a strong push with your hands. Keep your hips and back arched, head back, landing on either one or both feet.

Hand Balance

Place your hands a shoulder-width apart on the mat. Kick off with one foot, keeping your head up. In the final position your head should be up, your arms straight, your back arched enough to allow your feet to be directly over your head. Finger pressure must be constantly applied to maintain the balance. In learning this stunt use a wall to support your feet.

PYRAMIDS

The building of human pyramids is merely the art of having a group of people work as a unit with or without equipment to form artistic figures. This activity may be compared with a marching drill team. Each movement isolated by itself and done individually is unspectacular. However, when several of the movements are coordinated and done by several persons, it is most effective.

Good pyramid building requires attention to a number of factors, among which are the following:

1. It should not be attempted until you and your teammates have mastered the stunts covered in the balancing section of this chapter. Unless a number of these stunts can be done with ease, it is difficult to make pyramids. Afterwards, these stunts can be used as a basis upon which to design your own pyramids.

2. It is important to have the same groups work as units whenever possible. When a person is absent, or when one is asked to substitute for another position, the quality of the performance suffers. When you are

GYMNASTICS AND TUMBLING 199

nearing the date for a demonstration, each person should be assigned a specific position in the pyramid, and he should work on perfecting his role. There is as much team work in this activity as in many team sports.

3. The shape of the pyramid is usually concave or convex. This means that end and middle units are necessary, their height depending upon which type is desired. Time should be spent learning formations for one, two, three, and four people; and the way in which these, or their variations, will eventually be used will depend upon the symmetry finally decided upon by the leaders and the instructor. The following are examples of how single individuals may be used to give balance to the ends:

Examples of the use of two and three members appear on the following page. Examples of the use of four or more members may be found in the books listed at the end of the chapter.

When making large pyramids, either the instructor or middle member of the pyramid should give certain signals, such as "1, 2, 3, hold, down." There should be a maximum of four commands, with each command signifying that every member move into a specific position. When "hold" is given, the final posed position is reached simultaneously by all members to give the best effect. The position is held about five seconds, and on the command "down," each person returns to the attention position, preparatory to building the succeeding pyramid.

200 PHYSICAL EDUCATION FOR HIGH SCHOOL STUDENTS

Two Members

Three Members

GYMNASTICS AND TUMBLING

TRAMPOLINE

The first known trampoline was devised by a French acrobat named Du Trampoline in the Middle Ages. This fascinating piece of apparatus is probably one of the most popular in the schools of America today. It is a valuable piece of equipment in the development of poise, agility, and coordination.

Extreme attention must be paid to safety rules in connection with the trampoline. Have spotters on all sides of the trampoline when you work. Grasp the frame before dismounting; do not jump off. Seek optimum control of yourself before concentrating on height. Take frequent short turns rather than long ones. Do not work out alone.

Seat Drop

Sit on the trampoline bed, with your trunk erect, legs together, toes pointed, and hands next to your hips on the bed. Take low bounces landing in that position and returning to your feet.

Hands and Knee Drop

From a standing position jump into a table position in the air. Your hips should raise up in back and your hands should reach toward the mat. Land on your hands and knees simultaneously and push against the web bed to bounce back to your feet. Once you have learned to hit the bed evenly, perform this stunt from higher bounces.

Knee Drop

Kneel on the trampoline bed. With your toes pointed, body erect, and knees a comfortable distance apart, take low bounces landing in that position and then returning to your feet. Keep your hips and knees stiff when landing.

Back Drop

Lie on the trampoline bed with your feet at a 60-degree angle from the bed. Take low bounces and land in that position. As the springs thrust you upwards, quickly extend your legs and arch your back to reach a standing position.

Front Drop

Lie face downward on the bed with your arms bent so that your hands rest on the bed on each side of your chest, as if ready to commence push-ups. Take low bounces. Hold a semi-tucked position in mid-air, open up slowly, and land flat on the bed so that your toes, knees, and chest land simultaneously. Push up vigorously and reach a standing position.

Half Turntable

Land in a front drop, and while pushing off from the bed grasp a tuck and turn your head and shoulders. After having completed the turn, open up and land in a front drop position again. Push off with your hands and return to your feet.

Back Pull-Over

Land in a semi-tucked position on your back, a few inches below the belt (a position midway between a back drop and a seat drop). Hold a tuck with your hands, throw your head back, and bring your knees up to put you into a somersault. Land on your feet.

Swivel Hips

Land in a seat drop. As you near a standing position, quickly turn your head and hips. Thrust your feet out in front again, and land in a seat drop. Return to a standing position.

GYMNASTICS TERMS

Kip. A forward movement from the hips that throws the body from a hanging position to a support.
Pike. A position with the legs straight and the hips flexed.
Spotting. The art of guarding a performer, especially while a new stunt is being learned.
Tuck. Pulling the knees close to the chest. Also the act itself.

FOR MORE INFORMATION

American Association for Health, Physical Education, and Recreation, Division for Girls and Women's Sports. *Gymnastics Guide.* Current edition. Washington, D.C.: the Association.

Cooper, Phyllis. *Feminine Gymnastics.* Minneapolis, Minn.: Burgess Publishing Co., 1968.

Drury, Blanche, and Schmid, Andrea. *Gymnastics for Women.* Revised edition. Palo Alto, Calif.: National Press, 1965.

Morison, Ruth. *Educational Gymnastics for Secondary Schools.* London: Ling Bookshop (10 Bottingham Place), 1966.

Norman, Randi. *Gymnastics for Girls and Women.* Dubuque, Iowa: Wm. C. Brown Co., 1965.

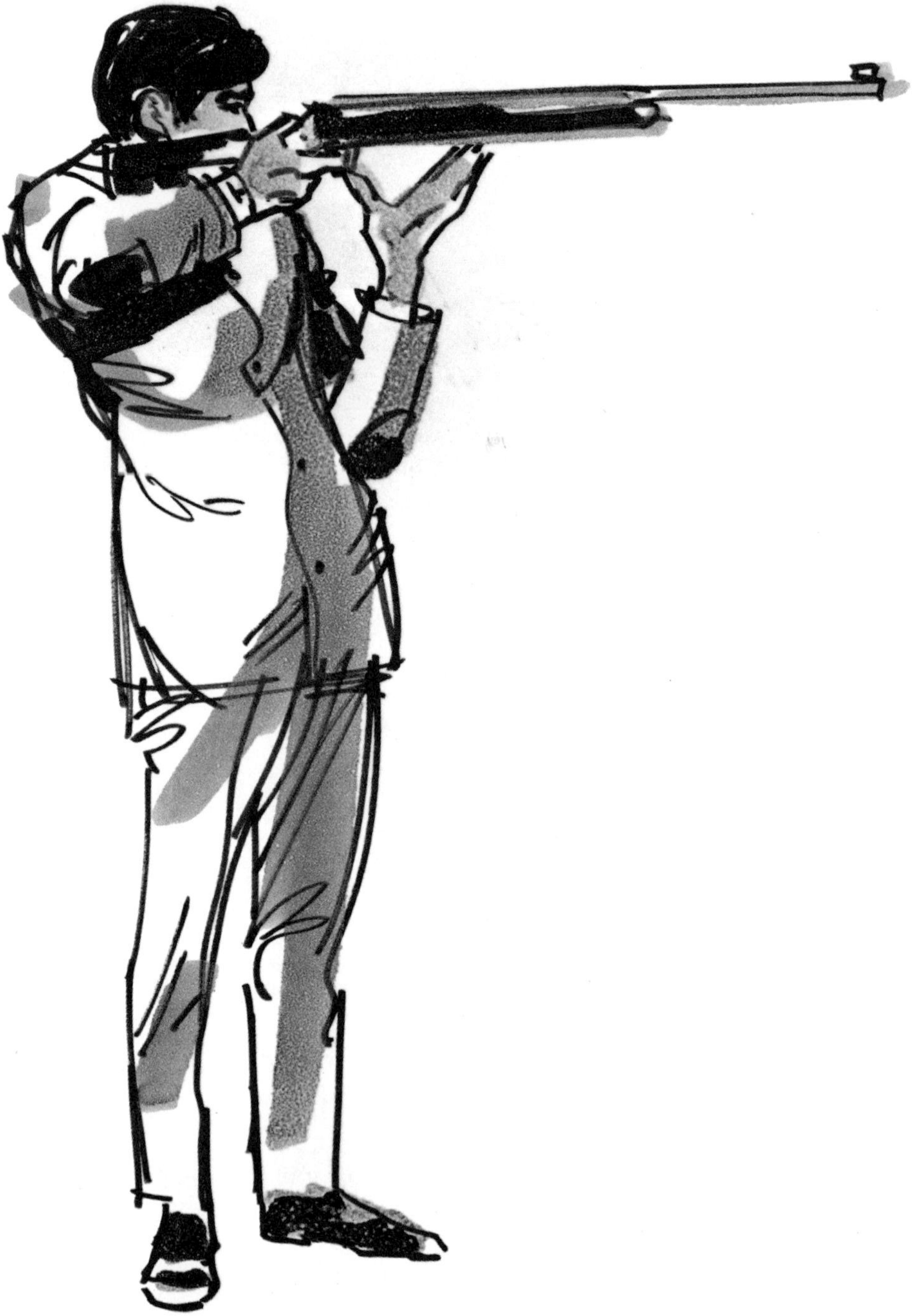

Riflery

The United States of America was built, it is said, with three implements: the axe, the plow, and the rifle. The axe, in the hands of the stalwart pioneer, felled trees to clear the way for fields of grain. It also provided timber to build the houses, barns, and fences of our farms. The plow cut into the virgin soil of our foothills, plains, and prairies to grow the food for a young and hungry country. The rifle brought down the deer, bear, and other game to give the hardy frontiersman and his family food and clothing. It also stood as the only means of defense against his enemies, both savage and civilized.

THE PIONEER AND HIS RIFLE

As towns sprang from the ground and our civilization moved westward, the rifle became even more important. The picturesque Indian scouts, like Kit Carson; the great fighters, like General George Custer; the speeding pony express rider; the prospector wandering in the desert lands—all had two traits in common: their desire to make America great and their marksmanship ability with a rifle. The American rifleman carved a place for himself in the history of America. His prowess and skill became known around the world.

A REWARDING PASTIME

The young American took the rifle hanging over his fireplace as a familiar and necessary item. Learning to use it well was part of his early training. Today, with our frontiers withered and our virgin forest shrunk, the rifle is no longer looked upon as an essential tool to provide food and clothing. Today it does provide Americans, young and old, boy or girl, man or woman, with one of the most satisfying and rewarding sports known. Rifle shooting, whether at a target or a game animal, is practiced by millions throughout the country today. It is a typical American sport. And it is the backbone of America's national defense.

Rifle shooting does not require special teams or groups. One person or a hundred, depending upon the facilities, can enjoy this fascinating sport. You need no particular uniforms or special equipment as in many sports, because rifle shooting can be practiced indoors as well as out.

The Range

The place where you shoot is called a range. The line from which you shoot is called the firing point, and the line on which your target is located is called the target butts. The distance between the shooter and the target varies. In the case of the .22 caliber rifle range, it will be 50 feet indoors and 50 feet, 50 or 100 yards outdoors. Most outdoor shooting is done at the latter distances. Pneumatic-type air rifles are fired at a range of 25 feet. Spring-type air rifles (the familiar BB guns) call for firing at 15 feet. In order to figure out how much space you need to have a range, merely add about 10 feet to these distances to provide room for the shooter and for the backstop.

To shoot safely outdoors, find a hill that slopes 30 degrees or so. Clear it of brush and rock to offer good visibility and prevent ricochets. Build a simple wooden frame on which to place your target and set this frame a foot or two in front of your earth backstop. A word of caution: Do not fasten targets to growing trees. Bullets will bounce from them.

Indoor ranges can vary from fine, permanent range installations with steel plate backstops, target carriers on trolleys, and fluorescent lighting systems to simple backstops easily constructed from a large packing case. Several commercial firms sell portable backstops (bullet traps). There are special plans that make it possible to use rooms like gymnasiums, school cafeterias, and auditoriums as part-time ranges without interfering with the regular use of the room. Plans for elaborate indoor ranges, or for part-time ranges, may be obtained on request from the National Rifle Association, 1600 Rhode Island Avenue, N.W., Washington, D.C. 20036. Specify the type of gun you will be using (.22, pneumatic air rifle, or spring-type air rifle) and whether shooting will be indoors or outdoors.

The Rifle

The rifle itself is the most important piece of equipment. There is a large variety of .22 caliber rifles which are safe and accurate. The prices

Simple Backstop

vary from very little to as much as you care to pay. A bolt action rifle is recommended. If you have a repeating rifle, always fire it during target practice as a single shot. That is, load and fire only one round (bullet) at a time.

The size and weight of your rifle are important. Young boy and girl shooters of less than high school age generally prefer a rifle weighing 6½ to 7½ pounds. Boys and girls in high school can handle rifles in the 7½ to 9 pound class.

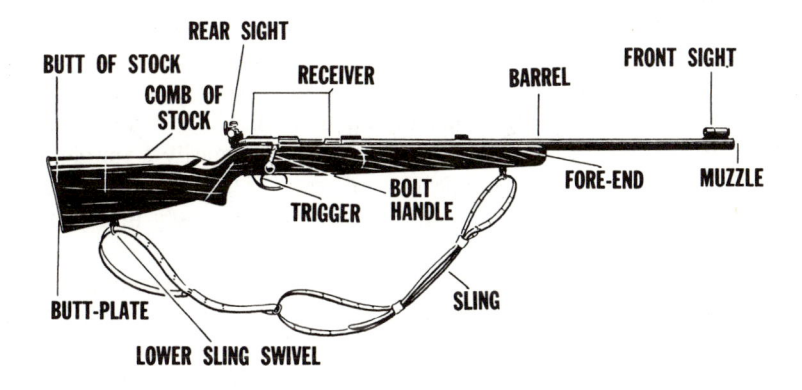

The Rifle

If your rifle does not have a sling, you can get one from your sporting goods store. If possible, get a rifle with a "peep" sight in the rear which can be adjusted up and down as well as from side to side. After you have become familiar with shooting, you will find these adjustments will mean greater accuracy.

For ammunition you can use any .22 caliber cartridge. Cartridges come in three sizes: shorts, longs, and long rifle. Target shooters find the long rifle the most accurate of the three.

There are several types of pneumatic air rifles. Some achieve the air pressure required by pumping devices; others use carbon dioxide gas to furnish the necessary propelling power. Most young shooters are quite familiar with the spring-type air rifle (the well-known BB gun).

Targets

It is best to use official NRA (National Rifle Association) targets, because as you progress in your ability you will probably want to shoot in competition from time to time. There are three types of targets for use at 50 feet. They differ mainly in the number of bullseyes on a single target card and are referred to as the "single bull," the "five bull," and the "eleven bull." The illustration shows the single bull and five bull 50-foot targets, the 25-foot pneumatic air rifle target, and the 15-foot target used for spring-type air rifle firing. Sporting goods stores generally handle these targets. If your dealer does not, he can get them for you.

Sighting and Aiming

Like other sports, rifle shooting has certain basic instructions for the new participant. The first lessons to be learned are those of sighting and aiming the rifle. There are generally two types of rear sights: the peep sight, which is actually a round hole in a piece of metal through which you look at the target, and the open sight, which is a square, V-shaped, or U-shaped notch. Front sights are customarily a simple post, a bead on top of a post, or an aperture or peep. If the front sight and the rear sight are properly aligned with the target, it is likely that you will score a bullseye.

The rear sight may be likened to a hole in a fence. The nearer your eye is to a knot hole the better you see what's on the other side of the fence. The same thing is true in aiming a rifle. You are not seriously concerned about the hole in the rear sight, once you find it, but in what is beyond, and you focus your eye on the front sight. When using the open sight, the top of the front sight should be held level with the top of

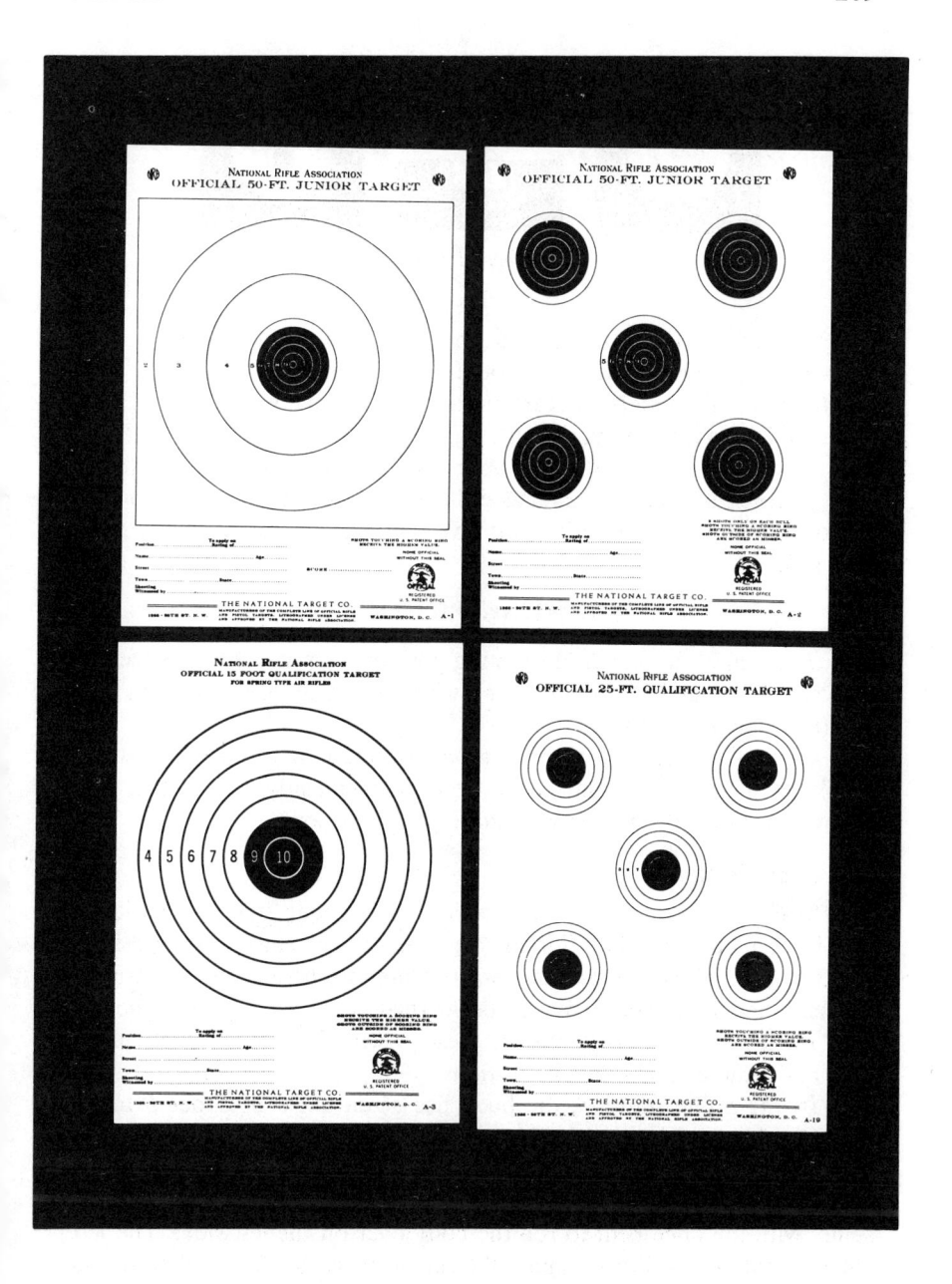

Bullseyes

Proper Sighting

the rear sight. Notice the dotted lines in the illustrated sights. They show exactly how the bullseye should be positioned with the three sight combinations shown: peep rear and aperture front, open rear and post front, and peep rear and post front.

Take care not to cant (tilt) your rifle to either side. Be sure to get your picture just as perfect and as uniform as possible each time you fire a shot. Great care in sighting will give you a good start on the way to high scores.

SHOOTING POSITIONS

There are four standard shooting positions: prone, sitting, kneeling, and standing—and several general variations that are described and illustrated on these pages.

Certain general rules apply to all of these positions. Study the following list carefully and check yourself frequently to see that you follow them every time you get into a firing position.

The Prone Position

The prone position is the steadiest of the four standard positions and is certainly the place for the new shooter to start. This position is easier to hold, so the fundamentals of aiming, breath control, trigger squeeze, and follow-through can be learned more readily. No shooter who makes errors consistently in these essentials should spend much time in the three more difficult positions.

In the prone position, the body lies at an angle of about 5 to 15 degrees with the line of aim. The spine is straight. The left leg is completely relaxed and is roughly parallel to the spine, toe pointed in. The left heel need not touch the ground. The right leg angles away from the spine, with the knee bent to roll the body over on the left side. The left elbow should be as directly under the rifle as possible. The weight of the upper body is supported by the triangles formed by the upper body and arms. The sling is adjusted tightly enough to give support and makes

RIFLERY

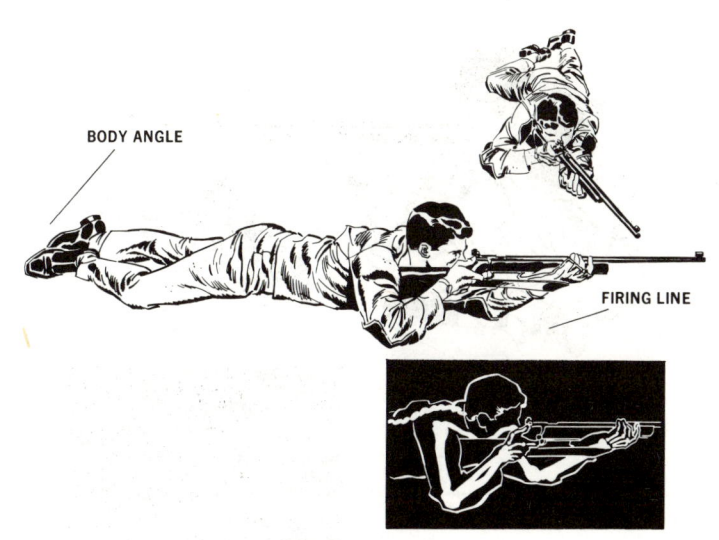

Prone Position

another triangle with the two parts of the left arm. The rifle is not actually gripped tightly in either hand. It should point naturally at the center of the target while the breath is being held. This position can be checked by closing both eyes and holding your breath. When the eyes are opened, if the rifle is pointing away from the center of the target, the body should be shifted, using the left elbow to pivot. Changes of position should not be made once firing has started.

Sitting Position

Next to the prone position, sitting is the steadiest of the shooting positions. The sling is used in about the same way as in the prone position except that some shooters shorten it slightly.

The sitting position is assumed by facing about 30 degrees right of the line of aim. The legs are crossed. The outside of each foot rests on the ground and supports the knees. The elbows are placed on or near the knees and form triangles to support the rifle. The left elbow is as directly under the rifle as possible. A variation not pictured is the high or open leg position. The feet are well spread, heels braced and the body leaned forward so the elbows may be braced over the knees.

In all positions the sighting eye should be close to the rear sight. The shooter should be relaxed and unhurried. The muscles should not be tensed with effort; rather, the long bones of the arms and legs—plus

Sitting Position

the sling—should support the rifle. The smooth easy rhythm of loading, breathing, sighting, squeezing the trigger, following through, and calling the shot should be practiced with every shot until they become habit. Better scores will be the result.

Kneeling Position

The kneeling position is more difficult from the standpoint of steadiness than either prone or sitting. However, the same basic principles of support are used. The sling is used as in sitting—slightly shortened in most cases—and the left arm is as directly under the rifle as possible. Relaxation is still important, although more difficult. There are two major variations in this position.

The kneeling position is reached by half facing to the right and dropping to the right knee. In the low position the left foot is extended as far forward as is comfortable, and the right leg is placed flat on the floor or ground with the foot flat also and rotated inward. The shooter sits on the side of his right foot. In the high position the shooter sits on the right heel.

In each case, the left knee supports the left arm two or three inches above the elbow. The right elbow is not supported and may be allowed to relax into the most comfortable position.

RIFLERY 213

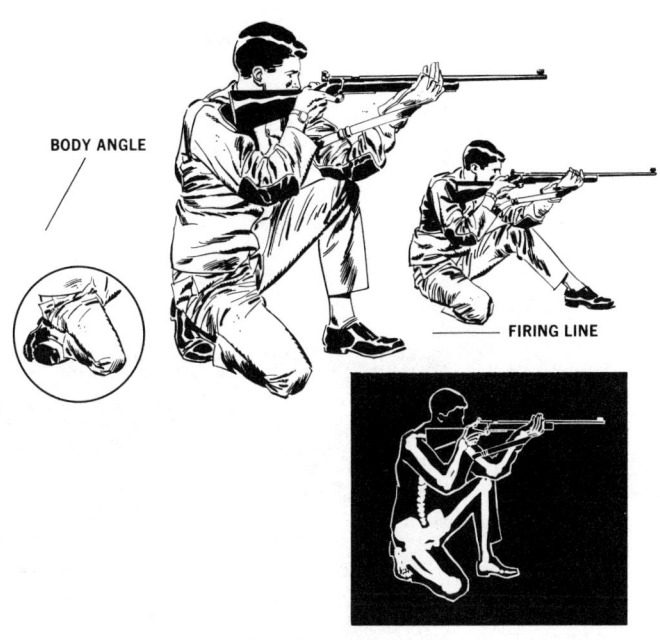

Kneeling Position

Standing Position

In the standing position, since support is at a minimum, the elements which contribute to good shooting are more important than ever. It is almost impossible to hold the rifle motionless. Rather than fight the movement, the shooter should devote his efforts to keeping the movement of the barrel to as small an area as possible. The movement should be natural and rhythmic, rather than forced or jerky.

The illustration shows a relatively high position. The weight is distributed evenly on both feet. The legs are straight, but the knees are not locked. The left elbow is directly below the rifle. The supporting hand is spread, with the thumb at the bottom of the trigger guard and the fingers extended along the fore-end. Some shooters prefer to double the hand into a fist and use it to support the rifle just ahead of the trigger guard.

Many shooters use a lower position in which the left hip is thrust forward in order to support the left elbow. The weight is shifted to the left foot and the upper part of the body is inclined somewhat away from the target. The sling is seldom used.

FIRING LINE

Standing Position

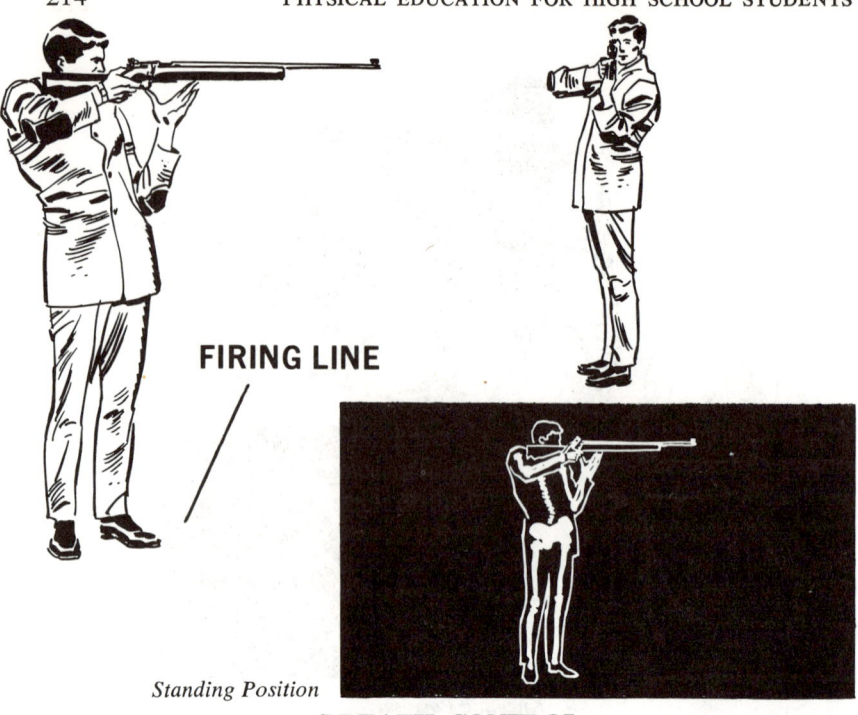

BREATH CONTROL

If you breathe while firing a shot, the muzzle of your rifle will go up and down with the movement of your chest. This will throw the shot far from the center of the target. For accurate results it is absolutely necessary to hold your breath while firing.

When you have your sights fairly well lined upon the target, draw in a normal breath, let out enough to be comfortable, and hold the rest easily until you get the sight picture you want and fire the shot. Don't try to hold your breath too long. That will only cause a rapid heart beat and pulse which will cause later shots to go wild. If you don't get a shot off soon enough, just relax, take a few more natural breaths, and then try again.

TRIGGER SQUEEZE

Proper trigger squeeze is the key to good shooting. There is only one correct way to start the bullet on its way; that is to *squeeze* the trigger with such a steady increase of pressure that you cannot tell exactly when the rifle will be discharged, all the while holding the sights as closely on the bullseye as possible. The trigger squeeze is carried out by a steady movement of the trigger finger only. If you notice that the sights are slightly out of alignment, maintain the pressure but apply no further pressure until the sights again line up properly with the bullseye. With the sights and the target in perfect alignment, increase the pressure until the rifle finally and unexpectedly discharges.

The good shot holds his aim on the target as accurately as possible and maintains a steady pressure upon the trigger until the rifle is fired. No one can become a good shot until he has learned the proper trigger squeeze.

CARE OF THE RIFLE

Like any other piece of sporting equipment, your rifle needs certain care to keep it in tip-top condition. A rifle can last you a lifetime if properly cared for.

A few years ago it was necessary to clean the barrel of a rifle every time it was fired. Today "noncorrosive" ammunition is available which eliminates this unpopular chore. Such ammunition is wholeheartedly recommended.

A little light oil will preserve the surface of your rifle, whether wood or metal. Wipe the surface with a rag moistened with a few drops of oil. Avoid squirting oil into the working parts, like the bolt and trigger.

If you are going to store your rifle for a long period of time, clean it thoroughly. Use a commercial solvent or cleaner on a cloth patch through the bore several times with a cleaning rod. Then run several dry patches of cloth through to clean and dry the inside of the barrel. Next put heavy gun grease on a patch and run it through the barrel. Rub the same type of grease on the outside metal parts of the rifle and store the rifle in a horizontal position. When you take the gun out again, clean it thoroughly and remove all grease before you fire it.

If there are small children around the house, be sure your rifle and ammunition are stored safely away where these youngsters cannot get them.

THE SAFEST OF SPORTS

Shooting is probably the safest of all sports. There are no sprained backs, split fingers, black eyes, or lost teeth. By practicing a few simple rules every shooter can become a safe shooter.

One of the greatest sources of pride for the National Rifle Association is the splendid record in the safe handling of firearms set by their junior members. Safe ranges, capable supervision, and, especially, adherence to the slogan that, "A real rifleman always handles a gun safely" has made it possible for nearly 9 million boys and girls, over a 43-year period, to take part in the NRA junior marksmanship program.

FOR MORE INFORMATION

American Association for Health, Physical Education, and Recreation. *Shooting and Hunting*. Washington, D.C.: the Association.

Briggs, Frank. *You Can Be an Expert Rifleman*. Laurel, Md.: Arthur Cook Supply Co.

National Rifle Association. *Shooters Guide*. Washington, D.C.: the Association.

National Rifle Association. *Shooting Handbook*. Washington, D.C.: the Association.

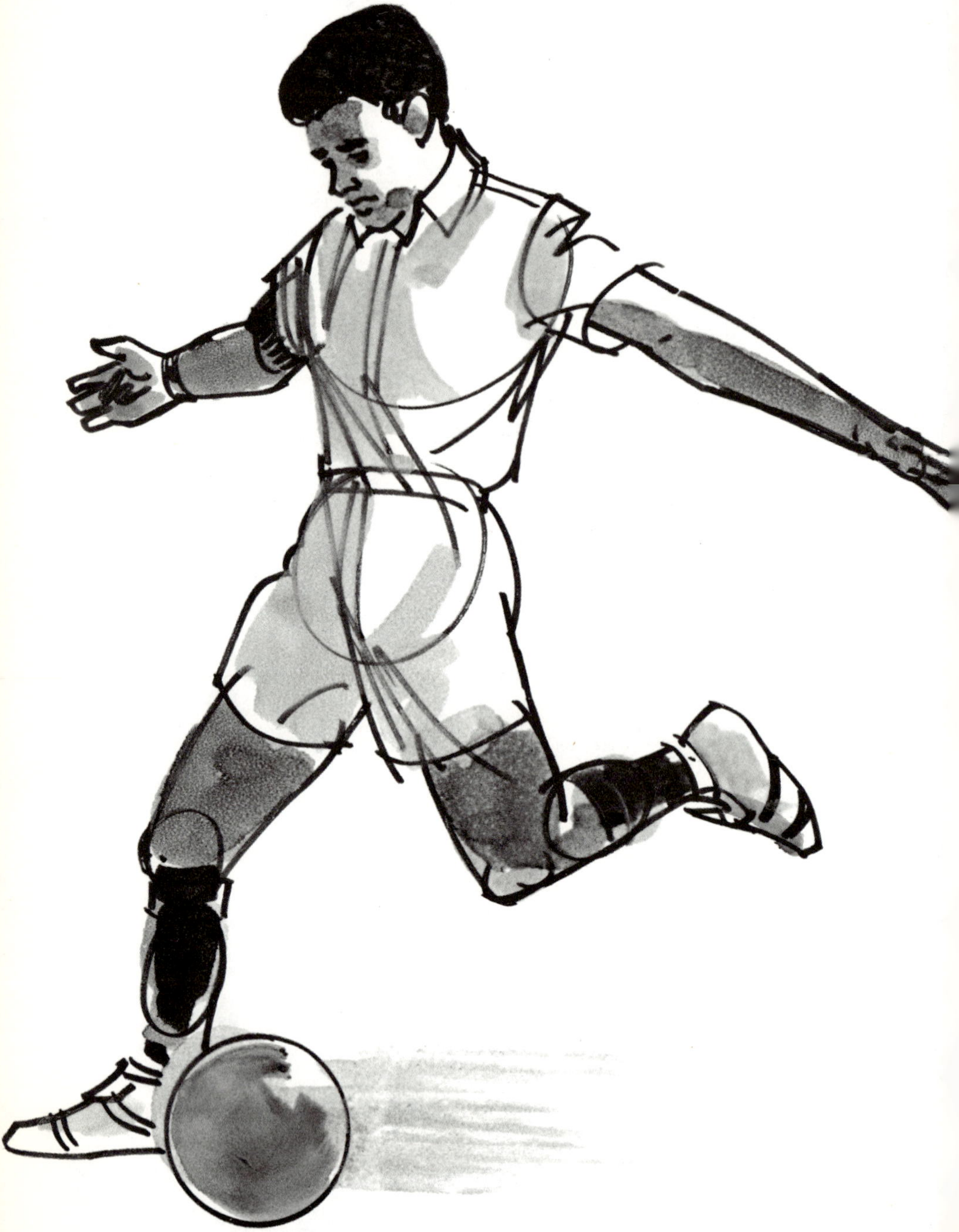

Soccer

Although attempts have been made to trace football to either a Roman or even an earlier Greek origin, there is little evidence for this. Football is as much an English game as baseball is an American one.

In 1851, Joseph Stutt wrote about a game the common people of England were playing on the greens. Two opposing teams tried to drive a ball—an inflated bladder cased with leather—through the goal of the rival team, the two goals being about 100 yards apart.

This game, which bears a close resemblance to our modern game of football, gave rise to two distinct kinds of football. In 1863, a number of English clubs formed the Football Association. Their rules provided only for a kicking game. One of the clubs, the Blackheath Club, protested against the rules and withdrew from the Association. Later the Blackheath Club was joined by other clubs who also wanted to use both hands and feet. This kind of football was called Rugby because those who favored handling the ball liked the style of game that was being played at Rugby School. In 1871, 17 clubs and 3 schools founded the Rugby Union.

From this time on, the Football Association and the Rugby Union went their separate ways. Each developed its own rules and each used a different shaped ball. The former used a round ball and the latter an oval ball. The American game of football developed directly from Rugby. Soccer has spread all over the world and in many countries has become the football game.

Recent events have played a part in making soccer one of the fastest growing sports in the United States today. First, many of our young men in the Armed Services have been exposed to the game in other countries through clinics and participation; second, our physical education schools are providing and preparing a better and more enthusiastic

Boys Field   *Girls Field*

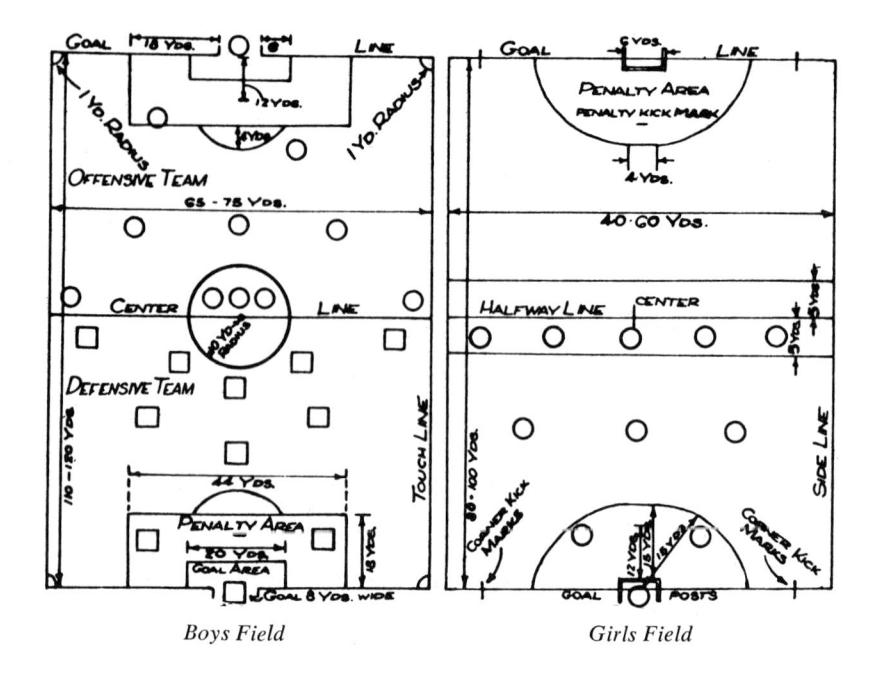

teacher of the sport; and third, the televising of the World Cup Soccer Match aroused so much interest in this country that professional soccer is making a real bid for a share of the overall sports picture.

THE GAME

Soccer is a running and kicking team game in which the ball is controlled mainly by the feet. In contrast to games in which the ball is caught and thrown, the soccer ball may not be touched by the hands or arms. The object is to advance the ball toward the opponents' goal by passing or dribbling the ball with the feet or body. One scores by sending the ball between the goal posts and under the cross bar.

The official playing field for girls is 100 yards long and 60 yards wide. For boys it is 120 yards long and 75 yards wide. The goal posts at each end of the field are 8 feet high and 8 yards apart for boys and 6 yards apart for girls, with goal nets attached to the rear. In the center of the field is a circle in which the ball is placed at the start of the game and after each goal is scored.

SOCCER

The soccer ball is an inflated leather or rubber covered ball with a circumference of not more than 28 inches. It is slightly larger than a volleyball and smaller than a basketball.

A team consists of 11 players: a goalie (the only player who can use his hands according to NCAA rules); a right and left fullback; a right, left, and center halfback; and 5 forwards (center forward, inside right, right wing, inside left, and left wing).

For girls, the game consists of four quarters of 8 minutes, with a 2-minute rest interval between quarters and a 10-minute interval between halves. For boys, quarters are 12 minutes in length in junior varsity and 15 minutes in varsity, with a 10-minute intermission between halves in both.

Girls Soccer

The game is started by a kick-off from the center of the field by the center forward. She may not play the ball again until it has been touched by another player. At the beginning of each quarter and after the goal has been made, the ball is put in play by a kick-off. Neither team may cross their lines until the ball has been kicked.

Let us suppose you are a player who has received the kick-off. Remember you cannot touch the ball with your arm or hands; so you must kick it to a teammate or you may dribble it down the field by kicking it a short distance ahead of you each time, tapping the ball with the inner part of your foot. One or more of your opponents may try to tackle the ball, but they are not allowed to touch you.

As the ball is passed or dribbled up and down the field, it occasionally will be kicked out-of-bounds. If it goes out over the sidelines, it is put back in play by a throw-in.

If it goes out-of-bounds over the end line and was last touched by a member of the defending team, it is put in play by a place kick by an attacking player from a spot on the goal line 5 yards from the nearest corner. This is called a corner kick.

When the ball is sent over the crossbar or over the goal line outside the goal post by a player of an attacking team, it is kicked in by a place kick by any player on the defending team from anywhere on the quarter circles marking the penalty area. This is called a defense kick.

If two opponents simultaneously cause the ball to go out-of-bounds, it is put in play by a roll-in. A roll-in is taken 5 yards in from the sideline or goal line, directly opposite the point where the ball left the field. An official rolls the ball between the two players who were responsible for causing the ball to go out-of-bounds. The two stand 5 yards in from the sideline facing each other and their opponents' goal, ready to kick the ball. All other players must be at least 5 yards from the ball.

As your team nears the goal, the opponent's goalkeeper gets ready to defend her goal. As a goalkeeper in her own penalty area, she may catch or pick up, then throw the ball, bounce the ball once and throw it, drop kick the ball, or punt. She may take two steps with the ball in her hands preceding a punt, drop kick, or throw. This privilege is denied if the punt, drop kick, or throw is combined with a bounce.

During the game you commit a foul if you trip, push, charge, or jump at an opponent; kick, strike, or hold an opponent; or touch the ball with your hands or arms. If you commit a foul, a free kick is awarded to any player on the other team, but it is usually taken by the halfback. All players stand at least 5 yards away from the ball until it has been kicked. If two opponents commit a foul at the same time, a roll-in is taken at the spot where the foul occurred by those involved.

If you are a member of the defending team and commit a foul in the penalty area, a penalty kick is awarded. The ball is placed on the penalty mark, 12 yards from the goal, and all players except the goalkeeper and player taking the kick are outside the penalty area. The ball is usually kicked by the center forward on the attacking team. After the kick has been taken, all players may rush in to play the ball if the goal is missed.

You may score in soccer by a field goal or by a penalty kick. A field goal counts two points; a penalty kick counts one point.

Boys Soccer

The game is started by the three inside forwards of one team who put the ball in play from the center circle—usually by the center forward's kicking the ball at least one complete revolution forward to one of his inside players. The opposition must remain outside the circle until the ball is touched. From that point on the ball is advanced primarily with the feet, but it may receive help from the head and body. You cannot touch the ball with your arms or hands unless you keep the ball in contact with your body or unless you are the goalkeeper. If the ball is kicked over the sideline, it is put in play by the opposite team from the one who played it last.

A halfback usually puts the ball in play from the sideline by a throw-in. In performing a throw-in part of both feet must remain on the ground; the ball is thrown with both hands, starting from in back of the head and following through.

When the ball is kicked over the goal line but not through the goal by the offensive team, the defense, usually the goalie or the fullback, takes a goal kick from 6 yards out. The other team must remain outside of the penalty area until the ball is kicked. When the defensive team last plays the ball going over their own goal line, the offensive team gets a corner kick. This is taken by the wing from the 1-yard arc in the corner of the field closest to where the ball went out of bounds. The offensive players position themselves in front of the goal where they are picked up by defensive players. A wing attempts to kick the ball to the spot in front of the goal where a teammate can receive it for a goal shot. Goals count 1 point.

Free kicks are awarded for various infractions of the rules, such as touching the ball with the hands or arms; kicking, striking, or jumping an opponent. Anyone can take a free kick, and the opponents must be 10 yards away until the ball is kicked. If a foul is committed within the penalty area by the defensive team, any player on the offensive team may take the penalty kick from the 12-yard penalty mark with all of the players except the goalkeeper outside the penalty area and 10 yards away.

In order to prevent massing in front of the goal, an offensive player must have two defensive players closer to the goal than himself when a teammate passes him the ball. He cannot be offside if he is behind the ball.

BASIC SKILLS

Soccer is a very different game for Americans. We are used to catching, striking, and throwing balls. Learning to control a ball without using one's hands or arms is a challenge. The most important skills for the game are ball control, speed, endurance, competitive spirit, and team play.

Kicking

Constant practice is necessary to develop a proper kick. Good soccer is played with the ball close to the ground. In learning to kick the ball, start with a stationary ball and progress to a moving ball and then to one moving and spinning.

Instep Kick. Place the nonkicking foot beside and about 6 inches from the ball. Keep the toe of your kicking foot down so you contact the ball

Instep Kick

with the instep or shoe laces. Get your power from the knee by snapping the bent leg forward. Follow through with your foot close to the ground. This will tend to keep the ball down. Learn to kick with either foot. Having to shift your stride to favor your best foot may result in losing the ball.

Side of Foot. Kicking with the inside of the foot makes it easier to control the direction of the ball and is effective in passing sideways or diagonally. Kicking with the outside of the foot will send the ball on the opposite diagonal. Though these two types of kicks are not distance gainers, they enable you to control and direct the ball.

Heel Kick. Kicking with the heel is used for passing backwards. It is good only for short distances.

Volleying. Once you have attained a certain amount of power and accuracy in kicking a stationary ball and a moving ground ball, practice kicking the ball just as it rises from the ground (half volley) and also in the air (full volley). The important things to remember on the half volley are to be over the ball, to keep your eye on the ball, and to kick at it with a short follow-through. To become efficient with a full volley, keep your eye on the ball, meet the ball squarely with the surface of the instep, and don't kick too hard.

SOCCER

Side of Foot *Volleying*

Punting. A punt is a kick that may be used only by the goalkeeper, since the ball must be caught and dropped to be kicked. The ball is held in both hands at arms length at about waist level in front of the body. One or two steps may be taken preliminary to kicking. The kicking leg swings forward and upward with the knee bent and the toe pointing forward, so that the ball is kicked on the instep. The bent knee and straight ankle position will cause the ball to travel diagonally forward and upward. The ball is dropped just before the kicking leg starts the forward swing. The follow-through is upward and forward, with the body bent forward and the arms out to the sides for balance. The weight is on the ball of the supporting foot.

Passing. Passing should be done with the sides of the feet because it will allow a greater surface of the foot to come in contact with the ball and thereby ensure a more accurate pass. Using the toe or heel is not recommended. Try to conceal where you are passing the ball until the last instant. Be sure to pass to a spot ahead of your teammate so that he won't have to slow down to receive it.

Trapping

Trapping is the art of stopping and controlling a moving ball. This is an essential skill of the game because if you can't stop and keep the ball close to you, you certainly can't pass or kick it.

Chest and Stomach Traps

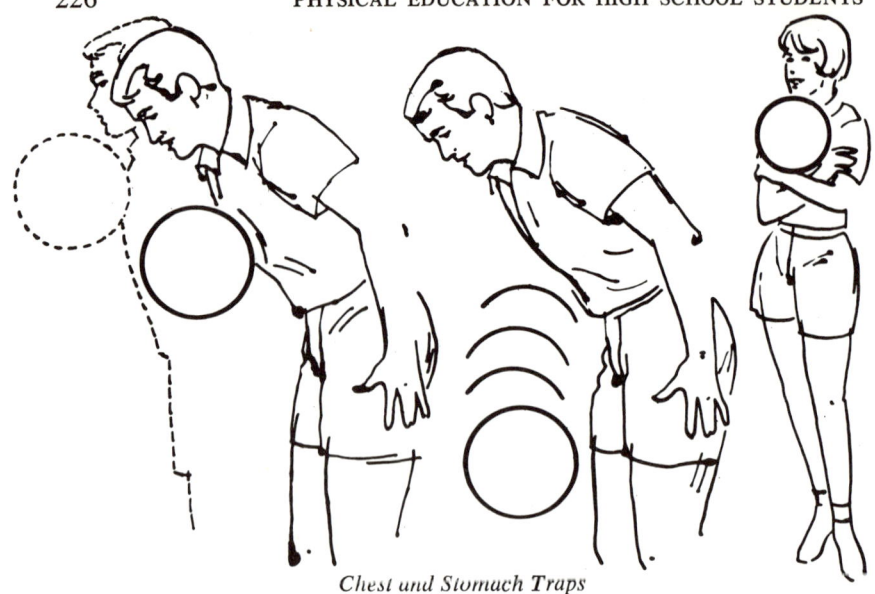

There are several ways to trap a ball, depending on how the ball comes at you. You can stop it with your head, chest, stomach, legs, shins, or feet. All of these ways require a lot of practice because no other game you have ever played has required this particular skill.

(In girls soccer, trapping the ball is stopping and controlling the ball with the legs or feet. If the ball is played off any other part of the body, the term used is *blocking the ball*.)

To practice the chest or stomach trap, have someone throw the ball at this part of your body—easy at first! The trick is to pull away from the ball at the right moment and speed to prevent the ball from rebounding. When a body trap is done right, the ball will fall at your feet. Use your arms for balance as you suck in your stomach or pull away with your chest. Girls do the chest trap with the arms crossed.

The leg trap is used when the ball approaches just off the ground. To take the speed from the ball, merely raise one leg with the knee bent and give with the speed of the ball as it contacts the inside of the foot, ankle, or lower leg. When properly done, the ball will drop directly in front of you.

For the foot trap, raise the leg and foot over the ball the instant it hits the ground and form a wedge by dropping the heel and raising the toe. Just as the ball rebounds it should be stopped by the wedge formed by the bottom of the foot. The trick is to place your foot over the ball at the exact moment of rebound.

Leg Trap   *Foot Trap*

Dribbling

Dribbling is a way to advance the ball until an opponent forces you to pass. It is an important phase of the game and often makes it possible to score. To dribble, you move the ball along with the sides of your feet, with deft movements of the ankles, always keeping it close to you. Never dribble with the toes because the ball will get too far ahead. Practice dribbling in and out between objects placed five yards apart. Use both the inside and outside of both feet to dribble. It takes experience to dribble well and at the same time watch an approaching player. Learn to dribble at two speeds so that your change of pace will fool the opponent trying to tackle you.

Heading

Many times during the game a ball approaches a player head high. Often goals are scored with the head, and many balls are brought back to the ground and under control with the head. The ball should be contacted with the thickest part of the skull, directly over the eyes. Always head the ball down to teammates or into the goal.

Tackling

Tackling is the art of taking the ball from your opponent by using your feet. First, you must not make the mistake of rushing in too fast and off balance. You should judge the time of your tackle so that the

Dribbling   *Heading*

ball will have just left the dribbler's foot when you move. The best tackle is made with the inside of one foot placed against the ball (not kicked). Crouch forward with the inside of your foot placed low against the ball. This will cause the dribbler to lose possession of the ball. Never leave your feet in making a tackle because it is dangerous to both you and your opponent.

TEAM PLAY AND STRATEGY

Although ball control is the most important skill of soccer, speed, endurance, and competitive spirit count for much. It is a distinct advantage to be faster than your opponent. But if speed is not one of your assets, you can compensate by developing the endurance to play in top form for an entire game. Competitive spirit is another thing that cannot be ignored. Many teams with more skill have lost to a team that had nothing more than an intense desire to win. The history of sports is filled with upsets because underdogs refused to accept defeat.

Every player on a team has 45 or 50 opportunities during a game to make his own decision as to what he will do with the ball. Team work and team strategy are among the most important factors in winning. Probably the most neglected area of the game of soccer is concerned with *what the player does when he does not have the ball.* Perhaps a coach can best emphasize this critical area by pointing out that the average player actually has the ball in his possession no more than three minutes during the course of a whole game. Therefore, it is important that he think about his duties to his team the rest of the time. *Anticipation* is a key, whether you are in a position to help defensively or offensively.

Ball control is essential to strategy. With the help of your physical education teacher, strategic plays can be worked out for kick-offs, free kicks, throw-ins, and other plays to give you an advantage. In the same way there are a number of defensive plays which can be worked out and practiced.

The common fault with most beginning players is not playing their positions. Forwards have an area which extends from their opponent's goal line to a point between the center line and their own goal line. The halfbacks go all the way back to their own goal line and toward the opponent's goal to a point halfway between the center line and the end line. Cover for the player beside you, but do not play his position unless he is out of position.

Tips for Forwards

1. Become a skilled dribbler, a fast runner, and a good dodger. The short pass and dribbling type of game full of little tricks will wear down and tire out the opposing team.
2. Develop speed and endurance.
3. Be aggressive.
4. Play ahead of your halfbacks. Center the ball as you near the goal.
5. Improve your ability to pass and shoot while moving at full speed.

Tips for Halfbacks

1. Develop endurance. Keep trying if your tackle is unsuccessful. Back up your forward line, but don't try to play on the forward line. Observe the style of play used by your opponent and adapt your tackling to it.
2. Become an expert in the art of tackling. Stay with your opponent until you get the ball or force him to pass it.

Tips for Fullbacks

1. Remember that defensive work is your primary job. Become efflicient in long accurate kicks and be sure you know just how and where the kicks should be placed.

2. Learn to kick accurately with both feet in order to avoid an opponent.

3. Practice tackling so that you can upset an attack.

Tips for Goalkeepers

1. Don't be afraid of onrushing players or the ball.
2. Be alert and ready to make a quick judgment.
3. Study the style of plays of your opponents.
4. Never use your feet in saving a goal when it is possible to use your hands. Develop skill in catching high balls and in punting and throwing.
5. Stand about two feet out from the line of the goal so that you have space in which to throw the ball out.
6. Learn to cut down on the angle of the opponents' shot so that less of the goal is visible.

COURTESY AND SPORTSMANSHIP

To be courteous and show sportsmanship does not mean that you cannot be an aggressive player. Play your game and save your breath. Sportsmanship is more than observing the rules or giving 15 "rahs" for your opponents. Your behavior is a reflection of your respect for the other fellow. Your true self shows in the things you do that are not in the rule book but are in the spirit of the rules. The following are unwritten rules which the good sport observes:

1. Raise your hand over your head when you know you were the last person to touch the ball before it went out of bounds.
2. Raise your hand over your head if you touch the ball with your hand or arm.
3. If you knock your opponent down accidentally, help him to get up.
4. Play for fun, but play to win.
5. Play your best. It is not fair to your teammates or your opponents to play half-heartedly.
6. Keep your temper.
7. Don't blame others for your own poor playing.
8. Don't be critical or fussy about the mistakes of others.
9. Don't alibi or boast. Be a good winner and a good loser.

SAFETY

You can protect yourself from injury in soccer by keeping physically fit, by developing proper skills, and by using body protectors. Soccer is a vigorous game for which the body should be conditioned gradually. Warm up completely every day before you practice or play a game. Take care of early season blisters and muscle pulls. Alternate tennis shoes with your soccer shoes the first week to help prevent blisters. Kicking too hard at the beginning of the season often results in serious strains in the groin.

You can protect yourself from injury by using shin guards and glasses guards—the latter a "must" for the player who has to play with glasses. Shin guards are worn inside knee-length socks.

Shoes are the most important part of the player's equipment. Regulation shoes are high, leather shoes, cleated with leather or rubber to protect the player against slipping.

It is recommended that the goalie wear a distinguishing color to enable forwards to recognize him easily as they attack. The privileges of a goalie may result in dangerous maneuvers if he is not known during an aggressive play.

Never kick a ball that is above the hips and never head a ball that is below the head.

SOCCER TERMS

Blocking. Intercepting the progress of the ball with any part of the body, except the arms and hands. (In girls soccer the arms and hands may be used if the ball is in contact with the body.)

Corner kick. Awarded the attacking team when the ball passes over the goal line other than between the goal posts and is last touched by a defender.

Defense-kick. Given a defensive team if the ball goes over the goal line other than between the goal posts and is last touched by an offensive player (girls game).

Dribbling. Advancing the ball by a series of short kicks.

Free kick. Awarded to the defending team for fouls committed by the attacking team inside the penalty area and to either team for fouls committed outside the penalty area.

Goal kick. In boys game, same as defense kick above.

Heading. Allowing the ball to come in contact with the head.

Passing. Kicking the ball to a teammate.

Penalty kick. Awarded the offensive team at the penalty kick mark if a defensive player fouls in his own penalty area.

Roll-in. Putting the ball in play after a foul by both teams, or after opponents have simultaneously kicked the ball out of bounds.

Tackling. Taking the ball from an opponent by use of the feet.

Throw-in. Putting the ball in play after it is out of bounds over the sideline.

Trapping. Stopping and controlling a moving ball (with legs and feet only, in a girls game).

Volleying. Kicking the ball while it is in the air (boys game) or playing a ball which is in the air with the shoulder, hip, leg, or foot (girls game).

FOR MORE INFORMATION

Allen, John. *Soccer for Americans.* New York: Grosset & Dunlap, 1967.

American Association for Health, Physical Education, and Recreation, Division for Girls and Women's Sports. *Selected Soccer-Speedball Articles.* Washington, D.C.: the Association.

American Association for Health, Physical Education, and Recreation, Division for Girls and Women's Sports. *Soccer-Speedball Guide.* Current edition. Washington, D.C.: the Association.

Athletic Institute. *How To Improve Your Soccer.* Chicago: the Institute.

National Collegiate Athletic Association. *Official NCAA Soccer Guide.* Chicago: the Association.

Nelson, Richard L. *Soccer.* Physical Education Activities Series. Dubuque, Iowa: Wm. C. Brown Co., 1966.

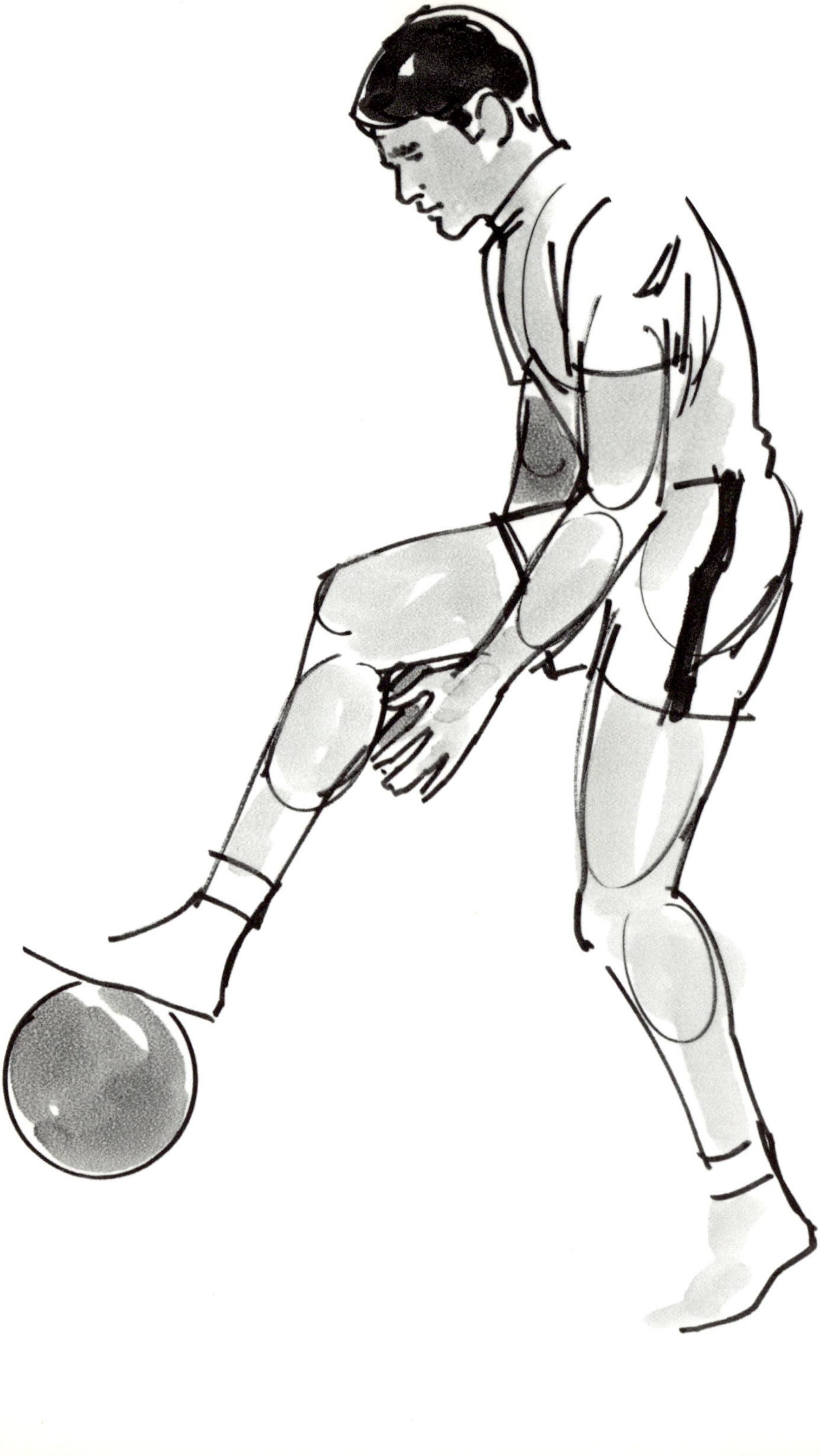

Speedball

Speedball, like baseball and basketball, is a game of American origin. The most recent of the three, it was invented in 1921 by Elmer D. Mitchell at the University of Michigan.

It is said that speedball got its name when an excited player yelled "Let's speed the ball!" Anyway, the name is certainly most appropriate, for fast footwork, handwork, and headwork are essential requirements for playing the game well.

And no wonder! Speedball is an ingenious combination of soccer and basketball. When the ball is a ground ball, it is played with the feet and body as in soccer; when it goes into the air, it is played with the hands as in basketball. The result of this combination is a game which is fast moving and provides plenty of opportunity for scoring.

From the University of Michigan it has spread all over the United States. Colleges and high schools have adopted it for their fall intramural program, for it is a good game for crisp autumn days. During World War II it was played in Army and Navy training camps as a conditioning sport, because it provides good all-around exercise.

Girls started playing speedball three years after it was invented. The National Section on Women's Athletics, now the Division for Girls and Women's Sports, in 1933 appointed a committee to make necessary revisions in the mens rules and develop a game suited to the needs and abilities of girls.

THE GAME

Speedball is a combination kicking and passing game. The object of the game is to advance the ball up the field and score. At times the rules permit the ball to be advanced by kicking only; at other times by passing only. An important part of the strategy of play is to get a

Girls Field   *Boys Field*

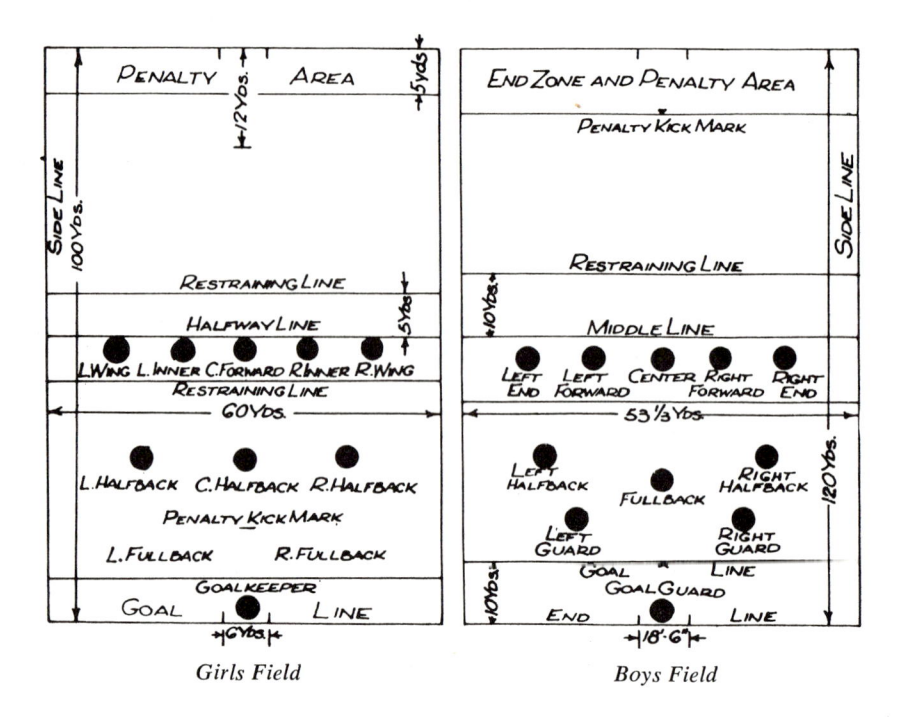

ground ball into the air and an aerial ball onto the ground when your opponents least expect it.

While the game of speedball for girls and that for boys are similar, boys play on a slightly larger field. The length of the playing field for the girls game is the same as that of a football field (100 yards). For the boys game the end zones are added to make an area 120 yards long.

Markings	Boys Field	Girls Field
Goal posts	Back line of end zone	Zero yard or goal line
Restraining line	10 yards from middle line	5 yards from halfway line
Penalty area	10 yard end zone	5 yards area in front of goal line
Penalty-kick mark	10 yards in front of goal posts	12 yards in front of goal posts

The 11 players on the boys team are 5 forwards (left end, left forward, center, right forward, and right end), two halfbacks (right and left), one full back, and three guards (right, left, and goal guard).

On a girls team the 5 forwards are left wing, left inner, center forward, right inner, and right wing. There are 3 halfbacks: left, center, and right. Right and left fullbacks and a goalkeeper complete the team.

Play starts with a kick-off from the center of the kicking team's restraining line. The toss of a coin determines which team shall kick off. The ball (a regulation soccer ball) is kicked by the center from a point on the middle or halfway line. Members of the defensive team must remain behind the restraining line and members of the kicking team may not cross the middle line until the ball has been kicked. By mutual agreement a basketball may be used for boys if the field used is less than 120 x 53½ yards.

The girl making the kick-off may kick the ball far down the field, but she is more likely to lift it diagonally forward so that a teammate can run forward to catch it and make the next pass.

After the kick-off the players who have the ball in their possession then try to advance the ball toward the opponents' goal by dribbling, kicking, and heading ground balls and throwing aerial balls.

A ball that has touched the ground is a ground ball and must be played according to soccer rules (that is, the hands may not be used) until such time as it is raised into the air by a kick. A ball may be caught directly from a kick, at which time it becomes an aerial ball. An aerial ball may be advanced according to basketball rules, with one exception. The basketball dribble may not be used because when the ball touches the ground it becomes a ground ball, and the hands cannot be used to recover it. As a substitute the juggle (overhead dribble), seldom used in basketball, is often used in speedball.

The defensive team tries to prevent scoring by their opponents and attempts to gain possession of the ball. In doing so the defensive techniques of soccer are used against ground balls and the guarding techniques of basketball are used against aerial balls.

Scores can be made in the following ways: by a field goal, a touchdown, a drop kick, and a penalty kick. By mutual agreement of both teams, boys may score one point by an end kick. An end kick is made when a ground ball is legally kicked over the end line but does not result in a field goal from within the opponent's end zone. You kick the ball between the goal posts and under the crossbar for a field goal. This is similar to the field goal in soccer. You pass the ball over the goal line to a teammate for a touchdown, just like the forward pass for a touchdown in football. Or you can drop-kick the ball over the crossbar as in football. The fourth method of scoring is the penalty kick. This is awarded as a penalty for certain fouls and is comparable to the free throw in basketball. However, it is a kick instead of a throw. In the boys game it is a place kick which must pass through the goal to count, as in soccer. In the girls game it is an unguarded drop kick which must go over the crossbar to score.

Speedball is played in four quarters, 10 minutes in length for boys and 8 minutes for girls, with a 2-minute break between quarters and a 10-minute half-time intermission for girls and 15-minutes for boys. If the score of a game is tied at the end of the regulation playing period, a 5-minute overtime period is played by boys. In the girls game the tie score stands.

At the beginning of each quarter the play is started by a kick-off, the teams alternating in taking kick-offs.

In the girls game if a team causes the ball to go out-of-bounds over the side line, a throw-in is given to the opposing team. Should the ball go over the end line without a score being made, the ball is given to the opposing team to put in play by either a pass or a kick.

Fouls and Penalties

There are two types of fouls. In the boys game they are called personal and technical. Personal fouls include the following: kicking, tripping, charging, pushing, holding, or blocking. Unnecessary roughness of any kind, such as running into an opponent from behind or kicking at a fly ball and thereby kicking an opponent, is a personal foul. A player with four personal fouls is disqualified.

Technical fouls include illegal substitution, more than five time-outs in a game, unsportsmanlike conduct, too many players on the field, and unnecessary delay of the game.

For boys there are other infractions of the rules besides personal and technical fouls. These additional infractions are called violations. The various violations are traveling with the ball, touching a ground ball with the hands or arms, double overhead dribble (juggle), offside on the kick-off, short kick-off, kicking or kneeing a fly ball before catching it, violating free-kick rules, violation of the out-of-bounds rule by offensive play, violating penalty-kick rules, and violating the tie-ball rule.

A violation outside of a team's own penalty area gives the ball to the opponents for a free kick at the spot where the violation occurred. If the violation occurs in a team's own end zone or penalty area, the opponents are awarded a penalty kick with a follow-up.

SPEEDBALL

In the girls game the fouls are called individual-type and team-type fouls. The individual type includes pushing, tripping, charging, handling a ground ball, and holding the ball more than 3 seconds; and the team type includes having more than 11 players on a team. Penalties vary depending on the foul and where it occurs.

In both the boys and the girls game the penalty for a foul is a free kick taken at the point where the foul occurred by a member of the team which did not commit the foul. The player taking the free kick puts it in play by a place kick, and all opponents must be at least 5 yards away. If the defense commits a foul inside its own penalty area or behind its goal line, the offense is given a penalty kick—an opportunity to drop-kick a goal from the penalty-kick mark.

FUNDAMENTAL SKILLS

The fundamental skills in speedball are kicking, throwing, and catching. There is, however, ample opportunity to use other common sports skills, such as running, dodging, jumping, pivoting, heading, trapping, volleying, and guarding. Most of these skills are common to other games—especially soccer and basketball—but several deserve special comment in connection with speedball. A few are special speedball skills.

Kicking

Kicking skill includes place-kicking, punting, drop-kicking, foot dribbling, and kick-ups. The first four types of kicking are common to football and soccer, and the correct ways of executing them are explained in the chapters on those sports.

The kick-up, however, is a skill definitely linked with speedball. The player kicks the ball so that he may catch it himself, with the purpose of starting a passing offense.

The one-foot kick-up is used on a rolling ball coming toward you. Let the ball hit the toe of your foot and lifting your foot flip the ball into the air so you can catch it. The ball must be free of the foot before it may be touched with the hands. This play may also be executed by having the ball touch your extended foot and then roll up your instep, ankle, and shin before being impelled into your hands.

There is a tricky variation on the one-foot kick-up. This is used on a stationary ball, usually on one that you have trapped. Start with your foot on top of the ball. Give your foot a quick move toward you. This

One-Foot Kick-Up

With Rolling Ball *With Stationary Ball*

will spin the ball so that your toe goes under it, and you can then flip the ball into the air and into your hands.

The two-foot kick-up is used when you have the ball trapped between your two feet. Jump into the air extending your knees forward. By a flipping action of the feet the ball will be flipped into the air for a catch.

The Overhead Dribble

The overhead dribble (juggle) is a special feature of speedball. You use it to get around an opponent. To execute it, you toss a looping gentle throw over his head and then run around him to recover the ball. You can also use it when you wish to gain ground without taking steps (traveling) and thereby incurring a violation.

Running

You must always remember that you cannot run when you have the ball in your possession. You must learn to come to a stop quickly in order not to incur a violation for traveling with the ball. The use of the overhead dribble will help you in this situation.

Jumping

This skill is employed in jumping into the air to catch or tip fly balls, in making throw-ins from out-of-bounds, in connection with toss-ups after held balls, and in combination with the skill of heading the ball.

SPEEDBALL

Two-Foot Kick-Up

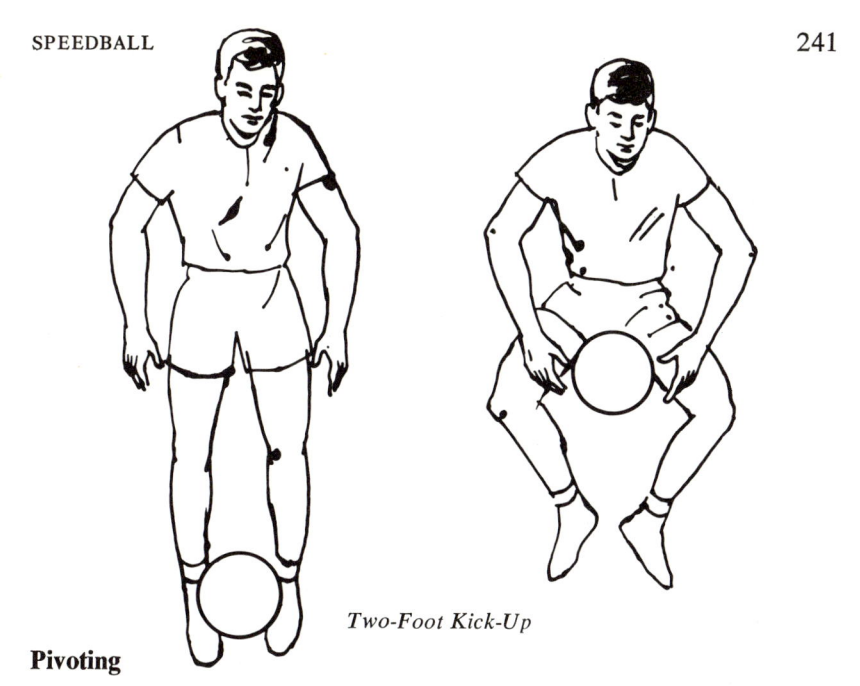

Pivoting

This skill is familiar if you have played basketball. You need it when you are confronted with an opponent. Since traveling with the ball is not permitted, you cannot elude your opponent by dodging; you must either pass the ball ahead to a teammate, make an overhead dribble, or pivot with the ball. By pivoting to either side you can turn your back to the opponent and keep the ball out of his reach while finding someone to pass to.

Heading

Most American players, unless they have played soccer, are unfamiliar with this particular skill. It consists of propelling a ball that is in the air by means of bouncing it off your head in a desired direction. In heading a ball, jump into the air with your neck rigid and your head slanted in the direction you wish the ball to go and play the ball off the thickest part of your skull, directly over your eyes.

Trapping

This is another skill common to soccer. It consists of trapping or blocking a moving ball with the foot or body so that it is stopped and can be controlled by the feet of the player who has trapped it. Sometimes you simply place your foot on top of a ball that is rolling on the ground toward you. Sometimes you use both feet, with one foot at an angle to stop the ball and the other foot then being clamped against it. Trapping is described more fully in the chapter on soccer, which you should turn to if you have not yet read it.

Volleying

This is another soccer skill. It is based on the same principle as heading. You use it to advance ground balls by letting them bounce off your body or by giving them added force by hipping, shouldering, or kneeing. Girls may volley with arms folded against chest. You can also use it to deflect aerial balls to the ground when you want to play a kicking game. This is an important skill, because ground balls may not be touched by the hands or arms.

Guarding and Checking (Marking)

You need variety in using these skills because the basketball-type of guarding is employed on aerial play, and the difficult checking (marking) tactics are employed in defending against the kicking game of the offense. The important thing when you are the defender is to play the ball and not your opponent. Also you cannot impede the progress of an opponent who does not have the ball; you can, however, stand still and force your opponent to run around you.

TEAM STRATEGY

Because of the nature of the game much of the play is impromptu. There are few "set" situations where rehearsed plays can be put into operation as is the case in football or basketball. Certain planned plays can be executed from the kick-off or from out-of-bounds, but usually the plays depend upon the ingenuity of the players themselves in sizing up the situation and in making the best response to it.

Offensive Play

In general a team that is adept at kicking will emphasize a kicking game and will tip all fly balls to the ground. Conversely, a team of tall players, expert at passing, will try to convert all ground balls into aerial play as soon as possible.

If your team is a fast, high-scoring team, concentrate on offense; if it is a slower, less experienced team, concentrate on defense to keep the opponents' scoring opportunities down.

Play your position on the field instead of running all over the field after the ball. When the offensive players are bunched, then there is no one free to play to in the open when the ball is secured. This tendency of players to chase the ball rather than to play in their own area on the field is one of the greatest faults of uncoached players.

A kicking offense is most likely to be successful if the ball is advanced up the sideline of the field and then, when the defense has been drawn out to cover, the ball is centered.

A passing offense has an advantage if the ball is advanced up the center of the field, as there is a better opportunity for scoring by a field goal or drop kick. Also there is the additional option of completing a forward pass in any part of the end zone that might be uncovered (except between goal posts in a girls game).

If a strong wind prevails, it is good strategy to select the goal with the wind. The punt is a good offensive weapon on windy days with the wind in your favor, because it gets the ball far down the field. Against the wind, long high passes or punts should be avoided. It is better to stick to ground kicks and low aerial passes.

The drop kick comes in handy when a player is alone with the ball in front of the goal and has no one to pass to.

It is a good plan to have a trailer for the man advancing the ball up the field. Then, if he is blocked ahead, he knows that he can always pivot and pass back to the trailer if in aerial play, or kick the ball backward if in ground play. In scoring tactics it is also advisable to hurry a man ahead of the play and have him in the end zone as soon as possible as a potential pass receiver.

Defensive Play

Three styles of defense are common: the man-to-man, the zone, and the combination. The zone or position style is generally favored as it cuts down on the amount of running and provides that someone be in each area of the field to accept passes. However, if your opponents' attack is centered around a few star players, you should use the combination style. In it, the opposing star players are covered man-to-man, but the other defensive players cover a specified area of the field. The threat of the opponents' attack is thereby checked doubly; for if an opponent who is covered man-to-man should break loose, he is almost certain to run into a second defender—the one who is playing position in the area invaded by the play.

In the man-to-man defense it is essential that the defender keep between his opponent and the threatened goal. This style of play is liable to be rougher than the position style and also causes more bunching of the players.

In the zone defense it is always important to follow the shifting principle. For example, if the ball is in play on the left side of the field, then the defending players on the right side of the field drop back toward their goal and also toward the center. By this method, the center defenders can move out in the direction of the play, knowing that the areas they are leaving will be protected; also, it ensures that the play does not get in behind the defense. If the ball should travel from the left to the right of the field, then the strategy is reversed. The right defenders move up the field and toward the sideline to meet the attack, and the left defenders fill in behind them. In this way, too, the offensive play is always being forced out to the edge, where there is much less chance of scoring.

The Front-Line Players

These players should be fast and active because they are the main scoring players. If possible, the ends should be tall, because they will have more chances to catch forward passes. The forwards and center should be especially adept at kicking field goals and making drop kicks. Also, they will have more chances to make penalty kicks and should devote special practice to this shooting skill. On penalty kicks it is important to disguise the direction of the kick beforehand. The best chance of success is to direct the kick to one side of the goal, after having feinted the goal guard off balance toward the other side.

The Backs

The second-line players (halfback and fullback in the boys game) have double duty in that they have considerable responsibilities both on offense and defense. They must, therefore, be more than skillful and versatile players—they must have stamina as well. Most of the throw-ins of the ball from out-of-bounds in their own half of the field are made by the backs. They are in the best position for this play. As a rule, one of the halfbacks should pass the ball in from the sideline out-of-bounds. This gives the forwards—the best scorers—a chance to take positions in scoring territory.

Because of their intermediate position on the field, the backs should have the intuition to size up the opponents' plays quickly and break these up if possible before they get too far under way.

The Guards

The third-line players (fullbacks in the girls game) are mainly defensive players. They should be good at making long kicks, punts, and passes in order to get the ball out of danger quickly.

The guards are in the best position to put the ball in play when the offense sends the ball out-of-bounds over the end line.

When starting offensive play, one of the guards should move up the center of the field and act as a trailer to the man who has the ball. The other guard should then fill in behind so that the three guards are somewhat in tandem formation. Under this plan, the guards may occasionally interchange sides of the field.

The goal guard in speedball has no advantages peculiar to his position. He can, therefore, interchange at will with any other player who needs a rest. This makes him an all-around player instead of a highly specialized player. It is an advantage to the goal guard to have a long reach. He must be quick-witted. He must decide quickly to leave the goal—sometimes a dangerous procedure—when he is sure he can beat an opponent to the ball. As a rule he plays his position correctly when he stands a few yards in front of the goal. By so doing, he cuts down the scoring angle—leaves less space to each side and above him through which a ball may score. In getting the ball out of danger he should be coached to clear the ball to one side instead of straight up the field.

SAFETY PRECAUTIONS

Since speedball is played on a large field, there is plenty of room to move about and few personal fouls need occur. It is a relatively safe game, but there are a few pointers which will help make the game a safer one to play.

1. Keep the field smooth and free from rubble.
2. Wear suitable clothing. Shin guards and eye glass guards if you need them are recommended.
3. Play your position. Avoid bunching and wild kicking.
4. Turn your side toward swift oncoming balls and play them off your shoulder or hip.
5. Girls should fold their arms across their chests when volleying balls or facing them for high play.
6. Direct your kicks. Don't just barge in and slam the ball.
7. Think as you play.

SELECTION AND CARE OF EQUIPMENT

You don't need much equipment for speedball. A soccer ball, shin guards for each player, and a regulation gymnasium uniform—or in cold weather a sweater and slacks—and you're ready for the kick-off. However, a few hints in this regard:

1. Select good leather balls and keep them properly inflated according to the manufacturers' specifications.
2. Dry them carefully and away from the heat after play on a wet field. Grease them if they get too dry.
3. Shin and goal keeper's guards are a necessity. They should be light in weight, well fastened, and *used*.
4. Rubber-shafted flags should be used to mark the corners.

SPEEDBALL TERMS

Aerial ball. One raised in the air by a direct kick from one or both feet. Includes the punt, drop-kick, and kick-up. It is also a thrown ball that has not yet contacted the ground. It is played with the hands.

Dribble. A series of little kicks by one player whereby the ball is moved forward along the ground.

Drop-kick. A play in which an aerial ball is dropped and kicked as it rebounds from the ground.

Free kick. A place kick awarded for certain fouls.

Ground ball. As the name implies, a ball rolling or bouncing on the ground. It is played with the feet.

Heading. Directing a ground ball, which is temporarily in the air, with a bounce off the head.

Kick-up. A play by which a player causes a ground ball to become an aerial ball.

Penalty kick. A play on the penalty-kick mark awarded the attack when the defense fouls in its own penalty area and under some other circumstances.

Place kick. A stationary kick, such as the one used to start the game at the kick-off or a free kick. Ball may be lifted into the air or kept on the ground.

Punt. Kicking a dropped ball before it touches the ground.

Trapping. Stopping and controlling the ball with the feet or body.

FOR MORE INFORMATION

American Association for Health, Physical Education, and Recreation, Division for Girls and Women's Sports. *Selected Soccer-Speedball Articles.* Washington, D.C.: the Association.

American Association for Health, Physical Education, and Recreation, Division for Girls and Women's Sports. *Soccer-Speedball Guide.* Current edition. Washington, D.C.: the Association.

Fait, Holles F., editor. *Speedball for Men.* Washington, D.C.: American Association for Health, Physical Education, and Recreation, 1967.

Vannier, Maryhelen, and Poindexter, Holly Beth. *Individual and Team Sports for Girls and Women.* Second edition. Philadelphia, Pa.: Wm. B. Saunders Co., 1968.

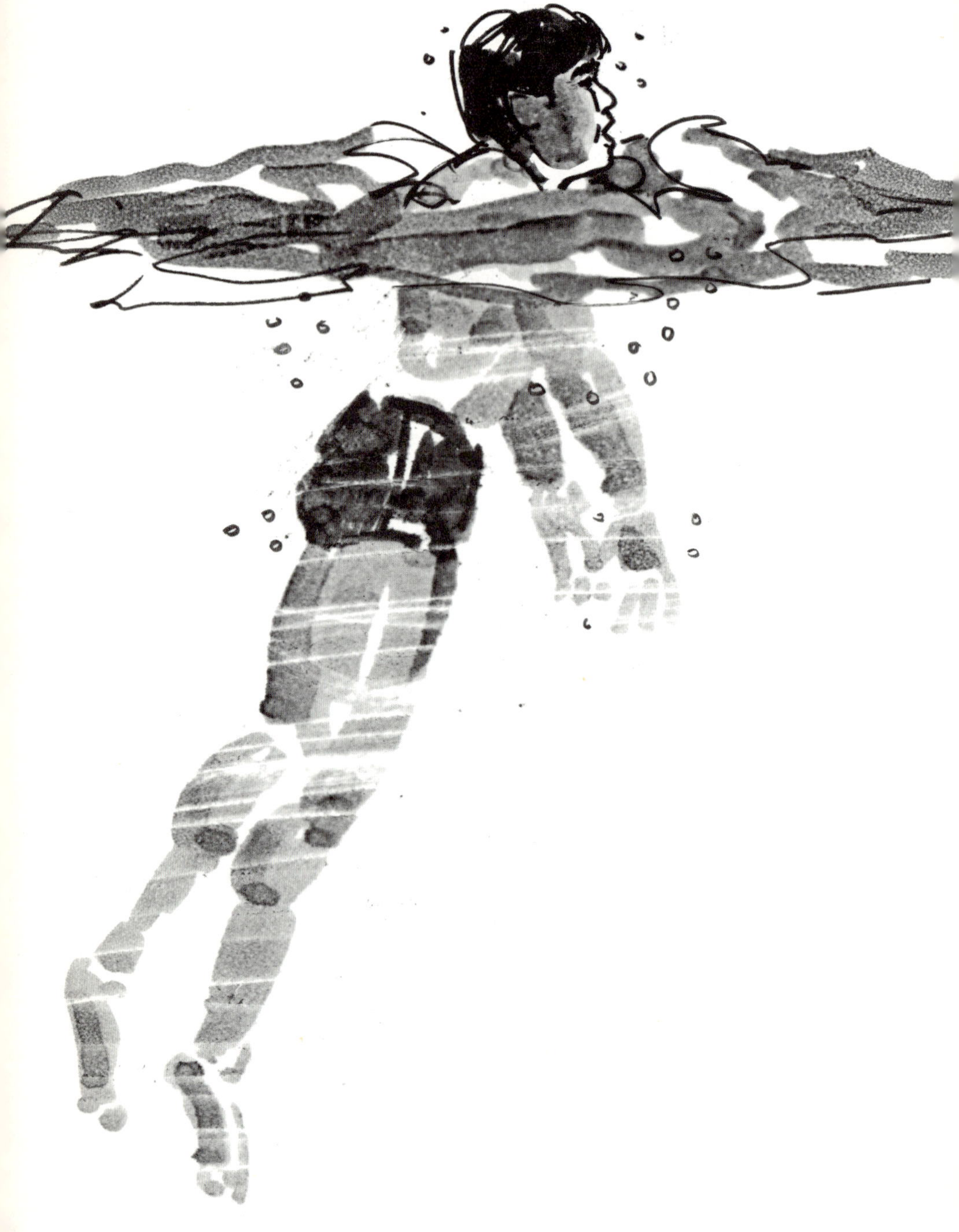

Swimming

The skilled swimmer has a whole exciting world of recreational aquatic endeavors that he can enjoy. Such related activities as boating, sailing, water skiing, skin and scuba diving, and surfing are very real attractions. It is important that the beginning swimmer have confidence in his instructor. The instructor builds this confidence by understanding the causes of fears, by never forcing a learner to attempt a skill unless he feels he is ready, and by always realizing that, until the adjustment process is complete, the fear is very real.

THE BEGINNING SWIMMER

For those unable to swim at all, and somewhat concerned about the water, swimming can be enjoyed by using artifical supports. It is advisable to have someone qualified work with you during this stage of development.

There are many very excellent artificial aids available for use in learning how to swim: zippered swimming vests of foam rubber with plastic covering, deflatable swim eggs, swim fins, and kick boards. All of these pieces of equipment enable the beginner to progress into deeper water on his own, while learning swimming skills. The artificial aids help in developing confidence faster and in enabling a quicker adjustment to the water.

CONFIDENCE AND ADJUSTMENT SKILLS

Climate, air and water temperature, body structure, and degree of skill determine your comfort on entering the water. Enter the water slowly and splash water on your torso, arms, and face to adjust your

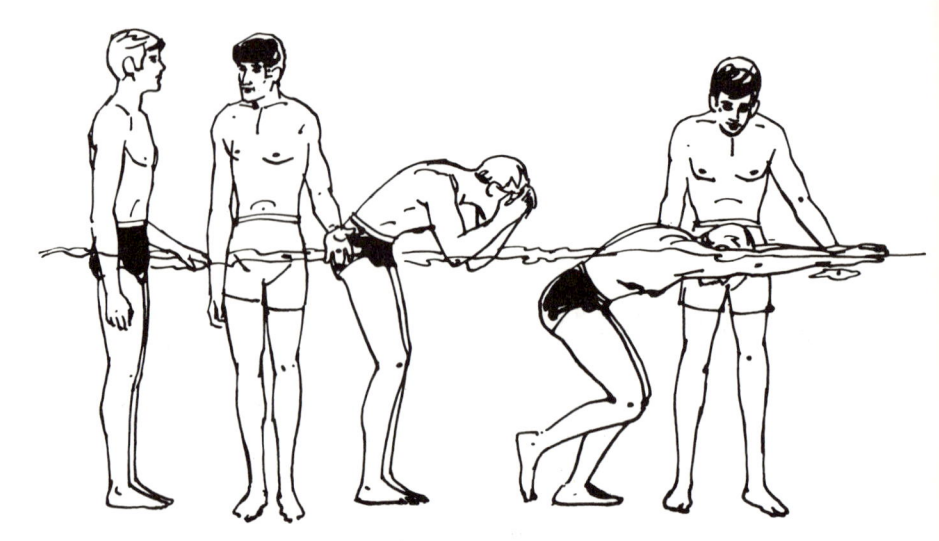

Adjusting to Water

body gradually to the change in temperature. You can reduce heat loss by executing a series of exercises before going into the water.

To accustom yourself to the upward force of buoyancy, wade into the water until it is waist-high. Move slowly up and down. If the water is not too deep, play games such as tag, keep-away, and simple relay races. Running in waist-deep water will help you to feel at home more easily. Let your arms help pull you through the water and use your feet and toes to push off the bottom. Learn to feel at home in the water.

BREATHING AND BUOYANCY

The secret of successful swimming is relaxation. One of the factors in learning how to swim is proper breath control. To be able to get a sufficient amount of air at regular intervals as well as to close the air passage so that no water enters the nose and mouth is a key to successful swimming.

The general rule for breathing, in swimming, is that air is inhaled through the mouth and exhaled through the nose and mouth. The timing for this cycle, inhalation-exhalation, depends upon the desired movement. The pattern of the breathing cycle is rhythmic and must be coordinated to the rhythm, speed, and purpose of the stroke or skill you plan to execute. You can begin the learning process at home.

SWIMMING

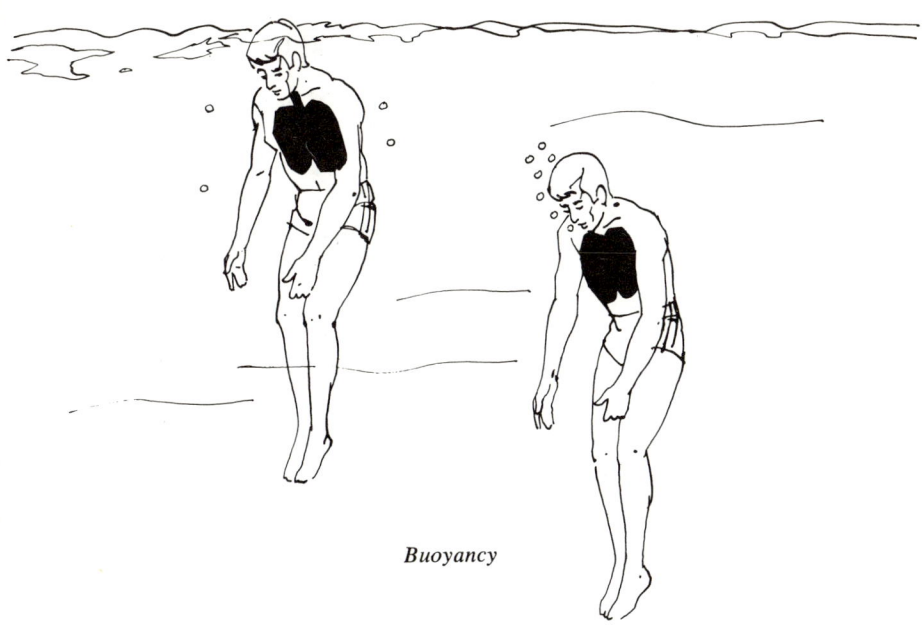

Buoyancy

Next time you take a shower or bath allow the water to run over your face. Keep your mouth closed and exhale through your nose. Try the same thing again, but this time exhale through both your nose and mouth. After you can do this easily, add rhythmic breathing. Move your face from the direct flow of the water and inhale through your mouth; then without hesitating put your face back under the water and exhale through your nose and mouth. Continue to do this until you develop a definite rhythm.

Now in the water. Stand in chest-deep water, take a breath through your mouth, bend forward, put your face in the water, and hold your breath. Practice this until you can keep your face under the water for at least 10 seconds. Now try exhaling below the surface through your nose, by blowing your nose or humming. Don't stop exhalation until your face returns to the surface again. When your face does break the surface, take a quick breath of air through your mouth, start exhaling through your nose, and let your face return to the water. Practice until you can do this continuously for at least one minute.

BOBBING

You can learn breath control faster by practicing bobbing. This is performed by starting at the wall in water slightly over your head.

Vertical Floating

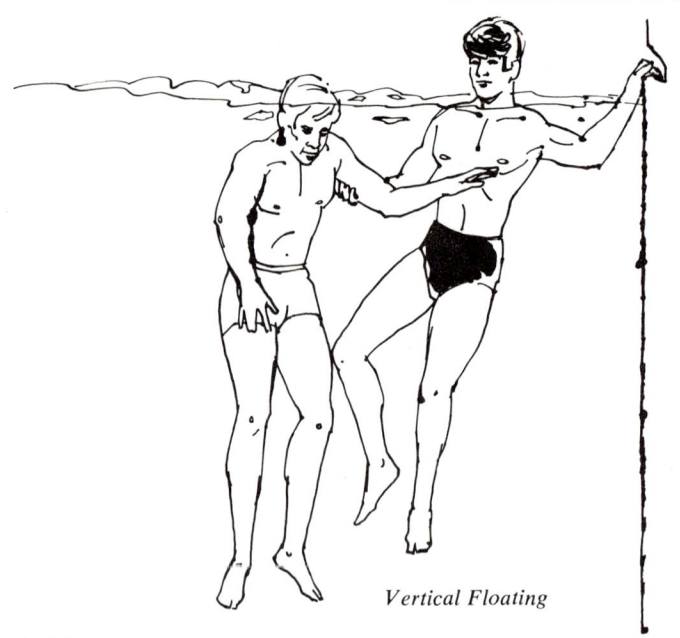

While holding on to the side of the pool, move your body so that your head alternates above and below the surface in a fixed rhythm. Take a breath of air through your mouth each time your face breaks the surface. Exhale through your nose as long as your face is in the water.

FLOATING

This skill is primarily a personal safety skill. Many times in an emergency it is more important to remain at approximately the same position on the surface rather than to swim far or fast. The mastery of this skill could very easily mean the difference between life and death.

Test your natural buoyancy by taking a deep breath of air and assuming a position in the water with your face submerged and the rest of your body hanging in a vertical or angular position. If some part of your head remains close to the surface, you have positive buoyancy and should be able to float.

THE BREATHING CYCLE

In the rest position your face is submerged, with the top of your head above the surface of the water. Slowly raise your face, exhaling the while. Avoid exhaling until your face is starting to break the surface

Breathing Cycle

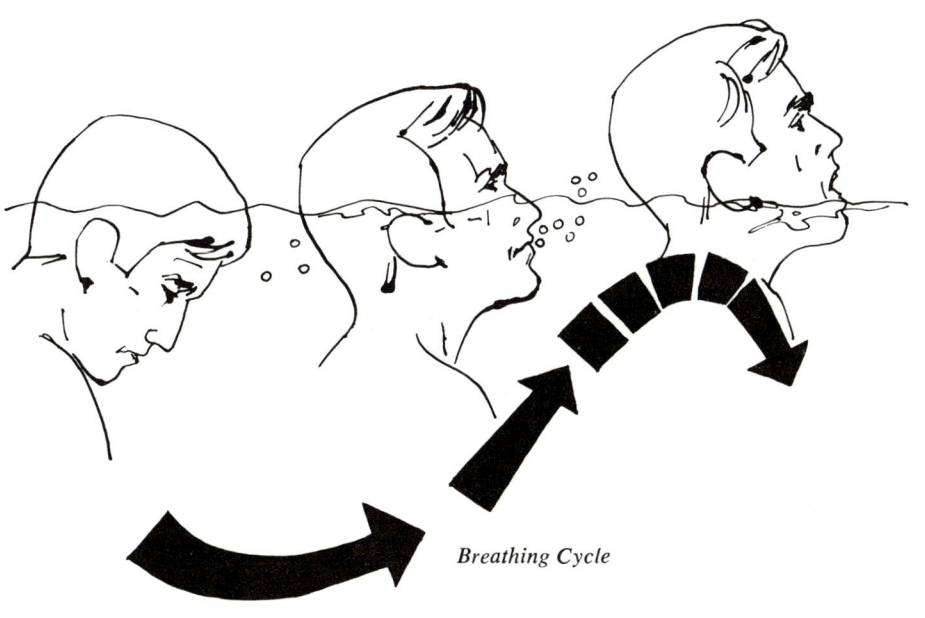

or your body may sink below the surface. Raise your face only high enough to inhale through your mouth. Again submerge your face and repeat the cycle.

BASIC ARM ACTION

At the beginning of the first phase, the arms and legs are motionless. The body is supported by its natural buoyancy. In the second phase, the arms are raised to a point where they extend straight out from the shoulders. In the third position, slowly press downward. This should not be done in too vigorous a fashion or the body will rise too high out of the water. Lower your hands no further than your waist. In the fourth phase, your head rises above the surface and air is exhaled. As your head breaks surface, the exhalation is completed and fresh air is inhaled. Note that the body is still in the vertical position.

BASIC LEG ACTION

This basic action is also known as the scissors kick. One leg is raised upward, while the other leg is brought downward. Spread your feet as far apart as possible. From this position, bring your feet back together again. In this action, water is pushed down by the back of one leg and the front of the other. As a result, your body will be pushed to

Basic Arm Action

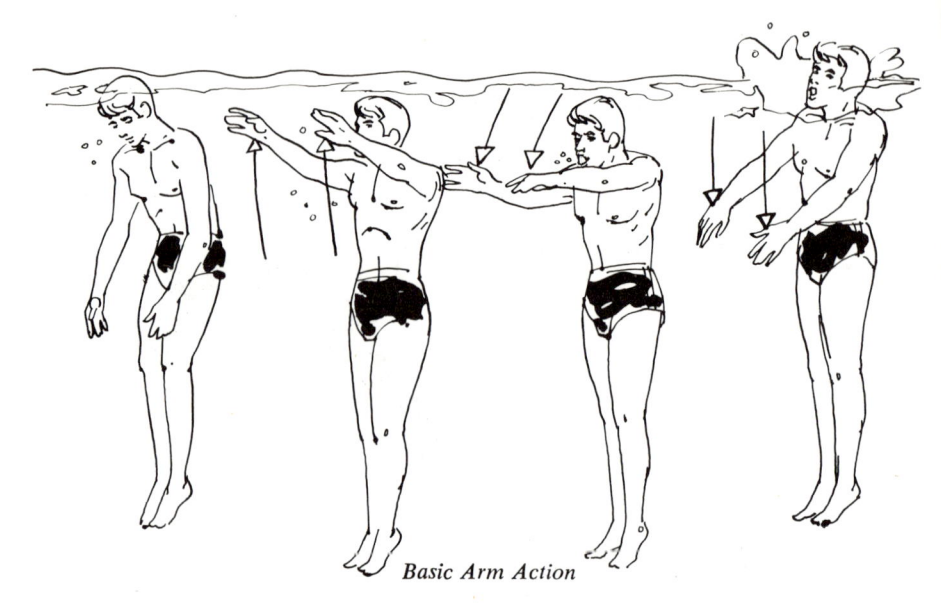

the surface. Exhale through your nose as your face breaks the surface. Inhale immediately through your mouth when your head clears the surface. Close your mouth immediately so that water from your hair does not enter your mouth. It is important that the leg kick not be so vigorous that the head rises too far out of the water.

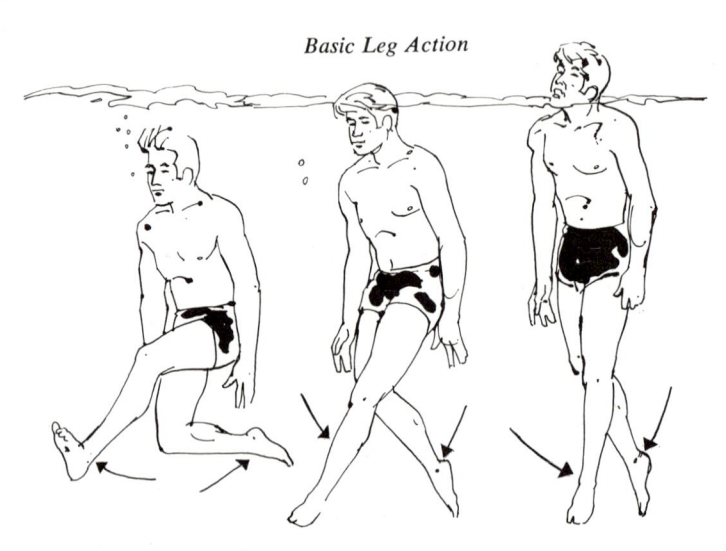

Basic Leg Action

SWIMMING 255

Coordinated Stroke

COORDINATED STROKE ACTION

The arm and leg actions are combined by raising your arms at the same time that you spread your feet apart. In the next phase, you lower your arms while you pull your feet back together. These simultaneous movements result in the head's rising above the surface of the water.

TRAVEL STROKE

This is one of the most practical strokes to use in any type of situation. It is especially good in rough, choppy water.

Position 1. The swimmer has just completed his inhalation and is about to sink back into the water.

Position 2. He has submerged and is starting to recover his arms and legs and to bend his trunk forward.

Position 3. His arms and legs have completed the recovery. His arms are extended forward, and his legs are in position to begin the power phase of the scissors kick. The trunk is bent forward at the waist.

Position 4. The legs have completed the scissors kick. The arms are about to be pulled through their range of movement. The leg action precedes the arm action.

Position 5. The legs are straight and held together. The arms are pulled slightly sideward and then downward. The pull ends with the hands alongside of the thighs. This is as long a pull as is possible.

Position 6. The hands have completed the pull, and the body is now in the glide position. This position, with the legs held straight and together and the hands at the side, should be held as long as possible. This is a very restful position.

Travel Stroke (cont.)

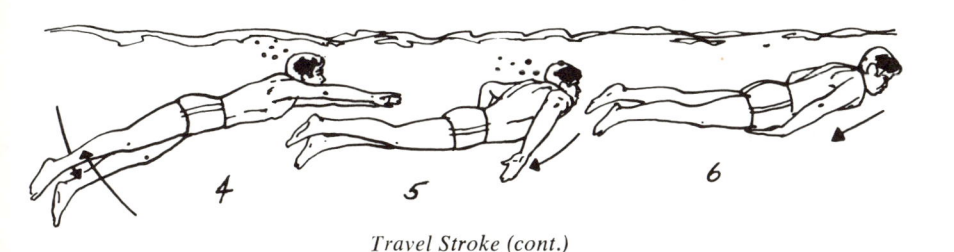

Position 7. The arms and legs are being recovered at the same time so that they will be in position for the power strokes.

Position 8. The legs are pulled together and the arms pulled downward. This action forces the head above the surface to facilitate breathing.

Position 9. The head breaks the surface and a breath is taken.

ENTRIES

There are, for the most part, four types of entries into the water from the side of a pool, dock, or boat. These include the compact, stride, roll, and plunge entries.

Compact

The compact, or streamlined, is a feet-first entry. It allows the swimmer to enter the water rapidly with little likelihood of injury to his head. This is especially important if the water is murky or the area unknown. Care should be taken to clear the edge of the pool by leaning forward slightly. The swimmer should exhale lightly through his nose during the entry to prevent water from rushing up his nose.

Travel Stroke (cont.)

Stride or Lifesaving Entry

This entry is especially important to the life saver, since it enables him to observe something or someone. A position is assumed at the edge of the pool with the toes of one foot curved over the edge of the pool, the arms raised sideways about shoulder height, and the body bent forward slightly. The eyes are fixed on something across the pool. When ready, a stride is executed with the rear leg, while pushing off on the foot that was on the curbing. The body enters the water with the arms outstretched and the legs in a scissors position. After hitting the water, the arms are forced downward against the water and the legs are drawn together vigorously in order to keep the head above the surface.

Roll Entry

Take a position at the edge of the pool with one or both feet hooked over the edge of the pool and your body in a tucked position. Roll forward toward the water making a 360° forward turn. The key to successfully executing this forward roll is to keep the feet in contact with the wall as long as you can, rather than pushing off as the movement is begun. This type of entry is very good for learning to dive from the edge of the pool.

SWIMMING

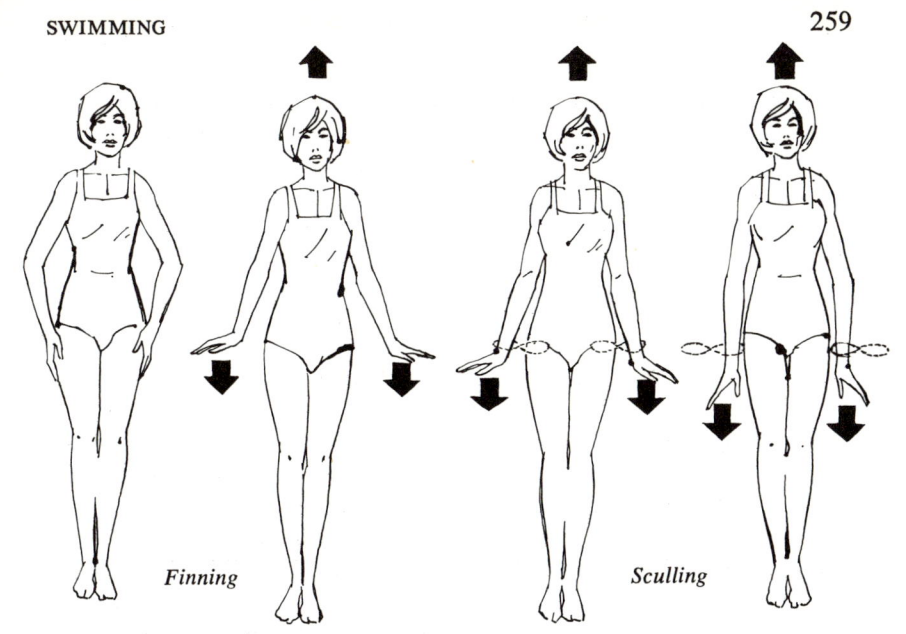

Finning　　　　　*Sculling*

Plunge Entry

The toes of both feet are hooked over the edge of the pool; the ankles, knees, hips, and trunk are flexed. The trunk is bent forward so that the back is parallel to the surface of the water. The eyes should be fixed on a point directly across the pool. When ready to dive, the arms are swung forward in an arc overhead. As the body moves forward toward the water with the trunk slightly flexed, the legs start to extend. If timed properly, the body will glide through the water about a foot below the surface, gradually moving toward the surface at the end of the glide.

FINNING AND SCULLING

Finning is usually thought of as a lead into sculling, which is slightly more complex than finning. Finning involves the use of the arms to move the swimmer head first. The starting position is on the back with the arms extended alongside the body. The hands are pulled upward slightly alongside the body, then the elbows are extended, straightening out the arms. In this maneuver the palms of the hands push against the water, thereby propelling the body head first through the water.

Sculling is not only valuable as a safety skill to propel yourself with minimum effort, but it is also very important in synchronized swimming, an advanced aquatic skill.

By executing a Figure 8 movement with your hands you can propel your body in whatever direction desired. The body is maintained in a back glide position with the arms alongside the body. The wrists are hyperextended to enable the palms of the hands to push water in the direction of the feet in a continuous motion. There is no stopping and recovering as in finning.

SUSTAINED SWIMMING

Not only will distance swimming prove to be a good body builder, but it will also serve you in good stead in the event you are forced to swim a long distance. There are a number of basic strokes that can be used in fairly calm water, such as the elementary backstroke, breaststroke, and side stroke. The elementary backstroke is probably the easiest to learn and the least tiring—as long as the water is calm. However, in water that is somewhat choppy none of the strokes just mentioned would be very practical because of problems of breath control. The most practical stroke to use in this type of situation is the travel stroke.

ELEMENTARY BACKSTROKE

As a resting stroke the elementary backstroke can be used to ward off extreme fatigue while providing slow but sustained progress.

There are three basic parts to the elementary backstroke:

Phase 1—Recovery. Start from a position on your back with your arms alongside your body and your legs together. Pull your arms up so that they extend straight out from the shoulders, with the palms of your hands facing downward. At the same time, bring your feet up on the side by spreading your legs and bending your knees. Do this phase slowly and inhale.

Phase 2—Propulsion. Before the pull-kick phase begins, the hands must be moved into position to effectively push against the water. This can be done by turning the palms of the hands so they are pointing in the direction of the feet. To execute this stroke, pull your arms and your feet down vigorously. The force that you exert to do so will propel your body head first through the water.

Phase 3—Glide. As soon as the propulsive phase has been completed, the glide begins with the feet together and the hands near the body. This position is held for two or more seconds or until there is no forward movement. Exhale during the latter part of this phase.

SWIMMING

Elementary Backstroke

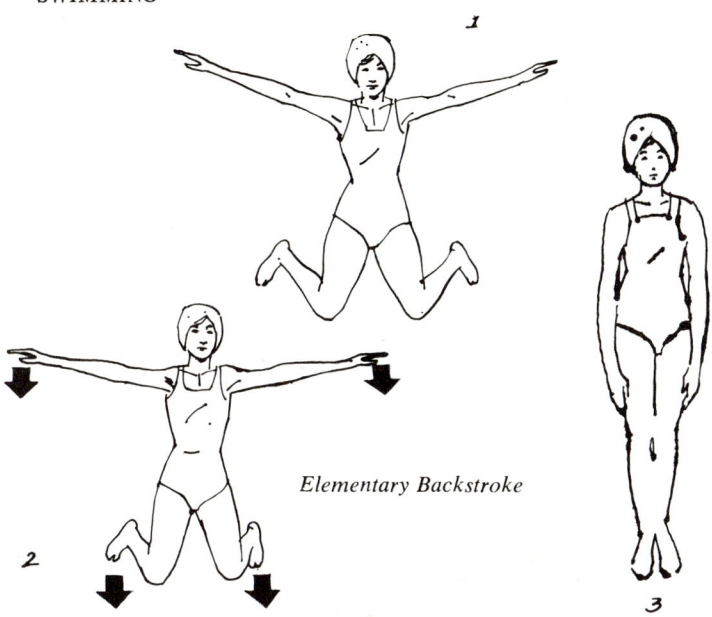

BREASTSTROKE

Another of the basic resting strokes is the breaststroke. It qualifies as a resting stroke because there is no recovery or propulsive movement during the glide phase.

Phase 1. The swimmer is in a prone position in the water with his legs stretched out and together. His head is almost completely submerged, and his face is looking slightly forward. His arms are extended in front of him, with the palms facing outward slightly.

Phase 2. The hand catch is made at a depth of about 6 inches. The hands begin to pull sidewards. At this point the swimmer begins to exhale through his nose and mouth.

Phase 3. The arms continue to pull out to the sides. Exhalation continues.

Phase 4. The elbows start to bend, and the upper arms rotate inward. The swimmer's head starts upward slightly to take a breath.

Phase 5. The arms have reached their maximum spread, with the elbows bent so that the hands move downward slightly. The high elbow position is evident at this point.

Phase 6. The head continues to rise, and the mouth rises above the surface. The hands start the inward sweep, finishing the last effective propulsive part of their action.

Breaststroke

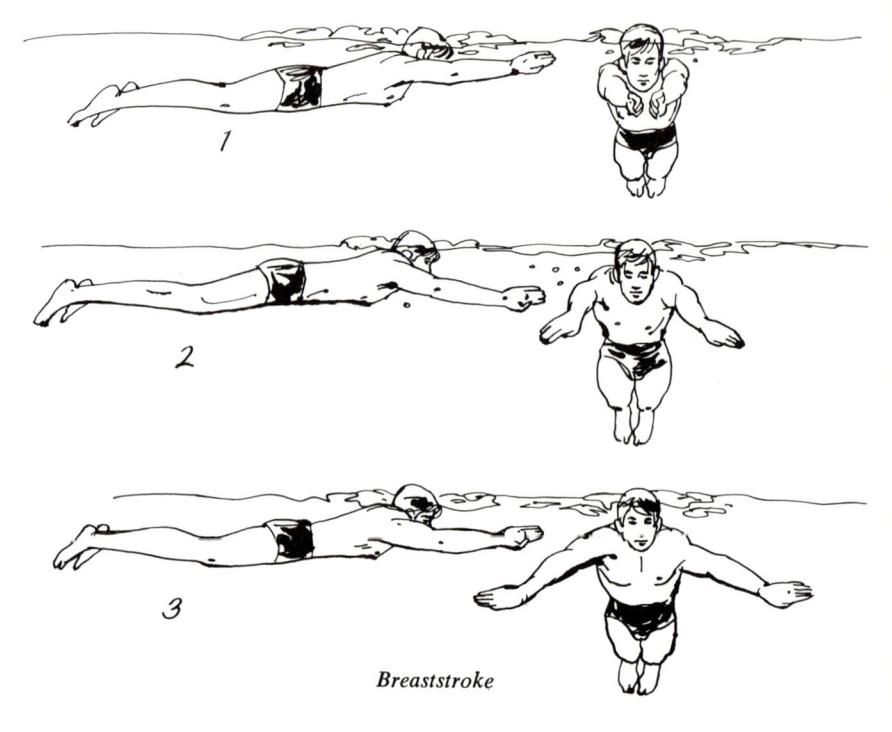

Phase 7. The swimmer inhales as the arms prepare to push forward. The elbows are not pulled into the ribs, as most swimmers tend to do. The knees start to bend, and the leg recovery is started.

Phase 8. The swimmer closes his mouth. His hands start to move forward as the leg recovery continues.

Phase 9. The face is lowered in the water. The feet are brought upwards toward the buttocks, as the arms continue to move forward.

Phase 10. The head continues to be tilted downward. The ankles are flexed as the backward thrust of the legs begins and the arms near completion of their recovery.

Phase 11. The swimmer starts to straighten out his legs. The breath is still being held.

Phase 12. The arms are now fully extended, with the hands slightly lower than shoulder level. The legs have nearly completed the kick.

Phase 13. The swimmer completes his kick and concentrates on getting his body into a straight horizontal alignment. He will hold this glide position for a split second and then, when he feels himself slowing down, will begin the stroke cycle again.

SWIMMING 263

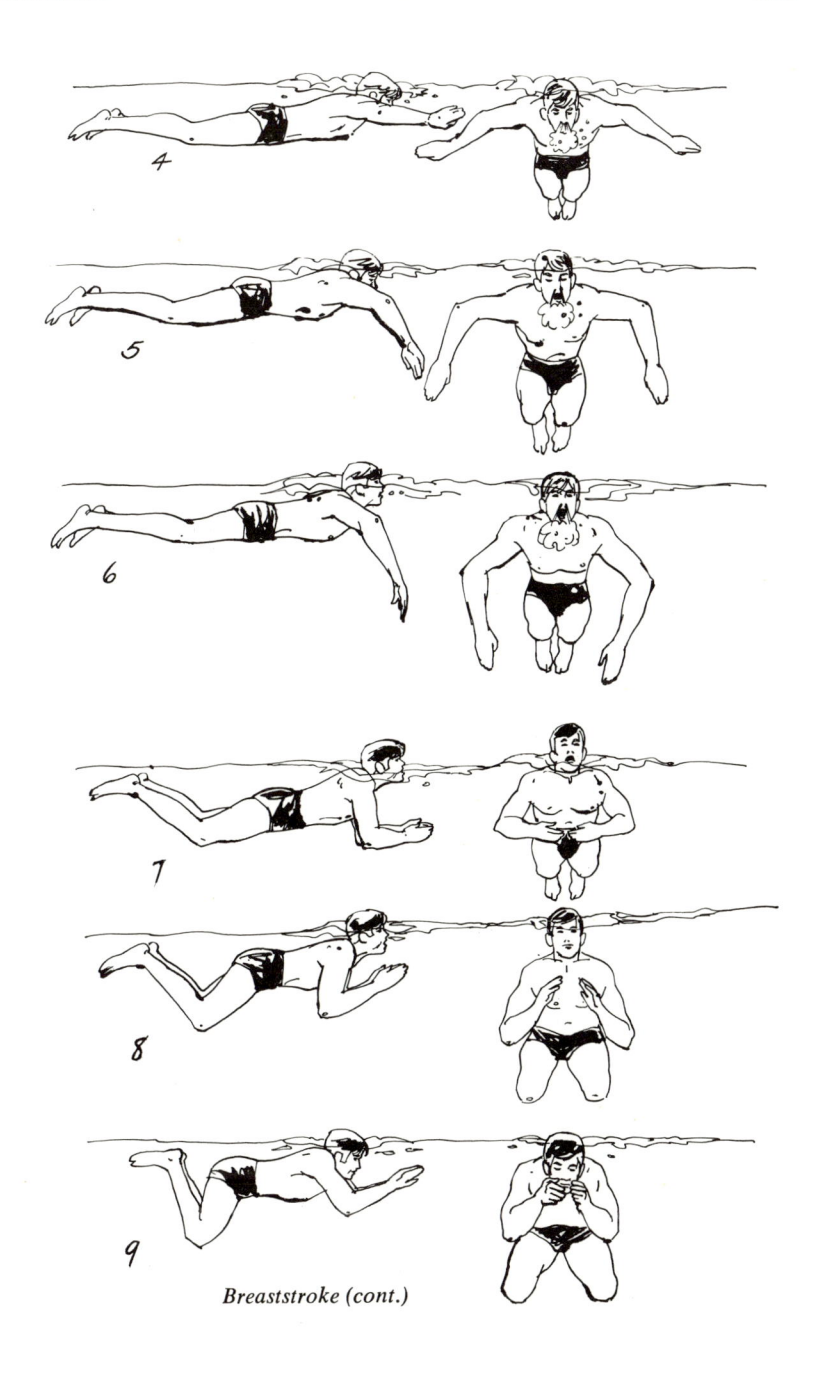

Breaststroke (cont.)

Breaststroke (cont.)

SIDE STROKE

You can practice the leg movement while lying on a bed, bench, or on the ground. Lie on your right side. (Stroke for the right side is described. Reverse directions if you prefer your left side.) Support your head with your right hand, elbow on the ground. Start with your legs straight and feet together. Slowly draw your knees upward toward your hips. When they have been drawn up as far as comfortable, and without stopping, extend your left leg forward and move your right leg back. As a continuation of the previous movement, and without stopping, snap your legs together. Rest momentarily when your legs are together. Continue until you develop a pattern of movement. This is the regular scissors kick.

To practice the arm movements lie on your side in the same position as for kicking. Rest your head on your right arm. Keep your left arm on your left hip. To start the stroke, move your right arm along the deck until it comes to rest in front of your right hip. Keeping your right hand in that position, move your left hand by bending it at the elbow forward and upward toward your left shoulder. Once the recovery has been completed, return both arms to their starting position to complete the stroke.

When actually performing the side stroke in the water, remember to keep your hands under water at all times; to maintain a long glide position; to recover your hands in a feathered position; and to keep both of your ears under water and your face above the surface throughout the stroke.

Phase 1—Propulsive action of right arm. The right arm pulls through the water 6 to 12 inches below the surface. It should not be pulled downward lest the swimmer bounce or ride up in the water.

Phase 2—Recovery of the top arm and legs. The left arm is recovered close to the chest to a point opposite the right shoulder, with the hand feathered, thumb side up. The hand is turned downward at the start. At the same time, the legs are recovered by moving them into a stride position with both knees bent. Inhale through the mouth at this time.

Phase 3—Propulsive action of legs and top arm and recovery of right or bottom arm. The knee of the top leg is extended at the start of the propulsive action. The right knee starts to flex at this time. These movements continue in the same plane until the feet are together. You should be able to feel the pressure of the water on the bottom of your

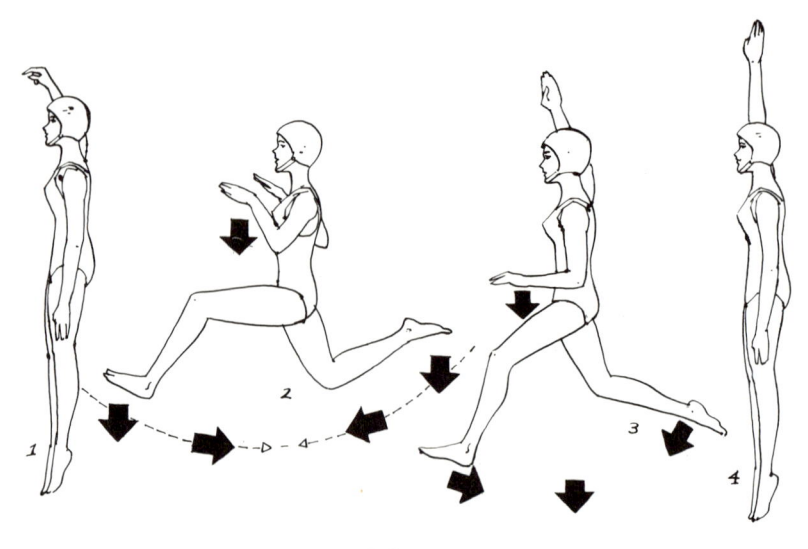

Side Stroke

left foot and the top of your right foot. As the kick is being completed, the left arm is pulled through a vertical arc close to the chest. The right arm is recovered by bending at the elbow slightly. The hand is feathered, and the arm moves to its starting position. Exhalation through the nose starts at this point.

Phase 4—Glide. As soon as the kick has been completed, the bottom arm has returned to its starting position over head, and the top hand is resting on the hip, the glide begins. This position should be held for at least two full seconds. Exhalation should continue during this final phase.

BACKSTROKE

Arm Pull

This stroke is started in a near horizontal, back-glide position. Extend both arms over your head, and then push off the wall, at which time the stroke is ready to begin. Either hand may be pulled through the water to start the stroke. The catch is made directly in line with the shoulders about 10 inches below the surface with a straight but not rigid arm. Just after the catch, the hand is put into position to push water backwards. The hand describes an "S" figure. This motion can best be accomplished with a natural, normal rolling of the shoulders.

This shoulder roll will do three things: (1) cause the shoulder on the pulling arm side to be raised so as not to catch water, (2) enable the opposite arm to move into a better position for a stronger pull, and (3) enable the elbow to more effectively push water. The angle between the pulling arm and shoulder can be decreased, thus strengthening the pull.

Kick

The flutter kick on the back is quite similar to the flutter kick on the front. The flutter kick should be thought of more as a stabilizer than as a means of propulsion. The up kick should be stressed, since this phase produces the major propulsive force.

The kick is executed while the hands move from the sides of the legs to an overhead position. Be especially careful that the knees do not break the surface on the up kick. A depth of approximately 12 to 14 inches is adequate. The knees and ankles are relaxed when kicking. On the downward kick the knee and hip are extended and the ankle flexed. On the up kick the knee and hip are flexed and the ankle extended. Every effort should be made to avoid overkicking, which will lead to fatigue and cramps in the feet and calves of the leg. No effort should be made to time the leg kick with the arms, but the legs should be permitted to move at will.

Breath Control

Full inspiration through the mouth should take place approximately once each complete arm cycle or once every two strokes.

Whole Stroke

The following drawings show the swimmer doing the bent arm back crawl stroke with a six beat kick. When trying to judge the depth of the arm pull, use the side view. The head-on view has greater distortion so far as the true position of the water surface is concerned.

1. The sequence begins as the left arm enters the water directly over the shoulder, with the little finger entering the water first. The right hand has finished its pull and is starting to move upward in its recovery.

2. The downward momentum developed by the left arm during the last half of the recovery phase causes the arm with the elbow still extended to sink downward into the water. The right hand has finished its pull and is starting to move upward in its recovery.

Back Crawl

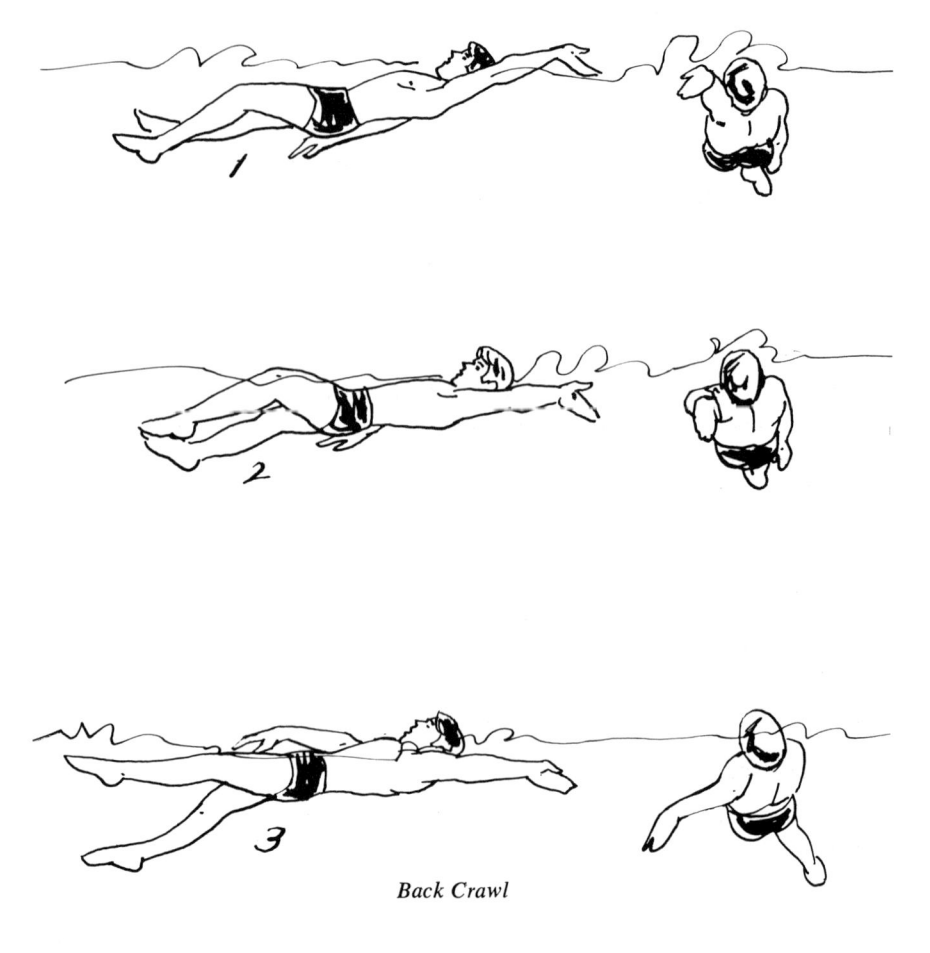

3. Muscular effort takes over control of the right arm as it is pulled downward. The right arm starts to break the surface, while the hand flexes at the wrist.

4. The left elbow begins to flex as the arm is pulled downward and sideward. The right leg which is at the bottom of its downbeat is ready to begin the upbeat at a slightly diagonal angle.

SWIMMING 269

Back Crawl (cont.)

5. The left arm pull continues as the flexion in the elbow is increased. The palm of the pulling hand faces almost directly backward. The right arm is recovered directly upward. The right leg starts to kick upward at a diagonal angle.

6. As the left hand passes by the shoulder, the elbow reaches maximum flexion of 90 degrees. The recovering arm starts to rotate, turning the palm outward away from the body.

Back Crawl (cont.)

7. The elbow of the pulling arm starts to extend as the hand goes past the shoulder. The recovering arm, directly over the shoulder, is rotated so that the palm of the hand faces directly outward. The swimmer closes his mouth to keep out the drops of water falling from his recovering arm. At this point in the stroke cycle, the body reaches its maximum roll of 40 to 45 degrees.

8. The left hand position is changed, bringing the palm of the hand closer to the body, and ready to begin its push almost directly downward. The recovering arm continues in its vertical path.

9. The left arm finishes its pull with the elbow completely extended and the hand palm down at a level of 3 to 6 inches below the hips. This downward push of the hand helps to elevate the right shoulder.

SWIMMING   271

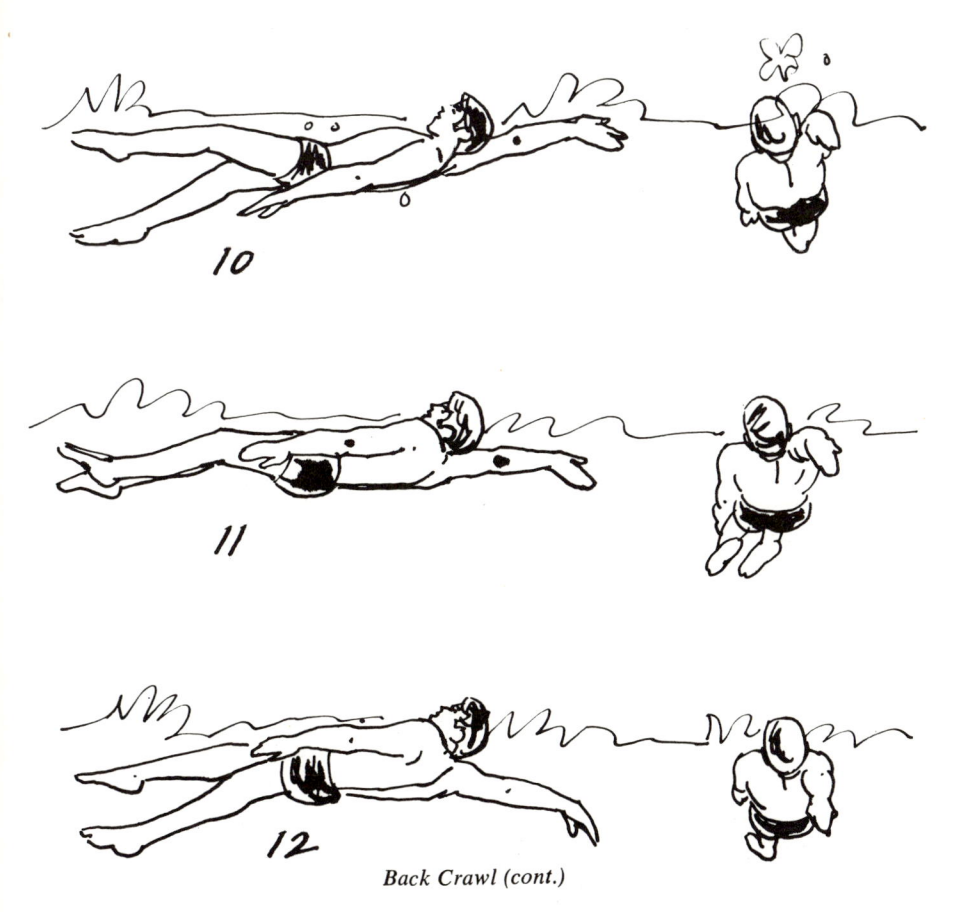

Back Crawl (cont.)

10. As the right hand enters the water, with the palm facing outward, the left arm starts its upward recovery. The swimmer pictured here is lifting his arm upward, with the palm facing downward. Many swimmers rotate this arm so that the palm of the hand faces inward toward the median line of the body. Both techniques are acceptable. At this point in the stroke neither hand is applying any propulsive force.

11. The left shoulder breaks the water prior to the out-of-water recovery of the left arm. The right hand sinks into the water, getting ready for its catch.

12. The catch of the right hand is made with a straight elbow as the left hand starts its out-of-water recovery. The left leg is kicked diagonally downward. Once again, the upbeat of the leg on the opposite side coincides with the final lift of the arm from the water.

Back Crawl (cont.)

13. The bend of the right arm becomes apparent as the arm is depressed sideward.

14. The right hand directly opposite the shoulder is applying its force directly backward. The left shoulder is lifted up and over the water, due primarily to the roll of the body.

15. The pulling arm has completed half of its pulling action. From this point on the hand will come in toward the body, tending to pull the hips in the opposite direction and destroy lateral body alignment.

Back Crawl (cont.)

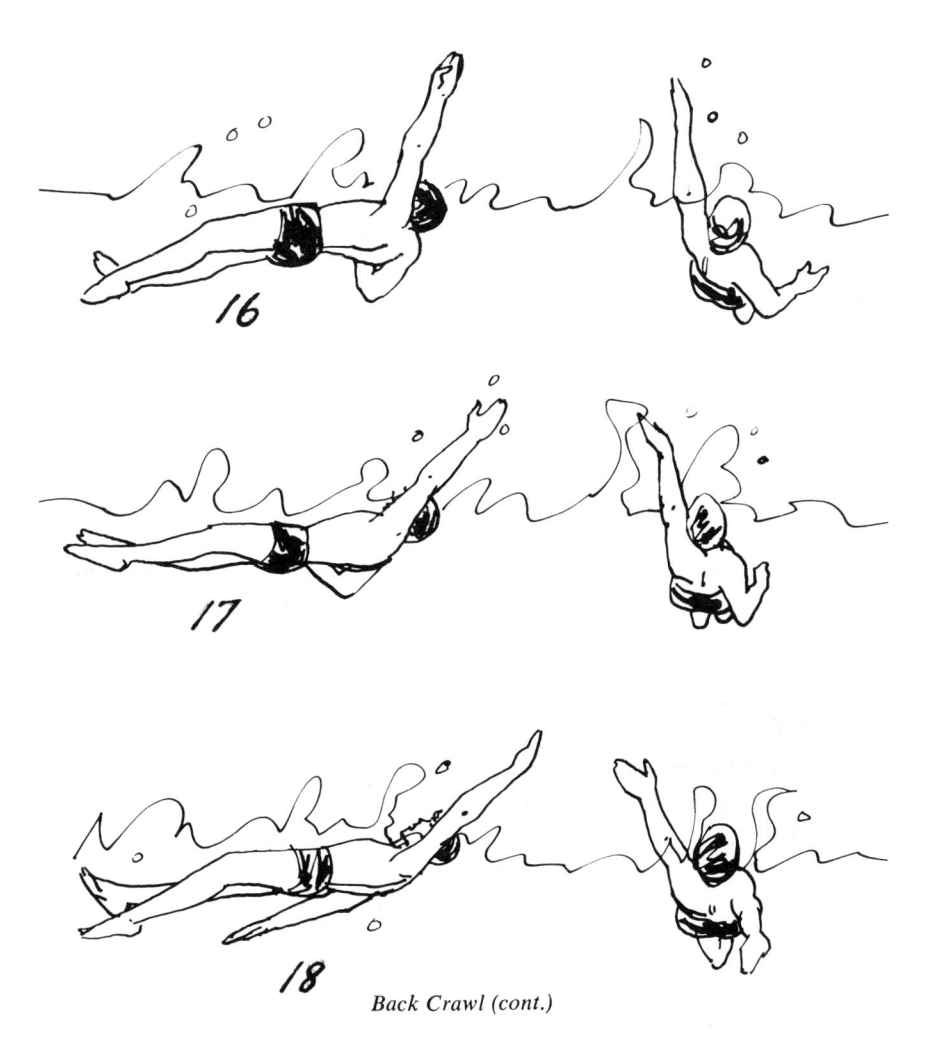

This action can be cancelled by the diagonal and upward thrust of the left leg.

16. As the right arm starts its downward thrust, the left leg continues to thrust diagonally upward.

17. The left hand, palm outward, continues its recovery action, as the right hand pushes back and downward.

18. The right arm finishes its pull, while the left hand has almost finished its recovery. The full stroke cycle is now complete.

BUTTERFLY STROKE

Body Position

There is a greater up and down movement in the butterfly stroke because the action of the down kick of the legs forces the hips up; the inertia of the recovering arms swinging causes the body to sink; and the start of the pull tends to cause the head and shoulders to rise. It is important that this movement not be inhibited if the stroke is to be performed properly.

Dolphin Kick

To start the dolphin kick, the knees must be somewhat relaxed on the down kick, bending to about a 45-degree angle. The hips start the movement downward. When the feet are snapped downwards to complete the down kick, they will cause the hips to rise. On the up kick, the feet move toward the surface with the knees straight and the ankles relaxed. This causes the hips to drop. The swimmer should make every effort to think about kicking downward rather than pushing backwards since the backward motion of the feet will tend to result in a pumping action or negative kick.

Arm Pull

The arms pull obliquely downwards and outward with the hands cupped. The arm rotators (medially) should come into play during this part of the pull to get the hand in a better position to push water backwards. This medial rotation will cause a higher elbow position while swimming, which is desirable. Dropped elbows cause the swimmer to push more water downward with his hands, which in turn causes the swimmer to move upwards. This should be avoided.

After the hands and arms press outward, they begin to come together until the hands almost touch under the body. The hand action is similar to that used in the crawl stroke.

Arm Recovery

The arm recovery begins with a slight elbow bend and, as the hands leave the water, the arms begin a swimming motion sidewards and forwards close to the surface and enter the water angled downward about shoulder level. It should be remembered that the head must enter the water *before* the hands enter in order to allow for the proper movement to occur.

SWIMMING

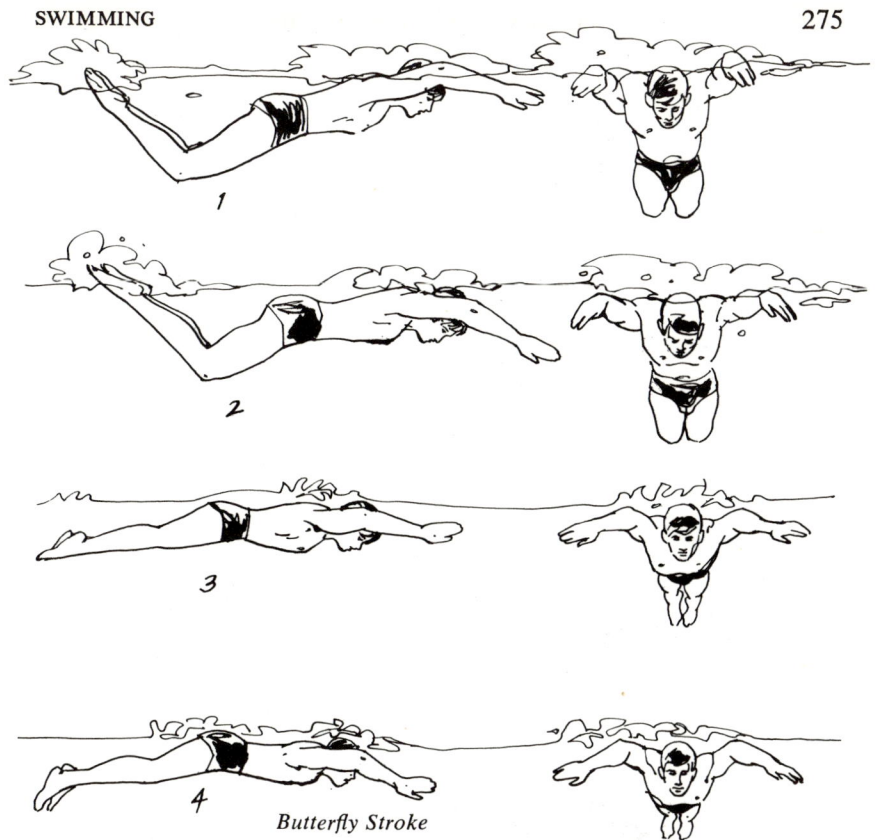

Butterfly Stroke

Sequence

1. The stroke cycle begins as the arms enter the water a shoulder-width apart. The legs, with the ankles extended, are ready to begin the downbeat of the kick. The head is not facing directly toward the bottom of the pool, but is tilted slightly forward.

2. As the momentum of the arms, developed during the recovery, causes the hands to sink downward, muscular effort is also applied to direct the pull diagonally outward. The downward thrust of the feet has begun.

3. The pull continues as the kick is almost completed. The reaction of the downbeat of the kick has caused the hips to come up to the surface.

4. The ankles flex as the legs begin the up kick. During the first part of the pull, even when the swimmer does not take a breath, he lifts his head as though he were looking forward. This action occurs naturally.

Butterfly Stroke (cont.)

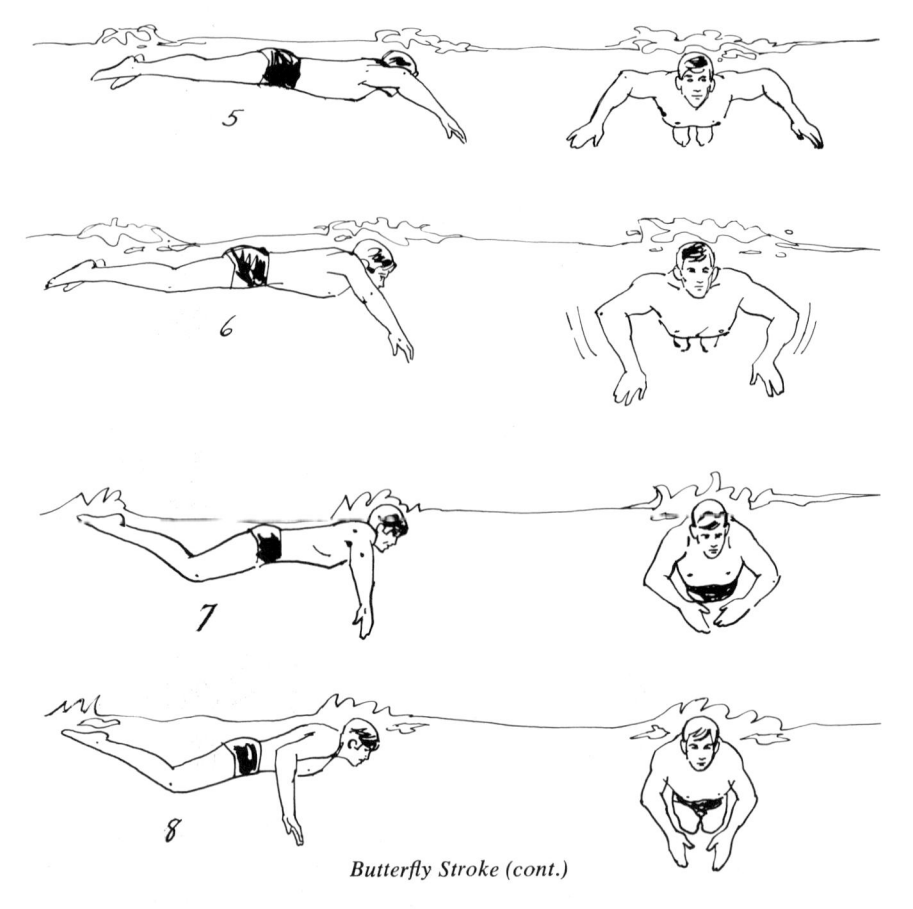

5. The arms (now at the maximum spread) are pulled down and backward in the elbow-up position. The legs have completed the first leg kick and are positioning themselves to begin the second beat.

6. The arms start to come closer together. The line of air bubbles indicates the general pattern of pull.

7. The hands come close to touching one another as they pass directly under the shoulders. The elbows bend—still held out away from the body at approximately a 90-degree angle.

8. The elbows are brought closer to the body as the hands pass under the shoulders. There is a downward thrust of the legs as the hands start upward during the last part of the pull. At this point the swimmer begins to flex his neck and to drop his head slightly.

SWIMMING

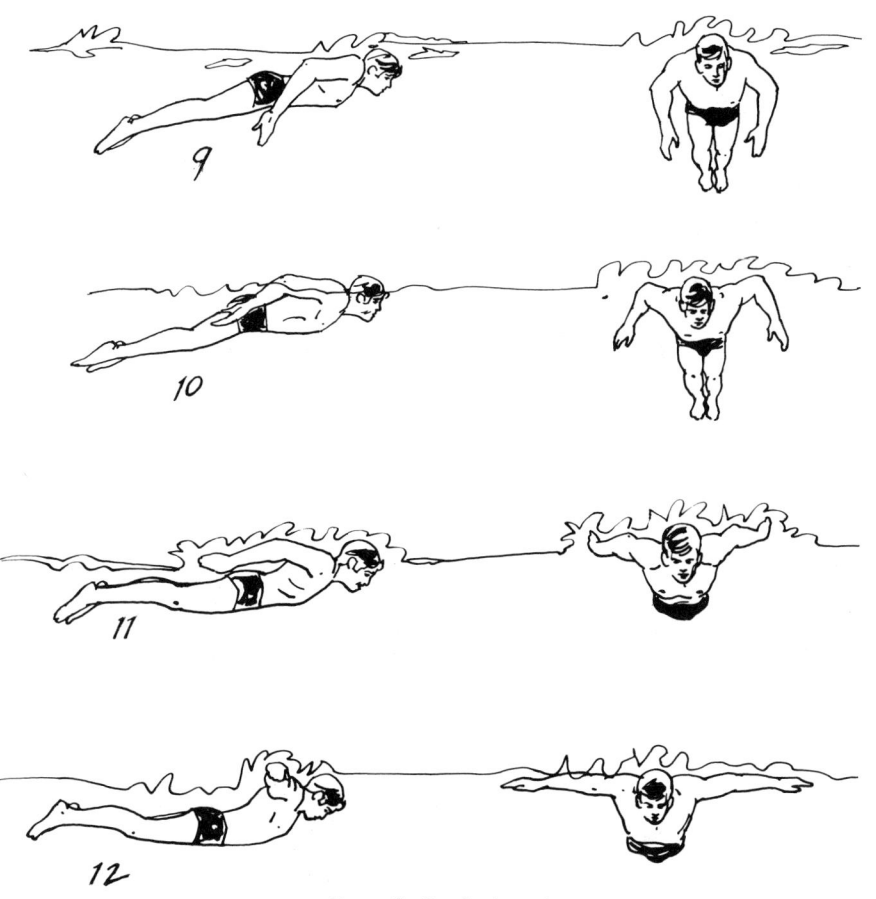

Butterfly Stroke (cont.)

9. As the arms near the end of the pull, they start to swing outward to prepare for the recovery. The neck continues to flex.

10. The legs complete their down kick slightly before the hands leave the water. The purpose of the second kick is to keep the hips near the surface so the body is in a streamlined position.

11. As the arms leave the water and begin their recovery, the legs are brought upward without bending the knees. The head is lowered so the face is almost parallel with the bottom of the pool. This action of the head facilitates an easier arm recovery.

12. As the hands swing past the shoulders, the palms are facing downward. The elbows are completely extended. The ankles start to extend as they near the top of the up kick.

Butterfly Stroke (cont.)

13. The upper arms start to hit the water, as the hands prepare to enter.

14. The hands become submerged as the upper legs start their movement downward. Flexion of the knees is increased. The feet almost break the surface as they start their down kick.

15. The down kick nears completion during the first part of the pull. The swimmer, who has been holding his breath during the previous arm cycle, begins his exhalation upon the beginning of the arm pull. The rotation of the upper arms results in an elbow-up arm position.

16. The swimmer continues his exhalation as he lifts his head upward.

SWIMMING 279

Butterfly Stroke (cont.)

17. The exhalation continues as the pull changes direction sharply and the hands are brought closer together.

18. The head is lifted, primarily by hyper-extension of the neck, and the inhalation begins before the arms complete their pull. The downward kick again coincides with the finish of the arm pull.

19. As the arms start to recover, the inhalation is completed and the second down kick is also completed.

20. After the inhalation, the face is dropped back under water and the arms complete their recovery as the legs start upward.

CRAWL STROKE

Body Position

The body should remain in a streamlined position with the back unarched. The shoulders should roll when swimming; this will aid in the recovery of one arm and the follow-through of the opposite arm.

Head Position

The face stays in the water, with the waterline somewhere between the eyebrows and hair line. With the head in this position, it is possible to take a breath by turning the chin toward one shoulder, keeping the opposite ear in the water. If the head is carried too high, it causes undue fatigue. If the head is carried too low, there will be too much drag over the back of the neck and shoulders.

Breath Control

The swimmer turns his head to the side, and as his mouth breaks the surface, he exhales through his mouth and nose rapidly. He then inhales immediately through his mouth and moves his face back into the water. One breath should be taken for each complete arm cycle (two strokes). The head starts its turning movement on the breathing side when the stroke has passed its midpoint.

Arm Catch

The catch or entry of the hand into the water is made directly in front of the shoulder about 12 inches below the surface with a slightly bent elbow.

Hand Control

You should make every effort to control the direction that your hand is traveling through the water. Your arm has an advantage over an oar in that it can bend during the pull, while the oar cannot. If you let your elbow bend during the midstroke, it will be much easier to move your hand through the water, enabling you to do a more effective job with less effort. The bend at the elbow should be at least 90 degrees. During the pull, the arm should be rotated inward slightly in order to keep the elbow high on the recovery and to make for a more effective pull while moving through the water.

SWIMMING

Crawl Stroke

Complete Follow-Through

The hand should complete its stroking motion by emphasizing a "push through" during the last third of the stroke. This follow-through combined with a natural body roll will allow the arm to swing clear of the water more effectively. You should avoid stop and go motions. Every effort should be made to maintain smooth, even, continuous stroking motion. This will result in far less fatigue in the end.

This sequence of drawings shows the swimmer performing a conventional six-beat crawl stroke with a continuous arm action.

1. As the right hand enters the water above the shoulder with the palm facing downward, the pulling arm has accomplished half of its pull. Air is being exhaled from the mouth and nose in a steady trickle, indicating a rhythmical breathing pattern.

2. The downward momentum developed by the hand during the recovery causes the right hand to sink downward for its catch. The pulling arm continues its pull backward with the palm still facing backward.

3. The right hand continues to move downward slowly as the pulling hand starts to come back toward the center line of the body.

Crawl Stroke (cont.)

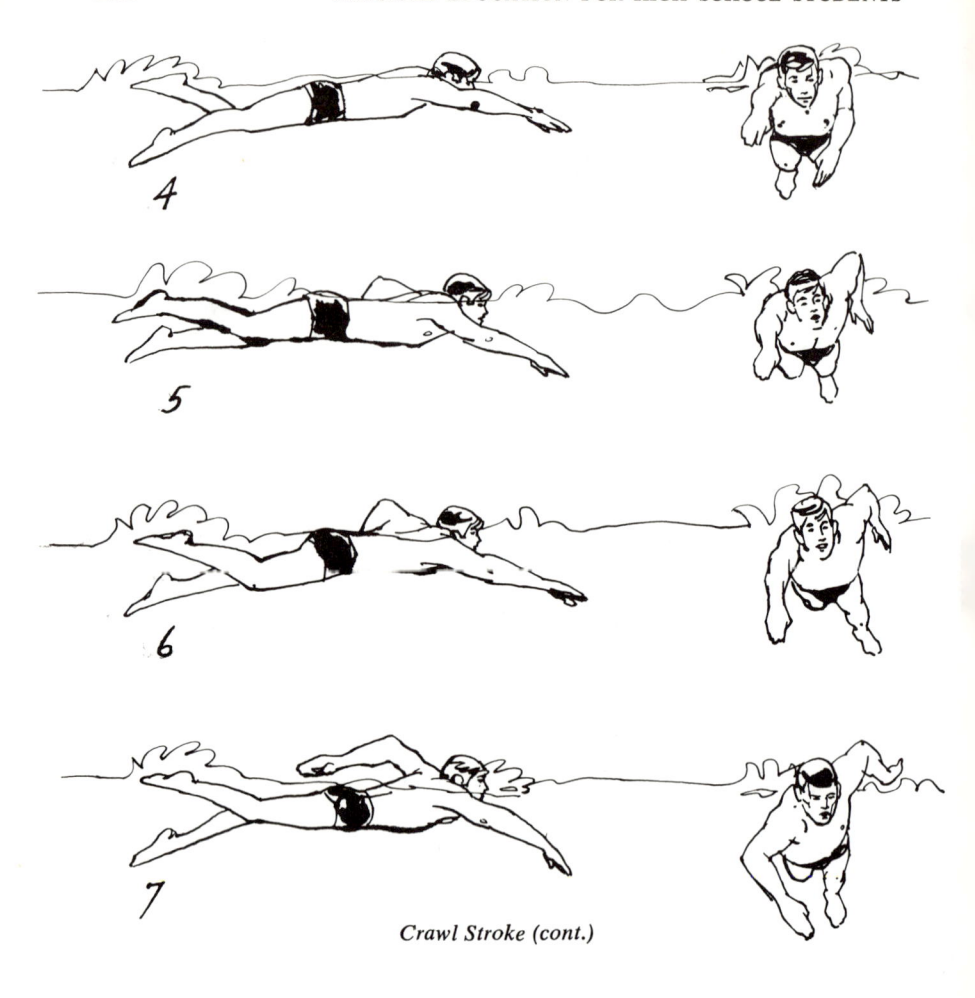

4. The arm depressor muscles now start to contract actively and depress the right arm downward.

5. The left arm has almost completed its pull and the swimmer is now applying force with both hands. The force of the right hand is not as yet directed backward sufficiently to contribute any forward propulsion to the body.

6. As the left arm finishes its pull, the left leg thrusts downward vigorously. This action cancels out the effect that the upward action of the arms has upon depressing the swimmer's hips.

7. As the right hand presses downward, the elbow starts to bend.

SWIMMING 283

Crawl Stroke (cont.)

8. The elbow-up position of both the recovery arm and the pulling arm is apparent.

9. The pulling hand has accomplished almost half of its pull and the head is getting ready to start rotating on the longitudinal axis. The amount of air being exhaled begins to increase slightly.

10. The pulling hand has accomplished half of its pull, and the head starts to rotate on its longitudinal axis. The amount of air being exhaled begins to increase still more.

11. The head continues to turn to the side as the chin appears to follow the action of the elbow as it goes backward. The pulling hand starts to round off and move back toward the center line of the body.

Crawl Stroke (cont.)

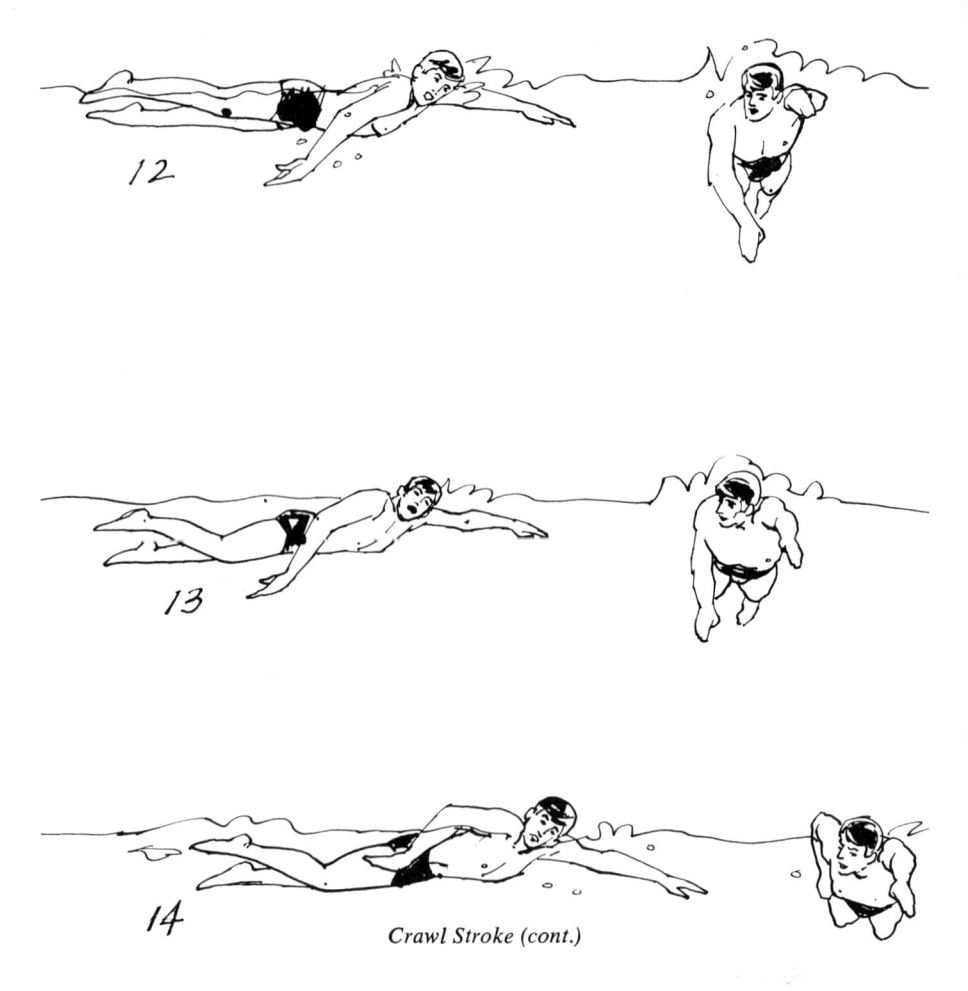

12. The swimmer's mouth is opened further as the volume of air exhaled is increased.

13. The pulling hand is no longer facing directly backward, but is held at an angle of about 45 degrees. The thumb-out position at this point is noticeable in many good swimmers; this is neither detrimental nor beneficial.

14. The downward thrust of the right leg starts as the right arm finishes its pull. The mouth finally breaks the surface of the water and the inhalation is about to begin.

SWIMMING 285

Crawl Stroke (cont.)

15. Immediately before the hand breaks the surface of the water, it is turned so the palm faces toward the body. The swimmer opens his eyes and starts his inhalation.

16. The downward thrust of the right leg ends as the swimmer starts his right arm forward. The inhalation is almost completed.

17. The head starts to rotate back toward the center line of the body as the recovering arm swings forward.

18. The swimmer starts to exhale as the face is almost submerged. The left arm is about to enter the water and complete the stroke cycle.

FOR MORE INFORMATION

American Association for Health, Physical Education, and Recreation, Division for Girls and Women's Sports. *Aquatics Guide.* Current edition. Washington, D.C.: the Association.

Arnold, Charles G. *Swimming and Survival Instruction.* Manual. Lexington, Va.: Virginia Military Institute, 1965.

Batterman, Charles. *The Techniques of Springboard Diving.* Cambridge, Mass.: MIT Press, 1969.

Campbell, William R. *Drown Prevention Techniques and Water Safety.* Instructors Guide. Washington, D.C.: Robert J. Brady Co., 1967.

Counsilman, James E. *The Science of Swimming.* Englewood Cliffs, N.J.: Prentice-Hall, 1968.

Harris, Marjorie M. *Basic Swimming Analyzed.* Boston, Mass.: Allyn & Bacon, 1969.

Lanoue, Fred. *Drownproofing.* Englewood Cliffs, N.J.: Prentice-Hall, 1963.

Spears, Betty. *Fundamentals of Synchronized Swimming.* Third edition. Minneapolis, Minn.: Burgess Publishing Co., 1966.

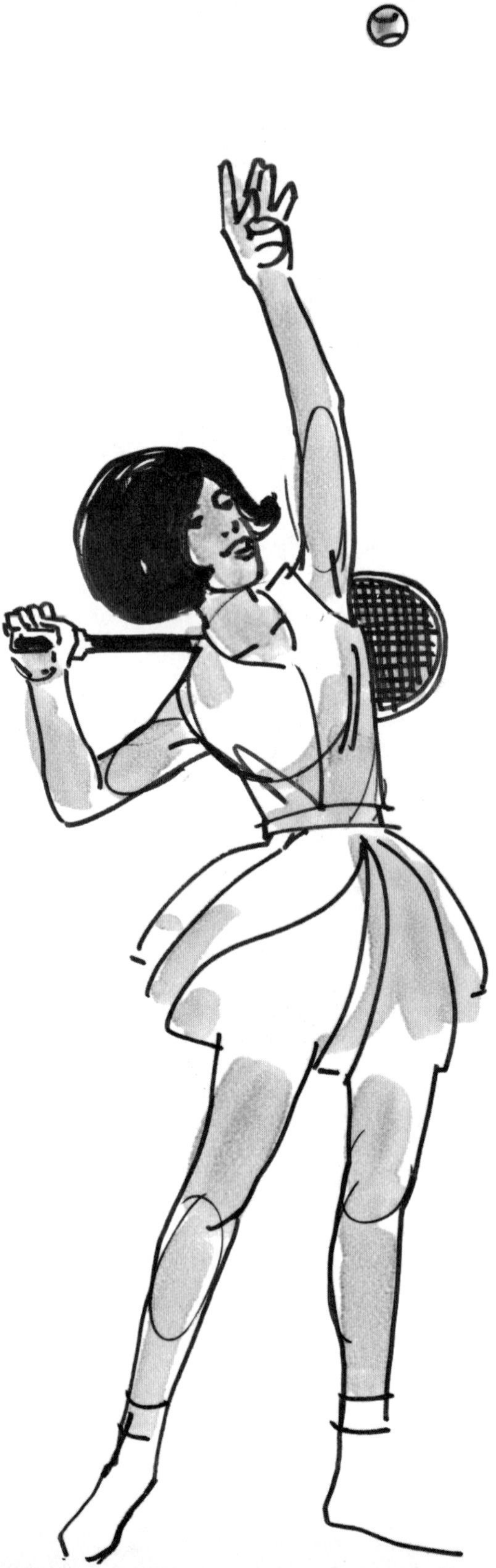

Tennis

Tennis has been discovered by people all over the world. It is a lifetime sport, one that is enjoyed by players of all ages and abilities. The game is so popular and interest has increased so much that many more tennis courts are being constructed at city parks, schools, resorts, clubs, camps, and recreation centers to accommodate the increased participation. It is a game that provides healthy exercise, a marvelous social environment, a challenge to your mental and physical ability, and an excellent opportunity to develop self-control.

The history of tennis is unique and colorful. From the days of the Greeks to the present time, the game has carried with it prestige and honor. Tennis actually started as handball in Greece. In the Middle Ages it changed to a game of batting the ball with the open hand across a cord or over a mound of dirt. The early court was shaped like an hourglass, and the balls were leather, stuffed with hair. The evolution of the racket is from hands, to glove, to a paddle, to a racket shaped like a snowshoe, to the present style. It is interesting to note that a very popular modern method of teaching tennis involves learning by stroking with the hand, a short racket, and finally a conventional racket. This progression provides appropriate equipment for the wide range of abilities in tennis, thereby making it possible for many more individuals to enjoy the game.

THE GAME

The idea of the game is to hit the ball with a racket over the net into the opposite court so that the opponents, or opponent, cannot return it to your court. A game between two individuals is called singles. Between teams of two it is called doubles, and when a boy and a girl play on each side it is called mixed doubles. Play is started when one player,

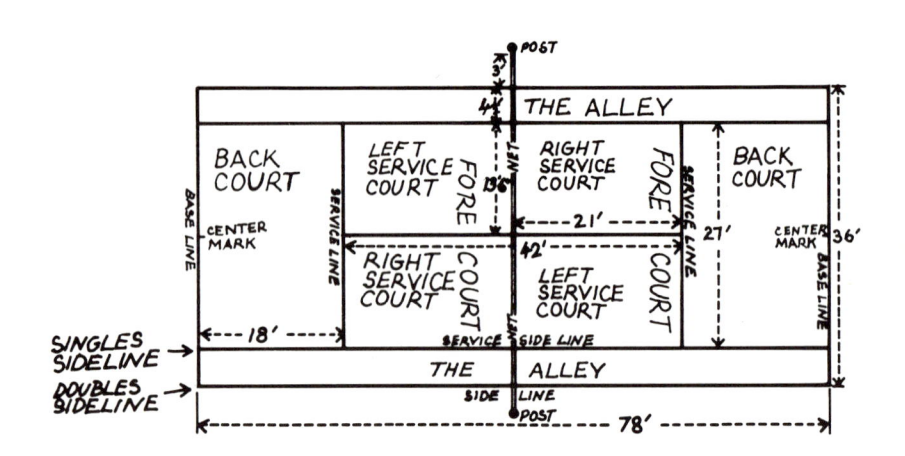

Tennis Court

called the server, standing behind the baseline, hits or serves the ball over the net so that it lands any place within the baseline and the singles sidelines, or in doubles, the doubles sidelines. After the return of service the ball may be hit either on a first bounce or before it bounces. The ball is then hit back and forth until a player makes an error, either by hitting the ball out of court, into the net, or by failing to hit the ball before it has bounced twice.

The basic strokes a beginner should learn are forehand, backhand, volley, serve, and lob. It is very important to learn the fundamental skills of each stroke. The parts of each stroke that will be described in the following pages are the backswing, forward swing, point of contact, and the follow-through. Gaining knowledge of each component part of the stroke combined with constructive practice will bring you earlier and greater success in mastering the strokes. (The following skills will be analyzed for the right-handed player.)

The Forehand Drive

The forehand stroke is used to return balls that come to the right side of your body. A beginner should learn to develop a deep forehand drive with topspin to use as an offensive weapon.

Learning the skills of the forehand drive—in which you use your right hand as you would the racket face to stroke the ball—will help you concentrate more on the basic body movements. Three movements

Forehand Drive

that should be given special attention are transfer of weight, body rotation, and arm swing. These will be incorporated in the instructional progression.

Stand with your left side to the net, drop the tennis ball with your left hand diagonally forward from your left side. Transfer your weight by taking a short step with your left foot toward the net. As you begin to transfer your weight, your right hand should be drawn back a short distance level with the court. As you step into the stroke, swing your right arm and hand forward to hit the back side of the ball with the flat of the hand. Be sure you contact the ball directly opposite your left side or forward foot. Finish the stroke by swinging your arm forward and upward to a point where your wrist is at about eye level. Your extended hand should be flat, on edge, and reaching forward toward the net. Your wrist should be firm throughout the stroke. Upon completion of the stroke check these points:

1. Did you contact the ball opposite your left side?
2. Is your left knee bent after completion of the stroke?
3. Is your wrist at about eye level, and is your hand flat and on edge?
4. Did your *body rotate* so that at the completion of the stroke you were facing the net?

Forehand Drive

    If you so desire, you may actually follow the above progression with the use of a paddle, short racket, or regular racket. For earlier success, it is recommended that you begin with your hand and then progress through the racket stages. When you begin using a racket, use the Eastern forehand grip; it has been found to be the best grip for stroking high and low oncoming balls. This grip is also known as the "shake hands grip." Hold the throat of the racket with the fingertips of the left hand. The racket should be perpendicular to the ground and held slightly away from the body. Place your right hand flat against the back side of the racket so the racket face and hand are in line with each other. The racket face is an extension of the hand. Spread your fingers slightly and wrap them around the grip portion of the racket. Your thumb should rest against the middle or second finger. Your other fingers will rest on the front portion of the racket. The "V" formed by the thumb and index finger is just to the right of the top plate, and the first knuckle of your index finger is on the top right level of the grip.

    The elements of the forehand drive are summarized below:

Backswing: The racket is taken back in line with the oncoming ball. A short backswing is recommended.

Forehand Grip

Backhand Grip

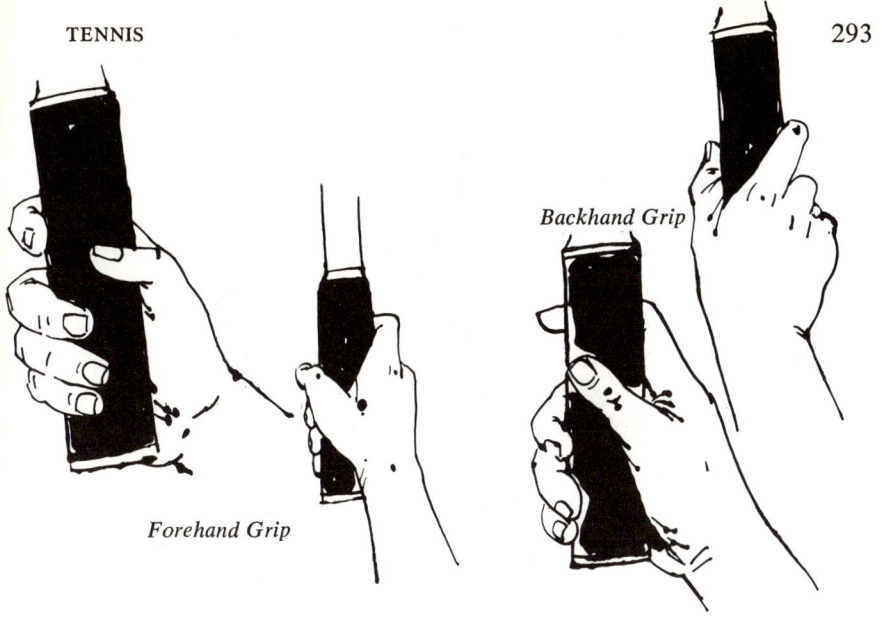

Forward swing: With the racket face flat, move the racket forward to contact the ball.

Transfer of weight: The weight is transferred from the right to the left foot just prior to the racket's meeting the ball. It is almost a simultaneous action. The step is taken toward the net.

Point of contact: The racket meets the ball opposite the forward left foot.

Follow-through: Keep the racket on the ball as you stroke forward. Finally the racket will travel upward as well as forward to impart top spin. The racket should finish with a flat racket face and the frame still on edge. Your wrist should remain firm throughout the stroke and should be at eye level upon completion of the stroke.

The Backhand

The backhand is the stroke played on the opposite side of the body from the forehand, or the left side. It is important to develop early in your game a deep flat backhand drive that imparts topspin.

For the Eastern backhand grip merely turn your hand from the Eastern forehand grip about a quarter turn to the left. The base of the thumb and the thumb support the back of the racket on impact with the ball. The palm of the hand is now on top of the racket. The index knuckle is on the top plate.

As in the progressions for the forehand drive you will discover you have increased control if you choke up on the racket during the learning

Backhand

stages. Move your hand down the shaft of the racket as you gain control of hitting. In performing the backhand, turn your right side toward the net. As the ball approaches take the racket back with your left hand placed at the throat of the racket. Be sure you have the correct grip with the right hand. The left hand helps pull the racket back and at the same time gives you more awareness of where the racket head is during backswing. The racket head should be taken back at about waist height and in line with the oncoming ball. With your knees flexed and your eyes on the ball start the swing forward so that the racket meets the ball at least 6 to 8 inches in front of your right side. Keep your wrist firm and follow through fully. The transfer of weight from your left to your right foot should be completed just prior to hitting the ball. Upon completing the stroke see if your wrist is at about head height. The end of the racket should be extended toward the net or reaching in the direction of the hit. Topspin is achieved by hitting slightly below the back side of the oncoming ball and finishing the stroke at head height. Although the racket travels from a low to high finish position, be sure you keep the racket

Ready Position

face flat and on the ball for as long as possible. Learn to hit through the ball.

Once you learn the two basic groundstrokes, forehand and backhand, you should learn the skills of a good "ready position" so you will be able to move easily to the right or left. The position is one whereby you face the net with your feet spaced about a shoulder-width apart, knees flexed, and your weight resting on the balls of your feet. The heels do maintain light contact with the court, but the weight is generally poised on the balls of the feet, ready to move quickly.

Footwork is oftentimes the key to good stroking. You must be able to get into position to hit an oncoming ball, and this is accomplished by short running steps, slides, pivots, skip-steps, or combinations of these steps. The important thing is to get to the ball early enough so you do not have to rush stroking the ball. After you gain confidence in the basic stroke you may experiment a little with timing, hitting the ball sooner or later, to enable you to vary the direction of the strokes, either across court or down the line.

The Serve

The serve is the stroke which puts the ball in play to start a game. It is a stroke in which you have complete control; only you are to blame if you make service errors.

The grip for the serve is about halfway between the Eastern forehand and backhand grips. With this grip and by hitting up and over the tennis ball you will impart a combination top and side spin to the ball. If you have great difficulty with this grip, you may use the forehand grip.

The left arm and hand place the ball into the air with great accuracy, while the right arm and hand begin the stroking action. The coordination of the two movements challenges the beginner, because the arms move in opposite directions.

The action of the right arm and body is very much like the overhand baseball throw. To develop a "feel" for the serve, stand behind the baseline and throw a tennis ball overhand into the service court. Notice how you transfer your weight, how your body rotates, and the necessity for getting a full smooth throw with wrist snap to get the ball to move forward and downward into the correct court.

In preparing to serve, stand with your left side turned toward the net. The feet should be turned diagonally toward the right net post, and spaced about a shoulder-width apart. The left toes should be placed about 2 inches behind the baseline, and not moved, during the serve. The weight is placed on the back foot, and the body is tilted back. The racket is held in front of the body about waist high with the tip end of the racket head pointing toward the opponent. As you start a full, relaxed backswing, the ball is placed into the air. The arms move down together and up together. As a follow-through the right arm moves down across the body and the left arm moves up and forward toward the net post. The ball should be placed about 6 inches to the right and 12 inches in front of the body. This placement of the ball allows room for the body to move forward for the transfer of weight to help you hit into the ball. The toss must be high enough to permit you to have a full reach with the racket and for the ball to be hit in the center of the racket face. The serve becomes relatively easy if you can control the toss. As the ball is tossed the right arm moves down and up to a cocked position with the wrist in back of the neck and the elbow about shoulder level. The hand and wrist lead as the racket is moved up to hit the ball. At the point of contact the racket travels over the ball and at this time the wrist comes into action. The wrist snaps and thereby actually throws the racket head out and over the ball, and the racket head continues downward to the left side of the body for a complete follow-through. At this time the racket head should lead on the follow-through. The left knee should be bent, and on some occasions the right leg swings forward.

Serve

Forehand Volley *Backhand Volley*

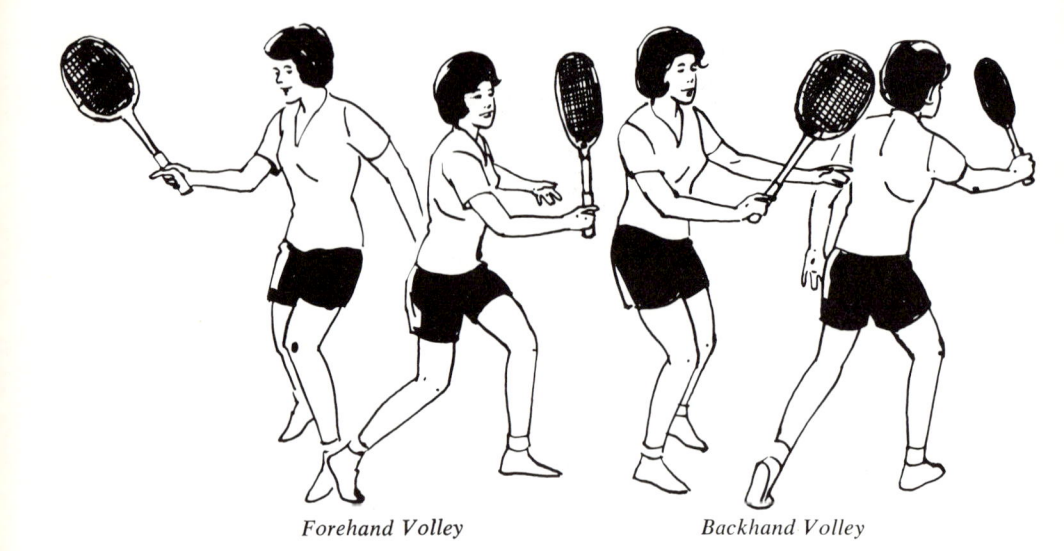

Success in serving is dependent upon the coordination of the toss and swing. The stroke must be a continuous, smooth movement, and therefore timing the motion of the racket head to meet the ball at the precise time is tricky, but necessary.

During your practice, try to develop a consistent stroke. Work on coordination rather than speed, form, and accuracy until you develop the stroke.

The Volley

The volley is used to hit the ball before it bounces. This stroke adds excitement and intrigue to the game of tennis. The proper use of this stroke speeds up the game and gives you more opportunity to angle a return shot. You take a position about 6 to 9 feet from the net with your knees flexed, ready to move quickly in any direction. Use the same Eastern grips as described for the forehand and backhand drives.

Assume the "ready position" facing the net. Hold the racket in front of you with the racket head at about eye level. As the ball approaches your forehand or backhand side, move to meet the ball well in front of your body. Transfer your weight as you do with the ground strokes. Keep the racket in front of you but turned so it is flat as you reach forward to block the ball. There is no backswing and very little follow-through. The follow-through should be in the same plane as the hit. In other words, the racket head should not drop forward. At the moment of impact the wrist should be locked. The punch comes from the locked wrist, shoulder power, and going to meet the ball. It is a short stroke, with the racket head held above or in line with the wrist, but never below the wrist.

If the oncoming ball reaches you at net level or below, you will need to open the racket face slightly, and thereby a little backspin will be imparted to the ball.

The Lob

The lob is the stroke used most frequently to hit balls over the head of an opponent who is playing at the net. It is played much like the forehand and backhand drives, except for the last minute deceptive move of opening the racket face to loft the ball into the air. Greater lifting action is required as you stroke the ball. You need to develop a feeling of carrying the ball on the racket face for control. Lobs should land close to the opponent's baseline. If possible, hit the lob just out of the reach of the opponent and low so there is not adequate time for him to run back and return the lob. On the other hand, make sure it is deep and high enough so your opponent cannot run back quickly and smash it away. On some occasions you may choose to hit a very high lob to enable you to get back into good court position. It is considered a safety or defensive action in these instances.

The overhead smash is used to hit lobs and high oncoming balls. It is played like a flat serve. The smash is usually a point winner and must be used with discretion. A well-placed smash with some speed is oftentimes a better return than a smash with great speed that may be out of control.

SCORING AND RULES

Rules are established by the International Lawn Tennis Association. The U.S. Lawn Tennis Association, being a member of the International Association, subscribes to their official rules.

A game is won when a player wins 4 or more points. Points in a game are referred to by the following terminology:

0 points	Love
1 point	15
2 points	30
3 points	40
4 points	Game

The score of 40-40 is called deuce. If the score goes to deuce, one player must take two points in a row to win the game. The first point following deuce is called advantage, but if the player does not win the second consecutive point after deuce the score goes back to deuce.

The player who first wins six games and is two games ahead of his opponent wins the set. If one player wins six games and is only one game ahead, play must continue until one player is two games ahead. For example, a set may be won by scores of 6-love, 6-1, 6-2, 6-3, 6-4, 7-5, 8-6, 9-7, and so forth.

A contest or match is won when one player wins two out of three sets, or in some tournaments three out of five sets for men and two out of three for women.

Starting the Game

Players determine who will be the first server or receiver by spinning a racket or tossing a coin. Normally rackets are marked to provide an option for the person given the choice of the call. The player winning the call has a choice of being first to serve, receive, or request the opponent to choose.

Some Basic Rules

1. The server serves one whole game, then alternates with his opponent for the rest of the match.

2. The server stands behind the baseline and starts a game from the right side serving into the opponent's right service court. He serves to alternate service courts throughout the game.

3. The server has two chances to serve into the proper service court on each point. If both serves are at fault, he loses the point.

4. The serve must bounce before the receiver may return it. All other balls may be hit before the bounce, or after only one bounce.

5. Players switch sides on odd games—after the first game, third game, fifth, and so on.

After the serve, play or rally continues when—

1. A ball lands on any portion of the line.

2. The ball is returned outside the net posts either above or below the level of the top of the net, provided it lands in the proper court, even though it touches the net.

3. A ball hits the net, but passes over it, and lands in the proper court.

4. A player returns the ball which hit a ball lying on the court.

After the serve, a player loses a point if—
1. He fails to return the ball into the opponent's court.
2. He fails to return the ball before it bounces a second time.
3. He plays the ball before it has passed the net.
4. He touches the ball with his body or clothing.
5. He contacts the ball more than once with his racket during a stroke.
6. He throws his racket at and hits the ball.
7. He returns the ball which hits a permanent fixture, before it hits the opponent's court.

DOUBLES PLAY

The order of service in doubles is as follows: The pair who have to serve in the first game of each set shall decide which partner shall serve. The opposing team shall decide which partner is to serve the second game. The partner of the player who served in the first game shall serve in the third, and the partner of the player who served the second game shall serve the fourth game. This pattern of rotation continues throughout the set.

A receiving order is established for each set. When the receiving team decides which player shall receive the first serve, that position must be maintained for all serves throughout each set. These are just a few of the basic rules, and you would greatly benefit by studying all of the official rules.

STRATEGY

Strategy in tennis requires using your strengths against your opponent's weaknesses. A few points which should help you out-play an opponent follow:
1. Learn to control and keep the ball in play. Let your opponent make the mistakes.
2. Hit balls deep to your opponent's baseline, and keep him back away from the net.
3. Keep your opponent running.
4. Figure out your opponent's weaknesses, and play to them.
5. Vary the spin, speed, and placement of your shots.
6. If you are winning, don't change your style of play. If you are losing, try something different.

7. Analyze your opponent's pattern of play. Try to anticipate where your opponent will return the ball.

8. Learn what is meant by safe and unsafe angles.

9. Try to make the first serve good, and serve the ball deep to the opponent's backhand.

10. In doubles, both players should be at the net or back of the baseline. Do not play one up and one back.

COURTESY AND SPORTSMANSHIP

The courteous and sportsmanlike tennis player is one who plays the game without trying to take unfair advantage of his opponents. A few rules of tennis etiquette follow:

1. Introduce yourself to your opponent before you begin your games.

2. Wear appropriate white tennis apparel, and strive for neatness and cleanliness in your appearance.

3. Show consideration for your opponent and partner.

4. Offer to play over again any doubtful decisions to your advantage.

5. Retrieve your share of balls.

6. Do not argue about decisions.

7. Don't lose your temper or make excuses for your play.

8. Limit conversation on the court as it may disturb your opponent as well as players on adjacent courts.

9. Before going onto another court to retrieve a ball, wait until play is completed.

10. If in doubt about a ball falling on the line, it is better to give your opponent the advantage than yourself. If a ball touches any portion of the line it is considered "in."

11. Upon completing a tennis match shake hands with your opponent and thank him for the games.

SELECTION AND CARE OF EQUIPMENT

Rackets, balls, and clothing should be chosen with care. Choose a racket that is appropriate for you, one that feels comfortable, and one you are able to control. Rackets are now made in different lengths as well as different weights and grip sizes. A shorter racket is more appropriate for beginners or younger players. As you acquire skill in stroking you can progress to a regular racket. Weight and grip sizes vary with the choice of the individual. Grip sizes vary from 4 to 4⅝.

When you select a tennis racket have your instructor or tennis pro assist you. Players often select rackets that have not been strung, and then select the type of string most appropriate for their skill level. A multifilament nylon is generally considered good because it withstands moisture, plays and wears well, and is less expensive than good gut. To prevent the frame from warping, store it in a press when it is not in use. It is also advisable to keep your racket in a moisture-proof case.

Tennis balls pressure packed in cans and approved by the U.S. Lawn Tennis Association (USLTA) should be purchased. It should be mentioned that some manufacturers are now producing balls that are not pressure-sealed and are widely accepted.

Smooth, rubber-soled tennis shoes are recommended. Tennis players wear white clothing. White has been a traditional color for many years. A tee shirt or other short-sleeved shirt, white shorts, and socks are acceptable for boys and girls. Some girls prefer tennis dresses.

TENNIS TERMS

Ace. A ball served so well that the opponent cannot touch it with his racket.

Ad. Abbreviation for advantage. The point following deuce is called advantage. "Advantage in" if the server wins the point; and "Advantage out" if the receiver wins the point.

Back court. Also known as "no-man's land." The area between the service line and baseline.

Backspin. The type of spin given to the ball by hitting down the back side of the ball. This spin tends to make the ball bounce back toward the hitter.

Cross-court. A ball which is hit diagonally across the net, from one corner to the other.

Drive. A forehand or backhand ground stroke.

Face. The hitting surface of the tennis racket (strings).

Foot fault. During the serve, a fault results if the server steps on or over the baseline.

Ground stroke. A stroke made by hitting the ball after it has bounced.

Head. The portion of the racket that includes the frame and strings and is used for hitting the ball.

Let. Interference or hindrance which calls for the point to be re-played. The most common let is a serve which hits the top of the net but is otherwise good.

Love. Zero in scoring.

Love game. One player wins four points; opponent—no points.

Love set. A score of 6 games to zero.

Opening. A mistake by the defense, which allows an opponent a chance to score a point.

Rally. Hitting the ball back and forth across the net.

Spin. A technique of hitting the ball by varying the angle of the racket face to cause it to rotate in different ways. Sidespin, forward or topspin, and backspin, are types of spin imparted to the ball.

FOR MORE INFORMATION

American Association for Health, Physical Education, and Recreation, Division for Girls and Women's Sports. *Tennis-Badminton Guide.* Current edition. Washington, D.C.: the Association.

American Association for Health, Physical Education, and Recreation, Division for Girls and Women's Sports. *Selected Tennis-Badminton Articles.* Washington, D.C.: the Association, 1970.

Gould, Dick. *Tennis Anyone?* Palo Alto, Calif.: National Press, 1966.

Harmon, Bob. *Use Your Head in Tennis.* Port Washington, N.Y.: Kennikat Press, 1966.

Heldman, Gladys, and Lumiere, Cornel. *The Book of Tennis and How To Play the Game.* New York: Grosset & Dunlap, 1965.

Johnson, Joan, and Xanthos, Paul. *Tennis.* Dubuque, Iowa: Wm. C. Brown Co., 1967.

Laver, Rod. *How To Play Championship Tennis.* New York: Macmillan, 1965.

Murphy, Bill, and Murphy, Chet. *Tennis Handbook.* New York: Ronald Press Co., 1962.

United States Lawn Tennis Association. *Official Tennis Yearbook and Guide.* Current edition. New York: the Association (51 E. 42nd Street, New York, N.Y. 10017).

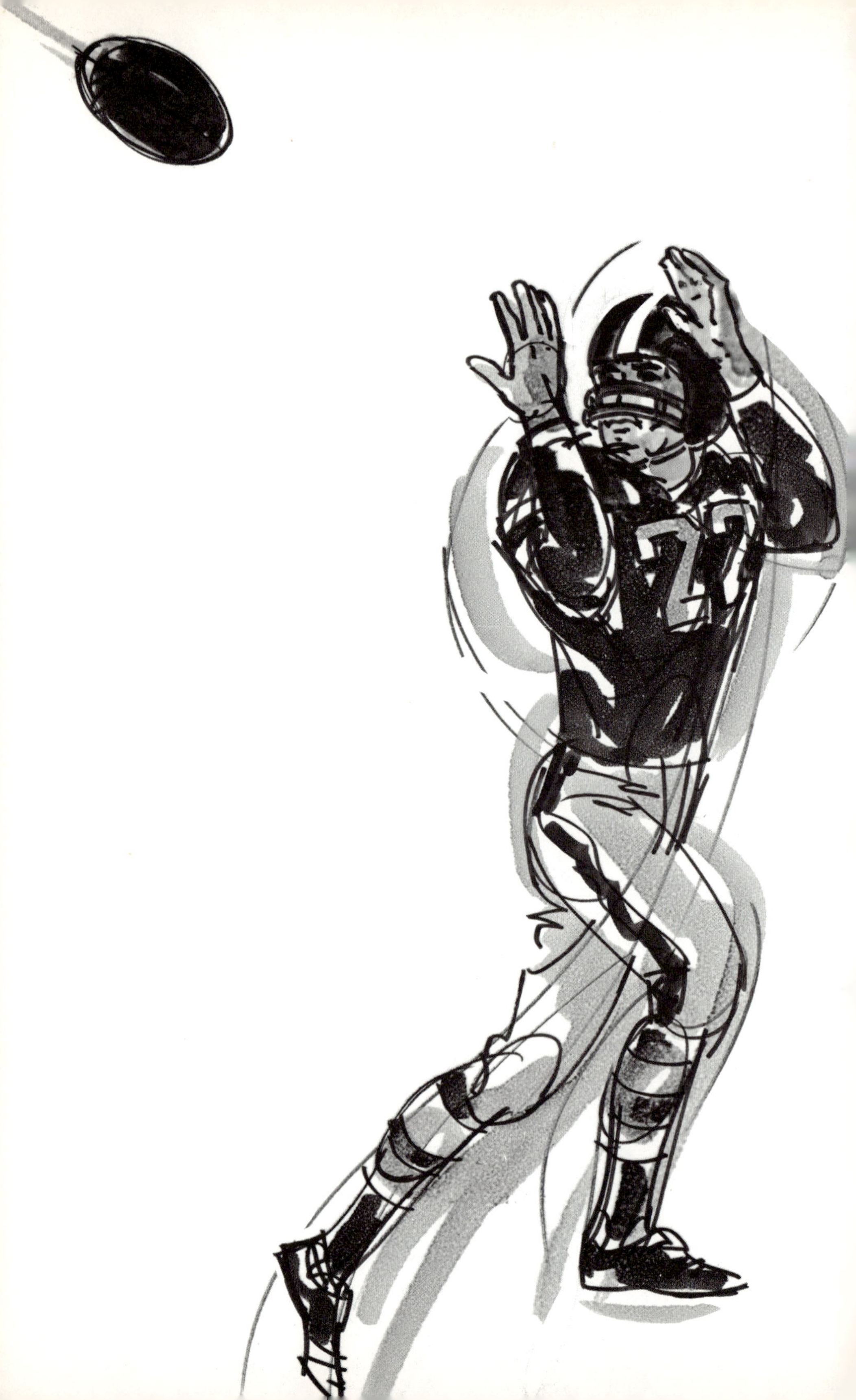

Touch Football

The game of football has grown since the first college game between Princeton and Rutgers University in 1869 to the point where today football is the king of school sports. Students who have not had an opportunity of playing varsity football have taken every opportunity to use the fundamentals of football in many invented games. Touch football has grown from an assortment of different games that used the football.

Touch football provides for the player many of the grand thrills that come from regulation football. It involves most of the fundamentals of tackle football, such as passing, running, kicking, pass catching, and carrying the ball. The big differences between tackle football and touch football are that a "touch" is substituted for a "tackle" and the block in which a player leaves his feet is not allowed.

The game of touch football should be included in your program of fall team sports. It requires little equipment, and almost any open field will serve as a playing area. Here is a game that will give you fun and at the same time contribute to your development of endurance, power, and coordination. A touch football player also gains a better understanding and appreciation of tackle football from his participation in touch football.

THE GAME

The game may be played in any open area, and the number of players may vary from 2 on a side to as many as 11 on a side. Equipment necessary to start the game consists of a regulation football.

The game is usually started in the same manner as tackle football—with a kick-off. However, in some areas a punt or a forward pass is used to put the ball in play.

Football Field

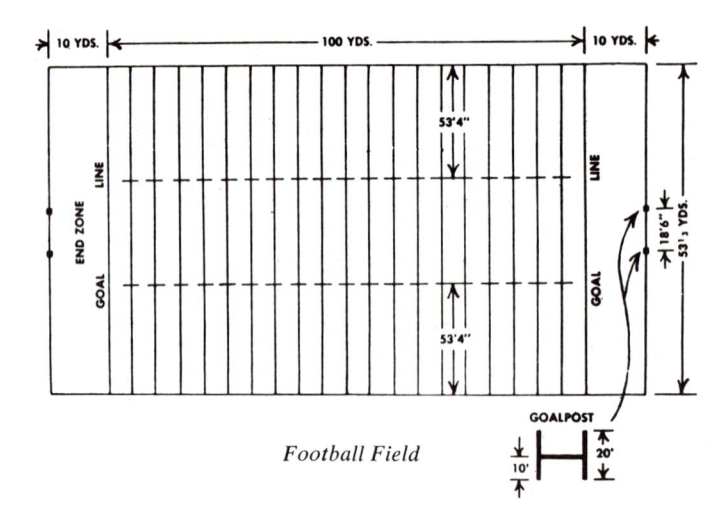

The team receiving the kick-off attempts to advance the ball by running and passing. Their object is to cross their opponents' goal line for a touchdown.

There are no limitations regarding who may catch a forward pass. A team in possession of the ball is allowed four downs to advance the ball a specified distance, usually X number of yards or into the next zone. When a team achieves the distance or the next zone, it receives four additional downs.

If the team in possession of the ball fails to make the distance or the next zone in four downs, it loses possession of the ball to its opponents.

The ball is downed or dead when the player carrying it is touched by an opponent. The touch may be one or two hands. In some sections of the country, the touch is made by removing a flag from the player with the ball. Scoring in touch football is the same as in tackle football.

RULES

The rules outlined here will be helpful in standardizing the rules for your class, league, or the informal games in your neighborhood.

1. Ball: Regulation football.
2. Field: Regulation football field when available; otherwise, goal lines as agreed upon by the captains.
3. Players: Seven men shall constitute a team. There is no limit to the number of players employed in the backfield, but only half the team may play on the line.

4. Downs and distance to be gained: The attacking team must cross center lines of the field in four downs in order to gain another series of four downs and not lose possession of the ball to the opposing team.

5. Tackling: No tackling is allowed. A clearly discernible one-handed touch of the runner, below the shoulders and above the knees, ends the forward progress of the ball. No player is allowed to leave his feet in order to complete a tackle. A 15-yard penalty is imposed if he does so.

6. Charging: Players shall not violently charge one another on either defense or offense. Offensive blocking must be done between shoulder and knee. Blocker must not leave feet. Fifteen-yard penalty.

7. Interference: No player may, on the offense, violently hip, shoulder, head, or trip an opponent. Fifteen-yard penalty.

8. Use of hands: Players on the offense under no circumstances are allowed to use their hands on opponents. Defensive players may push other players aside to make the touch; however, not with any show of violence. Fifteen-yard penalty.

9. Offside: Players must remain on their side of the scrimmage line until the ball is centered. Five-yard penalty.

10. Forward passes: One forward pass is allowed in each down. The forward pass must be made from behind the line of scrimmage (where the ball was put into play) for the ensuing down. The pass is illegal if the player making the pass is touched before the ball leaves his hand. Any player may make or receive a forward pass except the passer. A forward pass touched by two players of the offensive team is considered an incompleted pass unless it was touched by a defensive man between the touching by the two offensive men.

11. Backward pass: A backward pass may be made or received by any player at any point on the field of play.

12. Fumbled ball: A fumbled ball at any time is dead and belongs to the team that fumbled the ball at the point of the fumble, the down and point to be gained remaining the same. A fumbled forward pass is ruled as an incomplete pass.

13. Punt formation: When punt formation is announced the defense team may not attack and the offensive team must punt within three seconds after the snap of the ball. (Quick kicks are not allowed.) Penalty: Loss of ball.

14. Time of game: Forty minutes divided into two equal halves, or as agreed by the captains, shall constitute a game. A 5-minute rest between halves.

Three-Point Stance

Two-Point Stance

15. Personal equipment: No spikes or cleats on shoes are allowed. Head gear and shoulder pads are not permitted.
16. Scoring: Scoring is the same as in regulation football.
Touchdown—6 points
Field goal—3 points
Safety—2 points
Point(s) after touchdown—1 point if kicked from placement
2 points if successfully crosses goal line (run or pass)
17. Substitutes: Any number of substitutions may be made at any time during the game. Substitutes must report to the referee.
18. Blocked kick: A blocked kick that does not cross the line of scrimmage shall belong to the receiving team at the point where the ball hit the ground.
19. Delaying game: Failure to put the ball in play within 25 seconds after it is ready for play is delay in game. Penalty: Five yards.
20. Other rules: In any situation arising that is not covered by these rules, the intercollegiate football rules will apply.

BASIC SKILLS

To be an excellent touch football player, you must acquire skill in all of the fundamentals of the game. Players at one time or another use most of the skills described below, regardless of the position played.

Center Stance

Players Stance

1. Line stance: Your position is on the line of scrimmage, with both hands, both feet, or one foot and the opposite hand up to or within one foot of this line. Assume a comfortable position, enabling you to move forward, backward, or to either side easily and effectively without changing your position for the various types of play.

2. Center stance: As a center your stance should never change because this would cause telegraphing. You should never look at your opponent, but be aware of the tactical situation. You should be the first man to the line. Assume a stance that is comfortable for you.

3. Backfield stance: Your stance should be relaxed. You should assume a crouch or semistanding position, behind the line of scrimmage, on the balls of both feet. Spread your legs for quick blocking or receiving of the ball. Avoid telegraphing.

Blocking

Your job in blocking is to keep your body between the defensive player and the ball. Don't use your hands while blocking. Don't lose your balance. You should make contact with the defensive player first. Your job is to keep in your opponent's way at all times. Block with your shoulder and forearm. Remember your hands must be in contact with your body and you cannot use your forearm to block your opponent above the shoulder. You must not leave your feet nor place your hands on the ground.

Passing

Passing

Center Pass: In a pass from T-formation, the ball should be lifted with a stiff-armed sweeping motion. Get the ball to the quarterback's hands as soon as possible. The ball should be slammed up into the palm of the quarterback's upper hand. For direct passes you should draw a bead on the spot you wish to pass to. The pass should be of the soft spiral type and easy for the receiver to handle. In punt-formation passes accuracy and speed are essential. The center can obtain more power in his pass by using both hands and putting the ball farther in front with the lace of the ball rotated as far under the right hand as possible (left hand for left-handed centers).

Forward Pass: After receiving the ball from the center, place your fingers across the lacing. Spread your fingers out and keep a firm grip on the ball. Raise your arm and rock the ball behind your ear. Your other hand should come up to guide the ball and steady it. This hand should be kept in front of the ball. You should lift the ball in a smooth even motion. Keep both hands on the ball until you pass it. Your legs should be spread in a comfortable position. If you are right-handed, your right foot should be planted firmly but still able to move in any direction. Your left foot is the balance foot, also the direction foot. When you bring the ball forward to pass, the weight shifts from your right to your left foot. When delivering the pass your arm should follow through.

TOUCH FOOTBALL

Receiving

You should deliver the ball with a wrist snap. Short passes are thrown on a line; long passes are lofted. Time your passes with the speed of the receiver. Concentrate on your passing and give all your attention to your receiver. The passer's knees should be slightly bent and he should step with the left foot in the direction of the pass (for a left-handed passer, step with the right foot).

Receiving Forward Passes: You should always keep your eye on the ball. The ball is caught with the hands, not the arms or body. The hands should be extended, fingers spread and relaxed, giving easily as they touch the ball. Don't fight the ball. Long passes should be caught with arms extended over the shoulder. Short passes should be caught with the arms cradled, and the receiver facing the passer. Methods of catching the ball are the inverse catch—catching the ball like a baseball, with palms facing outward and away from the body; basket catch—catching the ball with both arms extended above either shoulder, palms facing in and elbows bent, forming a cradle for the ball; leaping catch—jumping high into the air to catch a high pass, both arms and hands completely extended overhead with palms facing toward the body; and reverse catch—when the pass comes to the opposite side of the receiver than that for which it was intended, he is forced to twist his body to the opposite side, catching the pass with his arms extended, without slowing down his speed.

Kicking

Carrying the Ball

The ball should be held with one end under the armpit, and the other end covered by the palm of the hand and firmly grasped by the fingers. The ball should be carried in the arm farthest from your opponent. Run hard and elude your opponents by learning to reverse your field, stop and go, change direction sharply, dodge, side step, and execute fakes. Follow your interference.

The Touch

Don't slap. Touch between the knees and the shoulder. Don't hold. Depending on the rules, use the one- or two-hand touch. Maintain good balance and body control at all times.

Punting

1. The one-step kick: Stand with both feet parallel or right foot slightly forward. Take one step forward with the left foot and kick.
2. The one-and-one-half-step kick: Your kicking foot should be slightly back. Bring your kicking foot up a half step; take a full step with your left foot; and kick the ball.
3. The rocker-step-kick: Have both feet parallel; take a backward step with the right leg, shifting your weight to this leg; then take a step forward with your left foot and kick.

4. Stepping back: With your left leg step back as the ball is being passed; then take a half step with the right and full step with the left leg and kick.

5. General hints on kicking: Keep your eyes on the ball until it is kicked. Extend your toe and snap your leg through the ball. Hit the ball directly on the middle of your instep with the lace of the ball to the right of center. Lay the ball on your foot. Never take more than two steps when kicking. Your feet should be about 6 inches apart and parallel when you prepare to kick. Your head and shoulders should be forward, and your fingers should be spread and relaxed to receive the pass from the center.

STRATEGY

Offensive and defensive strategy are very important parts of the game. You must learn to call the right play at the right time and be able to pick out the weak spots on the other team. Always have a reason for calling a given play. Save your surprise plays for an emergency. Mix up your pass and running plays, and above all know your teammates and what they can do. Follow a certain pattern when calling the plays and call them in a series with all the plays starting the same but having a different ending. Plan your attack with the following factors in mind: down, yardage, score, time, position, weather.

For an example, consider this situation: If the ball is on the other team's 30-yard line, second down, and 1 or 2 yards to go for the first down, here is how you figure out what to call. First, with 1 or 2 yards to go, you figure the defense thinks you are going to run the ball, but you say to yourself that you have two more downs to make it, so you call a pass play. If the pass fails, you still have the other team guessing what you are going to do on the next two plays. Now, if it is late in the game and your team is behind, don't be afraid to gamble with the ball—getting beat by 1 point or 20 points is immaterial.

Offensive Formations

The offensive formations are (a) single-wing, (b) double-wing, (c) T-formation, (d) punt formation, and (e) pro-set formation.

The single-wing formation is used when the tailback is a triple threat. An advantage of the double-wing formation is that the tailback can use the two other backfield men for fakes and single and double reverses.

Formations

Single-Wing (4 to 5 Yds.)

Double-Wing

T-Formation (5 Yds., 4½ Yds.)

Punt Formation (15 Yds.)

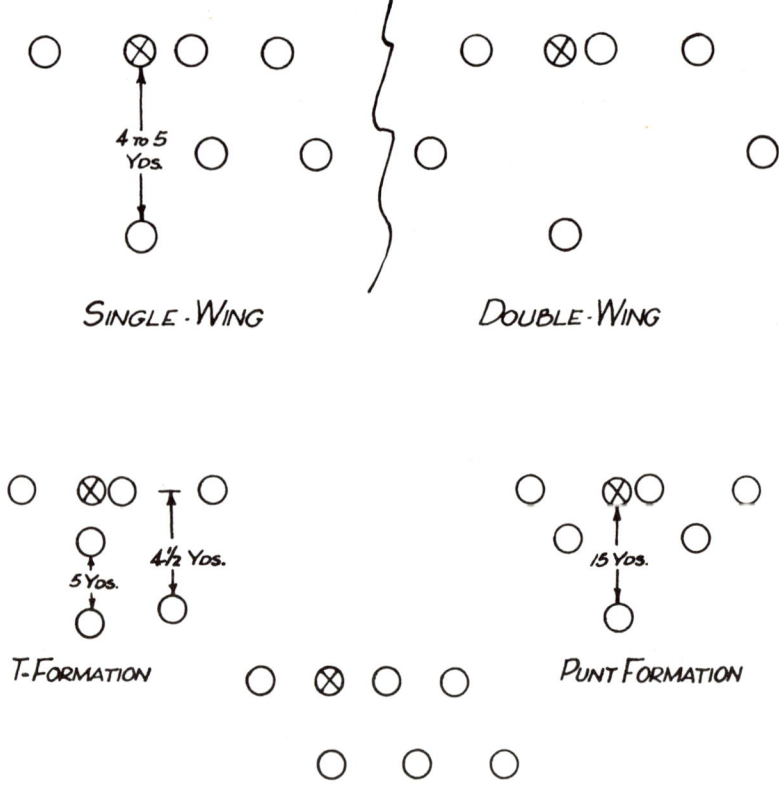

Pro-set Formation

Formations

The T-formation is a good one to use to fool the other team. But keep in mind that fast men are needed. The punt formation is used mostly for kicking, but can also be used for passing and running trick plays. Especially good for a surprise play is the pro-set formation. It also helps to loosen up the other team.

Defensive Formation

They say that the best defense is a good offense, but remember that after you score the other team gets the ball and this puts you on defense. As you planned your offensive attack, you must plan your defensive attack. The defensive team should have certain kinds of formations just as the offensive team has.

The defensive team has a quarterback just as the offensive team does, and he tries to figure out which formation and play the other team will use. With this information, he calls for a certain defensive formation. Here are some of the things you have to think about before calling the formation:

1. What part of the field is the ball on?
2. What down is it, and how far has the other team to go for a first down?
3. What is the score?

For example, if the ball is on the other team's 5- or 10-yard line, you could use your 4-2-1 defense. Why? Well, you have four men rushing hard, which will stop their running attack; and if they pass, it will have to be a quick, short pass.

Now, let us say that it is third down with 9 yards to go. You would use a defense to stop their passing, kicking, or wide-end runs. You could use a 2-3-2 defense, in which two men are pulled off the line and put in the backfield.

For another example, suppose your team is leading with only a few minutes to go, and you figure that the other team will throw long passes so that they can score before time runs out. You need more halfbacks so you would again use a 2-3-2 defense.

Now that your defense is set up, you must remember that if you are a lineman you charge low and fast and get into the backfield as quickly as you can. If you back up the line, you cover all running plays and short passes. The halfbacks guard against all passes; so they should watch the offensive ends and halfbacks. The safety man must remember never to let a man get behind him on a pass or a run.

The whole defensive team should be alert for little things that the offensive team does that will tip their hand. Watch the players' feet when they get into their stance. Watch their eyes when they come out of the huddle. Do they have a good passer, does he throw long passes, can he run, and what are his favorite plays? Know the other men in the backfield. Who usually runs? Which ones go out for passes? How fast are they?

SAFETY AND COURTESY

Touch football has been considered by many the most hazardous of all physical education class activities. These hazards can be reduced by practice of the fundamentals, by good officiating, by playing according to the rules, and by playing on a suitably surfaced area.

You can help eliminate the hazards of touch football by observing these fair-play practices:

1. Do not play rough because you may cause injuries and ill feeling.

2. Do not block or interfere with a player after he has gone out-of-bounds.

3. Accept decisions of the officials without argument.

4. Leave discussion of rule interpretations to your team captain.

5. Do not question the choice of plays of the quarterback during the game.

6. Do not talk in a huddle.

7. Do not intentionally hit someone with a foot, knee, or elbow.

8. Do not pile on after a man is down.

9. Do not use your hands while blocking.

10. Be appreciative of the progress and ability of those with whom you participate.

11. Consider suggestions of others.

12. Observe the rules and regulations of the game.

13. Do not make any insulting statements to your opponents.

SPECTATOR PARTICIPATION

By playing touch football you will be learning a great deal about tackle football. Whether you play the latter game or not, you will want to see and enjoy to the full the game as a spectator. To be a good spectator you should do the following:

1. Learn the rules of the game.

2. Learn the signals of the officials.

3. Watch the strategy of both the offense and the defense on certain plays.

4. At different times during the game pick out an individual player and watch how he plays both on defense and offense.

5. Notice the different types of blocking—in the line and downfield.

6. Put yourself in the quarterback's position and try to figure what play to use in various situations.

FOR MORE INFORMATION

American Association for Health, Physical Education, and Recreation. *Football Skills Test Manual.* Washington, D.C.: the Association.

Dodd, Robert L. *Bobby Dodd on Football.* Englewood Cliffs, N.J.: Prentice-Hall.

Gromback, J. U. *Touch Football.* New York: Ronald Press Co., 1958.

National College Physical Education Association. *Official National Touch Football Rules.* Chicago: The Athletic Institute, 1963.

Nelson, David M. *Football Principles and Play.* New York: Ronald Press Co.

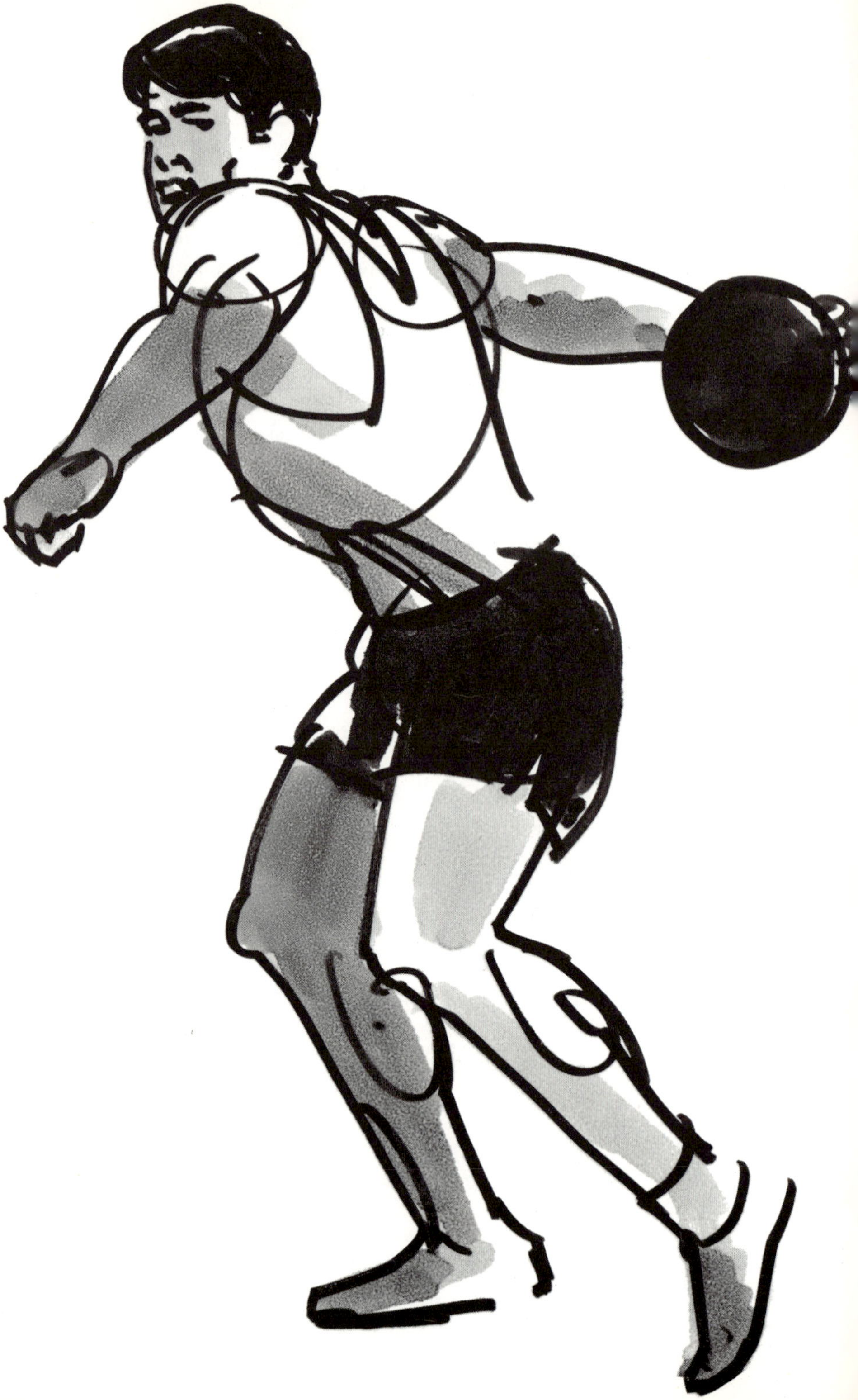

Track and Field

Before historical record some of the Greeks began holding foot racing contests on the plains of Olympia in Southern Greece. These contests grew in importance until all the Greek states participated in them, and victors in the games received the highest honors that a state could award.

The Greeks even based their calendar on the games, an Olympiad being the four-year interval between two festivals. If two states were at war at the time the games were to be held, a truce was declared so that both sides could attend the games. In 776 B.C. the Greeks began keeping a record of the victors at the games, and the games were held regularly thereafter until A.D. 394—nearly 1,200 years!

To the original foot races the Greeks added many of the track and field events that we know, plus wrestling, boxing, chariot and horse races, and even contests in poetry and drama. Victors at the games served as models for the great sculptors, and poets like Pindar made odes in honor of the winners. The Greek Olympics were truly a festival of athletics and the arts.

The modern Olympic Games were revived in 1896 in Athens, and with the exception of the years during the First and Second World Wars have been held every four years since then. In 1968, the nineteenth Olympiad was held at Mexico City, Mexico, with 7,500 men and women from 119 countries taking part.

Track events in a modern track and field meet now include sprinting, middle-distance running, distance running, hurdling, and relays. Field events include the running long jump, high jump, pole vault, triple jump, shot put, discus throw, javelin throw, and hammer throw.

Set Position

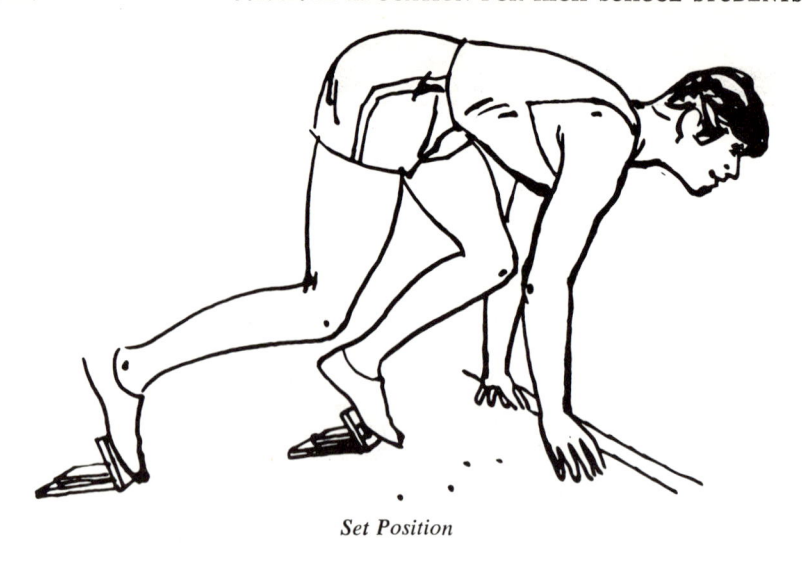

TRACK AND FIELD EVENTS FOR GIRLS

Dashes

If you like to run, you will be interested in the dashes of various lengths. Before you run a dash, you should warm up by some easy jogging and stretching exercises. Never run a dash without warming up beforehand because your are liable to strain muscles.

Junior high school girls participate in dashes of 50, 75, 100, 220, and 440 yards. For senior high school girls there are 50, 75, 100, 220, and 440 yard dashes, plus distance runs of 880 yards, 1,500 meters or 1 mile, or 1½ mile cross country.

The dashes are quite short and are over very quickly. For this reason the start is very important. A crouch start instead of a standing start gives you more drive and enables you to get away more quickly.

Let's go through a start. Remain standing, but relax until the official starter tells you to *Go to your mark.* To go to your mark, drop into a crouch position so that one knee is on the ground. If your right knee is down, the right foot will be farther back than the left foot. When you are down in a crouched position, your hands should be placed on the ground under your shoulders, with your fingers together pointing outward from the body and the thumb perpendicular to the surface of the track. Keep your arms straight.

On the command *Set,* bring your hips up to a level a little above your shoulders and lean forward. Hold this position until the signal

TRACK AND FIELD

Go

Go is given. The "go" signal may be given by a gun or by the word *go* and will come at least 2 seconds after the starter has the runners in the "set" position. On the "go" signal, bring your rear foot forward, drive your opposite arm forward, and swing your other arm back. Your first steps as you drive from your start position should be strong, and your body should be kept low. Many runners make the mistake of coming up straight on the start instead of starting out low. This means that they lose the advantage of a crouched start.

If the distance is no more than 75 yards, you should be able to run at top speed for the entire distance. Continue to run at top speed for at least 10 yards beyond the finish line to guard against slowing down as you cross the finish line. Don't sit down immediately after the race, but remain active until your body adjusts to lowered activity.

Relays

Relays require good teamwork. In shuttle relays, members of the same team line up opposite each other and run back and forth between the lines. In pursuit relays, runners cover a certain part of the distance around the track. There are four members on the team, and the next runner starts as she receives the baton from the previous runner.

Baton-passing is a skill which needs much practice. It is very important because poor baton-passing may lose the race. In the shuttle relay the runner carries the baton in her right hand. As your teammate approaches, you wait behind the line with your right arm extended to

Long Jump

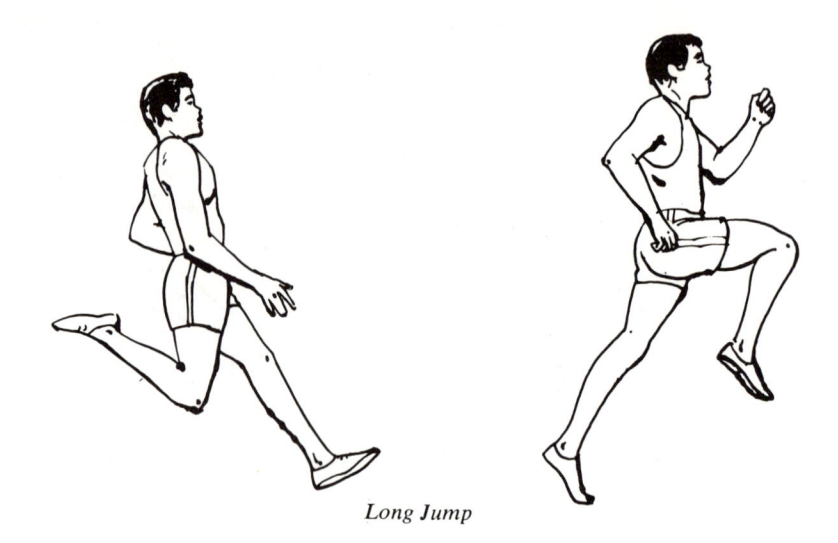

receive the baton. You must not step on or over the line until the baton is in your hand or your team will be disqualified. In this relay, if no baton is used, a hand touch is substituted, and you must wait behind the line until your hand or shoulder is touched by the preceding runner.

In pursuit relays the baton exchange must take place within a 22-yard exchange zone. If you are the runner to whom the baton is to be passed, you should wait inside the back line of the zone and you must

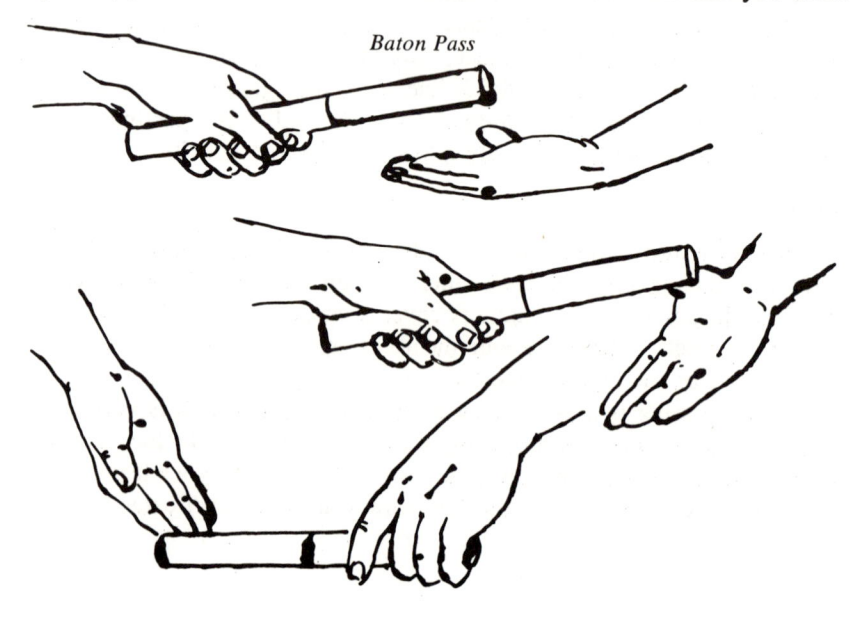

Baton Pass

Long Jump (cont.)

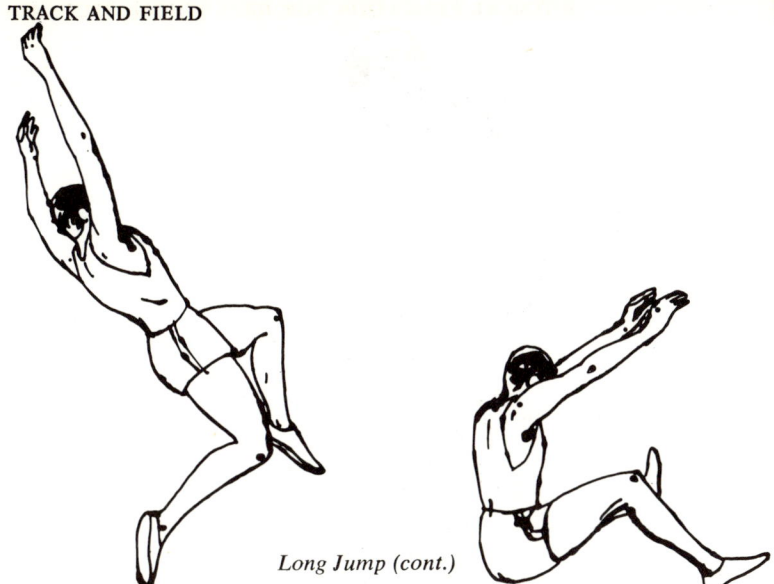

receive the baton while still in the zone. As your teammate approaches with the baton, you should begin running so that your speed equals hers as the baton is passed to you.

The passer carries the baton in her left hand and passes it to your right hand. You must time this so that the pass is completed before you reach the end of the 22-yard passing zone. Transfer the baton immediately to your other hand without breaking your stride. (The pass may also be made from right hand to left hand.)

The 440-yard pursuit relay is a standard event for junior and senior high school girls. This means that each of the four team members runs 110 yards.

The Long Jump

There are two types of long jump. Senior high school girls usually participate in the running long jump, while the standing long jump is an event for junior high girls.

There are four parts to the running long jump: first, the run for the take-off; second, the take-off; then the flight through the air; and finally the landing. Speed at the take-off point is as important as the jump itself. Approach the take-off board as fast as possible. Adjust your stride so that you can take off from the board without losing speed and drive. If you haven't judged this properly, it may be necessary to shorten your last step to keep from stepping over the take-off board and committing a foul, which usually results in a poor jump. Correct arm

Standing Long Jump

and leg movement add distance. Swinging the arms upward with force and springing with both legs will help to give you height and drive. Try to gain as much height as possible on your jump. When you land, be sure to fall forward because your jump will be measured from the nearest point your body touches.

In the standing long jump, as the name indicates, you start from a standing position with both feet on the take-off board. Place your feet comfortably apart and make certain that your toes are behind the front edge of the board.

Start with your weight on the balls of your feet and your arms extended forward. Swing your arms back and forth two or three times, and at the same time bend and straighten your knees so that you have a bouncing rhythm. Be careful not to lift your feet off the board. After a few preliminary swings, as your arms come forward, spring as high and as far forward as you can. As in the running long jump be careful to fall forward after you land.

High Jump

Most beginners will probably find the scissors type of jump easier, but it has certain disadvantages. You will find it more tiring than a layout type of jump, and you cannot gain as much height.

You approach the bar on a diagonal and gauge your approach so that you arrive at your desired take-off point with the proper foot. In the scissors jump, the spring and take-off are from the foot farthest from

TRACK AND FIELD   327

Scissors High Jump

the bar, and the nearer leg swings up and over the bar first. Be careful to swing your take-off leg up even higher than the forward one to avoid knocking off the bar.

Hurdles

In the hurdle course there is a 39-foot 4½-inch approach to the first hurdle; a 26-foot 3-inch space between hurdles; and a 31-foot 10½-inch finish. For high school girls there are 50- and 70-yard hurdle races. In the 70-yard race, the finish is 45 feet 9 inches. The hurdles are 2 feet high.

The important part in hurdling is to run over the hurdles, not jump them. To be a good hurdler you must consider carefully which leg you want forward on the crouch start, which is the same as in the dash. This decision will depend on how many strides you take before the first hurdle and which leg should lead over the hurdle. Take off far enough away from the hurdle so that your leading leg and your body must stretch forward in order to get over it. To get over the hurdle, push off with one leg and thrust forward with the other—the leading leg—keeping your toe up and your heel fairly close to the hurdle. At the same time, push your opposite arm forward toward the toe of your leading leg and swing the other arm backward, allowing your hand to go only as far as your waist. Keep your head up. As you clear the bar, snap the bent knee of your trailing leg forward and raise the lower part of your leg upward and away from your body. As your leading leg crosses the hurdle, push it down toward the ground close to the hurdle, then snap your trailing leg over the hurdle swiftly and thrust it forward to take the first step. Land on the balls of your feet and in normal running position. Between hurdles, try to equalize the size of your steps and gauge them so that you arrive at the next hurdle on the proper foot. Try to take 7, 5, or 3 steps between.

In finishing follow the instructions for the dash. Be careful that your trailing leg does not pass outside a hurdle or you will be disqualified.

Basketball and Softball Throw

The official basketball and league baseball are used for these throws. The throw is made from behind a line. You may make the throw from a running or a standing start, but you must not step over the line until your throw is measured.

Javelin and discus throws and the shot put are dealt with later.

TRACK AND FIELD EVENTS FOR BOYS

Every boy can find a track and field event in which his particular abilities will serve him well. There are few sports in which hard work and patient effort will pay off as in the events of track and field.

Sprinting

Sprinters seem to come in all shapes and sizes: short, tall, heavyset, and slender. The most important factors are quick reaction time, good leg speed, strength, coordination, and the ability to concentrate. Sprints include all distances up to and including the 440-yard dash.

One of the prime factors in good sprint times is a good start. This is the ability to propel the body into motion and accelerate rapidly to top speed. Starting blocks are used as an aid to the "blast-off." There are several starting positions, which involve different spacing of the feet. Research has shown that a position in which the knee of the rear leg is beside the instep of the front foot is the best. First, stand behind the starting blocks. On the starter's command, *Take your marks,* move forward of the starting line, place your hands on the track, and back into the blocks (front block first, then the rear block). Then place the hands a shoulder-width apart, back of the line but not quite touching it (the line is part of the distance to be run). Stay as high on your finger tips as strength will permit. Your shoulders should be directly over your hands or slightly forward of them, with the arms straight and elbows locked. In this position, your shoulders may actually be over or forward of the line. The body weight will rest on the fingers and the knee of the rear leg in this position. This is the "on the marks" position. The eyes should be focused near the starting line to keep the neck muscles relaxed. Then exhale, relax, and wait for the next command.

At the command *Set,* raise your hips to a position slightly higher than the shoulders. Inhale gently as you rise and hold it. In the "set" position, the angle between the upper and lower portions of the front leg should be about 90 degrees, and the majority of the weight should be on the hands and front foot You must concentrate on the actual mechanics of a good start rather than on the gun. When the gun goes off, you "blast-off" with a powerful drive of the legs. The forward leg contributes the most force because it is bent more and remains in contact with the starting block longer. There is an accompanying vigorous and speedy arm action forward and back to balance the movement of the legs and keep your body moving forward in a straight line. Try to maintain a good forward body lean so that the powerful driving action of the legs will push you forward. When your rear leg reaches the point of full extension while sprinting, it should be in a straight line with the spinal column and neck. The sprinter should land on his toes and the ball of his foot, dropping very lightly and momentarily to the heel to provide the leverage and drive needed for the next stride. All action should be straight ahead: knees, feet, arms, shoulders, and head. The arms move rhythmically with the legs. The legs will move only as fast as the arms. Normally the hands should not come above eye height on the forward swing or above the hip in the backward swing. Keep the elbows in. When the stride is properly done, you will have the appearance and feeling of gliding along. Always run at full speed across the finish line and for 10 yards beyond it; then slow gradually to avoid injury.

The 220 and 440 are both sprint races and require more strength. You develop this strength by repeated short, fast runs in training. The key to success in these races is "maximum acceleration, with a minimum of deceleration"; that is, run almost as fast as top speed and stay as relaxed as possible during the latter stages of the race to keep from slowing down drastically. The race is usually won by the runner who slows down the least. Stay relaxed and do not strain. The runner who often appears to be putting on a "kick" usually is only "slowing down the least."

Middle-Distance Running

The middle-distance runs include any race over the 440 up to and including the mile run. The stride of the middle-distance runner will be somewhat shorter than that of the sprinter as the conservation and economical use of energy (pace) becomes an important factor. Generally, the longer the distance to be run, the shorter the stride will be. When the middle-distance runner wishes to increase his speed, he increases the speed of the leg and arm action without overstriding, which is a slowing action. The speed of this action will regulate the stride length. The middle-distance runner should have a good knowledge and "feel" of pace so that he will be able to distribute his energy rather evenly throughout the race.

Distance Running

Races above the two-mile are generally classified as distance runs. The stride of distance runners will be shorter than that of sprinters and middle-distance runners. Economy of energy and running efficiency dictate stride length; shorter strides promote more efficient running over long distances. The distance runner has a different foot placement, also. He lands low on the ball of the foot, then allows his heel to come in contact with the track, and then rolls up off the ball of the foot for the next stride (ball-heel-ball action). This foot-plant is best because the distance runner's body is more erect, the forward knee lift lower, and the back kick higher than in shorter races. Distance runners let the leg come forward from the high rear kick position with little or no forward lift to conserve energy and to capitalize upon gravity to move the leg down and forward. Successful distance runners work year-round to develop the necessary endurance and strength.

Cross-Country Running

Cross country is distance running, usually over hilly, rough terrain, conducted over courses of up to three miles in high school. It is a team sport. The official team consist of seven competitors; the first five men to cross the finish line for each team score for their teams. Each scorer is credited with a number of points equal to the position in which he finishes—1 for first, 2 for second, 10 for tenth, 36 for thirty-sixth—and the team having the *lowest* aggregate score wins. The finish position of every man on the team is important; although the sixth and seventh men on each team to cross the finish line do not score for their team, they do push the opponents' score higher. Fifteen points are a perfect score and require a team to finish 1-2-3-4-5.

The same short stride and economical form described for distance running applies to cross-country running. When running on hills, adjustments must be made in form. Uphill running requires more forward lean, greater forward lift of the knees, higher landing on the ball of the foot, and more vigorous arm action. Downhill running necessitates opposite variations—more erect posture, less forward lift of the knees, higher rear kick of the legs, lower landing on the ball of the foot, and less vigorous and lower arm action.

Strategy often plays an important role in cross-country running. You learn to take advantage of wind breaks, such as hedges and buildings, and of other runners. Running with teammates will often help you do better. Most good teams attempt to stay together through at least three-fourths of the race. Some run in two groups of near equal ability. When your group is out of sight around a corner or over a hill, try to increase your lead over your opponents by speeding up for a while. It is very discouraging to them to unexpectedly lose ground that way. When you reach the top of a hill, speed up while your opponents are still climbing the hill. When you pass a runner, go by with a burst of speed and continue on for about fifty yards before settling back into your race pace. There is sometimes an advantage in running close behind an opponent since he sets the pace, acts as a wind break, and is often psychologically distracted by this maneuver.

Hurdling

High school boys compete in 180-yard low hurdle and 120-yard high hurdle races. In the low hurdles there is a 20-yard approach to the first hurdle, 20 yards between each of 2-feet 6-inch hurdles, and a 20-yard finish. In the high hurdles there is a 15-yard approach and finish and 10 yards between each of the 3-feet 3-inch hurdles.

The important point in hurdling is to run over the hurdles, not jump them. Spend as little time in the air over the hurdles as possible. Attack the hurdle. The start in hurdling is the same as in sprinting, except that you must decide which foot must be the forward one so that you can arrive at the take-off position for the first hurdle on the proper foot.

The chief difference in form between low and high hurdling is the angle of your body as you go over the hurdle. In the latter you lean forward more and your leading arm is more extended.

The take-off for the hurdle should be far enough away to permit a forward lift of the leading leg without touching the hurdle. Bring your leading leg forward with the knee slightly bent as in running, because once you have cleared the hurdle you must continue your run. The leading foot should continue straight forward and up to clear the hurdle

High Hurdles

as you lean forward. Your opposite arm and hand should be stretched forward to balance your leg. As soon as the toe of the take-off, trailing leg leaves the track, that leg is brought quickly forward with the knee bent. As it passes over the hurdle, it is lifted upward from your hip so that your thigh is almost parallel with the ground. Meanwhile, your leading leg is cutting down sharply as you are pulling the trailing leg through and around into running position for your next stride.

Remember that your legs go over the hurdle one at a time and that you must maintain your body-lean over the hurdle to keep from catching your knee or ankle on it. Adjust your stride so that you arrive at the next hurdle on the proper take-off foot. Finish as described for the sprints.

Relays

There are several different types of relays: sprint relays (4x110, 4x220, 4x440); distance relays (4x880, 4xmile); and medley relays, such as the sprint medley (440, 220, 220, 880), distance medley (880, 440, 1320, mile), and some other combinations of distances. The four runners on the relay team should be the fastest men on the squad in the distance required of them.

Of particular importance in relay running is the baton exchange or pass. Many sprint relays are won or lost on the efficiency of the exchange. The exchange or passing zone is 22 yards long, and the pass must be completed within this zone. The receiver starts from just inside

TRACK AND FIELD

High Hurdles (cont.)

the first line of the zone as the incoming runner reaches a point about 6 yards from the zone in the sprint relays. The incoming man will pass the baton from his left hand to the receiver's right hand (outside pass) or his right hand to the receiver's left (inside pass). In each case, each man will keep to his side of the lane so that the pass will be made straight-on with both men running at about the same speed. The baton is then changed to the opposite hand to prepare for the next exchange.

Passing the Baton

Many considerations are involved in the selection of the order in which the men will run. Standard procedure in the sprint relays is to run the second fastest man as lead-off, the slowest man second, while the third leg is usually run by the man who is a good competitor, with the anchor man being the fastest man on the squad. Very often this order is altered for purposes of strategy.

Running Long Jump

The main requirements for long jumping are speed, balance, and fine coordination. Measurement of the jump is made at right angles from the take-off board to the nearest mark on the ground made by the athlete or his clothing. Long jumping starts with a run of between 90 and 125 feet. You attempt to reach maximum speed about 45 feet from the toeboard.

To make sure that your approach to the take-off point is always the same, you will need two check marks: one at a point about 100 feet from the take-off board where you begin your run, and the other about 45 feet from the take-off point. The step-off at the first mark should be with the take-off foot, and the second check mark should be reached on the same foot. These two check marks can be adjusted so that you reach the take-off point on the correct foot.

At the take-off, you should jump up and not out. Your take-off foot hits the board with the knee slightly bent, and by taking a shorter, final stride, your body is directly over this foot. With an upward swing of your free leg and a rocking motion on the toes of the take-off foot, you concentrate on getting your chest as high as possible.

You should reach your maximum height with your chin and chest up and your feet trailing slightly. Your arms should be forward and out. Bring your hips forward and your feet about level with them. With your arms forward, "sit" in the air, with your feet about a foot apart and your knees slightly bent.

Land with your feet a foot or so apart so that your body will fall between your knees and over your feet. To keep from falling back into a sitting position, drop your chin on your chest, lean forward on your hips, flex your knees, and swing your arms downward and backward.

Triple Jump

The approach in the triple jump, formerly known as the hop, step, and jump, is similar to that in long jumping. The length of the run varies with the person but usually is from 70 to 100 feet. Two check marks

TRACK AND FIELD

Hop, Step, and Jump

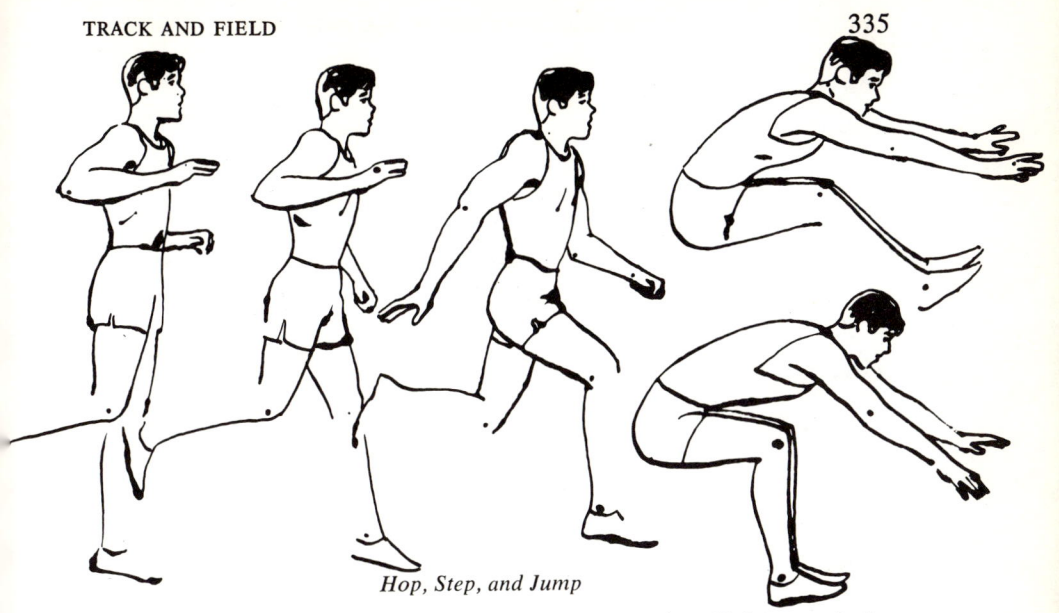

are used, one marking the starting point of the take-off foot, and the second marking the position of the take-off foot, about 45 feet from the take-off board. Your last few strides will probably be shorter than previous ones so that your body is directly over the take-off foot at the end of the board.

In this event, maximum height is not desired as it is in the broad jump since you are attempting to maintain forward speed. You can hop about 14 feet, step about 12 feet, and jump about 15 feet, so that the hop is roughly 40 percent of the total distance covered. In the hop you land on the take-off foot, maintaining forward momentum. Now you swing your other knee up, feeling that you are floating through the air with your knee up, your take-off foot trailing, and your body bent slightly forward. When your foot touches the ground, you are ready for the jump phase. Use good long jump technique and land so that your body falls forward.

The Pole Vault

You need strong arms, a strong shoulder girdle, good coordination, and speed to be a pole vaulter. Many good pole vaulters develop early; some ninth grade boys have been able to make 11-foot jumps.

Learning pole vaulting starts with careful attention to the grip on the pole. If your hands are placed too high, it takes greater momentum to get you up, and if too low, you can't get enough height. You need to learn by experience the maximum height for you to grip the pole. The

Pole Vault

location of your top hand is more important because the other hand may be 2 or 3 feet lower on the pole.

During the run toward the bar you should carry the pole with the tip about head high and slightly across the body and pointed in the direction of the run. You will need two check marks for your run: one to mark the position of the take-off run about 100 feet from the vaulting block (where you place the pole) and the other about 45 feet from the vaulting block, where the take-off foot touches. The speed of your run will depend on your ability to use it in the vault. The faster you run the higher your grip can be and the greater vaulting height you can reach.

In holding the pole, your right palm faces out and your left palm down. As you approach the bar, bring your right hand forward past your hip and push the pole forward and upward through the left hand until it is over your head. Raise your right knee to add upward momentum from the push of your take-off foot, with your arms and legs extended. The take-off must be made from the left foot directly behind the pole and with the pole along the middle of the body.

Letting the pole do most of the work, you start a pendulum swing upward. Raise your hips above your shoulders, with your feet back above your head, while still "hanging" with extended arms from the pole. As the pole reacts and straightens, pull up with your arms to raise your body higher until you are in a handstand on the pole with feet above the bar. Let your right leg scissor across the top of your left leg and keep your right shoulder as close to the pole as possible. Keep

TRACK AND FIELD 337

Pole Vault (cont.)

on pushing until you can look down and see your hands and arms in full extension. Now, to avoid hitting the bar, push the pole away from you and throw your hands over your head. You may land on your back in the pit unless the pit is made of shavings or sawdust, in which case you should land on your feet.

When a competitor in the pole vault has three consecutive misses, he is eliminated from the competition. Usually he will take all three jumps at the same height.

High Jumping

Leg spring or bounce is needed for high jumping. An athlete's natural spring can be improved through a well-planned program in weight training and jumping exercises. You may go over the bar anyway you want to, but you must leave the ground from one foot only.

You approach the bar with several easy, relaxed strides, usually between five and nine, from approximately a 45-degree angle. Smooth, uniform strides are essential.

There are several clearance styles in the high jump. The Western roll is a good basic form to use for beginners; the straddle or "belly" roll has proven to be the most efficient; and the latest style, the "Fosbury Flop," was made popular by the 1968 Olympic champion. We advocate the use of the Western or straddle rolls for beginners.

The Western roll requires a firm plant of the left foot with a swing of the right leg and foot through and upward. The take-off point will

Running High Jump

be approximately 30 to 36 inches from the crossbar. The body weight should be directly over the take-off foot at the moment the jumper leaves the runway. He should strive for as much lift and height as possible. When your take-off foot leaves the ground, move it up even with your right foot. Your head and shoulders should be at about the same level as your feet when you cross the bar. You should look as if you are laying on your left side just above the bar. Roll slightly to the right by dropping your right arm so that you will drop face down. After clearing the bar, you should land on both hands and the take-off foot.

The approach for the straddle roll is the same as for the Western roll. The take-off is also the same. The difference between the two forms is in the manner of bar clearance. Your body rolls over the bar so that you are facing down as you are over the bar, as if rolling over on your belly. The body roll is imparted simply by turning toes and knee of your left (trail) leg toward the sky and dropping your right arm toward the pit.

After clearing the bar you should land on your right foot, side, or back, depending upon how much roll your body develops. As in the pole vault, a jumper is allowed three consecutive misses before he is eliminated from the competition.

The Shot Put

Shot putting requires strength, speed, and coordination. A 12-pound shot is used in high school, and an 8-pound shot in junior high

TRACK AND FIELD   339

Running High Jump (cont.)

schools. The secret of putting the shot is to push it, not throw it, from the shoulder. To gain momentum for the put, you can travel across a 7-foot circle before releasing it.

The shot should be held in the fingers with the thumb on the outside for balance and held against the neck and shoulder. You should face away from the direction in which the put will be made (your back should be to the landing area). Your weight should be over your right leg, with your left arm at shoulder height across the front of your chest. Your

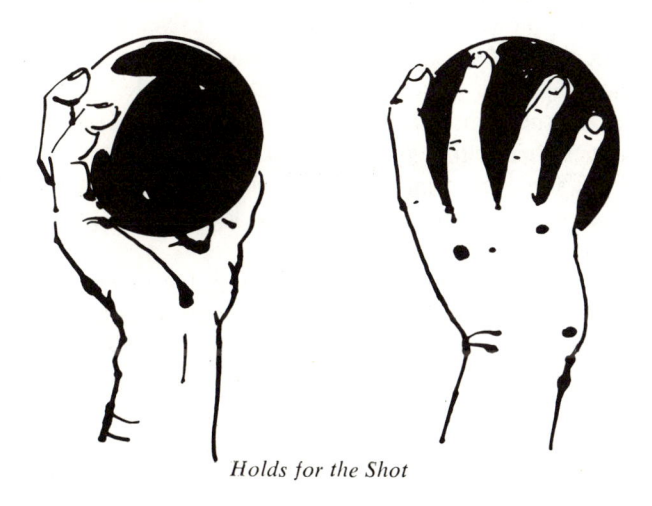

Holds for the Shot

Putting the Shot

body should balance over your right foot as your upper-body bends forward. Your right leg should bend until your chest is at about waist height. Your left leg should swing up to the rear at the same time for balance. At the low point of your body at the rear of the circle, bring your left knee up beside your right knee, with the lower left leg parallel to the ground. Then this leg is kicked vigorously back toward the front of the circle. This will pull your body momentarily off balance so that there must be an immediate push off of the right foot and then a rapid pulling of the right foot across the circle back under the center of your body weight. This should put your right foot at about the mid-point of the circle, from which there is an immediate drive up and around off your right foot while the weight is still centered over it. Your left foot in the meantime strikes the toeboard slightly to the left of the center of the board. As the right side of your body is driven (pushed) up and around, your weight will begin to shift to your left foot as the right side of your body, shoulder, arm, and hand push the shot forward and up at a 40-degree angle. Straighten your left leg just before the shot is released.

Your head and chest must be up during the delivery. Keep your left shoulder up to avoid dipping to the left and pulling away from the shot. All of your power and strength must be directly behind the shot precisely at the moment of release! The forward momentum developed by your body will tend to carry you through and out of the circle, which would be a foul. To avoid this and to control your body after delivery, make a rapid reverse from your left foot onto your right foot. Relax and

Putting the Shot (cont.)

regain body control and balance by bouncing on your right leg to stay in the circle.

The whole action of the put must be continuous, without any hesitation from the rear of the circle until the delivery of the shot at the front of the circle. The action must be one of setting the shot in forward motion and then adding as much power as you possibly can to it before you release it. You cannot touch the top of the 7-foot circle or any thing outside of the circle once the action has started, and you must leave the circle through the rear half once the put has been completed and the official gives you permission. You are given four trial throws, one of which must be a legal throw of sufficient distance, compared with your competitors, in order to advance you to the finals, where you receive three more throws. The best distance that you achieve throughout the competition will determine your final standing in the competition.

The Discus Throw

For high schools the discus weighs 3 pounds 9 ounces and is thrown from a circle 8 feet 2½ inches in diameter. Measurement in the discus throw, as in the shot, is taken from the nearest edge of the mark made by the implement to the nearest point on the circumference of the circle (inner edge). All throws must fall within a 60-degree sector marked on the ground. You must not touch the top of the circle or outside of the circle with any part of your body or clothing.

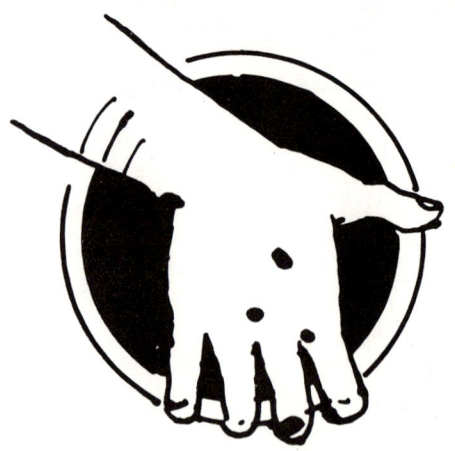

Grasping the Discus

The discus is held with the fingers hooked over the rim—just enough to control it—and the thumb along the side of the discus. You should first learn to throw the discus by scaling it from a standing position. Practice putting clockwise spin on the discus by whipping your arm forward and snapping your wrist. The discus should leave the index finger last. The flat side should be nearly parallel to the ground (at about a 30-degree angle), because if it is thrown at too great an angle air pressure will keep it from achieving distance.

Throwing the Discus

As in the shot put, the thrower starts at the rear of the circle with his back facing the direction of the throw (the thrower facing to the rear of the circle). Make a couple of preliminary swings by extending your right arm backward at shoulder height and then bringing the discus around to a point in front of your left shoulder. At the moment it comes around, use your left hand to check its forward movement.

When you make the turn for the throw, pivot 180 degrees on the ball of your left foot and then shift your weight to the ball of your right foot to complete the turn. As you pivot, keep your throwing arm well back of your right hip. Make the throw by driving off the ball of the right foot to lift the whole right side of the body as in the shot put. As the right side is driven up and around, a full, straight right arm is whipped or pulled forward with a final snapping of the wrist just prior to the release. The discus should leave the hand slightly above shoulder height. The angle of the discus and the angle of the delivery should be about 30 degrees. To maintain your balance and keep within the circle, let your body swing on around after you have made the throw so that you have reversed the position of your feet, with your right foot now parallel to the edge of the ring and controlling the remaining momentum of your whirling body. The problem in throwing the discus is to develop a lot of momentum by whirling the body without any serious loss of balance and control, and to keep the body weight centered over the right foot as the delivery in started. The same number of trials and final

Throwing the Discus (cont.)

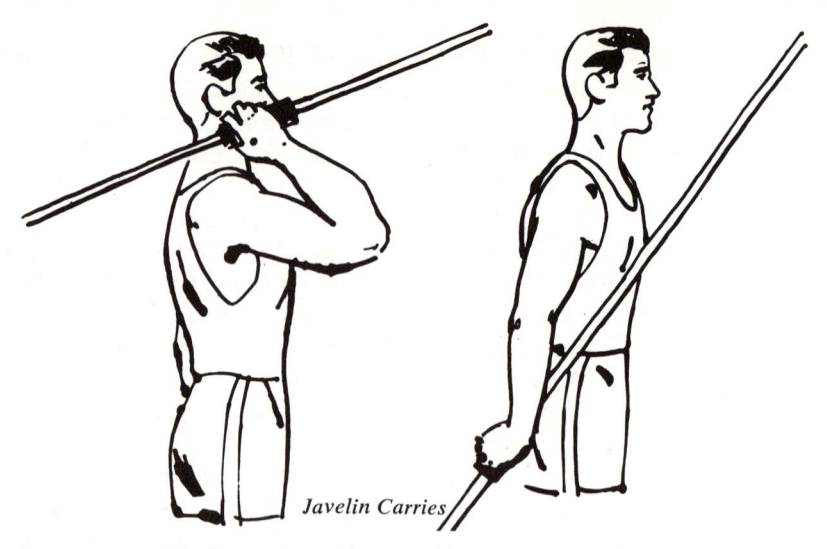

Javelin Carries

throws are allowed in the same manner as in the shot put. The discus thrower must also exit from the rear half of the circle.

The Javelin Throw

To be successful in the javelin throw you should have a strong arm, strong legs, a well-developed upper body, and good coordination. The javelin is thrown from behind a scratch (foul) line, which actually is an arc of a circle with a radius of 26 feet 3 inches. The javelin must

Throwing the Javelin

hit the ground point first, but does not have to stick up. The throw is measured from the scratch line to the nearest point made by the point of the javelin.

The javelin is gripped across the palm of the hand with the thumb over the rear edge of the grip cord. The index finger may also wrap around the shaft at the rear of the grip or it may be along the shaft with the second finger around the edge of the grip. The thrower should use the grip that is most comfortable to him and most powerful.

The javelin is carried over the shoulder during the run-up so that the throwing arm is free to contribute some motion to the running action. The approach to the throw varies according to the thrower, but is usually between 60 and 120 feet.

Most throwers use two check marks for the approach run: one about 90 feet from the scratch line, and the second about 30 feet from it. The length of the run will vary according to the thrower. The left foot lands at the first check mark and the thrower runs with good speed—not full speed—to the second check mark which is also hit by the left foot. He then takes five steps leading to and including the throw. His feet and body must face forward during the first step on the right foot. The right arm starts to draw back straight from the shoulder directly in the line of intended flight. On the second step the left foot hits the ground turned slightly to the right. The right foot is turned out and crosses over the left leg. The body is now turned slightly to the right, in

Throwing the Javelin (cont.)

the third step. At this point the throwing arm is now fully extended behind the right shoulder, and the javelin point is at about eye level. On the fourth step the left foot extends forward and is planted firmly, heel first, directly in line with the intended flight. On this step the throwing arm starts to pull the javelin forward. With both feet planted firmly, the throw is made by pulling the javelin straight through over the right shoulder with the elbow leading the hand. The right leg drives the body forward and up over the planted left foot which has acted like a brake to convert the speed of the run into the whip-like action of the throw. The throw is made at about a 40-degree angle as the body pivots up and over the left foot. The fifth step is the natural follow-through as you land again on your right foot and halt your forward momentum by bounding on your right leg to stay behind the scratch line. The action is more of a pulling action from the extended position behind the shoulder than a throwing action, since the javelin is over the shoulder. To avoid injury to the elbow and throwing arm, be sure to lead the throw with the elbow forward of the hand as it is pulled over the right shoulder.

SAFETY IN TRACK AND FIELD EVENTS

Keeping yourself in good condition is the first requirement for safety in any sport. Warm up thoroughly before any event or practice. Early season workouts should be progressive so that you do not run too hard before your muscles are ready for it. After you have finished a race, don't stop immediately. Come to a gradual stop by slowing down and jogging several yards further. This may prevent strained muscles and will help your body adjust itself to lessened activity. Before and after track and field events and during long waits for your trials in field events, keep your sweat suit on to avoid chilling. Otherwise the excessive tensing of muscles may result in a pulled muscle or strain.

Do not leave spiked shoes laying around with the spikes sticking up as you or someone may accidentally step on them. In the field events, look before you jump or throw. Make sure that the runway is clear or that the landing area is clear and that no one is approaching it. Do not "horse around" with implements; they are not playthings and can cause death if used carelessly. Do not throw implements back and forth. Do not go to retrieve your implement until the area is clear and no more throws are to be made. Always be alert around the field event areas and keep your eyes on the circles and runways. Do not let your vaulting pole drop to the ground or leave it laying on the ground where someone may accidentally step on it and spike it. Take good care of your vaulting pole and protect it from injury so that it will not break in the middle of a vault.

Do not cut in too soon on other runners that you are passing. Many spike wounds are caused this way. Avoid pushing and shoving during a race.

Keep as relaxed as possible at all times, since muscle tenseness may invite injury.

EQUIPMENT

The most important item of equipment that the runner has is his shoes. These should fit snugly but not tightly. A shoe with a soft, pliable upper, such as kangaroo leather, is best. Above all the shoe should feel good on you without pinching, feeling heavy, stiff, or loose. There are many different kinds of track surfaces in use today, from cinder, clay, to all-weather and board tracks, so shoes which have replaceable spikes are the most economical since they can be used on any surface simply by putting in the correct length and type of spike. The spiked shoe is necessary for racing. You should also have a pair of flats (rubber soled shoes) for use in going to and from the locker room and for some of your training. The rubber soled shoe with canvas upper is good for this use. The field men often require somewhat different shoes. The shot putter and discus thrower need a good rubber-soled shoe for use on concrete and asphalt surfaces. Here a broader based sole is best, with a soft, pliable upper, such as Kangaroo. The javelin thrower uses a field shoe with two spikes in the heel. Javelin shoes are also made as "boots" as compared to "low-cuts." The boots come up over the ankles and give added support. The spikes in the javelin shoe are generally longer. Football shoes often make a good shoe to throw in, especially when the grass is wet and the field muddy. The high jumper wears a shoe with one or two heel spikes on his take-off foot and a regular shoe or none at all on the lead foot.

Keep your shoes dry if possible. If you do get them wet, do not dry them over direct heat. Stuff them with newspaper and let them dry normally at room temperature; then apply some leather preservative to them to keep them soft. Do not let your spikes wear down so far that you cannot get them out. Replace them when they bend or are blunted. Always make sure that your shoe strings are in good order and not frayed. Many races have been lost because of a broken shoe lace.

A good shot (for shot put) is one that you can grip well. The larger iron shots are best if you can grip them, and they have the advantage of being less expensive.

In high school and junior high, the use of a rubber discus is permissible and somewhat safer. The wooden metal-rimmed discus is still the best implement, however, as it has better sailing qualities. The discus should be kept in good shape and clean. Do not allow a lot of dirt and grass to build up on it as it will add extra weight and affect its sailing qualities.

There are several kinds of javelins. One company even makes a javelin with a rubber tip. Aluminum javelins usually cost more but are more consistent, last longer, and have better aerodynamic qualities. If you buy a wooden javelin, look it over closely to make sure that it is not warped and that it meets all of the rules governing the javelin. Javelins—especially wooden javelins—should be stored in a cool moist place and should be hung from the tail rather than left laying on the floor or standing in a corner. Keep the javelin clean and protect it from abuse.

Vaulting poles are quite expensive and quite varied. If you plan to buy a pole, you should seek the advice of a coach to make sure that you get the one best suited to you and your vaulting techniques. When not in use, poles should be stored in a firm tubular case. This case should also be used in transporting poles. Off season, your pole should be stored in a tube and out of the way of damage.

TRACK AND FIELD ETIQUETTE

You should have a strong desire to win at all times, but never take unfair advantage of an opponent or create any distractions for him. Do not make noise, talk loudly, or move around when a thrower is in the circle and trying to concentrate or a jumper is preparing for a jump. This also is true around the starting line when the starter has called the runners to their marks.

Do not use unsportsmanlike tactics in a race, such as elbowing, pushing, or boxing a man in. Quite often such tactics detract from the performance of the offender rather than the offended. An athlete should not use another athlete's implement, pole, or equipment without the consent of the owner. You should not attempt to use any piece of equipment which does not meet all of the legal requirements for that item.

Report to your event on time and properly warmed up, with shoes on and tied so that you do not cause unnecessary delay of the event.

Do not take too much time in completing a trial in field events or in moving from one event to another if you are in more than one event at the same time.

Be a humble winner and a gracious loser. Be polite and courteous to all officials, and do not argue with their decisions.

Be careful not to disturb the marks along runways or on the track that other competitors have placed there.

Track and field is a gentleman's sport, and everyone should be accorded the opportunity to do the very best that he can without distractions or the less-than-fair tactics of others.

FOR MORE INFORMATION

American Association for Health, Physical Education, and Recreation, Division for Girls and Women's Sports. *Track and Field Guide.* Current edition. Washington, D.C.: the Association.

Doherty, J. Kenneth. *Modern Track and Field.* Second edition. Englewood Cliffs, N.J.: Prentice-Hall.

Foreman, Ken, and Husted, Virginia. *Track and Field.* Dubuque, Iowa: Wm. C. Brown Co., 1966.

Foreman, Ken, and Husted, Virginia. *Track and Field Techniques for Girls and Women.* Dubuque, Iowa: Wm. C. Brown Co., 1965.

Jordan, Payton. *Track and Field for Boys.* Chicago: Follett Publishing Co., 1960.

Luke, Brother G., F.S.C. *Coaching High School Track and Field.* Englewood Cliffs, N.J.: Prentice-Hall.

Miller, Kenneth D. *Track and Field for Girls.* New York: Ronald Press Co., 1965.

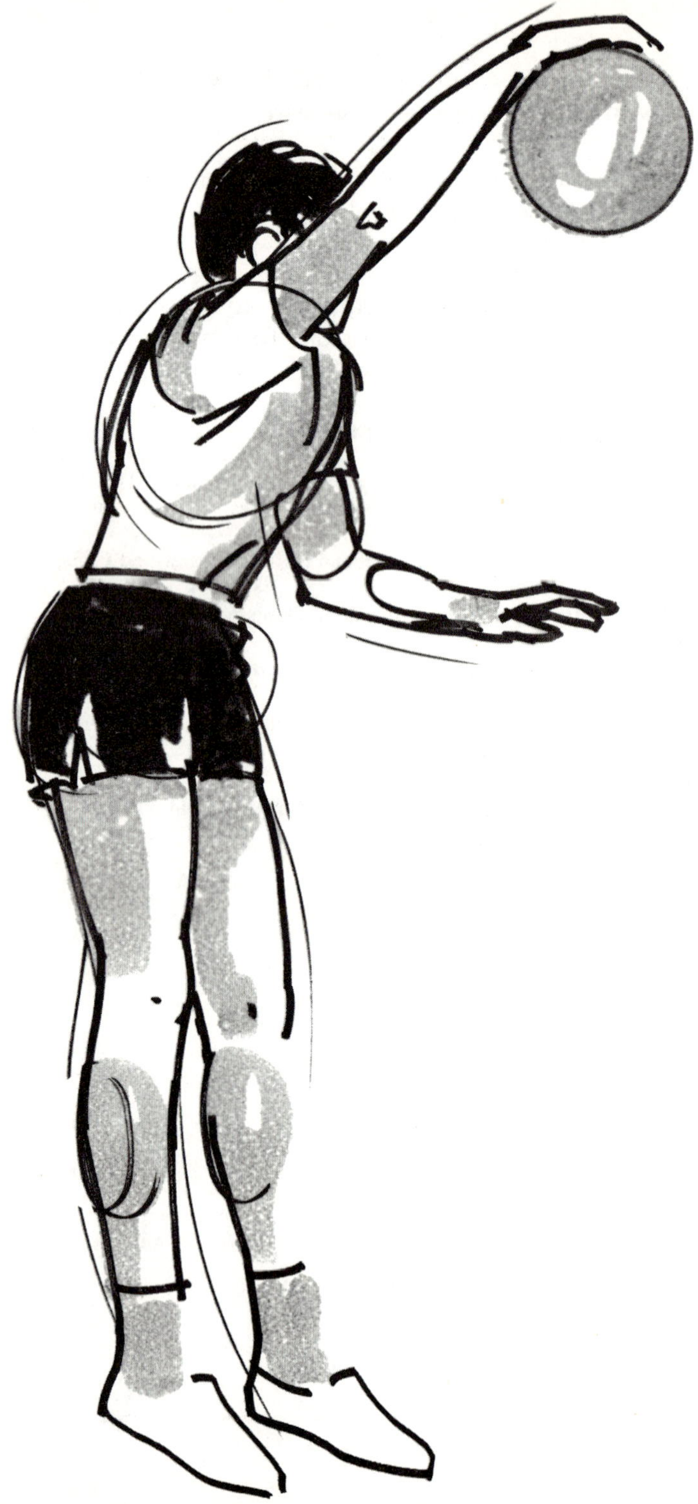

Volleyball

Volleyball is one of the few popular games developed in the United States. In 1895, William Morgan, while working in a YMCA in Holyoke, Massachusetts, developed it as a team game to play indoors. Morgan first used a tennis net stretched about 6½ feet from the floor. For a ball he first tried the bladder of a basketball, but that was too light and slow; a basketball was too heavy and large. Finally he decided on a ball similar to the present volleyball, and a sporting goods manufacturer made one for him.

The object of the game was to keep the ball going back and forth over the net without its touching the floor. At first the game was divided into innings, and any number of people could play.

In 1924, seperate rules for girls were published by the organization that is now known as the Division for Girls and Women's Sports of the American Association for Health, Physical Education, and Recreation. In 1928, the United States Volleyball Association was formed, and this Association has helped make volleyball a familiar game all over the country.

During World War II, American servicemen played volleyball for recreation in many different countries. This caused a rapid spread of interest and participation in the game in various parts of the world. In 1964, volleyball was played in the Olympics for the first time, with both men's and women's teams competing. Currently, it is felt that, except in the United States, volleyball is second only to football soccer in popularity throughout the entire world. Moreover, volleyball continues to show increased popularity in the United States. A survey conducted in 1966 revealed 40 million participants, just double the amount a similar survey indicated in 1961. Currently, many schools and colleges offer competitive athletic programs in volleyball for both boys and girls in addition to the regular instructional program.

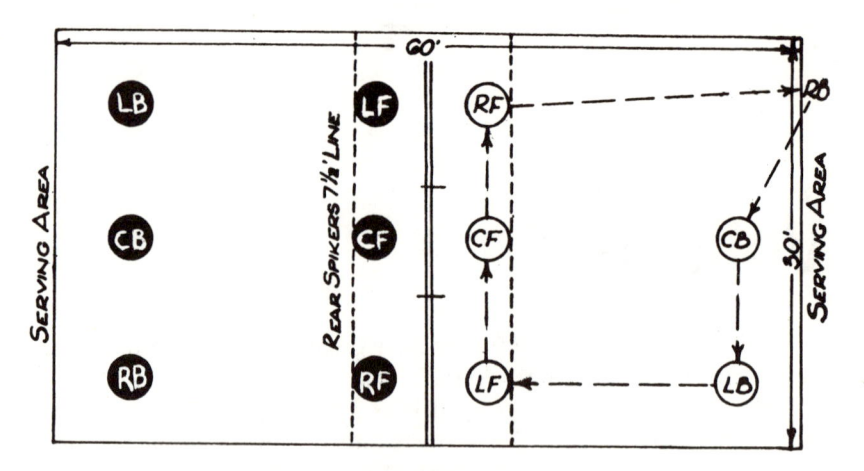

The Court, Players, and Order of Rotation

THE COURT

Volleyball is played on a court 30 feet wide by 60 feet long. The court is divided by a net 3 feet wide, the top of which is 8 feet above the floor for boys and 7 feet 4¼ inches above the floor for girls. This height may be lowered 6 inches to 1 foot in accordance with the ability of the players. The space above the court should be unobstructed for at least 25 to 30 feet. The official ball has a 12-panel, light-colored leather cover and must be approximately 26 inches in circumference and weigh not more than 9 ounces.

THE GAME

A volleyball team consists of six players: left forward, center forward, and right forward at the net (or front areas); left back, center back, and right back behind the frontline players. The player in the right back position is called the server.

The team starting the play is referred to as the serving team. Only the serving team may score points. If the receiving team fails to legally return the ball over the net, a point is awarded to the serving team. When the serving team fails to serve the ball legally into the opponent's court, or return the ball into the opponent's court, a "side-out" is called, and the other team becomes the serving team. (No point is awarded to either team when a side-out is called.) When a team is awarded a side-out, the players on that team rotate one position clockwise. The player who rotates into the right back position becomes the server.

A game is completed when one team has scored a total of 15 points and has a 2-point lead, or if at the termination of eight minutes of actual playing time, a team has a 2-point advantage. The team that is first to win two out of three games is declared the winner of a match.

Basic Rules for Volleyball

1. Team captains toss a coin for choice of serve or court.
2. The server may strike at the ball with the hand in any manner—underhand, sidearm, or overhead. The server may not touch the end line while serving the ball. The ball must not touch the net on the serve.
3. When playing the ball, the player must clearly hit or bat the ball.
4. The ball must be played before it touches the floor.
5. The boundary lines are considered part of the court. Therefore, a ball that lands on or touches part of any of these lines should have been played.
6. Some part of the ball must pass over or between the side boundary lines as it crosses the net.
7. Other than on the serve, it is legal for the ball to touch the net.
8. No player may touch the opponent's court. The center line under the net may be stepped on but not over.
9. No player may touch the net. Players may, however, reach over the net on the follow-through of a hit.
10. A player may leave his own court to play a ball, but may not enter his opponent's court.
11. Each team may play the ball as many as three times before returning it to the opponent's court.
12. No player may play the ball twice in succession. A player may play the ball on the first and third hit.
13. A backline player may not come up to the net to spike the ball.
14. Teams exchange courts at the end of each game and in the middle of the third game.
15. The team that served first in the first game may not serve first in the second game.

Rule Differences for Boys and Girls

1. In the girls game, neither team rotates from its original starting positions until after each team has had its first term of service.

2. Girls may serve from anywhere behind the end line; boys must serve from within a 10-foot distance from the right side line.

3. Boys, except on the serve, may play the ball with any part of the body above and including the waist; girls may use only the hand(s) or forearm(s) in playing the ball.

4. The 10-foot spiking line is not included in the marking on the girls court; other rules covering spiking are approximately the same.

5. After the serve, boys are allowed some interchange of relative court positions in order to utilize some offensive and defensive team play patterns; girls are responsible primarily for their own approximate one-sixth of the court.

NOTE: Rules are continually under study for change. Therefore, it is strongly suggested that you consult the most up-to-date edition of rule guides as a means for determining the most current rules in effect. Such guides are listed at the conclusion of the chapter.

Rules for Co-Recreational Volleyball

Volleyball is an excellent game for boys and girls to play together. Some suggested rules for this co-recreational game follow:

1. The team shall consist of 3 girls and 3 boys who alternate positions on the floor.

2. The net height for senior high school students should be 7 feet 4¼ inches; for junior high school students it should be 7 feet. (Boys should be restricted to the use of a "soft spike" or the net height should be raised to 8 feet for high school and 7 feet 4¼ inches for junior high play.)

3. When the ball is played by more than one player before going over the net, one of these must be a girl.

4. Except for the serve, the ball may be contacted with any part of the body, above and including the waist.

BASIC SKILLS

Serving

Play is started by a serve made from behind the end boundary of the court by the player in the right-back position. The serve must go over the net on the first attempt.

Underhand Serve

The Underhand Serve. This is an easy serve to learn, but it is also easy to return. If you are right-handed, place the ball in the palm of your left hand and hold the ball toward the right side of your body. Have your left foot ahead of your right and both knees slightly bent. Swing your right arm back and up behind you. Then as you swing it forward, straighten your arm and hit the ball with the heel of your hand. After hitting the ball, let your arm swing up and forward in the direction you want the ball to go. This is called *follow-through*. Contact with the ball may be made in one of several ways. The open-hand serve is the easiest for beginners. Force can be given either with the palm and fingers or with the heel of the hand. Others may wish to use a fist in contacting the ball, but, in this method, the ball is not easily controlled.

The Overhead Punch Serve. This is one of the most popular and widely used serves among players today. You should stand facing the net with your feet in a slightly stride position, your left foot just ahead of your right. Hold the ball well out in front of your body. Toss the ball straight up in front of you to a height of 12 to 18 inches above your head. Using an open hand, contact the ball with the heel of your hand as the ball drops to a point just above your head. Follow through with a straight punch action of your right arm, bringing your weight forward as you step onto your right foot. You will be more successful in controlling your serve if you focus, during the entire serve action, at the point on the ball where you wish to contact it.

If you wish to make your serve more difficult to receive, you can cause the ball to "float," that is, to wobble back and forth or swerve

Overhead Punch Serve

suddenly as it crosses the net. To develop this action of the ball, you must toss the ball from the holding hand so that it will not be spinning at the time it is contacted. It is also important that you hit in a line straight through the ball.

Volleying

One of the first skills you need to learn is how to volley the ball (that is, keep the ball in the air) without holding, lifting, pushing, throwing, or scooping it. The ball must be clearly batted.

Overhead Volley. This skill is most often used to send the ball to a teammate and is quite commonly referred to as the chest pass. To perform this skill, you must use your fingertips to contact the ball, keeping your wrists firm and cocked well back. Practice hitting a balloon into the air several times. This will give you the feeling of volleying with your fingertips rather than pushing or lifting it with your hands. In hitting the balloon, you must give a little flick from your fingers and wrists to get it up into the air. Although the volleyball is heavier than the balloon, you do the same thing to play it. Keep your fingers spread with your hands in front of your face and with your knees slightly bent and wait for the ball to come to you. Just before contact, begin to straighten your knees. With a slight wrist snap and straightening of your arms the ball should rebound immediately off your fingers. Follow through in the direction you want the ball to go. Make a habit of using both hands on every volley. Concentrate on learning to control low as well as high passes.

VOLLEYBALL

Overhead Volley

During game play, direct all passes up and in a line toward your teammate. If the pass is high enough, your teammate will have time to get under the ball and can then easily make the next play. You must be alert at all times so that you can move quickly toward the ball. It is important that you be crouched beneath the ball well before contact. The poorer player reaches out for the ball. The good player gets under it and waits for the ball to come to him.

Setting is the art of passing the ball fairly high and close to the net so that the spiker can spring into the air and smash it into the opponent's court. The chest pass, or overhead volley, is the skill that is most frequently used to set the ball. Since the success of the spike often depends upon how good the set-up is, it is very important that the set-up be accurate. The center forward is usually designated as the setter. As a setter, you should try to deceive your opponents in passing the ball to the spiker by trying to fake a set-up to one spiker but passing it to another. This is sometimes done by passing the ball back over your head, using the same hand position in contacting the ball. In this way you do not telegraph your intentions. It is important, however, that you arch your back as you contact the ball. This will cause the ball to go high and behind you, dropping straight down over the designated spot for the spiker to come in and hit. You should set the ball at least 12 feet high and from 1 to 2 feet from the net, to either of the side net positions. This will give the spiker enough time to get into position, jump up, and hit the ball.

Underhand Volley

Underhand Volley. When it is impossible to get into the proper position to use an overhead volley to play the ball, you will find it necessary to use an underhand volley instead. This skill is referred to as either a bump or bounce pass, and is commonly used to receive serves (especially the low, close-to-the-net, hard-hit serves), to recover a ball as it drops from the net, to pick up a spiked ball, as well as to make a save.

To perform the skill, place the palms of the hands together and grasp the back of one hand with the fingers of the other, with the thumbs forward and the arms extended and downward. This will bring the forearms close together in a parallel position and provide a fairly flat hitting surface. The ball should be hit 3 or 4 inches above the wrist with a controlled upward motion. Face the direction in which you wish the ball to go. Bend your knees deeply to get low and well beneath the ball as it comes toward you. Extend your legs and body upward to meet the ball, keeping your elbows and shoulders in a somewhat fixed position at the time the ball rebounds off the forearms. Bending your elbows or allowing too much lift of the arms from the shoulders usually causes the ball to rebound from your forearms and go backwards over your head. The important thing is to try and get the ball high in the air so that a teammate has plenty of time to move in under the ball and make an accurate set pass. Even though it is legal to use a one-hand underhand volley, it is easier to control the ball by using both arms.

VOLLEYBALL

Spike

Spiking

The spike is a hard hit which sends the ball directly downward over the top of the net into the opponent's court. The spike is made with an open hand by hitting the ball off the heel of the hand, with a quick whip action of the shoulder, arm, and hand.

The ball must be set up by a teammate so that you can spike it. If you are right-handed, the set should be made by the player to the right of you whenever possible, because this puts you in a better position to play the ball. The set-up should be at least 5 feet above the top of the net and parallel to it, and from 1 to 2 feet away from it. As you face the net, you should be about an arm's distance from it. Bend your knees, keeping your weight somewhat forward. Swing your arms upward to help you get height as you spring into the air. Hit the ball at the highest point of your jump. At the height of your jump, your hitting arm should be bent with your hand behind your head. Quickly whip your hitting arm up and toward the ball, straightening your arm and snapping your wrist downward as you contact the top of the ball with the heel of your hand. Hit the ball downward across the top of the net, being careful not to touch the net. You will have much more control if you hit the ball with your open hand rather than with your fist.

Blocking

The block is a defensive maneuver used against a spiked ball. When one of your opponents is spiking, you should try to stop or slow down the hit by blocking the ball with your hand above the net. After deciding where the spike is coming from, you should go to that area at the net—about 2 feet from it. Jump with the spike at the same time as the spiker. Straighten your arms to reach high above your head, thumbs together, with fingers spread and pointing upward. The ball will rebound from the straight fingers and be deflected back toward your teammates. Be careful not to swing your arms forward, as you might hit the net and commit a foul. You will need to practice the timing of your jump.

Recovery from the Net

The ball may be recovered from the net if it is hit before it touches the floor. You must think and act quickly. Bend your knees to get well under the ball, letting the ball fall from the net so that you can bump it high enough into the air so that your teammate has time to get under it.

Footwork

Good footwork is a big part of successful volleyball. You must be active within your own position and shift with the play and be ready to assist a teammate, but be sure to cover your own position. Use short, quick steps or slides. Learn to jump. Keep your eyes on the ball at all times. Always try to get in line with the ball in order to play it. Never play the ball underhand when you can get into the proper position to use an overhead volley.

STRATEGY

Basic strategy of the modern game of volleyball is known as "1-2-3" attack. This is the pattern of play used to maneuver the ball into position for an offensive play at the net. The expression "1-2-3" refers to the three hits that each team is allowed to return the ball across the net into the opponent's court. Ideally, the first hit should be the serve receive, by means of a bump or overhead volley. This, then, is a pass, preferably to the center forward who, on the second hit, sets the ball to either the player on his right or on his left. The third hit, coming from the right or left forward, should be a spike. If, on the third hit, the ball is not in a good position for one to spike, then the third player should merely save it. Again, preferably, this should be a hit off of the heel of your open hand.

COURTESY AND SPORTSMANSHIP

Each sport has unwritten rules of courtesy and etiquette that are as important as the written rules of the game. For instance, in volleyball you should roll the ball to the next server. The ball will be easier to handle, and you save time. Be courteous to officials, opponents, and teammates. Volleyball is a game in which players are expected to call their own fouls, especially at the net. When you touch the net or step over the line, you should raise your hand to inform the referee. Be a good sportsman both in respect to your opponents and your fellow teammates. Play your own position always, and don't criticize your teammates for making mistakes. Compliment them as well as your opponents on good plays.

FOR MORE INFORMATION

American Association for Health, Physical Education, and Recreation, Division for Girls and Women's Sports. *Selected Volleyball Articles.* Washington, D.C.: the Association, 1970.

American Association for Health, Physical Education, and Recreation, Division for Girls and Women's Sports. *Volleyball Guide.* Current edition. Washington, D.C.: the Association.

Egstrom, Glen H., and Schaafsma, Frances. *Volleyball.* Dubuque, Iowa: Wm. C. Brown Co., 1966.

Odeneal, William T., and Wilson, Harry E. *Beginning Volleyball.* Belmont, Calif.: Wadsworth Publishing Co., 1962.

Thigpen, Janet. *Power Volleyball for Girls and Women.* Dubuque, Iowa: Wm. C. Brown Co., 1967.

Trotter, Betty Jane. *Volleyball for Girls and Women.* New York: Ronald Press Co., 1965.

Walters, Marshall L., editor. *Official Volleyball Guide.* Berne, Ind.: United States Volleyball Association.

Welch, J. Edmund, editor. *How To Play and Teach Volleyball.* New York: Association Press, 1966.

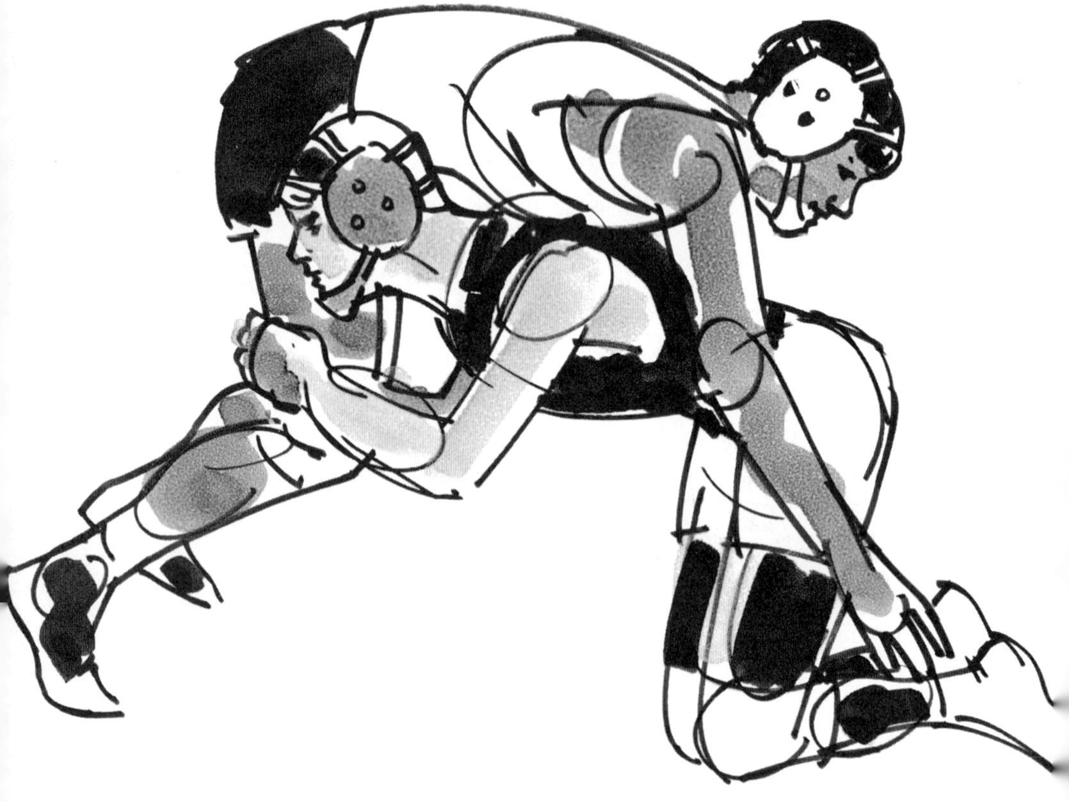

Wrestling

One of man's first forms of physical combat took place in the form of wrestling. From its beginnings in the ancient world through the Grecian civilization the art of wrestling increased not only in popularity, but also in skill and technique. The Egyptians developed many maneuvers and holds that we are still using today. In the Roman era wrestling was an art of self-defense, whereas the Teutonic people viewed it as a form of recreation. In Asiatic countries—principally Japan—wrestling has been a popular activity since 2000 B.C.

In the United States, the University of Pennsylvania and Yale conducted the first intercollegiate wrestling match in 1900. Since then, amateur wrestling has spread throughout the country. The sport is very popular among youth because it lends itself to all sizes and shapes of boys. Wrestling strongholds in this country are in the Midwest, the Northwest, and the Middle Atlantic states.

The creation of a National Rules Committee in 1927 rendered many changes in rules that resulted in wrestling's becoming a great spectator sport. Wrestling in this country is primarily the catch-as-catch-can style. It is a free style of wrestling that permits a contestant to trip and use holds above or below the waist. The objective is to pin or hold an opponent's shoulders to the mat, which terminates the individual bout with the defeat of the pinned man. The Rules Committee developed a point system which is used to determine winners in bouts where no fall occurs. It developed the weight classification system which is a safeguard to the sport, and it set a time limit on individual bouts, which adds greatly to the interest of contestants and spectators.

Wrestling provides an outlet for boys of varying physical qualities; and although some individuals would contend that strength is a prerequisite to success, this is not true. In the short time that contestants wrestle there is constant physical and mental exertion. Wrestling is individual sport at its finest. When a wrestler is able to pin his opponent, he knows that he has done it himself and finds this thought rewarding.

RULES

Scholastic wrestling matches are divided into three 2-minute periods, the objective being to secure a fall (or pin) by holding the shoulder area of your opponent to the mat for 2 complete seconds. The National Rules Committee has established uniform rules which enable coaches, teachers, and wrestlers to establish a worthwhile program. The first period starts from a standing (or neutral) position, with the objective being to get your opponent down on the mat. This is the "takedown." If no fall occurs during the first period, the second period then starts from the "referee's position," which has both wrestlers on the mat in a kneeling position. If there is no fall in the second period, the third period again starts from the referee's position.

A fall or pin is scored as five points for the winner's team. A decision is scored as three points for the winner's team, and a draw is scored as two points for each team.

The point system used in scoring an individual bout is as follows:

two points	*takedown*
two points	*reversal* from the bottom to the top position, called the position of advantage
one point	*escape,* in which the bottom wrestler either breaks away from his opponent or obtains a neutral position
three points	*near-fall,* in which the wrestler in the position of advantage is able to hold his opponent's shoulders to the mat, but is unable to hold them for the complete two seconds
two points	*predicament,* in which one or both shoulders are held near the mat, but the offensive wrestler is unable to force them to the mat
one or two points	*time advantage,* in which the wrestler in the position of advantage is able to control the bottom wrestler for one complete minute (one point) or a maximum of two complete minutes (two points) longer than his opponent was able to control him.

Upright Position

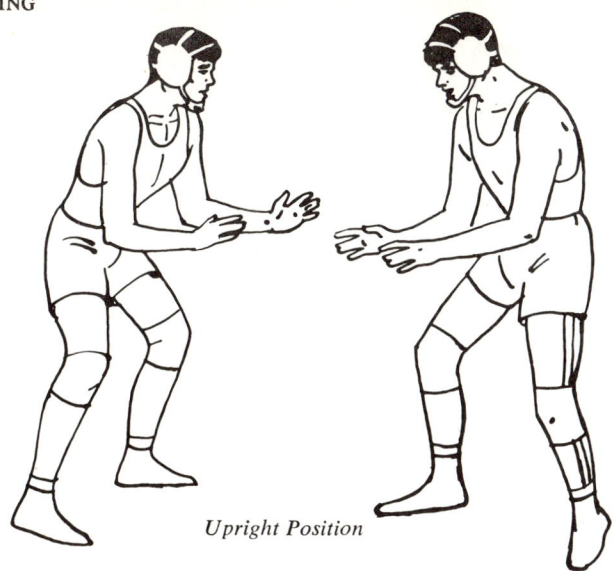

The Rules Committee has established various precautions that help to prevent serious injury. The use of the hammerlock above a right angle is illegal, as are strangleholds; full nelsons; toeholds; holds over the mouth, eyes, or nose; the interlocking of hands or arms around the legs or waist while the defensive contestant has both knees on the mat, unless the offensive wrestler has a pinning combination; bending or twisting the fingers for punishment or to break a hold; or any hold used for punishment alone. There shall be no striking, gouging, kicking, hair pulling, butting, or anything that endangers an opponent. The contestant who lifts an opponent clear of the mat is responsible for the safe return of that opponent to the mat.

BASIC STARTING POSITIONS

There are three basic wrestling positions, and you must be thoroughly familiar with all three.

The Upright Position

There are two basic upright stances. The wrestler on the left has more of a closed stance but is well balanced over his knees and has his arms extended so that he is prepared both for an offensive move as well as a defensive move. His left foot is slightly extended; thus he is able to defend one or both legs. It is easier to defend one leg than it is to defend two. The wrestler on the right has an open stance with one

Tie-Up Position   *Referee's Position*

foot back. This permits him to generate speed from a drop-step action without giving away his intentions.

The "Tie-Up" Position

This technique is used by wrestlers attempting to work at a closer range—generally used by individuals who do not possess the speed to work from the outside, without tieing up.

Referee's Position

The bottom man is down on all fours with the palms of his hands 12 inches from his knees. The offensive wrestler then assumes a position on one side of his opponent. One arm must be loosely placed around his opponent's waist and the hand of the other arm at the bend in the elbow of his opponent. The offensive wrestler may have either his front knee or his back knee off the mat as long as his foot stays outside the nearest plane of the defensive wrestler.

TAKEDOWN SKILLS

There are several ways of taking an opponent down to the mat. As you gain skill, you will want to add additional skills to the ones described here. As in all wrestling maneuvers, takedowns are effective only when you move rapidly and catch your opponent off guard. Practice is required in all these movements. When learning and practicing,

Leg Dive

have your opponent offer almost no opposition. He should increase the amount of opposition as your skill increases.

The takedown is probably the most important maneuver, except for a pinning combination, in wrestling. More practice time should be allowed for this phase of wrestling than many of the other techniques.

The Single Leg Dive

From either an upright position or a tie-up position this maneuver is attainable. From the upright position make a quick thrust toward the knees of your opponent and grab behind your opponent's knee joint. The same technique can be used from the tie-up position. Remember, on all tie-up techniques you must shrug your arms free of your opponent before attempting to get at his leg and body area. Drop on both knees with your head on the same side as the leg you grasp. At the same time bring your outside leg forward and pivot on your knee in order to move behind your opponent. Move your left arm up around his waist and straddle his right leg as he goes forward to the mat.

Double Arm Drag

Double Arm Drag

From the tie-up position, slide your left arm over your opponent's right arm and grasp him just above the elbow. Bring your right hand across and grasp your opponent just below the right armpit. At the same time slide your left hand down to your opponent's right wrist. Pull his right arm to your side, applying most of the power with your right hand. At the same time move to his right side and hook your right leg around his right foot. Release your left hand and grasp his right leg at the knee. Pull forward and down with your right hand, at the same time swinging your left leg over his right leg. You must throw

Heel Pick-Up

yourself into this maneuver because your weight will initiate your opponent's fall toward the mat, to complete the takedown.

Heel Pick-Up

Grasp your opponent's neck with your right hand, and, at the same time, slide your left hand to the inside of his right arm and grasp his upper arm. Drop to your right knee, at the same time grasping your opponent's left heel with your left hand. Pull his left heel to your left, and, at the same time, snap down hard with your right hand on your opponent's neck. As your opponent touches the mat, release your hold and secure an inside crotch position or other advantage hold depending on what he does. Maintain leg control over your opponent, thus preventing him from regaining his balance and possibly breaking your hold.

Head Drag or Duck Under

From a tie-up position reach for your opponent's neck with your right hand. At the same time slide your left hand to the inside of his right arm and grasp his upper arm. Holding his right arm in place with your left hand, duck quickly under his right arm so his elbow is resting

Head Drag

on your neck. You must practice the ducking phase of this move because it enables you to get behind your opponent much easier. Don't try to go through his arm; go under. At the same time throw your head back, pull down on his neck with your right hand, and swing around behind. If you pull hard enough on your opponent's neck with your right hand, your opponent will go forward to the mat.

BREAKDOWNS

From a referee's position on the mat the man with a position of advantage must control the defensive wrestler. The objective of the bottom man is to reverse his position and gain control of his opponent. Therefore, it is important to learn basic breakdowns in order to bring your man under control if you are to obtain a fall. This is the preliminary step to securing a fall. Your first objective should be to flatten your opponent out in a prone position. This prevents his escaping and puts him in a position which allows you to maneuver for a fall. When on top you must remember the man underneath has four points of support. The object is to destroy one or more of these supports and get

Far Arm and Double Bar

your opponent off balance. Use your weight and leverage on the breakdown and conserve your strength and energy when possible. Keep your body weight over your opponent's hips in order to tire him.

Far Arm and Double Bar

From the top position of the referee's mat position, hook your left leg around your opponent's right ankle. (Remember: Always attempt to control the legs of your opponent.) Throw your right arm under his right armpit and grasp his left arm just below the elbow with your right hand. Pull his left arm toward you. At the same time push him forward toward his left shoulder where the support has been removed and grasp

Far Ankle and Near Waist

both hands around his left wrist. Be careful not to roll him too far or he will roll you over.

Far Ankle and Near Waist

Reach across with your left hand and grasp your opponent's ankle, at the same time placing your right arm around his waist. Pull his left ankle forward. This will either break your opponent down or keep him under control.

Far Ankle and Far Arm

Hook your left leg around your opponent's right ankle, shoot your right hand across under your opponent's right armpit, and grasp his left arm just above the elbow. Pull his left arm toward you, grasping his left wrist in both hands. Bring your left arm back and grasp your opponent's left ankle, forcing his left shoulder to the mat.

Stretcher

Hook your left leg around your opponent's right ankle; put your right leg to the inside of his right leg. Step over his back and shove your left leg inside his left leg. Both your legs are now inside of his. Pull his elbows forward with your hands as you drive all of your weight

WRESTLING 373

Far Ankle and Far Arm

The Stretcher

The Switch

forward to flatten him. As you lift your hands to put pressure on the small of his back, he will move forward into a prone position on the mat.

REVERSES AND ESCAPES

The real test of your wrestling ability is how well you can escape from underneath. You must try to lure your opponent by a series of rapid maneuvers.

Since an escape counts one point and a reversal counts two, it is always important to combine a reversal or takedown with the escape.

The Set Out

Often when a reverse is secured, the opponent is placed in a situation that will result in a fall or near fall. Four basic escapes combined with their reverses are discussed below. Additional ones may be learned after the simple ones are mastered.

Switch

Knock your opponent's left hand off your left arm with your right hand. Bring your left hand across to your right side to counter for loss of support. Shift all your weight to your left hand and right foot, raising your right knee off the mat at the same time. Pivot on your right foot and bring your left leg through to your right. At the same time, throw your right arm over your opponent's right arm, grasping the inside of his right thigh. Lean back on your opponent's right arm and swing your body out from under your opponent. Take your left hand and reach for a rear crotch hold, pulling your opponent forward as you come on top.

376 PHYSICAL EDUCATION FOR HIGH SCHOOL STUDENTS

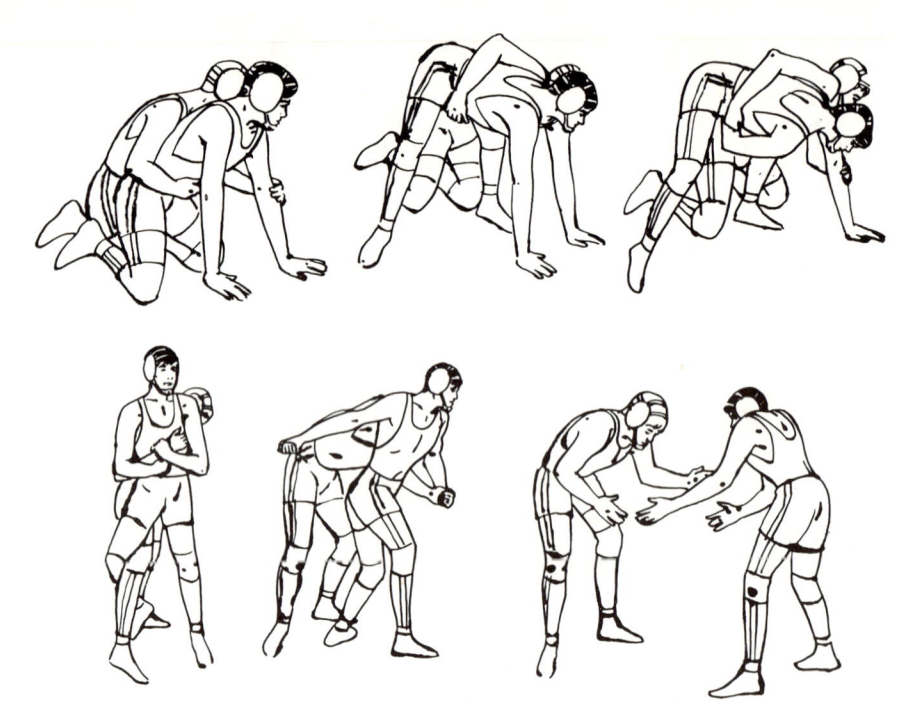

Standing Escape

The Set Out

Bring your right foot forward and shift your weight to your right foot and left hand. Throw your left foot forward as far as possible and drop on your left elbow. Pivot on your left knee and elbow and turn to face your opponent. Throw your arms out forward ready for action.

Standing Escape

Jump to both feet, at the same time keeping both hands on the mat. Grasp your opponent's right hand with your right hand, being sure to grasp all four fingers. Stand up on both feet and grasp your opponent's left hand with your left hand. At the same time hook your right foot over his right leg so that he can't lift you. Pull the hands apart and face him. Immediately take the on-guard position.

Hiplock Escape

Hook your left arm over your opponent's right arm. Pull him forward and down, at the same time snapping his right knee off the mat

Hiplock Escape

and throwing him with your left hip. Pivot on your right knee while your opponent is still off balance and come even with him.

Hiplock and Whizzer

Hook your left arm over your opponent's right arm. Pull him forward and downward as in the hiplock escape. Pivot on your left knee, putting your right arm across and under your opponent's head and left armpit. The right leg is straightened out and ready to drive off. Throw your left leg out from under. At the same time you push with the right leg, forcing your opponent backward and to the left. As your opponent falls on his back, you can hold him down with the weight of your body.

PINNING COMBINATIONS

After you have developed a fair degree of skill in takedowns, reverses, escapes, rides, and breakdowns, you are ready to start work on pin holds. It is very important that you have control over your opponent before attempting to pin him. Failure to do so may result in

Hiplock and Whizzer

a reversal or a wild tumble with the result that you are pinned. Four of the fundamental pinning combinations are described here.

Bar Arm and Half Nelson

From the top referee's position hook your left leg around your opponent's right ankle. Take the far arm and double bar position described under breakdowns. Take your right hand off your opponent's left wrist and apply a near half nelson to force your opponent on his side. As you start to turn your opponent on his left side, unhook his right ankle from your left leg. Increase the hold to a full half nelson and apply pressure to force your opponent on his left side. The pit of your elbow should now be at the back of your opponent's neck. Now grasp his left wrist with your right hand. Both hands are now on his left wrist. Keep driving until both of his shoulders are on the mat. Keep your body perpendicular to your opponent and your legs spread. This will prevent him from hooking your legs with his.

Crotch and Half Nelson

From the top referee's position, hook your left leg around your opponent's right ankle. Pass your right arm across under your oppo-

WRESTLING

Bar Arm and Half Nelson

nent's right armpit, grasping his left arm just above the elbow. Pull his left arm toward you as you reach with your left hand for a rear crotch hold near your opponent's right knee. Pick your opponent up and put him on his left side. Use your right arm to place a half nelson, sliding it around the neck until you can grasp his left arm with your right hand. At the same time change your left hand from a rear crotch to an inside crotch hold. Keep your body perpendicular to your opponent's and your feet well spread. If he turns toward you, drive his shoulders back to the mat. If he turns away from you, flatten him out.

Three-Quarter Nelson

From the top referee's position hook your left leg around your opponent's right ankle. Bring your left arm from around your opponent's waist and put it through from under his right side so that it comes out on the left side of his neck. Grasp your own left with your right hand. Clamp down on your opponent's neck, keeping your left leg hooked around his right ankle and at the same time pulling his right foot forward. Keep pulling his head downward and backward and his legs forward until his head is almost between his legs. As your opponent's shoulder touches the mat, shift your own weight backward to prevent him from kicking you over.

380   PHYSICAL EDUCATION FOR HIGH SCHOOL STUDENTS

Crotch and Half Nelson

Three-Quarter Nelson

Counter to Leg Dives

COUNTERS FOR TAKEDOWNS

Counter to Leg Dives

As soon as your opponent drops under you on both knees, fall on him with your legs straight out and well spread, making him carry all of your weight. Grasp his farther ankle with both hands. After he is under control, cross his face with your right hand, grasping his arm above his left elbow. Free your leg by pulling on his arm and leg. Swing behind and straddle to a riding position with your right arm across his face and your left hand grasping the farther ankle.

Counter to Double Arm Drag

After your opponent has pulled you forward, step across his body with your right leg, followed by your left leg. This will put your body perpendicular to his.

Counter to Heel Pick-Up

As your opponent ducks his head under your right arm to go his right arm. As he reaches for your left foot with his left hand, pry

Counter to Double Arm Drag

up on his right arm and grasp his left arm just above the elbow with your right hand. Throw your legs backward with your weight, causing your opponent to fall on his back.

Counter to Head Drag

As your opponent ducks his head under your right arm to go behind, hook your right arm around his right arm. Jerk down to bring his right shoulder and hip to the mat. At the same time throw your own right leg high over your opponent, followed by your left leg. This is a good pinning position if your body is perpendicular to your opponent.

Counter to Switches

As your opponent pivots out to switch, catch his near arm at the elbow with your right hand. As you pull his arm out from under him, throw your left shoulder and left arm into him, forcing him down on his right side. This is an excellent position to ride.

When your opponent pivots out to a position where he is sitting on his buttocks, keep your left knee against his left hip, at the same time shifting all of your weight to your left foot and right hand. As he

WRESTLING

Counter to Heel Pick-Up

Counter to Head Drag

Counter to Switches: Near Arm Tie-Up

turns to come on top, apply the same pressure to his left arm by prying up on it. Keep your left knee against his hip and off the mat. Start to pivot on your left foot. Move your right leg through, putting pressure on his left shoulder. All of your weight is now on your left foot and right hand. As you put pressure on him, swing away from him to keep him from recountering. You must put enough leverage on your opponent's left shoulder to force it to the mat; then swing away wide and come up on top.

STRATEGY

To make wrestling satisfying and appealing one should learn just what to do during a match. First you should be in good physical condition and should master basic skills. An effective conditioning program can be accomplished by calisthenics, running, and wrestling. Your wrestling must be learned by drills. Holds, riding, and pinning combinations should become a matter of reflex to the individual wrestler. You should practice the maneuvers that you feel confident in and learn them well. Some techniques will work well for one boy and not as well for another.

Learn the takedowns well; this phase of wrestling will give you control over your opponent. Do not attempt a lot of different takedowns at the beginning; rather, two or three will enable you to get an opponent to the mat and will increase your confidence in your own ability. After you master these few, you can add to your knowledge of takedown techniques. When you get control over your opponent use your best holds and rides. If you learn to control an opponent, you have the opportunity to relax and conserve your energy for later in the match when it is needed.

By working on various moves and developing these moves into an automatic reflex you will develop the offensive techniques that will help you win matches. Chain wrestling involves the putting together of a series of moves that will keep your opponent off guard. By working just one maneuver it is easy for your opponent to counter you and stop you; the more movement you give him the harder it is for him to stop you.

WRESTLING TERMS

Arm bar. A lock on the arm of an opponent obtained by circling his arm with yours and holding your hand against his body.

Arm drag. A quick pull on an opponent's arm, usually above the elbow, in an attempt to pull him to the mat.

Breakdown. The top wrestler forcing his opponent to the mat by taking away his supporting points.

Bridge. Elevating the body by use of the neck. Sometimes called a *wrestler's bridge.*

Crotch hold. Holding an opponent by the upper leg near the crotch.

Drag. A pulling motion on the upper arm in an attempt to either pull the opponent to the mat or to go behind him.

Drill. Working on a series of maneuvers.

Escape. An action by which the wrestler on the bottom breaks free of the top wrestler.

Fall. Occurs when a wrestler is held in contact with the mat for an "appreciable time"—two seconds in scholastic wrestling.

Half-nelson. A pinning hold that occurs when one arm is placed under an opponent's armpit and comes out over the top of his neck.

Helmet. Protective covering used to protect a wrestler's ears from being rubbed—thus eliminating the "cauliflower ear."

Hold. The technique of grasping an opponent. The grip on an arm or leg which will keep an opponent from moving.

Neutral position. Both wrestlers are either standing or are locked in the same hold.

Pin. Occurs when both shoulders of a contestant are held to the mat.

Pinning combination. The technique of securing a "hold" which will result in a pin or fall.

Referee's position. The down position on the mat, in which the bottom man is on his knees with the palms of his hands 12 inches from his knees. The offensive wrestler is on top with one knee up or both knees on the mat and one arm around the opponent's waist and his other hand at the bend of the elbow of his opponent.

Reversal. Occurs when the bottom wrestler maneuvers himself to the top position, or the position of advantage.

Ride. An action in which the offensive wrestler effectively counters the moves of the defensive wrestler.

Sit-out. A maneuver in which the defensive wrestler assumes a sitting position in order to escape or reverse his opponent. The beginning of a chain maneuver.

Takedown. A situation where one wrestler gets his opponent down to the mat and gains control over him.

Tie-up. Obtaining a hold or grasping an opponent in order to work for a takedown.

FOR MORE INFORMATION

Dratz, J.; Johnson, M.; and McCann, T. *Winning Wrestling.* Englewood Cliffs, N.J.: Prentice-Hall, 1966.

Kapral, Frank. *Championship Wrestling.* Englewood Cliffs, N.J.: Prentice-Hall, 1964.

Sasahara, Shozo. *Scientific Approach to Wrestling.* Japan: Chuo University Co-operation Press, 1960.

Organization of Competition

The competitive element adds a great deal to sports, whether individual or team sports. Various systems have been worked out to give all contenders an opportunity to compete under fair conditions. Competition within a league or other athletic organization usually is organized in the form of tournaments.

TOURNAMENTS

The types of tournaments most generally used are the elimination, the consolation, the double elimination, round robin, and the ladder, and other challenge-type tournaments. In setting up tournament play you will need to know something about methods of eliminating contestants.

Byes

An elimination tournament can be set up with any number of players or teams. In order to have a single winner, the final round must have only two contestants or teams. In each preceeding round of play one-half of the total group is eliminated. This means there must be 4 in the semifinals, 8 in the quarter-finals, 16 in the round before that, and so on.

When the number of contestants is not a perfect power of 2, the number eliminated in the first round must be such that a perfect power of two remains for the second round of play. This means all players will not participate in the first round. Those advancing to the second round automatically without playing are said to have received *byes*.

To determine the number of byes for the first round apply the formula, $2^n - N = X$, where N equals the number of teams or contestants and 2^n is the next perfect power of 2 greater than N. For example, with 12 entries you would have 16-12 or 4 byes.

One half of the byes should be placed in the upper half of the bracket and the other half in the lower.

Lot and Seeding

Entries given *byes* are selected by "lot" or "seeding." If they are to be chosen by drawing lots, place the numbers representing the entries in a container and have them drawn by a person in such a manner that the entries drawn are by pure chance.

The "seeded" entries are considered to be the best teams or individuals and are "seeded" or intentionally placed in the order of their estimated strength and may be favored with *byes* as opponents. The system of "seeded" entries is used to stack the places so as to ensure that what appears to be the better entries will meet in the later rounds

Single elimination with eight entries

	Round 1	Round 2 or semifinals	Round 3 or finals	
Upper bracket	A B C D	A D	A	
				H (Champion)
Lower bracket	E F G H	F H	H	

of the tournament. Tournaments with 8 entries will "seed" at least 2 players, and those with 16 entries at least 4 players.

In a tournament of 8 entries the number-one seeded entry is placed in position one in the upper bracket and the number-two seeded entry is placed in position eight in the lower bracket. In the case of 16 entries, seeded numbers one and three would be in the upper bracket and two and four in the lower bracket. All other positions are determined by lot.

The number of entries should not be too large. A better plan is to set up flights of 8 or 16 entries. The winners of the various flights can then play each other. This arrangement by flight also provides an opportunity to play on an ability basis. The winner without further play establishes himself as the champion of a particular flight, such as the novice, intermediate, or expert flight.

Single Elimination

A graphic representation is given of single elimination play in a tournament made up of eight entries: A, B, C, D, E, F, G, and H, in which A was seeded number one and H was seeded number two.

In the next illustration we have an example of the same type of play involving five entries: A, B, C, D, and E, in which A was seeded number one and E number two.

Three byes and entries A and E were seeded and given byes in the first round.

As you see, the winners advance to the next round, and the losers are eliminated from play. This process continues until two entries meet in the finals for the championship. This type of play determines a champion quickly, but eliminates a loser from further participation.

Ladder or Challenge Tournaments

In this type of play the entries are placed in position either according to ability or by lot. They are generally placed like rungs on a ladder. The illustration involves six entries: A, B, C, D, E, and F.

There are many variations of the basic rules of play in this type of tournament, some of which follow:

1. An entry may challenge an entry one or two positions above him on the ladder.

2. The entry challenged must play this contest before he can challenge any entry above his position.

Single elimination with five entries

```
                 Round 1      Round 2 or    Round 3 or
                              semi-finals   finals

                   A
                                  A
                  Bye
 Upper
 bracket                                       A
                   B
                                  C
                   C
                                                          A
                   D                                   (Champion)
                                  D
                  Bye
 Lower                                         E
 bracket
                  Bye
                                  E
                   E
```

3. The entry in the number-one position is generally not challenged more than once during a stated period of time—for example, within one week.

Illustration of ladder tournament arrangement
TENNIS

- • A •
- • B •
- • C •
- • D •
- • E •
- • F •

4. When the challenger wins, he exchanges positions with the loser.

5. If the entry challenged does not play within a stated period of time, positions are exchanged with the entry who issued the challenge.

6. Other rules state such things as the hours in which play is to be conducted and the date on which play will cease.

ORGANIZATION OF COMPETITION

This kind of play is used most frequently in connection with such activities as tennis, handball, golf, bowling, and badminton. All entries remain in the running throughout the length of the tournament, and relative ability of the players can be more nearly established. Many coaches of the single- and dual-type activities use this method for the purpose of determining positions on teams.

Round-Robin League Play

Round-robin league play is used when ample play areas and time are available. All entries play each other one or more times. It is generally used with team activities such as baseball, basketball, field hockey, and touch football. Leagues are generally restricted to no more than eight teams. The winner and other positions are determined on a percentage basis of wins and losses.

The percentage for a team's standing is worked out by dividing the number of games won by the number of games played. This is ordinarily expressed as a decimal of three places. For example, if a team played nine games and won three, it would have an average of .333, the decimal value of nine divided into three. If we used a percentage, it would be 33.3 percent.

In drawing up a league schedule for round-robin play, you should do the following:

1. Assign a number to each of the entries.

2. When there are an even number of entries, put as many numbers as there are teams in two vertical columns. Start with number one and go down the first column and up the second.

3. Each set of opposite numbers represents two teams that play each other on a certain date determined by the schedule maker.

4. To complete the required rounds of play keep number one always in the same position and rotate the other numbers in a counter-clockwise manner.

The following is an example of an eight-team round-robin schedule:

Round 1	*Round 2*	*Round 3*	*Round 4*	*Round 5*	*Round 6*	*Round 7*
1 vs. 8	1 vs. 7	1 vs. 6	1 vs. 5	1 vs. 4	1 vs. 3	1 vs. 2
2 vs. 7	8 vs. 6	7 vs. 5	6 vs. 4	5 vs. 3	4 vs. 2	3 vs. 8
3 vs. 6	2 vs. 5	8 vs. 4	7 vs. 3	6 vs. 2	5 vs. 8	4 vs. 7
4 vs. 5	3 vs. 4	2 vs. 3	8 vs. 2	7 vs. 8	6 vs. 7	5 vs. 6

When there are an odd number of entries, the foregoing plan is used except that bye is placed in the position now held by number one.

Like number one, bye stays in the same position while the other numbers rotate counterclockwise. The first three rounds for seven teams would be as follows:

Round 1	*Round 2*	*Round 3*
Bye vs. 7	Bye vs. 6	Bye vs. 5
1 vs. 6	7 vs. 5	6 vs. 4
2 vs. 5	1 vs. 4	7 vs. 3
3 vs. 4	2 vs. 3	1 vs. 2

The number of games to be played to complete a round-robin schedule can be obtained by using the formula $[N(N-1)] \div 2$, in which the number of entries is substituted for the letter N. A seven team league would play 7×6 or 42 divided by 2, which gives us 21 games.

Meets

This type of participation is used in such activities as swimming, cross country, track and field, and skiing. Results are determined usually within a day or two. The meet is organized by events which are run off at stated times according to a program worked out in advance. When there are more entries for an event than can be accommodated by the facilities available, heats (also called qualifying trials) are arranged and run off. Generally, those who win first and second place in a heat qualify for the final running of the event. The "seeding" of entries is also used in the qualifying heats. The best performers are chosen as the leaders of different heats so that they will not compete in the same heat. This procedure greatly increases the possibility of having the winner of the final of an event come from among the most capable contestants.

Keeping Physically Fit

This book has presented basic information about a great many sports and physical activities. You should have learned something about the rules and skills of games which you can play with satisfaction and enjoyment the rest of your life.

But is this the main objective of your physical education course? An even more significant goal is to become physically educated. This involves more than knowledge of rules and strategy, more than sports skills. The physically educated person knows the contribution which regular and vigorous activity makes to total well-being; he knows the effects of activity on mental health; he is knowledgeable about the structure and function of his body systems; he knows how to achieve and maintain physical fitness—and he acts on these understandings.

WHAT IS FITNESS?

There are many definitions of fitness, including those which encompass the physical, spiritual, mental, emotional, and social aspects of total fitness. There are even many definitions of *physical* fitness.

The President's Council on Physical Fitness and Sports has stated that "physical fitness is a broad quality involving medical and dental supervision and care, immunization and other protection against disease, proper nutrition, adequate rest, relaxation, good health practices, sanitation, and other aspects of healthful living. Exercise is an essential element to achieving physical fitness. Strength, stamina, endurance, and other desirable physical qualities are best developed through vigorous activity. Physical fitness is achieved through a sensible balance of all these provisions adapted to age, maturity, and capability of the individual."

Other definitions of physical fitness include the following facets:

good health	flexibility
strength	coordination
ability	cardiorespiratory endurance
muscular endurance	proper body weight
speed	general motor achievement
balance	neuromuscular skill

A simple but useful definition is that fitness is a personal sense of well-being.

There are physical activities designed to help develop all the qualities listed above. Your physical education class will help you learn about them and assist you in selecting those to round out your own developmental needs. Your progress through your physical education experience in school will help you understand the concept of physical fitness.

KEEPING FIT

You will find that you need a strong and healthy body to enjoy such strenuous activities as tennis, tumbling, or dancing. In your physical education class you can learn how to keep your body fit for both play and work. You need to learn, first, how your body is constructed and how it performs most efficiently; then you find out what keeps your systems operating at top level. You learn how to move more freely and easily so that you stand straighter, look better, and work and play more efficiently. You will learn that vigorous activity releases the tensions caused by the stress and strain of modern-day living. Instinctively, you know you feel better after exercise. Study of human physiology teaches you why.

When you exercise, your body is affected immediately. Certain changes take place in order for your body to accommodate the exercise. When you engage in vigorous activity regularly, every day and throughout the year, more gradual changes occur in your body as it adjusts to the continued demands of exercise. The immediate effects of activity include an automatic increase in the rate and depth of breathing and an increase in the rate of heartbeat. The faster heartbeat results in (a) an increase of the flow of blood to the muscles, supplying them with the oxygen and nutritional items necessary for increased energy expenditure, and (b) an increase in the rate and amount of waste material removed.

Both effects operate to make the muscles more efficient. Another immediate effect is the production of heat, which serves to "warm up" the muscles and help make them less susceptible to injury.

Long-term effects of exercise are apparent on the muscular system, the cardiovascular system, and the respiratory system. Results include increased endurance, quicker recovery from fatigue, greater mechanical efficiency in breathing, increase in strength and resiliency. The physically fit person performs work with a relatively smaller expenditure of energy than the poorly conditioned individual.

Scientific research has demonstrated that regular participation in vigorous activity influences in a favorable manner all components and functions of the human organism.

You continue to be physically fit only if you continue to exercise. Fitness levels are improved when the activity in which you participate becomes progressively vigorous. Once a desired level of physical fitness is achieved, it is no longer necessary to increase the exercise load; but in order to maintain that level it is essential to continue exercising regularly.

The benefits of physical activity are not permanent. All of the immediate and long-range accommodations are lost if participation stops. Both endurance and strength are lost when exercise is abandoned. The muscles atrophy; the pulse rate decreases; the lungs become less efficient. A lack of exercise acts in a negative fashion upon the body. An important lesson to be learned is that once a satisfactory degree of physical fitness has been developed, it is much easier to maintain that condition than to try to reach it again if fitness levels decline.

Exercise is essential to proper body functioning. It is of value, however, only on a regular basis. Playing tennis in the summer and watching TV in the winter does not add up to fitness. The benefits of exercise are not cumulative; you must be active every day, all year round, to maintain top physical condition. Even brief periods of activity every day are more effective than "crash" programs of violent, prolonged exercise once a week.

OTHER CONDITIONS FOR FITNESS

Becoming physically fit demands activity on a regular basis, but this is not enough. It is also necessary to get adequate rest and relaxation. Proper sleeping habits are important to give your body time to recover from exertion and fatigue. Cleanliness and medical and dental attention are also essential for keeping fit.

Proper nutrition is basic. A steady diet of hot dogs and soft drinks won't build the kind of body you want for a healthy life.

A balanced diet, one which contains a variety of foods, is the most favorable for the achievement of physical fitness. High school students require a diet which utilizes the four basic food groups—milk and dairy products, meats, bread and cereals, and fruits and vegetables. There is no special diet or combination of foods uniquely capable of producing good physical condition.

The amounts of food eaten depend upon the need of the individual. People who are very active burn more energy and therefore need more food, as measured by calories, to maintain weight. Proteins, carbohydrates, fats, vitamins, minerals, and water are essential nutrients for everyone.

Why is physical fitness desirable for you? Why should you go to the trouble of maintaining a high level of fitness? The benefits derived from being physically fit have been studied and enumerated. There is scientific evidence to prove that physical activity plays an important role in preventing heart attacks and degenerative diseases and in assisting in recuperation from their effects. It has also been shown that regular participation in vigorous activity helps to keep the body weight within the normal range and to prevent the ill effects of obesity. Because exercise improves the tone of skeletal muscles, it helps to develop good posture. The physically fit person is identified by his erect body posture. Regular exercise also favorably influences physical growth during childhood and youth. It increases muscular skill so that less energy is expended in performance, causing activity to be less fatiguing and more enjoyable.

There is also considerable evidence that physical activity aids in the release of tensions. Certain sports provide acceptable outlets for feelings of aggression and other emotions ordinarily restrained.

The sum total is a feeling of well-being—an acceptance of self—that is worth the effort involved.

EVALUATING FITNESS

It is important to assess your own physical condition from time to time. Medical examinations are a part of this, but it is also possible for the student to evaluate his physical fitness level with a series of tests

KEEPING PHYSICALLY FIT

prepared by the American Association for Health, Physical Education, and Recreation (AAHPER), the professional organization for teachers of physical education.

The test battery includes seven items: pull-up (with flexed-arm hang for girls)—for judging arm and shoulder girdle strength; sit-up—for judging efficiency of abdominal and hip flexor muscles; shuttle run—for judging speed and change of direction; standing broad jump—for judging explosive muscle power of leg extensors; 50-yard dash—for judging speed; softball throw for distance—for judging skill and coordination; and 600-yard run-walk—for judging cardiovascular efficiency. Altogether these tests form a basis for determining physical fitness.

Forms for recording the scores on all test items are available from AAHPER. A Personal Fitness Record makes it possible for each student to record his scores on two trials; the profile record then provides space to plot a graph which will show changes in performance from one test period to the next.

Test scores should be recorded in order that they may be put to use. The results are useful in measuring your individual progress, in identifying specific weaknesses which can then be improved, and in comparing your performance levels with a nationwide standard. AAHPER, through a testing program involving approximately 9,200 boys and girls, aged 10 to 17, has established national norms for each of the seven test items. It is thus possible for you to compare your score with that of others of your age and general physical characteristics. The comparisons are in the form of percentile tables, showing just where you stand with relation to all others who have taken the test. For example, if you are 16 years old and jumped 6 feet-10 inches on the standing broad jump, by locating your score on a specific table you discover that you have done as well as 70 percent of all those who took the test.

AWARD PROGRAM

AAHPER has prepared a series of awards for those who participate in a regular testing program. Those taking part in the testing may receive certificates and emblems indicating their performance level on the AAHPER Youth Fitness Test.

There is an achievement award certificate for boys and girls who attain the 50th percentile on all items in the test. An embossed gold merit seal is available for this certificate for boys and girls who attain the 80th percentile on all test items.

There are also other awards for those who have a keen incentive to improve their fitness standards. Separate sew-on embroidered emblems are available for three levels: elementary, junior, and senior.

The Presidential Physical Fitness Award, established by President Lyndon B. Johnson in 1966, honors students who demonstrate exceptional physical achievement. Boys and girls who score at or above the 85th percentile on all seven items of the Youth Fitness Test are eligible. They must be students in good standing and recommended by their school principals. Information about all these awards may be obtained by writing to AAHPER, 1201 Sixteenth St., N.W., Washington, D.C. 20036.

There is a thrill to be experienced in making the best use of your body and trying for maximum performance. Participating in physical activities in high school starts you on the road to maintaining good condition and getting the most out of life.

Career Information

As you think seriously about your choice of a career during your high school years, you should attempt to find out whether you possess interests and abilities which would help you succeed in a career in physical education or the closely related field of recreation.

What are some of these interests and abilities?

1. Do you like to do things to help other people?
2. Do you have strong leadership qualities and enjoy working with people?
3. Does your personality attract others, and are you skillful in getting along with various types of people?
4. Do you possess above-average sport skills?
5. Do you have a sense of humor, enthusiasm, and a concern for the development of people?
6. Do you have imagination and creative power?

HOW DOES HIGH SCHOOL PREPARE YOU?

Physical education classes, sports programs, and other extra-class activities will naturally be most interesting to you, but the main job is to get a good background in fundamental courses, such as English, social studies, and science. You should also explore other interests through electives.

Getting ready for college means taking those courses that will give you a good basic training for more advanced work. Participation in a variety of school activities also is important to show that you are developing interests other than in the field of sports. It means that you have taken advantage of opportunities to go to camp, perhaps even gaining a position of junior counselor; or you have worked on the city playground in the summer; or you have taken the neighbor's children under your wing and taught them to play a new game. Through your leaders club or scout troop, you discovered that it was fun to teach others how to do things.

HOW DO YOU CHOOSE YOUR COLLEGE?

Choice of your college should be made most carefully. The factors of size, location, and the type of institution are not so important as the quality of instruction, the opportunities for guidance, and the institution's interest in development of the student. It is well to consider several schools. Be sure that the colleges you are considering are members of one of the regional accrediting associations for general education.

WHAT ARE THE EMPLOYMENT OPPORTUNITIES?

A great variety of positions are open to men and women who have completed college degrees in physical education or recreation. These include coaching, recreational leadership, camp work, research, and various types of teaching positions in schools and colleges. The opportunities for both men and women in the elementary schools are increasing rapidly.

Employment opportunities are also found in organizations, such as the YMCA, YMHA, YWCA, YWHA, Boys Clubs, Boy Scouts, Campfire Girls, and church recreation programs. These may be permanent year-round positions or summer jobs in the camping programs sponsored by the organizations.

As the man or woman advances professionally and gains varied experience, administrative, supervisory, research, and teacher-education positions on the college level become available. For positions of this type, it is necessary in most cases to have wide experience and a doctor's degree or its equivalent.

Thus opportunities are many and varied for well-qualified young men and women. With the rapidly expanding school enrollments of the next few years, properly prepared educators will be increasingly needed.

For additional information contact the American Association for Health, Physical Education, and Recreation, 1201 16th Street, N.W., Washington, D.C. 20036.